E DUE

D0498422

WITHDRAWN
UTSA LIBRARIES

Economics and the Social Sciences

Economics and the Social Sciences

Boundaries, Interaction and Integration

Edited by

Stavros Ioannides

Associate Professor of Economics, Department of Political Science and History, Panteion University, Athens, Greece

Klaus Nielsen

Professor of Social Sciences, Roskilde University, Denmark and Senior Lecturer of Management, Birkbeck College, University of London, UK

Edward Elgar

Cheltenham, UK • Northampton, MA, USA

© Stavros Ioannides and Klaus Nielsen 2007

All rights reserved. No part of this publication may be reproduced, stored in a retrieval system or transmitted in any form or by any means, electronic, mechanical or photocopying, recording, or otherwise without the prior permission of the publisher.

Published by
Edward Elgar Publishing Limited
Glensanda House
Montpellier Parade
Cheltenham
Glos GL50 1UA
UK

Edward Elgar Publishing, Inc.
William Pratt House
9 Dewey Court
Northampton
Massachusetts 01060
USA

Library
University of Texas
at San Antonio

A catalogue record for this book
is available from the British Library

Library of Congress Cataloguing in Publication Data
Economics and the social sciences : boundaries, interaction and integration /
edited by Stavros Ioannides.
    p. cm.
  Includes bibliographical references and index.
  1. Economics.   2. Social sciences.   I. Ioannides, Stavros.
  HB71.E2677 2007
  330–dc22
                                            2006016807

ISBN 978 1 84064 790 7

Printed and bound in Great Britain by MPG Books Ltd, Bodmin, Cornwall

Contents

Contributors

Markus C. Becker, Department of Marketing, University of Southern Denmark, Odense, Denmark

Guido Buenstorf, Evolutionary Economics Group, Max Planck Institute for Research into Economic Systems, Jena, Germany

Geoffrey M. Hodgson, The Business School, University of Hertfordshire, Hatfield, UK

William A. Jackson, Department of Economics and Related Studies, University of York, York, UK

George Liagouras, Laboratory of Industrial and Energy Economics (LIEE), National Technical University of Athens, Athens, and Department of Finance and Management Engineering, University of the Aegean, Greece

Desmond McNeill, SUM (Centre for Development and the Environment), University of Oslo, Oslo, Norway

Eyüp Özveren, Department of Economics, Middle East Technical University, Ankara, Turkey

Irene van Staveren, Feminist Development Economics Institute of Social Studies (The Hague), and Economics and Christian Ethics, Nijmegen University, Nijmegen, the Netherlands

Jack Vromen, Erasmus Institute for Philosophy and Economics, Erasmus University, Rotterdam, the Netherlands

1. Economics and the social sciences: synergies and trade-offs

Stavros Ioannides and Klaus Nielsen

ECONOMICS: QUEEN OF THE SOCIAL SCIENCES OR A DISCIPLINE IN DIRE STRAITS?

On the one hand the history of economics as a scientific discipline is one of undoubted success. Its extended reproduction has been impressive. It is now widely seen as the most advanced of the social sciences with its mathematical formalization, public prestige and Nobel Prize awards.

On the other hand mainstream economics can also be seen as having developed an autistic condition; that is, 'withdrawal, fantasies and delusions stemming from an inability to relate to and perceive the environment realistically' (Levey and Greenhall, 1984: 56). It is characterized by a withdrawn state in relation to both real-life economic problems and the social science disciplines. Journal articles, education and training have degenerated into exercises in applied mathematics with little or no practical relevance. Since the 1970s it has increasingly written itself out of policy relevance, most emphatically the new classical macroeconomics with its policy ineffectiveness implications based on the idea of rational expectations. Furthermore, 'fantasies and delusions' follow from widespread imperialistic efforts to extend the application of the core model of constrained maximization to phenomena and problems that were previously considered the prerogative of other social science disciplines. Mainstream economics has failed to develop language and social behaviour that makes possible the kind of interaction or even integration of disciplines that is necessary in order to solve real-life problems. The language of modern economics makes dialogue with other disciplines impossible, and the self-image of the discipline makes it unnecessary. Furthermore, the dominance of one paradigm implies that heterodox approaches within the discipline have in effect been excluded from its core institutions through the neoclassical purification of economics departments and the main journals, and the refuge of dissidents to business schools, interdisciplinary departments and policy institutes.

1

There is a need for a post-autistic, more pluralist economics, and luckily evidence of promising efforts to develop such a new creature abounds. New international organizations such as the EAEPE (European Association for Evolutionary Political Economy), SASE (Society for the Advancement of Socio-Economics) and AHE (Association for Heterodox Economics) promote a pluralist agenda and are openly interdisciplinary, with considerable success. Heterodox economists are increasingly becoming involved in policy advice and policy implementation in think tanks, interest associations, regulatory institutions, government offices and international organizations. Furthermore, students have responded to the excessive application of mathematics and the autistic withdrawal of mainstream economics from real-life economic problems through exit as well as voice. Recruitment to the study of economics has fallen, and important incidents of student revolt and efforts to promote alternatives have occurred in Sorbonne, Cambridge, Harvard and many other places. Crucially, these efforts are no longer isolated incidents after the establishment and growth of the post-autistic economics network, initiated by French economics students at Sorbonne in Paris (see www.paecon.net/).

One of the central ingredients in the efforts to develop a pluralist, post-autistic, practically relevant economics is the reinsertion of economics in the context of the social sciences. Mainstream economics has become increasingly uninterested in and isolated from the other social science disciplines. This is a deplorable state, for reasons that will be explored in detail in this volume. The established boundaries of economics as an academic discipline have become increasingly irrelevant. Future progress in the study of the economy requires not only openness and dialogue with other disciplines but also cooperation and integration across the boundaries of disciplines. The development of such a reformed, pluralist and interdisciplinary economics requires multi-dimensional efforts at many levels. Advancement of knowledge of other disciplines and the history of the social sciences in the education and training of economists would be an important step in order to create mutual understanding and joint problem-solving tools. An attention to the limitations of deductive application of general theories and the necessity of theory-building and problem-solving attuned to the historically specific context in question would be another important step (see Hodgson in this volume).

Such integrative efforts no doubt promise intellectual as well as practical synergies but they come at an expense. The teaching of other disciplines takes time away from activities such as mathematical sophistication and field specialization. Disciplinary specialization and narrow-mindedness involve benefits as well as costs. A degree of formalization is necessary in order to advance understanding and problem-solving. The power of mathematics is unchallenged in dealing with situations where many influences make themselves felt simultaneously. If the relevant social causes and consequences can be operationalized properly, no doubt the use of simultaneous equations greatly enhances the problem-solving capacities of social science. In general, analytical depth may suffer when efforts to stress broad knowledge gain prominence. Such arguments are widely used by mainstream economics to legitimize the current trend of specialization and formalization. However, the costs of counteracting this trend should not be exaggerated. The benefits of deepening specialization and formalization are illusionary when it is built on dubious assumptions and the neglect of influences and effects that cannot be handily operationalized. Anyway, in addition to the obvious beneficial synergetic effects of a proper re-insertion of economics in the context of the social sciences there are evidently also costs, and there are trade-offs between benefits and costs.

This volume is based on the premise that mainstream economies has developed too much in the direction of an excessively specialized and formalized state of de facto withdrawal from the study of the economy in favour of exercises in applied mathematics. The editors believe that there is much scope for synergies by engaging in an encounter with the other social sciences and the articles of this volume offer important new contributions to such a development.

What is needed in order to develop a new pluralist economics is not only a re-insertion of economics in a proper social science context. It is also crucial to counteract the exclusion of heterodox approaches to the study of the economy. In this volume economics is seen as encompassing both the heterodox and the mainstream versions. The split between mainstream and heterodox approaches is constituted by alternative assumptions concerning actor behaviour, coordination mechanisms, information, and the role of technology, power and institutions, and so on. These differences are closely linked to different conceptions of economics as well as its relation to the other social sciences. The boundaries of economics are wider and more porous in heterodox versions compared to mainstream economics. Heterodox economics are more open to dialogue and input from the other social sciences. Consequently, the need for re-insertion into the context of social sciences is primarily related to mainstream economics. However, heterodox approaches may also benefit from a more deliberate and explicit positioning concerning the boundaries of economics and the contributions from the other social sciences to the study of the economy

This introduction is an attempt to place the contributions of this volume into a wider context. The remaining part of the chapter is structured in the following way. First, the history of economics as a discipline is briefly outlined in the overall context of the history of the social sciences. Second, the issue of the boundaries of economics as a discipline is discussed, which makes it necessary to clarify what economics is and to confront different answers to this question. Third, the focus is directed towards the conceptualization of the relations between economics and the other social sciences. How is it possible to distinguish exogenous versus endogenous factors in studies of the economy? Fourth, recent developments in the relationship between economics and the other social sciences, and the consequent future challenges for mainstream as well as heterodox economics, are briefly outlined. The fifth and final part of the introduction presents the structure of the book and brief summaries of the chapters.

ECONOMICS AND THE OTHER SOCIAL SCIENCES – A BRIEF HISTORY

The constitution of the social science disciplines is a relatively recent phenomenon. The contemporary division into distinct and separate disciplines may seem natural and 'cut in stone' but it has not existed for much more than a century (see Wallerstein et al., 1996). The current disciplines and the divisions between them were established in the period 1850–1914. Before 1850, none of the current disciplines existed in their present form. Rather, there was a modest level of specialization around a number of topical areas. In addition, there were a few broad pre-disciplinary approaches (Sum and Jessop, 2001), such as political economy and 'staatswissenschaft'. The constitution of the social science disciplines in the form we know today was closely linked to the late nineteenth century growth of universities and the increasing demand for state employees with specific skills. The new disciplines quickly established and reproduced themselves and their mutual boundaries through academic journals, professional associations, promotion systems, library classifications, and so on.

The modern discipline of economics originated from classical political economy that broadly focused on the dynamics of growth and distribution in capitalist economies and included within its analytical focus a lot of phenomena that are today considered the topics of other disciplines. From the 1870s political economy was transformed into 'pure' economics. Landmark contributions by Walras, Jevons, Menger, Marshall and others were particularly instrumental in this process. Value theory was substituted by marginalism and the topic was narrowed down to the analysis of the functioning of abstract markets as an effect of the optimizing behaviour of market agents under scarcity, the interaction of supply and demand, and the role of prices and competition. Modern economics soon developed clear boundaries towards the other social sciences although there have always been a number of contacts and interaction with other disciplines (Erreyghers, 2001).

Most of the other social science disciplines were established later than economics. The constitution of sociology as a new discipline was closely linked to the increasing interest in the social consequences of modernity and the rise of social reform movements. From the beginning it had the whole of society as its field of study and the ambition of becoming the queen of the social sciences. In practice its topical area became rather focused on social relations and institutions that were not covered by the other social sciences, that is, civil society. This ambiguity is reflected in the persistent split within sociology between the macro-theories covering society in its totality (Habermas, Bourdieu, Foucault and others) and micro-theories covering specific topical areas such as the sociology of stratification, crime and sports. The establishment of political science as a modern discipline happened even later. Previously the study of the structure and the functioning of the state was part of either political economy or the study of law. However, the emergence of modern 'pure' economics excluded the 'political' from political economy and created a space for a new discipline organized around the study of the state and the struggle for influencing the structure and the activities of the state.

Economics, sociology and political science all became nomothetical, that is, oriented towards the development of universally valid, law-like knowledge, independent of time and space. Part of the reason why they became nomothetical disciplines was the outcome of the so-called 'methodenstreit' that concluded with a victory for a positivistic approach to social science knowledge that sought to copy the natural sciences as far as possible in terms of epistemology and methods of inquiry. Previously, predominant approaches such as the historical school had to a large extent been ideographic, that is, oriented towards the development of contextually specific knowledge rather than general knowledge. However, such approaches lost out in the 'methodenstreit' and were relegated to the fringes of the social sciences.

The discipline of history itself, on the other hand, became clearly ideographic. Historians are studying unique historical events and are accordingly anti-theoretical, if theory is understood as general theory independent of context. Economics, sociology, political science and history all implicitly assumed the superiority of the European culture and studied only the developed countries. The study of countries 'lagging behind' became the domain of anthropology. Psychology, law and geography are other disciplines that were also established in the same period. However, it may be argued that they never became institutionalized as social science disciplines to the same extent as economics, sociology, political science, history and anthropology (Wallerstein et al., 1996).

In the mid-twentieth century there was a clear division of labour between disciplines, with clear boundaries. Each discipline studied separate fields of society with specific and separate methodologies (Wallerstein et al., 1996). This was the Golden Age of the disciplinary division of labour in the social sciences. Since then the blurring of boundaries, overlap and attempts to adopt new interdisciplinary ways of study have made the relationship between the institutionalized disciplines far more complex. The nomo-thetical disciplines have entered the traditional domain of anthropology through area studies, development studies and other activities developed in order to satisfy the increasing need for specific and practically relevant knowledge about the new nation states in the so-called Third World. The traditional distinction between the study of history and the nomothetical disciplines oriented towards the study of the present also became blurred. Increasingly, economics, sociology and political science began to study their subject matters from a historical perspective, and, simultaneously, history has become more like the social sciences in the sense that underly-ing general trends and general explanatory factors, rather than discrete events, increasingly have come into focus.

Furthermore, the disciplines of economics, sociology and political science increasingly overlap in terms of field of study and also, to some extent, in relation to methodology. The mainstream economics approach of rational choice has been applied in fields that were previously the exclu-sive domain of either sociology or political science. This 'economic imperi-alism' includes theories of public choice and social choice and has reached its most general expression in the form of Gary Becker's economic approach to human behaviour (Becker, 1976). Countervailing tendencies characterize recent developments within sociology. The socioeconomic approach of Etzioni seeks to include neoclassical economics as a special case of a broader social theory that integrates the 'I' of economics (indi-vidual utility maximization) with the 'We' of sociology (the rule-following behaviour of the socialized individual) (Etzioni, 1988). New subdisciplines in sociology (political sociology and economic sociology) are examples of new forms of overlap that extend the field of the disciplines beyond traditional boundaries. Within political science the field of study has also been extended to cover not only the traditional domain of the state and government policies but rather collective action in general, includ-ing organization, mobilization and discourse. The methodological differ-ences between the social sciences have also become less clear, especially as far as sociology, political science and heterodox economics are con-cerned, whereas mainstream economics still applies methodologies (formal modelling, deductivist reasoning and econometric testing) that are only modestly used outside the field of economics.

Thus, on the one hand, increasing overlap, blurred boundaries and the emergence of new multi- or interdisciplinary fields have made the established division of social science into clearly distinguished disciplines still more problematic. On the other hand, strong institutional dynamics within academia still reproduce and reinforce the existing disciplinary boundaries. The institutionalization of the social sciences is to some extent a process of increasing autonomy from external social connection. One of the consequences of the development that sociologists have conceptualized as the differentiation into societal subsystems (Luhmann) and the rise of expert systems (Giddens) has been a strong self-reinforcing dynamics within largely autonomous institutions of research and education, primarily universities. However, the institutionalization of the social sciences has never been fully autonomous (Wagner, 2001). Government policies and new social needs and practices have modified the autonomy and the self-reinforcing dynamics of the strengthening of disciplinary boundaries. In the last decades the counteracting initiatives include the establishment of policy-oriented research institutes, interdisciplinary education and training, and targeted funding for interdisciplinary research projects. The central role of universities in academia as undisputed centres of research is even increasingly being contested by new separate elite institutions for research and education.

Although university departments of economics have become increasingly dominated by neoclassical economics, there has been room for other approaches in business economics and other more practical applications of economics. In addition, economists outside of academia seldom apply the deductive reasoning of neoclassical economics in their daily practice. The current strength of the forces counteracting the self-reinforcing dynamics of mainstream economics necessitates that the institutions of the discipline adapt or alternatively accept the increasing irrelevance of the ivory tower.

WHAT IS ECONOMICS: A METHOD, AN OBJECT, A SYSTEM, OR A FIELD?

The borderlines between the social science disciplines are permeable and the definition of economics is not clear. In order to clarify the issue of the boundaries of economics as a discipline it is necessary to clarify what we mean by economics and to confront different answers to this question.

Four general types of answers to the question can be identified. Economics can be understood as (1) a method or an approach; (2) an object or a subject matter; (3) a system; or (4) a field (Hausner and Jessop (2000) use a similar categorization although they define some of the categories differently and do not include all of these). The explicit definitions of economics typically adopt one of the four possible types of answers. Here we shall briefly outline and discuss the different answers. The main purpose of the exercise is to broadly outline the general understanding of economics as perceived by mainstream economists and to confront this with the general heterodox positions. The differences between mainstream and heterodox economics can be seen as different positions along four dimensions corresponding to the four types of answers.

The first type of answer defines economics as a specific method, or a specific approach. Economics can be defined, as in the famous definition by Lionel Robbins, as 'the science which studies human behaviour as a relationship between ends and scarce means which have competing ends' (Robbins, 1935: 16). This is a very general definition relating to the nature of the problem to be solved without any reference to substance. Economics is the science of (rational) choice, a specific approach to understanding social interaction in general. Gary Becker explicitly prefers this definition to substantial definitions (Becker, 1976, Chapter 1). Most mainstream textbooks subscribe to this definition, although sometimes in combination with a reference to a specific subject matter. The method of constrained maximization based on rational choice is what has made possible a much higher level of formalization and application of mathematics than in other social sciences. This is the foundation of the recent trend of economic imperialism, which has of course provoked criticism and resistance from the other social sciences (Archer and Tritter, 2000). The methodological issue also divides the mainstream from heterodoxy within economics. Heterodox economics advocates methodological pluralism and rejects an identification of economics with a specific methodology, or one specific approach.

The main alternative is to see economics as the study of the economy. This is how heterodox economics typically understands economics but some mainstream economists do so as well, sometimes in combination with reference to the method of constrained optimization. This alternative has two variants. One alternative defines the economy as an object, or a subject matter. The other alternative sees the economy as a system.

Before Robbins, all economists typically understood economics as the study of a specific object or subject matter. Nowadays some mainstream economists still do and all heterodox economists seem to do so as well, although often implicitly rather than explicitly. In these definitions the specific subject matter can be defined in many different ways. Gary Becker discusses two types of substantial definitions. The first refers to the allocation of goods to satisfy material needs whereas the second refers to the market sector as the area of study. According to the first definition, economics is the 'social science that deals with the ways in which men and societies seek to satisfy their material means and ends' (Becker, 1976: 3). The second definition focuses on social interaction that takes the form of market relations. This is connected with money in the sense that market relations include activities that can be directly or indirectly measured in money.

Becker criticizes both types of definition. The first is considered as the narrower and least satisfactory. Becker certainly has a point. It is and has increasingly become difficult to distinguish between material and non-material wants, as well as between tangible and intangible goods. The second definition is more to Becker's taste, although he rejects this as well. If the market sector includes all activities that can indirectly be measured in money terms this definition is clearly broader than the first definition; it relates to material as well as immaterial wants, and it opens a door for an expansive application of economics by reinterpreting social relationships as exchange relationships guided by shadow prices. Anyway, the definition is still narrower than the definition of economics as a method (a science of choice) that is not restricted to the market sector, however widely this is understood. However, the location of the boundaries of economics is not at all clear if it is said to include all that can indirectly be measured in money. If you can reinterpret or imagine social interactions as market relations then they are part of the subject matter of economics independent of any objective distinctions. The boundaries of economics then become a question of imagination rather than substance, or a social construction if you wish.

Other substantial definitions similarly escape any reference to ontology. This is the case if economics is understood as 'what economists do', which is often implicitly the case. Economics may also be defined institutionally, such as '(the study of) the social interaction within economic institutions' (Caporaso and Levine, 1992: 28–31). However, this merely shifts the problem into distinguishing between economic and other institutions instead.

All the ambiguities related to definitions of economics as an object are reflections of a general problem with substantial definitions. The problem concerns the location of the exact boundaries of the object/subject matter. What is endogenous and what is exogenous? The next section will explore this problem in more depth. Maybe the character of the problem makes it unsolvable in principle. A clear demarcation of the subject matter necessarily comes at the price of ignoring several important aspects, linkages and relationships. However, this is not in itself a sufficient reason for escaping a definition of the economy as a subject matter and preferring a definition of economics as a method instead.

The third type of answer understands the economy as a system. The economy is seen as an interlinked set of interactions. It is a system in the sense that it has elements, relationships, boundaries and emergent properties. The system can be seen as either closed, open, or open/closed (autopoietic). A closed system focuses on a limited set of variables and conceptualizes the role of the environment as constant parameters or exogenous variables. The environment provides input to the economic system but external changes do not influence the structure and the dynamics of it. On the other hand, in an open system the environment can have structural impacts on the economic system. Rather than a fully holistic view of the economy/society, an open system uses tentative closure but is aware of structural impacts and consequently of the unpredictability of the system. An autopoietic system is both open and closed at the same time. It is open in the sense that it receives external input from the environment and it is closed in the sense that it can only understand the external input by means of its own logic/code. The system can be economic or socioeconomic. An economic system includes only economic variables and forms of interaction, whereas a socioeconomic system integrates political, social and other variables and forms of interaction.

Mainstream economics sees the economy as a closed system of market relations with political, social and other external input in a form that can be taken as 'given'. However, the methodological approach has been extended to explain the internal relations of firms and other 'black boxes' as well as some of the 'given' variables. Heterodox economics typically perceives the economy as an open system. The autopoietic view of the economic system is related to the idea of increasing functional differentiation of societal subsystems. It has been pioneered by Luhmann (Luhmann, 1984; 1995) and has also been applied in a Gramscian–Marxist reinterpretation of the role of the economy in society (Jessop, 1990).

There are obvious dilemmas and trade-offs in relation to systemic openness. On the one hand, openness increases relevance but reduces possibilities for modelling. On the other hand, a closed system is more susceptible to modelling but is less relevant. If the economy is seen as a closed system, it is assumed that all the exogenous variables (including political and social variables) can be considered 'given' and stable. Mainstream economics sees preferences, technology, resources and institutions as exogenous. These exogenous factors provide input to the system and influence the outcome of the systemic interactions, but they are not formed by these interactions, and the internal dynamics of the system is independent of the exogenous variables. The problem with this approach is related to the assumption that all these variables are 'given' and stable. If preferences and technology are actually formed by the economic system they are endogenous rather than exogenous, and an approach that perceives them as exogenous implies ignorance of important linkages and mechanisms. The problems with the autopoietic view of the economic system are two-fold. First, it cannot deal with disembedding/re-embedding processes. It is blind to processes that disembed the economy from society as well as processes that re-embed the economy in society (Polanyi, 2001 [1944]). Second, it is also blind to mixed forms of allocation or decision-making, such as negotiations (Willke, 1992).

There is a fourth possible way of defining economics. As an alternative to methodological and substantial definitions, economics can be seen as a field, that is, defined by a set of institutionalized rules and norms of practices, common understandings, evaluation criteria, guardians of standards, communities of practice (professions, journals, scientific societies, educational and research standards, prizes, textbooks, and so on) (Di Maggio and Powell, 1991). This is based on an understanding of the social science disciplines from a 'sociology of science' point of view. Disciplines are seen as scientific communities of practice. Boundaries between disciplines are based on practice and convention and they are not necessarily natural or based on clear differences as far as subject matter and methodology are concerned. The daily practice of economists is to a large extent formed by an implicit understanding of economics as a field. Boundaries between subject areas and methods may be blurred but the institutions of the disciplines still clearly define affiliations.

In this sense there is a clear distinction between the disciplines of economics and sociology, which is otherwise not easy to see. It has become increasingly difficult and may not at all make sense to distinguish between the subject matters of the two disciplines (Hodgson, 2007) but there are clear institutional differences (Baron and Hannan, 1994). Mainstream economics tends to understand the field of economics more academically and rather narrowly, even to the extent of excluding heterodox economics in some cases. Heterodox economics sees the field as more inclusive, encompassing everybody that studies the economy broadly defined, including the new interdisciplinary 'disciplines' (for example, economic sociology and economic psychology) and interdisciplinary practices as well. Developments in the relationship between economics departments and business schools/policy analysis are interesting in the context of understanding economics as a field. Business and policy orientation seem to induce a broad understanding whereas economics departments represent the narrowest interpretation of economics as a field.

In conclusion, mainstream economics embraces mainly a methodological definition of economics, although many economists combine this with a substantial definition. The economy is seen as a closed system and the understanding of economics as a field is narrow and serves the exclusion of non-conformists. From a heterodox perspective the methodological stand is pluralist and a definition based on one method or one approach is rejected. Economics is rather defined as the study of a specific subject matter, that is, the economy, although it is often implicit and unclear as to what this implies. The economy is most often understood as an open system and the discipline is seen as an inclusive field. The heterodox position has an evident critical potential. However, it is crucial from a heterodox perspective to develop a clear substantial and (open) systemic understanding of economics in order to strengthen its analytical power. In this context it is important to define the boundaries, to develop a meaningful tentative closure of the system, and to articulate and/or model the structural impact of the environment in the context of an 'open system' understanding of economics.

EXOGENOUS AND ENDOGENOUS FACTORS IN STUDIES OF THE ECONOMY

The issues of boundaries, closure and structural impacts can all be seen as related to the distinction between exogenous and endogenous factors in economics. It may be advantageous to review briefly a study of the relationships between economics and the other social sciences that took this distinction as its point of departure. IDEA (Interdisciplinary Dimensions of Economic Analysis) was a research project that was initiated by the International Social Science Council and took place in the years 1983–88. The results of the research are reported in Himmelstrand (1992a) and in special issues of *Social Science Information* (24 (3) 1985; 24 (4) 1985; 25 (1) 1986) and *International Social Science Journal* (113, 1987). IDEA was an interesting study, although more for its approach and some of its evidence than for its conclusions. Revisiting the study is in many respects revealing. In general, it documents how difficult it is to communicate across disciplines but it also shows that fruitful interaction is easier in some instances than in others. It shows the variety of approaches within economics and it also reveals some of the causes for the strength of mainstream economics and the challenges of heterodoxy. Furthermore, it shows how the framework of a study to a large extent predetermines the results.

The initiation of the research project can to a certain extent be seen as an attempt to counteract the flawed interdisciplinarity of economic imperialism. The IDEA project did not aim at the endogenization of exogenous factors in formal economic models. This would mean, for instance, that the behaviour of politicians, public employees and voters would be subject to

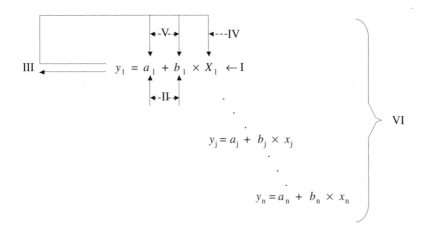

Figure 1.1   Various types of 'plug-ins' in economic processes (IDEA project)

explanations in terms of economic theory. The aim of IDEA was quite contrary, that is, to identify economically relevant exogenous variables, and to find ways of building them into economic theory without sacrificing the substance and form of non-economic theories that cover the exogenous domain (Himmelstrand, 1992b). The study was organized around the model seen in Figure 1.1.

The model presents the economy as a system of simple linear functional equations with independent variables (x), dependent variables (y) and parameters (a, b). The model is used to formalize what kind of inputs other disciplines can contribute to the analysis of economic processes, and what kind of outputs of economics can be made useful in other disciplines. The conditions and processes covered by other disciplines can be seen as plug-ins (I and II), spillovers (III), mediated feedback (IV and V) or structural impacts (VI). The plug-ins refer to either exogenous independent variables (I) or exogenous parameters (II). It is easy to see how contributions from psychology and law, for instance, can be seen as exogenous independent variables, plug-ins (preferences, legal regulation) or exogenous plug-ins on parameters such as price elasticities (cognition) and costs of tax avoidance (enforcement of tax rules). The spillovers are the social, political, environmental and other effects of economic interaction.

Some of the feedbacks (multiplying effects, forward and backward linkages, and so on) can be accounted for purely in terms of economic variables, but other feedback loops are mediated through non-economic processes. For instance, the environmental effects of economic change may feed back into the economy in terms of changing relative prices. The structural impacts are exogenous influences that extend beyond the plug-ins, spillovers and feedbacks. The idea is that the given social structure and other non-economic conditions may influence the working of the economy, not in terms of isolated effects on variables or parameters but in a more structural and wholesale fashion. Structural impacts include, for instance, the tendency for some combinations of variables to occur easily whereas others do not, independent of the predictions based on the logic of the economic system in itself. This is similar to the mechanisms described by other scholars as structural selectivity (Offe, 1984) and strategic selectivity (Jessop, 1990). Other structural impacts are transformation of equations or the event of novelty in terms of new variables and parameters, or even new equations.

The IDEA project was to be executed in four phases: (1) economists from different economic schools conceptualize how the concept of exogenous factors was used in their approach; (2) scholars from other disciplines should conceptualize their input to economics; (3) a theoretical attempt at integrating the various contributions was planned; and (4) the new integrated approach should be applied in studies of cases of common concern across disciplines. Whereas the first two phases were executed according to the plan and resulted in several interesting papers, the third part was not implemented apart from a brief attempt by the project coordinator (Himmelstrand, 1992c). Several case studies were made but not in the intended form of application of a novel methodology.

Mainstream economists were most comfortable with the model although they generally seemed to ignore the possibility of structural impacts of exogenous factors. Some other disciplines (for example, demography and law) could easily use it as well. It was much less so for heterodox economics and for disciplines close to economics in terms of subject matter. They found it difficult to conceptualize their contributions by means of the elements and relationships of the IDEA model. Generally, they perceived the model as a 'straitjacket' and often found it necessary to conceptualize their contributions to the analysis of the economy in other ways. Some found the model implicitly adapted to the conceptual logic of neoclassical economics with its perception of 'given' exogenous factors. The participating mainstream economists did not advocate economic imperialism with its implicit negligence of contributions from other disciplines. They recognized the importance of other disciplines and expressed willingness to take into account their contributions – but they were unhappy with these contributions, in particular those from sociology and psychology. According to the mainstream economists the neighbouring disciplines do not provide inputs about, for instance, norms and preferences, in a form that is usable for economists in their modelling. The contributions from the other disciplines were typically characterized by complexity and thick description, which are not easy to integrate in formal models.

The contributions from heterodox economists can be divided into two parts. First, the Marxists stressed the structural impacts on the economy of the capitalist system and also that the internal logic in Marxist economic analysis cannot be understood by the IDEA model. Second, the institutionalist economists basically favoured endogenization of all the most relevant exogenous factors. F. Gregory Hayden advocated a holistic approach, which implies that the boundaries of analysis should be defined, not by whatever predetermined set of concepts are available in given formalized models of economic processes, but rather should be 'designed to encompass the analysis necessary to understand the problem' (Hayden, 1985: 874). In his contribution to the project, Geoffrey Hodgson focused on the rejection of the neoclassical assumption of the given individual in neoclassical economics and the attempts to endogenize preferences in institutionalist economics. In another contribution, he concludes that institutional economics is characterized by endogenization of preferences, technology and institutions (Hodgson, 1988: 16; see also Himmelweit et al., 2001: 15). It is difficult to conceptualize and operationalize such complex relationships and maybe impossible to model them.

There is an inherent bias in the IDEA model against the approach of heterodox economics. Efforts to endogenize 'non-economic' factors are not easily accounted for in the IDEA model that, motivated by its opposition to economic imperialism, seems to implicitly favour interdisciplinarity in the form of cooperation between distinct disciplines rather than integration of elements in a holistic analysis. The strength of mainstream economics is its rigorous approach and narrow focus with clear boundaries and a clearly identified internal logic, which makes it easy to conceptualize its relation to other social science disciplines. Heterodox economics gives priority to relevance and integrates aspects that are the primary focus in other disciplines. The problem with mainstream economics in this respect is its failure to take into account the richness and complexity of the contributions from other disciplines as inputs to its rigorous formal models. However, heterodox economics has also problems in its relationships to the other social sciences. It is basically unclear whether heterodox economics manages to properly take into account the contributions from other disciplines. The mere willingness to integrate the aspects that are the primary focus in other disciplines is not a guarantee against amateurism in the actual efforts to take this into account. It is one of the major challenges of heterodox economics to develop a proper interdisciplinary approach to the analysis of the economy.

RECENT TRENDS AND FUTURE TRAJECTORIES

The last 50 years has been a story of the decomposition of the boundaries between economics and the other social sciences as far as subject matter and method are concerned. At the same time the separate disciplines have been reinforced as institutionalized fields, although this is being counteracted by efforts of governments and business (supported by some academics and student groups), to strengthen interdisciplinarity, practice orientation and policy relevance. However, communication across disciplinary boundaries is still rather undeveloped and knowledge of neighbouring disciplines is modest. This is so even in the case of disciplines that are close and overlapping, such as economics and sociology. Citation data show that sociologists seldom refer to the work of economists; they tend to refer exclusively to a few contributions such as Marxist economists in the 1970s and Gary Becker's work in the 1990s, and citations have not grown from the 1970s to the 1990s (Baron and Hannan, 1994). A similar study of economists' citation practice would no doubt reveal even less attention, among mainstream economists, to the work of sociologists.

The contributions to this book begin to fill this gap of knowledge and to build much needed bridges between economics and the other social sciences. However the gap is wide, and the book cannot, of course, contribute more than fragments of what is needed. In recent years there have been interesting developments outside of economics that are either directly or indirectly relevant to the study of the economy. We shall briefly summarize what we consider to be some of the most interesting developments within sociology, psychology and political science.

The emergence of new economic sociology means that we now have a parallel (sub)discipline with exactly the same object of study as economics. The new economic sociology takes its point of departure in a fundamental critique of microeconomics. Economic man is seen as undersocialized. New economic sociology offers an alternative conception of economic actors as embedded in networks and partly formed by normative, cognitive and cultural forces (Granovetter, 1985; Smelser and Swedberg, 2005 [1994]; Swedberg, 2003). Microeconomics is also criticized for failing to take into account the implications of fundamental uncertainty that is seen to characterize all important economic decisions. In situations of uncertainty economic actors have no basis for making rational decisions in isolation, which necessitates social communication and conventions, and consequently a sociological dimension in the study of the economy (Beckert, 1996). Even if new economic sociology is a relatively new phenomenon, many highly interesting studies have been made within this tradition of, for instance, shareholder capitalism (Fligstein, 2001), money (Ingham, 2002), job markets (Granovetter, 1995 [1974]) and economic networks (Powell and Doerr-Smith, 2005 [1994]).

The emerging literature on social capital is another example of the increased interaction between economics and sociology. The concept 'social capital' was originally developed by sociologists (Bourdieu, Coleman, and so on) as a way of conceptualizing the beneficial effects of an individual's social relations, and was later taken up by political scientists (Putnam, and others) in attempts to understand the societal effects of the prevalence of trust, social norms and civic participation. There is powerful evidence of the existence of a correlation between social capital and economic performance (Knack and Kiefer, 1997; Durlauf and Fafchamps, 2005), and many economists have taken up the concept as a possible 'missing link' in the literature on development, growth, transition, regional development and a lot of other areas (Dasgupta and Serageldin, 2000). The acceptance by economists of the economic role of social relations not only makes possible new and more cooperative relations between economists and sociologists. It may also make economists inclined to adapt their approach to take into account sociological findings and perspectives that have traditionally been ignored by economists. However, some scholars believe that the social capital literature rather trivializes and distorts the research of social relations by subsuming them under the concept of capital (Fine, 2001).

Psychology systematically explores human judgment, and findings of psychological research show how humans differ from the way they are traditionally described by economists. Neoclassical economics is built on assumptions of human behaviour that have long been rejected by psychology. For more than a century the findings of psychological research were generally ignored by mainstream economists but this has changed. In recent decades contributions by psychologists (Daniel Kahneman and Amos Tversky) and by an economist strongly inspired by psychology (Herbert Simon) have received the ultimate recognition of the profession, that is, the Nobel Prize award. Simon has applied cognitive psychology as well as findings from other disciplines to the study of decision-making within economic organizations (Simon, 1997 [1947]). This has led him to reject the assumption in the classical economic theory of the firm of an omniscient, rational, profit-maximizing entrepreneur. He substitutes this with an assumption of a number of cooperating decision-makers, whose capacities for rational action are limited, both by a lack of knowledge about the total consequences of their decisions, and by personal and social ties. These decision-makers cannot choose the best alternative and have to be content with a satisfactory alternative. Individual companies, therefore, strive not to maximize profits but to find acceptable solutions to acute problems ('satisficing').

The prevailing view in psychology in general, and in cognitive psychology in particular, is to regard a human being as a system that codes and interprets available information in a partly unconscious manner via emotions, perception, mental models for interpreting specific situations, and memories of earlier decisions and their consequences. Kahneman and Tversky and other psychologists have applied this perspective in surveys and experiments that call into question the assumption of rational choice, in particular in situations of uncertainty (Royal Swedish Academy of Sciences, 2002; Kahneman et al., 1982; Kahneman and Tversky, 2000; Rabin, 1998). One of the striking findings is that individuals are much more sensitive to the way an outcome deviates from a reference level (often the status quo) than to the absolute outcome. Kahneman and Tversky have developed an alternative theory of decision-making under uncertainty, known as prospect theory (Kahneman and Tversky, 1979). In addition to biases in judgment under uncertainty, findings in psychology have also shown that preferences are often incoherent, and that motivations often depart from pure self-interest. Economists who are sensitive to this evidence have developed an interest in bounded rationality and mental models, and other alternative approaches that challenge core assumptions of mainstream economics.

Mainstream economics has more impact on contemporary political science than it has on sociology (Miller, 1997). The application of microeconomics in studies of politics has been a significant trend in political science in recent decades. Public choice theory and principal–agent models have been widely adopted. They have challenged traditional understandings of the behaviour of voters and politicians, and the role of public agencies and interest associations, and have formed the theoretical background for public sector reform. On the other hand, other developments in political science have the potential for making an impact in economics. Political science has not only been influenced by economics but also by what has been termed the cultural, discursive, cognitive, and institutional 'turns' in the social sciences. Neo- and post-Marxists and others have focused on the role of hegemony in political struggles and the increasing importance of cultural relative to material reproduction. Various strands of discourse theory (Torfing, 1999; Fairclough, 1995) and an emerging 'cultural political economy' (Jessop, 2005) have emerged as a result. Political scientists have also tried to take into account insights from cognitive psychology and, in general, the role of cognitive frames, meaning and ideas in political discourse (Campbell, 1998). A highly influential new trend in political science is the new institutionalism initiated by contributions from March and Olsen (1989). They stress the normative and cognitive role of institutions and the role of the logic of appropriateness in understanding policy outcomes. Economists may benefit from adopting a similar attention to the normative and cognitive role of institutions rather than the exclusive focus on their constraining, regulative role, or what is termed by March and Olsen the logic of consequentiality, in understanding human behaviour. Recent developments in political science may also inform the efforts of economists to come to terms with the role of mental models in economic decision-making.

Mainstream economics is based on an expansive research programme with a strong core and a flexible protection belt. The core is constituted by assumptions of optimizing behaviour, equilibrium and informational characteristics that makes optimization possible. The protective belt is practically everything else. The concepts and theories that constitute the protective belt may easily be substituted with alternative concepts and theories without compromising the strong core. However, the core needs to be protected and cannot be substituted with something else if the research programme shall be maintained. This is the reason why so much effort is being made to interpret bounded rationality, rule-following and trust as optimizing behaviour and to interpret uncertainty as probabilistic risk.

Mainstream economics has expanded significantly in recent years. Significant developments are public choice, social choice, Becker's economic theory of human behaviour, and, more recently, the rise of information economics/cognitive economics, evolutionary games theory, social capital theory, and new institutional economics. The expansion shows the strength of the mainstream. To a large extent, these are examples of economic imperialism. However, the expansion also to some extent represents efforts to integrate evidence and perspectives from other social science theories, and the encounter with the other disciplines implies cracks in the core of the neoclassical research programme. Social capital theory challenges methodological individualism. Cognitive psychology challenges the assumption of given and stable preferences as well as the assumption regarding the informational characteristics of decision-making situations necessary for maintaining the assumption of optimizing behaviour. The recognition of the importance of perception and mental models makes impossible the idea of the representative agent and introduces variety and the possibility of novelty and surprise. Bounded rationality and satisficing make the assumption of optimizing behaviour as well as the assumption of the given individual untenable. Mainstream economists and the founding father of the concept of satisfying (Herbert Simon) maintain the link between the phenomenon of satisficing and optimization. However, how is it possible to see satisficing as optimization with scarce time and attention when there is no basis at all for calculation of the costs of alternative choices? Obviously, the perception of what is satisfactory is dependent on aspirations and expectations based on social interaction and social norms, which makes it necessary to abandon the assumption of the free-standing individual with given preferences and to include the social as a sphere that cannot be reduced to effects of individual behaviour.

Heterodox economics is more open to interaction with the other social sciences and compared to mainstream economics it is in a situation that makes it easier to integrate the new insight from the other social sciences. The pluralist inclinations of heterodoxy make it difficult to identify the core and protective belt (following Lakatos's characterization of research programmes), although some strands of heterodoxy certainly have core assumptions. The vagueness of the core assumptions implies less resistance to integrating contributions from other social sciences on their own terms. This is also facilitated by the open systems approach of heterodoxy to the study of the economy and its inclusive understanding of economics as a field. However, heterodox economics has fundamental problems, which are to some extent reinforced by the increased interaction with the other social sciences. When economics is defined by an object of study it is crucial to clarify its boundaries. It is also crucial to establish the criteria for meaningful tentative closure of the open system of the economy in order to make possible a more advanced level of analysis. Furthermore, how is it possible to operationalize the economy as a socioeconomic system rather than an economic system?

However, recent developments imply not only challenges but also opportunities for heterodox economics. Part of it is connected to the emerging cracks in the neoclassical core. Part of it is linked to the opportunities for providing concepts and theories that offer better explanations and policy guidance in relation to a range of economic phenomena where the following characteristics prevail: extensiveness (overload of information), complexity and uncertainty (Hodgson, 1997); cognition and learning; intersubjectivity (Fullbrook, 2002); path dependence and context specificity (see Chapter 5); networks and trust; and hegemony and logic of appropriateness. Interdisciplinarity is crucial in order to take account of these characteristics. The role of institutions is also crucial in relation to all these aspects, but that is another story.

THE CONTRIBUTIONS TO THIS VOLUME

This book is novel and important because it builds bridges over the hitherto far-too-silent waters between economics and the other disciplines. The book analyses various aspects of the relationship between economics and the other social sciences. Some of the contributions focus directly on the relationships between economics and one or more social science disciplines such as sociology, anthropology or psychology. Others focus on phenomena that reflect the need for overcoming the barriers between economics and the other social sciences. These contributions take their point of departure in the analysis of a specific economic problem and offer new perspectives and new analytical tools by means of integrating contributions from the other social sciences in the analysis. A variety of inputs from a wide range of disciplines (sociology, anthropology, psychology, cognitive science, history, philosophy, and even evolutionary biology) are being applied in efforts to bring new light on concepts and phenomena such as utility maximization, production activities, the environment, social relations, flexibility and routines. Most of the contributions discuss and critique mainstream economics in the context of the social sciences and bring in evidence and perspectives from other social sciences in developing novel approaches to the studied phenomena. Some of the contributions do so in the context of the institutional and evolutionary strands of heterodox economics.

The rest of the book is divided into three parts. Part I consists of contributions that focus on the relationships and boundaries between economics and the social sciences. Chapter 2 actually goes beyond the social sciences and relates to biology as well. Chapter 3 discusses the changing relationships between economics and sociology. Chapter 4 covers the various institutionalist approaches in the social sciences. Chapter 5 is about the role of generality and specificity in economic and social theory and brings the role of history into focus.

The intricacies that invariably crop up in any exchange between economics and the social sciences are addressed by Jack Vromen in Chapter 2, 'What can be learnt from "serious" biology and psychology?' Vromen begins by exploring the intricacies that are entailed in any effort by economists to 'learn' from other social sciences. In his view, there are at least three issues involved in attempts at such cross-disciplinary learning: (1) what disciplines to turn to; (2) what aspects to concentrate on; and (3) how to interpret their implications for economics. However, difficulties emerge also in instances in which scientists from other disciplines attempt to recommend to economists where to turn to for inspiration. Vromen explores the recommendation offered by the sociobiologist Edward O. Wilson, that economists should turn to 'serious' psychology and biology – where the adjective 'serious' is supposed to refer to biologically-informed psychology, or evolutionary psychology as it is commonly known. For Wilson, this recommendation stems from his conviction that all disciplines, social sciences included, must be anchored to the 'hard' natural sciences. However,

Vromen argues that it is precisely this conviction that cannot be easily accepted by economists, as both mainstream and heterodox schools of thought will have serious, albeit conflicting difficulties with it.

In Chapter 3, 'Economics and sociology in the transition from industrial to post-industrial capitalism', George Liagouras analyses the different phases in the relationships between economics and sociology by referring to the broader socioeconomic environment, characterising each phase. From this standpoint, classical political economy and classical sociology are seen as two opposed conceptions of civil society related to distinct phases of industrial capitalism. The former has been founded in the beginnings of industrial capitalism and it assumes that material reproduction is the basis of societies and that free markets are self-regulating mechanisms promoting economic development and social welfare. The latter has been founded during the turning point from the liberal to the late capitalist (1890–1920). It asserts that it is moral and intellectual beliefs that determine social dynamics and that constitute the main source of social order. Then the author interprets the blurring boundaries between economics and sociology during the last two decades in the context of the rise of post-industrial capitalism. In post-industrial capitalism the main sphere for the valorisation of capital moves from the material to the symbolic reproduction of individuals and societies. The above shift undermines the autonomy of the sociological conception of civil society, and at the same time compels economists to investigate a series of issues – institutions, knowledge, trust, values, culture – that stand at odds with the postulates of possessive individualism underlying the dominant economic discourse. This in turn results in a serious vacuum in our representation of civil society, which, according to the author, can be overcome only by addressing the major socioeconomic challenges put forward by the rise of post-industrial capitalism.

The idea that 'institutions matter' can now be found in many approaches within various social sciences. In Chapter 4, 'The "institutional turn" in the social sciences: a review of approaches and a future research agenda', Klaus Nielsen begins with a critical discussion of the attempts to review the various approaches and to develop general typologies across disciplines. Following this, Nielsen sets out to explore the possibilities of cross-fertilization among various institutionalist approaches. A set of preconditions for cooperation is outlined and six different approaches that share general methodological and theoretical assumptions are identified: institutional–evolutionary economics, American institutionalism, new economic sociology, new institutionalism in political science, historical institutionalism and the cognitive–institutional approach. These institutionalist approaches all share an open system, post-positivist and realist methodology. Furthermore, they are also seen to share a set of theoretical assumptions: a perception of behaviour as intended rational; an emphasis on the constitutive importance of the cultural and cognitive framework; a recognition of the pervasive role of power and conflict; and an emphasis on the role of habits, norms and routines in coordination of behaviour.

In Chapter 5, 'The problem of historical specificity', Geoff Hodgson re-interprets the relationship between nomothetic and ideographic approaches in the social sciences. The explanatory power of general theories is seen as overrated and detailed analyses of particular events, structures and circum-stances of the past are seen as needed. In economics, a general theory is seen to be always better than one with a narrower domain of analysis. However, this is not always the case because of the phenomenon of historical specificity. The lure of a general theory is seen as in part responsible for the degree of neglect of history in contemporary economics. Hodgson discusses the limits of general theories. There are different socioeconomic systems and it is shown that applications of a single, general theory in terms of mere differences in parameter values are not sufficient to capture the complexity of economic phenomena in each system. In conclusion, the social sciences in general, and the economic in particular, must combine general principles with theorizing that is aimed at specific domains. These operate on different levels of abstraction and a philosophically informed meta-theory must address the relationship between these levels.

Part II of the book includes contributions that throw new light on core phenomena in the social sciences such as rationality (Chapter 6), social relations (Chapter 7) and the environment (Chapter 8). The approaches of mainstream economics to these phenomena (utility maximization, social capital and environmental economics) is criticized and confronted with other approaches inspired by the other social sciences (Aristotelian ethics, sociality and Polanyi's institutional economics).

For orthodox economics, the principle of utility maximization consti-tutes the basis for the explanation of rational behaviour. Irene van Staveren challenges this view in Chapter 6, 'The irrationality of utility maximisation or the *Death of a Salesman*'. She bases her argument on a metaphor: the theatre play *Death of a Salesman*, by Arthur Miller. The behaviour of the play's protagonist illustrates that utilitarianism is unable to distinguish between rational and irrational behaviour. On these grounds, the concept of commitment is suggested as an alternative to utility. Van Staveren intro-duces here Aristotle's virtue ethics: different commitments (or virtues) are realized through the allocation of scarce resources via different allocation mechanisms. Rational economic behaviour then can be understood as the balancing of various types of allocation mechanisms in such a way that they mutually support each other. Thus she concludes that the Aristotelian mean is an endogenous balance depending on the mutual supportive relations between liberty, justice and benevolence, which take the shape of positive externalities.

In Chapter 7, 'Social capital or sociality? Methodological contrasts between economics and other social sciences', Desmond McNeill raises the question whether it is possible to achieve a synthesis between economics and anthropology/sociology, in view of the contrasts in the fundamental assumptions underlying the two disciplines, and especially the emphasis on the individual in economics. The author starts from a critique of recent research on social capital, which reveals the individualist base of this concept as it is used by economists. Based on literature from anthropology and psychology he shows that a case can be made for rejecting the presumption that human beings are individualistic and for instead seeing sociality as a basic human drive. McNeill concludes with the exploration of a more radical approach, in which human beings are conceptualized as fundamentally social beings and the emphasis in economics on individuals is replaced by an emphasis on social relations.

In Chapter 8, 'Where disciplinary boundaries blur: the environmental dimension of institutional economics', Eyüp Özveren explores the environmental dimensions of institutional economics, and especially the works of Karl Polanyi and William Kapp. Special emphasis is given to concepts such as 'embeddedness', 'fictitious commodity' and 'social cost'. On these grounds, Özveren argues that the 'arrow of time', that is, the irreversibility of time, makes a major difference for economic processes. This has profound implications for the manner in which economists may approach the problem of the environment. In essence, and unlike the short-term approach of mainstream economics, the approach of institutional economics allows the economist to adopt a long-term perspective and thus to theorize about the long-term effects of economic development on the environment. Therefore Özveren claims that a combination of institutional and evolutionary approaches has much to offer for the cross-fertilization of economics with other social sciences and that this nascent alternative can well challenge further the dominance of the mainstream approach over the terrain of economic enquiry.

Part III consists of three contributions that all take their point of departure in concepts that either have attracted a lot of interest recently – flexibility (Chapter 9) and routines (Chapter 10) – or have been ignored in spite of its central importance – production (Chapter 11). The three concepts are reconstructed through the application of perspectives from other social sciences or an evolutionary perspective inspired by biological metaphors.

In Chapter 9, 'Economic flexibility: a structural analysis', William Jackson investigates the meaning of the concept of flexibility, which has become commonplace in recent economic discussion. Neoclassical economics often interprets flexibility as the absence of social structure impeding the operation of free markets. However, from a non-neoclassical perspective this interpretation of flexibility is inadequate, since markets are inherently structural and founded on role-playing. Jackson argues that recent work in sociology is relevant here, as it seeks to provide more fluid versions of social structure. These versions allow the recognition of the interplay between structure and agency and among different types of social structure, which create a broader framework for social and economic analysis, capable of envisaging many forms of flexibility.

In Chapter 10, 'Routines: a brief history of the concept', Markus C. Becker argues that, despite its frequent use in economics, the concept of a routine is still quite unclear and many ambiguities and inconsistencies still prevail. Thus it is argued that a history of the concept can provide a contribution to its understanding and to a conceptual progress. On these grounds, the chapter attempts to reconstruct the history of the concept in economics and related social sciences from the Enlightenment onwards.

In Chapter 11, 'Complementarity, cognition and capabilities: towards an evolutionary theory of production', Guido Buenstorf attempts to put forth an evolutionary theory of production. The author builds on a number of concepts developed in evolutionary economics, economic history and cognitive science. The starting point of the analysis is the notion of complementarity caused by technological interdependences. Due to compatibility problems, these interdependences favour incremental over radical change, which is implied by the properties of cognitive and communicative processes that have been identified by psychologists. Based on this line of reasoning, a framework for modelling production is suggested, which is based on localized learning and the switch between technologies.

REFERENCES

Archer, M. and J.Q. Tritter (eds) (2000), *Rational Choice Theory. Resisting Colonization*, London and New York: Routledge.
Baron, J.N. and M.T. Hannan (1994), 'The impact of economics on contemporary sociology', *Journal of Economic Literature*, **XXXII** (September), 1111–46.
Becker, G. (1976), *The Economic Approach to Human Behaviour*, Chicago: The University of Chicago Press.
Beckert, J. (1996), 'What is sociological about economic sociology? Uncertainty and the embeddedness of economic action', *Theory and Society*, **25**, 803–40.
Campbell, J.L. (1998), 'Institutional analysis and the role of ideas in political economy', *Theory and Society*, **27**, 377–409.
Caporaso, J. and D. Levine (1992), *Theories of Political Economy*, Cambridge: Cambridge University Press.

Dasgupta, P. and I. Serageldin (eds) (2000), *Social Capital. A Multifaceted Perspective*, Washington, DC: The World Bank.

DiMaggio, P.J. and W.W. Powell (1991), 'The iron cage revisited: institutional isomorphism and collective rationality in organizational fields', in W.W. Powell and P.J. DiMaggio (eds), *The New Institutionalism in Organizational Theory*, Princeton: Princeton University Press, pp. 63–82.

Durlauf, S. and M. Fafchamps (2005), 'Social capital', in P. Aghion and S. Durlauf (eds), *Handbook of Economic Growth*, North Holland: Elsevier, pp. 1639–99.

Erreyghers, G. (2001), *Economics and Interdisciplinary Exchange*, London: Routledge.

Etzioni, A. (1988), *The Moral Dimension. Towards a New Economics*, New York: The Free Press.

Fairclough, N. (1995), *Critical Discourse Analysis: The Critical Study of Language*, London: Longman.

Fine, B. (2001), *Social Capital Versus Social Theory*, London: Routledge.

Fligstein, N. (2001), *The Architecture of Markets: An Economic Sociology of Twenty-First-Century Capitalist Societies*, Princeton, NJ: Princeton University Press.

Fullbrook, E. (ed.) (2002), *Intersubjectivity in Economics. Agents and Structures*, London: Routledge.

Granovetter, M. (1985), 'Economic action and social structure: the problem of embeddedness', *American Journal of Sociology*, **91**, 481–510.

Granovetter, M. (1995 [1974]), *Getting a Job. A Study of Contracts and Careers*, 2nd edition, Chicago: University of Chicago Press.

Hausner, J. and B. Jessop (2000), 'Is the economy an object, a system, or a field?', paper for the EAEPE (European Association for Evolutionary Political Economy) Conference 2000, Berlin, 2–5 November.

Hayden, F.G. (1985), 'A transdisciplinary integration matrix for economic and policy analysis', *Social Science Information*, **24** (4), 869–903.

Himmelstrand, U. (ed.) (1992a), *Interfaces in Economic and Social Analyses*, London and New York: Routledge.

Himmelstrand, U. (1992b), 'Project IDEA: an introduction', in U. Himmelstrand (ed.), *Interfaces in Economic and Social Analyses*, Routledge: London and New York, pp. 3–16.

Himmelstrand, U. (1992c), 'In search of an interdisciplinary approach for economic and social analysis', in U. Himmelstrand (ed.), *Interfaces in Economic and Social Analyses*, Routledge: London and New York, pp. 281–311.

Himmelweit, S., R. Simonetti and A. Trigg (2001), *Microeconomics. Neoclassical and Institutionalist Perspectives on Economic Behaviour*, London: Thomson Learning.

Hodgson, G.M. (1988), *Economics and Institutions*, Cambridge: Polity Press.

Hodgson, G.M. (1997), 'The ubiquity of habits and rules', *Cambridge Journal of Economics*, **21**, 663–84.

Hodgson, G.M. (2007), 'Epilogue', in K. Nielsen and C.A. Koch (eds), *Institutionalism in Economics and Sociology: Varieties, Dialogue and Future Challenges*, Cheltenham, UK and Northampton, MA, USA: Edward Elgar.

Ingham, G. (2002), 'New monetary spaces?', in OECD, *The Future of Money*, Paris: OECD, pp. 123–46.

Jessop, B. (1990), *State Theory. Putting the State in Its Place*, London: Polity Press.

Jessop, B. (2005), 'Cultural political economy, the knowledge-based economy, and the state', in A. Barry and D. Slater (eds), *The Technological Economy*, New York and London: Routledge, pp. 144–66.

Kahneman, D. and A. Tversky (1979), 'Prospect theory: an analysis of decisions under risk', *Econometrica*, **47**, 313–27.

Kahneman, D., P. Slovic and A. Tversky (eds) (1982), *Judgment Under Uncertainty: Heuristics and Biases*, Cambridge: Cambridge University Press.

Kahneman, D. and A. Tversky (eds) (2000), *Choices, Values and Frames*, New York: Cambridge University Press and the Russell Sage Foundation.

Knack, S. and P. Kiefer (1997), 'Does social capital have an economic payoff? A cross-country investigation', *Quarterly Journal of Economics*, **112** (4), 1251–88.

Levey, J.S. and A. Greenhall (1984), *The Concise Columbia Encyclopedia*, Harmondsworth: Penguin.

Luhmann, N. (1984), 'Die wirtschaft der gesellschaft als autopoietisches system', *Zeitschrift für Soziologie*, **13** (4), 308–23.

Luhmann, N. (1995), *Social Systems*, Palo Alto, CA: Stanford University Press.

Mäki, U., B. Gustafsson and C. Knudsen (eds) (1993), *Rationality, Institutions, and Economic Methodology*, New York: Routledge.

March, J.G. and J.P. Olsen (1989), *Rediscovering Institutions: The Organizational Basis of Politics*, New York: The Free Press.

Miller, G.J. (1997), 'The impact of economics on contemporary political science', *Journal of Economic Literature*, **XXXV** (September), 1173–204.

Offe, C. (1984), *Contradictions of the Welfare State*, Cambridge, MA: MIT Press.

Polanyi, K. (2001 [1944]), *The Great Transformation. The Political and Economic Origins of Our Time*, Boston: Beacon Press.

Powell, W.W. and L. Doerr-Smith (2005 [1994]), 'Networks and economic life', in N.J. Smelser and R. Swedberg (eds), *The Handbook of Economic Sociology*, 2nd edition, Princeton, NJ: Princeton University Press, pp. 379–402.

Rabin, M. (1998), 'Psychology and economics', *Journal of Economic Literature*, **XXXVI** (March), 11–46.

Robbins, L. (1935 [1932]), *An Essay on the Nature and Significance of Economic Science*, 2nd edition, London: Macmillan.

Royal Swedish Academy of Sciences (2002), *Foundations of Behavioural and Experimental Economics: Daniel Kahneman and Vernon Smith*, see www.kva.se/KVA_Root/files/newspics/DOC_2003213145652_104967873867_ecoadv02.pdf.

Simon, H. (1997 [1945]), *Administrative Behavior: A Study of Decision-Making Processes in Administrative Organizations*, 4th edition, New York: Free Press.

Smelser, N.J. and R. Swedberg (eds) (2005 [1994]), *The Handbook of Economic Sociology*, Princeton, 2nd edition, NJ: Princeton University Press.

Swedberg, R. (2003), *Principles of Economic Sociology*, Princeton, NJ: Princeton University Press.

Sum, N.L. and B. Jessop (2001), 'The pre- and post-disciplinary perspectives of political economy', *New Political Economy*, **6** (1), 89–101.

Torfing, J. (1999), *New Theories of Discourse : Laclau, Mouffe and Zizek*, Oxford: Blackwell.

Wagner, P. (2001), *A History and Theory of the Social Sciences. Not All That is Solid Melts into Air*, London: Sage.

Wallerstein, I. (ed.) (1996), *Open the Social Sciences. Report from the Gulbenkian Commission on the Restructuring of the Social Sciences*, Stanford, CA: Stanford University Press.

Willke, H. (1992), *Ironie des Staates: Grundlinien einer Staatstheorie Polyzentrischer Gesellschaft*, Frankfurt: Suhrkamp.

PART I

Economics and other social sciences:
relationships and boundaries

2. What can be learnt from 'serious' biology and psychology?

Jack Vromen

INTRODUCTION

In these times of postmodernist irony and anarchy, Edward O. Wilson's *Consilience: The Unity of Knowledge* (1998) stands out as a bold, grand prophecy and advocacy of the nascent convergence of our knowledge in fields that hitherto were worlds apart. Wilson envisions a future in which 'all great branches of learning', ranging from the several natural sciences over the social sciences to moral theory and religion, are connected with one another in a comprehensive and coherent way. Economics is dealt with only cursorily in Wilson's book. Though not entirely dismissive, Wilson is quite critical of the present state of the art of economics. In his opinion, economics is lacking in particular in relevance for practical and policy issues. Economists can overcome this deficit, Wilson argues, by taking to heart what 'serious psychology and biology' tell us about human behaviour.

Wilson's argument raises several questions. Why should economists turn to psychology and biology rather than to sociology and cultural anthropology, for example? What parts or branches of psychology and biology are 'serious'? What distinguishes serious from facetious and 'trivial' psychology and biology? And, finally, what precisely is there for economists to learn from serious psychology and biology? This chapter not only sets out to discuss Wilson's answers to these questions and the arguments behind them; an attempt is made also to put Wilson's answers in the wider perspective of a general discussion of the peculiarities, vicissitudes and pitfalls of cross-disciplinary learning.

VICISSITUDES OF CROSS-DISCIPLINARY LEARNING

Many economists lately are engaged in cross-disciplinary learning, in attempts to learn from other disciplines. Many economists have started to reach out to other disciplines, looking for things they can learn from them. To an outsider it may seem obvious that economists should do this, but economics has long lived in 'splendid isolation' from other disciplines. It is as if for most of the previous century economists collectively signed a declaration of independence from other disciplines (Lewin, 1996). This seems to be changing lately. It seems one can only welcome this. By closing their own discipline off from 'input' from other disciplines, potentially interesting and fruitful insights developed in these other disciplines may have been foregone. Yet opening up the borders with adjacent disciplines not only creates new opportunities for mutually beneficial trade. It also raises several vexing problems. What other discipline(s) to turn to, for example? Nowadays we can see some economists venturing into psychology, for example, whereas others try sociology, (cultural) anthropology, (evolutionary) biology or literary criticism.

When it comes to cross-disciplinary learning, disagreement among economists abounds. As we shall see, massive disagreement pertains not just to what disciplines are to be chosen (or consulted), but also to what aspects of other disciplines economists can learn something from and what implications the chosen aspects of the chosen disciplines have for economics. Let us start by having a look at how different economists treat the two disciplines Wilson singles out as *the* disciplines economics should turn to: biology and psychology.

Biology (or more generally, evolutionary theory) lately has become a source of inspiration to many economists. Here we can think of evolutionary game theory entering economics, for example, and of the Nelson and Winter (1982) type of evolutionary economics. This already suggests that we can find different views among economists on what lessons biology holds for economics. On the one end of the spectrum we have Paul Krugman (1999) arguing that mainstream economics and mainstream evolutionary theory are very much alike. Krugman is struck by the similarity, if not identity, in 'basic method' between standard economics and evolutionary theory (1999, p. 19). Both standard economics and evolutionary theory follow what Krugman calls the maximization-and-equilibrium approach (ibid., p. 21). 'Maximization' and 'equilibrium' are useful fictions, Krugman argues, that allow economists and evolutionary theorists alike to cut through what might otherwise be forbidding complexity (in their respective subject matters).[1]

At the other side of the spectrum we find, for example, Geoff Hodgson (1999) arguing for 'NEAR' (Novelty-Embracing, Anti-Reductionist) evolutionary economics. Clearly, Hodgson finds many faults in the maximization-and-equilibrium approach of standard economics. Neither in economics nor in biology, Hodgson argues, are 'maximization' and 'equilibrium' useful notions to study dynamic evolutionary processes. Hodgson holds that the 'biological metaphor' is suitable for economics only to the extent that evolutionary biology hosts anti-reductionist, non-mechanistic and non-individualist approaches. These approaches show economists possible new avenues to explore. Hodgson is aware that reductionist, mechanistic and individualistic approaches also abound in evolutionary biology (Hodgson, 1999, p. 75). But as economics itself already is dominated by such an approach and suffers from this dominance, these latter approaches are best viewed as blind alleys for economists.

What this shows is that economists apparently assign opposite implications for their own discipline to some chosen discipline (in this case biology); one 'pro' and the other 'con' standard economic theory. It is no coincidence, I submit, that the maximization-and-equilibrium approach in evolutionary biology that is quite akin to the approach followed in standard economic theory catches the eye of Krugman. And it does not come as a surprise either that Hodgson, who is much more hostile to standard economic theory than Krugman, is looking for other approaches in evolutionary biology; approaches that could help evolutionary economists further develop a NEAR variant. It is the difference in their preconceived beliefs about (standard) economic theory that makes them go their different ways here.

Other economists have paid attention to other aspects of biology. Becker (1976), Hirshleifer (1977) and Coase (1976 and 1978), among others, have argued that the primary relevance of (socio)biology for economics does not lie so much in the approach(es) biology follows as in the view of man it implies. In particular, these economists believe that biology can tell economists what preference patterns people have. Note that in their academic careers these economists have defended and applied standard economic theory extensively. In their view biology provides data that standard economic theory needs if it is to be operationalized and applied. The relation between biology and (standard) economics envisioned is thus a highly reconciliatory one. Again, I think this is no coincidence. Their preconceived pro-attitude towards standard economic theory makes them look for ideas and insights in other disciplines that are compatible with it.

Becker *cum suis*, we could say, focuses on an ontological aspect of biology. Generally speaking an ontological aspect relates to the issue of what relevant properties relevant entities (within some disciplines) have. In the case under discussion we can say that evolutionary biology is assumed to shed some light on the issue of what preferences real people actually have. Krugman and Hodgson seem to be primarily interested in epistemological and methodological aspects of biology. How do biologists approach the phenomena they address? What sorts of notions do they apply in doing this? What is their explanatory strategy?

Roughly the same picture emerges if we look at how economists treat psychology. Perhaps what has drawn most attention from economists over the last few decades is the Heuristics and Biases Program pioneered by Kahneman and Tversky (see, for example, Rabin, 1998). Many economists, especially heterodox ones, take the experimental results established in this program to be devastating for standard economic theory (and for expected utility theory in particular). Others warn against drawing over-hasty conclusions. Findings in experimental economics suggest that standard economic theory predicts well in some situations (such as in laboratory experimental markets) but not in others (Smith, 1991).[2]

Others add to this that it should not have come as a surprise that people do not reason flawlessly in unfamiliar, artificial laboratory situations. People can only be expected to do well if they are given enough time to become acquainted with these situations and to find out, through some sort of trial-and-error learning, the best way to behave. Furthermore, if the stakes in experiments are low (which they typically are in psychological experiments, these economists hold) then subjects are not sufficiently motivated to learn how to perform well (see, for example, Binmore, 1999). Thus, these economists assume that if only the incentives provided and the time given to subjects are sufficient for them to learn, the biases in decision-making identified by experimental psychologists will go away.

Thus, as with biology, some economists concentrate on what psychology entails for the ontological issues that economists are (or at least could be) interested in. Are 'irrational' biases in actual learning and actual behaviour omnipresent and ineradicable, so that expected utility theory effectively is refuted? Or do these biases only appear in artificial situations, so that at most qualifications about the applicability of expected utility theory are needed? Other economists such as Frey (1992) argue that one of the main contributions of psychology to economics could lie in its demonstrations of how to test theories empirically. Economics, which does not have the strong empirical orientation that psychology has, could benefit from paying attention to how psychologists put their theories to experimental tests. Frey also argues that, conversely, (social) psychology can learn (and de facto already has learned) from economics. Frey notes that even though they largely developed independently of one another, 'economic man' and man as depicted in contemporary social psychology exhibit striking similarities. Social psychology started off with an approach centred on the notion of attitude. This notion turned out to be too vague and confounded to explain human behaviour. But later on social psychologists unpacked the notion of attitude into preferences and constraints as two separate categories. According to Frey (1992) this means that social psychology in this respect has moved in the direction of mainstream economics. Frey's ideas on the possible mutual improvements economics and psychology could bestow on one another clearly relate to methodological aspects of cross-disciplinary learning.

Why Biology and Psychology?

So far the discussion has focused on the possible contributions biology and (evolutionary) psychology can make to economics. But why biology and psychology? Why not other disciplines, such as sociology and (cultural) anthropology? Lewin (1996) argues that all the fuss about whether or not economic theory rests on sound psychological assumptions has detracted attention from a much more fundamental sociological shortcoming of economic theory: how do social forces affect human decision-making (and its basic categories, such as preferences and beliefs)? This suggests that there is greater need for economics to turn to sociology than to psychology or biology. Many economists seem to share Lewin's view. What attracts a lot of attention nowadays (especially in the field of industrial organization) is the new economic sociology developed by Mark Granovetter (1985) and others. The new economic sociology stresses the social embeddedness of individuals, organizations and their behaviour. In doing so, it tries to steer a middle course between an undersocialized view of man, as endorsed in mainstream economics, and an oversocialized view of man, as exemplified in classical sociology. Thus Granovetter's new economic sociology entails a different view on how individual agents with their behaviour interact with their social environment than the one implicit in mainstream economics.

More radically, the 'rhetoric' movement has new literary criticism, postpositivistic (and pragmatist) philosophy, postmodernism and deconstructionism among its sources of inspiration. Amariglio and Ruccio,[3] for example, have consistently been working toward a radically different economics inspired by some sort of a synthesis of Marxism, postmodernism and deconstructionism. The 'rhetoric' movement itself is internally divided. Its aims range from civilizing and enriching mainstream economic discourse to overthrowing it. Some want to change the style of economic reasoning, whereas others want to make room for a plurality of different styles of reasoning and discourse in economics.

This is not a complete overview of the several disciplines economists consult or turn to as sources of insight and inspiration. Far from that. But it suffices to make the point that it is not at all self-evident that biology and psychology (whether 'serious' or not) should be the chosen disciplines that economics has to turn to. Many other options are available.

Is this Genuine Learning?

Thus there are at least three different issues involved in attempts at cross-disciplinary learning by economists. First, what disciplines to choose? Second, what aspects to concentrate on (or, what exactly is looked for)? And third, how to interpret their implications for economics? How, and on what grounds, do economists settle these issues? As already indicated, I believe that economists are most of the time led by prior attitudes towards and prior beliefs about their own discipline. There need not be anything wrong with this. If one fully appreciates the intricacies involved, and especially if one acknowledges that it is almost impossible to oversee all options at the supply side then it is quite understandable, reasonable and perhaps even inevitable that cross-disciplinary learning is demand-driven. Yet beyond some critical threshold demand-driven learning deteriorates into an effort to amass whatever evidence one can find to support one's prior beliefs. Still calling the latter learning strains credulity.

A first obvious reason for believing that cross-disciplinary learning can legitimately be driven by demand considerations is that it does not make sense to embark on cross-disciplinary learning unless one has the expectation (or feeling) that something is to be gained by doing so. There are lots of economists who believe that there is nothing wrong (or at least nothing seriously wrong) with mainstream economics as it is right now.[4] Led by the motto: 'If it ain't broke, don't fix it', they do not see any need for economists to engage in attempts to learn from other disciplines. Perhaps not all of them do believe that economics in its present state does not leave anything wanting. But they are complacent enough to think that economics can be (and de facto is) self-reliant. Whatever the shortcomings of economics, it is felt that economists can overcome these without help from neighbouring disciplines. Insofar as mainstream economists look at other disciplines at all, and insofar as they want to learn something from them qua economists, they are likely to be attracted to disciplines and to interpretations of aspects of them that seem to confirm their prior pro-attitude towards mainstream economics.

By contrast heterodox economists, who are much less satisfied with mainstream economics, tend to be attracted to disciplines and to interpretations of aspects of them that seem to confirm their con-attitude towards mainstream economics. If they have outspoken ideas about how heterodox economics should look, they tend to be attracted to disciplines that support these ideas (and if possible provide models or styles of reasoning that could help them to elaborate these ideas). As we have seen, these ideas can relate to different aspects. The belief, for example, that individuals and their essential properties co-evolve with the social structures in which they are embedded relates to ontology. The belief that the approach to be followed is non-reductionistic pertains to epistemology.[5] In between these two competing camps there are economists who do not want to discard mainstream economics altogether, but who, with the aid of other disciplines, want to improve it where necessary and possible.

All this is quite understandable. To some extent at least this also seems reasonable. It seems only reasonable that other disciplines are resorted to only if one sees a need to do so. Looking around in other disciplines is a waste of time, it can be argued, unless it is warranted by the expectation that some added value to economics is to be found there. And ideas about what can count as added value are most likely (and rightly so) to stem from one's prior beliefs about the strengths and weaknesses of prevailing economic theory. Prior beliefs may even be indispensable in cross-disciplinary learning – for the array of possibilities on the supply side is so vast that one easily gets lost if one is not led by prior beliefs. If one does not have a clear idea about what one is looking for, the complexity is bewildering.

Even if we confine our attention to psychology and biology, we encounter a vast array of different subdisciplines and doctrines or schools of thought. Within psychology we can find cognitive psychology, social psychology, developmental psychology, personality psychology, clinical psychology and cultural psychology. And within biology we have evolutionary biology, ecology, organismic biology, cellular biology, molecular biology and biochemistry (Wilson, 1998). It is an understatement to say that neither in psychology nor in biology do the subdisciplines form a fully coherent whole. So which one of the subdisciplines is chosen can make quite a difference.

To make things even more complicated, there is not consensus within the subdisciplines either. Typically different doctrines, traditions and schools of thought co-exist for extended periods of time (and often not in an altogether peaceful way). For several decades now there has been a heated controversy going on in evolutionary biology. Some even speak of 'Darwin wars' (Brown, 2000). Writers such as Maynard Smith, Dawkins and Dennett belong to the one camp, while Gould, Lewontin and Rose belong to the other.

Given all these considerations, I believe it is only fair that cross-disciplinary learning is primarily demand-driven. Lest economists get lost in the overwhelming variety in (sub)disciplines and doctrines, there seems to be a need for guidance. Prior beliefs about what possibly could improve current economics can legitimately guide what economists are looking for. And assuming initial ignorance of where to find this, these prior beliefs may also guide where (at what (sub)disciplines) economists start looking. An economist dissatisfied with the atomistic agents featuring in mainstream economics, for example, is more likely to have a look at sociology than at biology. But this is reasonable only up to a point. When economists put their prior beliefs beyond all doubt, when they only pay attention to what confirms their prior beliefs, for example, and disregard the rest, something serious seems to be amiss. If this is what is going on, then one may rightly wonder whether this still has anything to do with genuine learning.

One gets the uneasy feeling that this critical point is trespassed sometimes. Biology and psychology sometimes seem to serve as some sort of a 'grab bag' from which economists choose at will. The foregoing discussion also suggests that these disciplines are not in short supply of providing 'ammunition' for economists of all sorts of persuasion. It seems that if one searches long enough in these disciplines, one can find support for virtually anything one already believes in. Economists of (or close to) the mainstream display a preference for the types of psychology and evolutionary biology that allow for reconciliation with (or an enrichment of) received economic theory. By contrast, heterodox economists appear to favour types of psychology and evolutionary biology that undermine received economic theory. On this rather sceptical reading the added value other disciplines bring to economics cannot go beyond suggesting models of how to elaborate already firmly established beliefs. It is ruled out in advance that other disciplines call such pre-established beliefs in question, let alone that they show these beliefs to be wrong.

Genuine learning seems to require some mental open-mindedness. Sometimes such open-mindedness seems to be lacking altogether. It is lacking, for example, when economists are blinded by their own prior beliefs for contradictory (or incompatible) views. Often economists seem to confer expertise in some matter onto practitioners of some other discipline (signalling that they know best). But sometimes the fact of the matter is that those practitioners in other disciplines are chosen by economists who voice ideas, models, findings or results that best befit the economists' own preconceived views (signalling that I know best). This seems in particular to hold for disciplines that do not rank highly in the implicit hierarchy (or pecking order) in academic circles.[6] It may happen, of course, that some discipline is held in low esteem. But what is the point then of discussing this discipline at all? Turning to another discipline and subsequently conveniently ignoring everything that does not accord with one's own preconceived views makes a travesty out of learning.

This is not to argue that economists had better leave it to practitioners of other disciplines to determine what repairs or improvements (if any) economics needs. Who else than economists themselves should be able to identify what is amiss (if anything) in their own discipline? Nobody, perhaps. Existing divisions of labour within the scientific community at large should not easily be annihilated. Division of labour here is a double-edged sword, however. Economists may be best equipped to tell what 'outside' infor- mation and knowledge their own discipline needs most. But then they should also listen with an open ear to what relevant specialists in other dis- ciplines think of it (and also if that contradicts their own preconceived beliefs). When specialists speak with different voices, however, which voice should be listened to? Should economists listen to the majority view, then? This is not at all obvious. Especially for heterodox economists, who by definition belong to the minority in their own profession, the mere fact that some view is the majority view in other disciplines will not count for much. Sometimes, then, it seems economists cannot escape from adjudicating views in other disciplines. But caution is recommended. For in cross- disciplinary learning the danger of dilettantism is always nearby.

In short, cross-disciplinary learning is a difficult and tricky affair. Hard- and-fast guidelines for successful cross-disciplinary learning do not seem to be forthcoming. Unsuccessful cross-disciplinary learning is guaranteed, by contrast, if one is blinded by one's own preconceived view. Or, rather, one can learn next to nothing by suitably ignoring possibly contrary beliefs and disconfirming evidence in other disciplines.

WILSON ON WHAT IS WRONG WITH ECONOMICS AND HOW TO CURE IT

Many issues were raised in the preceding section. It may be helpful to cluster them under three headings. One cluster of issues pertains to the question of whether cross-disciplinary learning should be demand- or supply-driven. In particular, is it legitimate for economists to be led by their own preconceived views as to whether economics has weaknesses and shortcomings in need of repair? A second cluster of issues is about the question of what (if any) (sub)disciplines to turn to. Why should econo- mists turn to some school of thought within some (sub)discipline rather than another? Finally, the last cluster relates to the things to be learnt from the school of thought. What aspects of the school of thought should be focused on and what are their implications for economics?

Although so far no clear and definite answers were given to these ques- tions, something like the following picture emerged. It is perfectly legitim- ate for economists in cross-disciplinary learning to be led by their own prior views on their own discipline. Their prior views may not only guide their choices about whether other (sub)disciplines are to be consulted, but also about what (sub)disciplines to consult. Economists can rightly claim to have special expertise in their own field. But they cannot rightly claim to have special expertise in other fields. Some critical threshold is trespassed if economists only have an eye for those things in other disciplines that confirm their own preconceived views. If economists do not 'buy' other things in other disciplines for no other reason than that these other things do not fit well with their own preconceived views, one can no longer meaningfully talk about cross-disciplinary 'learning'. Instead, traverses into other disciplines become an exercise in self-indulgence and self-congratulation.

Let us now turn to Wilson's *Consilience*. It is possible, it seems, to read Wilson's remarks about economics in a way that runs counter to the picture just sketched. Wilson's remarks about economics seem to be supply-driven. After all, Wilson is an outsider to economics. His areas of expertise are in evolutionary biology and in sociobiology. Although only very few would dare to call Wilson's expertise in these areas into question, his own views (especially on sociobiology) have sparked off a lot of controversy. Far from being a detached and disinterested observer, Wilson has been a major participant in the 'Darwin wars', voicing views that are much closer to those of the Maynard Smith–Dawkins–Dennett camp than that of the opposing Gould–Lewontin–Rose camp. Not surprisingly, the 'serious biology and psychology' Wilson urges economists to have a look at closely resemble the sorts of theories and views that Wilson has been advocating throughout his professional career. The picture emerging here, then, is one of a major player in one specific (sub)discipline trying to sell his own preconceived controversial views to economists.

We should not rush to premature conclusions, however. Let us postpone discussion of the second and third clusters of issues to succeeding sections and first concentrate on the first cluster. Is Wilson's plea to (re)connect economics with 'serious biology and psychology' supply-driven rather than demand-driven? It is useful to distinguish between Wilson's diagnosis of the strengths and weaknesses of current economics and his cure to remove its weaknesses (while retaining its strengths). While Wilson's cure can be argued to be primarily supply-driven, it is less clear with his diagnosis. It is obvious that Wilson cannot claim special expertise in economics. Yet his diagnosis seems to accord pretty well with what many practising economists and methodologists of economics alike have been arguing over the last decades. Wilson characterizes strengths and weaknesses of economic theory in a way that, I shall argue, many economists not only will recognize but also will subscribe to. Furthermore I shall also argue that his diagnosis is reasonably well informed and balanced.[7]

Wilson's stand towards economics is ambivalent. On the one hand Wilson argues that economics deserves to be called the Queen of the Social Sciences. Its emphasis on rigorous mathematical model-building – that makes economics unique among the social sciences – has paid off in terms of some useful insights and guides for economic policy. Wilson also takes the most advanced of (what he calls) the micro-to-macro models to be on the right track. But by and large Wilson seems to believe that economists cannot be particularly proud of the successes they have achieved so far: 'The esteem that economists enjoy arises not so much from their record of successes as from the fact that business and government have nowhere to turn' (Wilson, 1998, p. 219).[8] Despite its occasional successes, Wilson argues that economics is mostly irrelevant for practical matters (ibid., p. 224).

Why is economics mostly irrelevant and why does it have a poor record of successes? Wilson hints at several reasons. But the reason that is given most prominence is that economists have sealed off their theory from serious biology and psychology:

> But the theorists have unnecessarily handicapped themselves by closing off their theory from serious biology and psychology, comprising principles drawn from close description, experiments, and statistical analysis. They have done so, I believe, in order to avoid entanglement in the formidable complexities of these foundation sciences. Their strategy has been to solve the micro-to-macro problem with the fewest possible assumptions at the micro level. In other words, they have carried parsimony too far. Economic theories also aim to create models of the widest possible application, often crafting abstractions so extreme as to represent little more than exercises in applied mathematics. This is generality carried too far. The result of such stringency is a body of theory that is internally consistent but little else. (Wilson, 1998, pp. 223–4)

In these few lines Wilson in effect does three things. First, he identifies the major cause of the weaknesses of economics: economics failed to keep track with developments in 'serious biology and psychology'. Second, he explains why economics steered away from these disciplines: economists did not want to get entrapped in intricacies of these 'foundation sciences'. And third, he characterizes its unfortunate consequence: by over-emphasising parsimony and generality, models in economics are little more than exercises in applied mathematics.

Even though some would argue that it needs some qualifications and refinements, the third thing Wilson argues for – let us call this Wilson's diagnosis – is shared by many commentators. What is wrong with economics is that it has lost itself in a never-ending pursuit to cover ever more phenomena (generality) with as few assumptions possible (parsimony). The result is some kind of applied mathematics (Rosenberg, 1992), 'blackboard economics' (Coase, 1993), or a journey through the hyperspace of assumptions (McCloskey, 1994), that has little if any bearing on 'the real world'. As said, the general thrust of this diagnosis is shared by many methodologists and economists (mainly but not exclusively heterodox ones) alike. What

perhaps distinguishes Wilson's diagnosis from some others is that Wilson
acknowledges that generality and parsimony are theoretical virtues in their
own right. Other things being equal, general and parsimonious theories are
to be preferred over theories that are wanting in these respects. It is just that
economists have over-emphasised these virtues. As a consequence economists lost sight of the other qualities good scientific theories should also
have, such as consilience and predictiveness (Wilson, 1998, pp. 219–20). If
we understand consilience (for the time being) as the quality of a theory to
cohere well with adjacent disciplines, and predictiveness as its quality to
yield precise and empirically accurate prescriptions, then this part of
Wilson's diagnosis also is shared by many commentators (see for example
Hausman, 1992 and Rosenberg, 1992).

The second thing Wilson argues for does not seem to be controversial
either. Indeed, a cogent historical narrative can be told (and is sometimes
told) that in the twentieth century economics gradually but steadfastly
moved away from psychology.[9] And Wilson may well be right that one of
the main reasons for this was that economists did not want to burn their
fingers on intricate and controversial psychological issues. For Bentham,
for example, utility clearly was a psychological magnitude. And the *homo
oeconomicus* of classical economics, as portrayed by J.S. Mill (1836) for
example, reflected a particular and substantive psychological view. Mill
may have thought this view to be self-evidently true. But subsequent developments in psychology called this into question. By arguing that economic
theory no longer assumed that economic man is only interested in his own
material well-being, Robbins (1932, 1936) already loosened the connection
between economics and psychology. Far from being a foundational science
for economics, psychology was relegated the task by Robbins to describe
and explain what are given data for economic theory: the preferences of
individuals. Samuelson's (1938) revealed preference theory and Savage's
(1951) influential subjectivist interpretation of expected utility theory can
be seen as attempts to further shy away from a dependence of economic
theory on any psychological doctrine. Thus Wilson's depiction seems to be
basically right (and uncontested): throughout most of the twentieth
century economics and psychology went their own separate ways, with little
or no contact (see also Hogarth and Reder, 1987). Indeed, economics developed as if it signed a 'declaration of independence' from psychology
(Lewin, 1996).

What is 'Serious Biology and Psychology'?

What is original in Wilson's analysis, and what is likely to meet more
resistance, is his identification of the major cause of the weaknesses of

economics and the cure based on it. Wilson ventures that economics suffers from its weaknesses because economists have closed off their theories from 'serious biology and psychology'. Accordingly, his cure is that economists should reconnect again with these two disciplines. Many readily agree that renewing contacts with adjacent disciplines could help economics in overcoming its problems. But many are likely to disagree that the type of 'serious biology and psychology' Wilson had in mind are the disciplines economics should turn to. For Wilson, serious biology and psychology is evolutionary biology and psychology. To be more precise, it is a hybrid of evolutionary biology and cognitive science: evolutionary psychology (henceforth abbreviated as EP). Wilson approvingly discusses some core ideas in the work of Herbert Simon and Daniel Kahneman and Amos Tversky. These ideas could serve as first steps in helping economists understand better how people actually reason and think, Wilson argues. But he expects major breakthroughs to be coming not from these authors but from evolutionary psychologists.[10] Wilson argues that EP is best regarded as identical to the discipline he himself called into existence: human sociobiology (Wilson, 1998).

Now what is EP and what sorts of insights does it offer? Wilson argues that EP can help us understand better how people behave in different situations and why they do so. The key to the understanding of how people behave, Wilson argues, is provided by the notion of an epigenetic rule. Throughout the book Wilson repeatedly states that '*Behavior is guided by epigenetic rules*' (ibid., p. 213, [italics in original]). Wilson has a lot to say about epigenetic rules, but never comes up with a comprehensive definition. The following pieces can nevertheless be put together. Epigenetic rules are prescribed by genes and are inherited by the individual brain. Epigenetic rules '. . . *are the neural pathways and regularities in cognitive development by which the individual mind assembles itself. The mind grows from birth to death by absorbing parts of the existing culture available to it, with selections guided through epigenetic rules*' (ibid., p. 139, [italics in original]). Wilson compares epigenetic rules with gravitational centres pulling the development of mind in certain pre-figured directions (ibid., p. 248).

Thus epigenetic rules guide the developmental trajectory of the human mind. Epigenetic rules themselves are in turn guided by emotions (ibid., p. 251). Wilson contends that epigenetic rules, like emotions, operate at two levels:

> Primary epigenetic rules are the automatic processes that extend from the filtering and coding of stimuli in the sense organs all the way to perception of the stimuli by the brain. The entire sequence is influenced by previous experience only to a minor degree, if at all. Secondary epigenetic rules are regularities in the integration of large amounts of information. Drawing from selected fragments

of perception, memory and emotional coloring, secondary epigenetic rules lead the mind to predisposed decisions through the choice of certain memes[11] and overt responses over others. (ibid., p. 166)

Primary epigenetic rules typically translate otherwise continuous sensations into discrete units. Thus the human brain classifies visible light of continuously differing wavelengths into four basic colours. Drawing on this, secondary epigenetic rules predispose humans to behave in certain ways. An example of this is the so-called 'Westermarck effect': people tend to abhor the idea of having sexual intercourse with individuals with whom they were closely associated in early life (such as parents). Together our primary and secondary epigenetic rules determine what behavioural output is evoked by which stimuli.

Most of the time epigenetic rules do not trigger 'mature' responses in people right from their birth. Rather, epigenetic rules predispose newborn infants to learn in such ways that they will pretty soon arrive at 'mature' responses. Epigenetic rules enable children to learn in a fast and reliable way. This is also known as 'prepared learning'. A well-known example of this is the Garcia effect. Garcia showed that rats can quickly learn some things, while there are other things they can hardly learn. It turned out, for example, that rats have no problem in learning that eating certain types of food 'causes' nausea. But they do have great trouble in associating nausea with buzzers and light flashes.[12]

What this suggests is that rats (and organisms in general) are in some way 'pre-programmed' to learn some things quickly and reliably, whereas learning other things is difficult if not impossible. Wilson argues that humans are similarly equipped with epigenetic rules that both facilitate and constrain our learning efforts.[13]

Wilson argues that acknowledging that our behaviour is guided by epigenetic rules implies that both folk psychology and the Standard Social Science Model (SSSM) are to be discarded. Wilson describes folk psychology as the grasp of human nature suggested by our common sense (ibid., p. 203). We think we know how we ourselves think and behave and how others think and behave. But according to Wilson we are wrong in thinking this. Wilson's main reason for thinking so seems to be that he believes that the findings of serious biology and psychology have not yet found their way in our common sense views.[14]

The SSSM essentially says that the human mind and, consequently, human behaviour, is shaped by cultural phenomena. Wilson does not deny that cultural phenomena, the prevailing complex system of symbols, meanings and values, have an impact on how individuals think and behave. What he denies, *pace* SSSM, is that the human mind and human behaviour are shaped exclusively by culture; they are shaped also by our biologically inherited human nature. Wilson is at pains to argue that he is not a genetic determinist. He does not hold that 'it is all in our genes'.[15]

Our genes prescribe our epigenetic rules. But our epigenetic rules do not fully determine how we behave. How we behave does also depend on our personal experiences and on the culture of which we are a part. Wilson holds that next to biological evolution there is also cultural evolution going on. And cultural evolution is not just an epiphenomenon of biological evolution. Biological and cultural evolution, rather, go hand in hand. They mutually affect one another. There is 'gene–culture coevolution', as Wilson calls it. Our inherited epigenetic rules channel human behaviour and herewith also cultural evolution. But conversely, culture feeds back on which genes survive and multiply in subsequent generations (ibid., p. 173).

Wilson's notion of gene-culture coevolution also allows for the possibility that processes of cultural evolution unfold without there being corresponding processes of biological evolution. There may be fast cultural evolution with no repercussions for changes in gene frequencies (ibid., p. 140). Thus the connection between biological and cultural evolution can be quite loose. But the connection can never be broken altogether. Epigenetic rules will never cease to have their inescapable, constant influence on human behaviour and cultural evolution. In this sense we can speak of a universal and intransient human nature biasing anything we do. Sometimes this influence is so vast that universals of culture (ibid., p. 162) – common features all cultures we know thus far share with one another – are generated. But most of the time they allow for cultural diversity.

Wilson's epigenetic rules are what evolutionary psychologists call special-purpose modules (or algorithms; see, for example, Cosmides and Tooby, 1992). They emerged as responses to the many different evolutionary problems our ancestors in the Pleistocene era were faced with. The special-purpose modules (such as the one for rapid and reliable language acquisition, or for cheater detection) may have been well-adapted to those problems, but they need not be well-adapted also to the problems facing us today (ibid., p. 250). However, they nevertheless may still be triggered by suitable stimuli. The Stone Age modules of our mind still predispose us to behave in certain ways.

Wilson admits that EP still is in its infancy. For one thing, there are many different pathways running from genes to epigenetic rules. A one-to-one correspondence between a gene and an epigenetic rule seems to be an exception rather than the rule (ibid., p. 171–2). For another, epigenetic rules themselves are largely still unexplored (ibid., p. 190). And, furthermore, it is not yet clear to what extent epigenetic rules predetermine human behaviour and culture. There seems to be a great variety in the types of epigenetic rules identified so far. Some are rigid and specialized, whereas others are rational and generalized (ibid., p. 190).

Putting the bits and pieces discussed so far together, the picture that emerges from EP and biology (as Wilson sees them) is the following. It is acknowledged that there is much variety or diversity in human thinking and behaviour. This variety cannot possibly be subsumed under one general law. EP and biology do not so much stress the variety between or among humans, but the variety of behavioural patterns all individuals display. This variety does not have its ultimate origin in culture. First of all, contrary to what many hold nowadays, different cultures do not differ in all respects; there are also striking similarities between cultures. And second, to the effect that cultures do differ, Wilson tends to argue that this is due to the different developmental pathways the cultures went through: the same human nature interacted with different types of environments. One can meaningfully speak of a universal human nature. But human nature itself is not of a piece. It consists of a multitude of epigenetic rules, each of which is activated by a distinct set of stimuli.

The reader may rightly wonder what all this has to do with economics. It is clear that Wilson holds that the insights of EP that might be relevant for economics are of an ontological rather than of an epistemological or methodological kind. EP can help us improve our understanding of rules and mechanisms underlying human behaviour, rather than teach us how to approach economic phenomena. But for the remainder, EP's more specific implications for economics are yet to be sought out. Before we come to that, however, I want to discuss issues that are also still awaiting resolution. We did not address the issue yet, for example, as to why Wilson singles out psychology and biology as the chosen disciplines that economics should reconnect with. Furthermore, why does Wilson treat EP as 'serious biology and psychology'? By virtue of what features is EP serious? It is to these issues I now turn.

CONSILIENCE

Wilson's notion of consilience provides the key to understanding why Wilson believes it is EP that economics should turn to in order to learn more about actual human behaviour. Wilson's 'consilience' explains why Wilson believes it is biology and psychology that economists should connect with, and why it is more specifically EP that economists should turn to. As we shall see, Wilson's notion of consilience entails a complete overview of all disciplines based on a grand metaphysical picture. EP is singled out by Wilson because it makes it possible to connect the social and natural sciences in a way that is compatible with the grand metaphysical picture.

Backhouse has argued that Wilson's notion of consilience does not require economists to turn to EP in particular (Backhouse, 2000). Wilson's 'consilience' would leave open the possibility that economists could also learn from other disciplines. I believe Backhouse is at most partly right here. Wilson's notion of consilience is not unambiguous. Wilson puts forward at least two different interpretations of 'consilience'. The two notions of consilience present two different models of what disciplines to engage in with the cross-disciplinary transfer of ideas and of how this transfer is to proceed. Only on one interpretation – the one that is *not* given much prominence in the central argument in Wilson's book – is Backhouse right.

The notion of consilience that does not single out EP as the discipline economics should learn from is a rather moderate one. This is the notion Wilson invokes when writing about what sets 'real science' apart from mere pseudoscience (that is, when he puts forward his own 'demarcation criteria') and about the qualities that theories in general and mathematical models in particular ought to have. Consilience here entails that explanations of different phenomena should be connected and proved consistent with one another (Wilson, 1998, p. 57). It also implies that units and processes should conform with solidly verified knowledge in other disciplines (ibid., p. 219). Key words here are 'connected', 'consistent' and 'conform'. Explanations in different disciplines should not only be linked with one another,[16] they should also be shown to be consistent with one another.

Two things deserve special mention. First, Wilson considers consilience to be a virtue or quality (of a theory, model or explanation) in its own right (ibid., p. 57, p. 210, p. 219). Consilience is not seen as a mere means to improve other virtues or qualities that theories can have, such as their explanatory or predictive power. It is a goal *sui generis*. Second, note that Wilson does not specify what other disciplines are to be consulted. This could be any discipline. The only thing he demands is that conformity should be sought only with solidly verified knowledge in other disciplines.

Contrast this with the much stronger notion of 'total consilience' that Wilson also advances. Wilson argues that total consilience amounts to a transcendental world view: '. . . nature is organized by simple universal laws of physics to which all other laws and principles can eventually be reduced' (ibid., p. 59). Total consilience implies a particular type of reductionism.[17] It entails the claim that laws and principles at higher levels of organization can ultimately be reduced to universal laws at the lowest, most fundamental level of organization: those of physics. As such total consilience envisages a hierarchical ordering of knowledge (ibid., p. 201). Note that physics here is singled out as the discipline providing the laws that the laws of all other disciplines must be reducible to in the end.

Total and moderate consilience are akin to Hacking's (1996) notions of singleness and harmonious integration respectively. Hacking argues that singleness and harmonious integration are two different aspects of unity that can, but need not, go together. Two disciplines allow for harmonious integration if they fit together well. Singleness goes further in claiming that two seemingly different things (such as disciplines) at bottom are one. Thus it is claimed that animate and inanimate matter share the same basic physical constituents. In this case we can say that biology (as the study of living things) is claimed to be reducible to the disciplines studying inanimate matter (chemistry and, ultimately, physics). Wilson's total consilience is a clear example of what Hacking calls metaphysical singleness.

EP is assigned a prominent role in 'total consilience'. EP explicitly and systematically links psychology (and cognitive science in general) with evolutionary theory. In Wilson's grand scheme of things, EP bridges the gap between the natural and the social sciences. EP makes it possible for the social sciences to connect first to the brain and neurosciences and then further, via cellular and molecular biology, all the way down to chemistry and, finally, physics. Vice versa, EP facilitates investigating how our evolved innate constitution in interaction with the environments surrounding us affect how (and what) we feel, think and do and, finally, all the way up to how cultural processes (including possible changes in our values and ethical principles) unfold.

This indicates that Wilson takes 'serious' biology to be a kind of biology that allows psychology to be connected with chemistry, and finally physics. Serious biology should provide an important link in the reduction of psychological processes to chemical and physical processes. Throughout his book Wilson sketches the contours of a hierarchically ordered ontology of adjacent levels of organization. Although the full picture is nowhere drawn in its entirety, it in any rate entails the following entities: culture, behaviour, organisms, mind, organs (such as the brain), tissues, cells (such as neurons in the brain), molecules (such as genes), atoms and subatomic particles.[18] Wilson argues that a causal chain connects the behaviour of lower-level entities with that of higher-order entities: '. . . causal events ripple out from the genes to the cells to tissues and thence to brain and behaviour' (ibid., p. 182).[19]

Not surprisingly, Wilson goes on to argue that evolutionary biology fills the bill. Evolutionary biology is able to shed interesting light on the causal connections between processes at adjacent levels of organization. Evolutionary biology points out, for example, that our brain and sensory system contain several prefigured configurations that guide our learning behaviour. It does so by identifying evolutionary pressures impinging on our ancestors in a distant past. Wilson leaves no doubt that the most persistent and forceful agent in evolution (including the evolution of us, human beings, see ibid., p. 141) has been natural selection. In the end only natural selection can explain why we got to be the sophisticated, yet limited and fallible creatures that we are.

Wilson's views can rightfully be called 'reductionist'. His invocation of a hierarchically ordered ontology of adjacent levels of organization joined with his emphasis on the ubiquity of natural selection justifies this. Actually, Wilson himself does not resent being classified as such. On the contrary, he is proud of it. Reductionism is the cutting edge of science, Wilson argues (ibid., p. 58). We cannot hope to begin understanding complex things unless we break them apart into simpler constituents. So at least in the explorative stages a reductionist strategy is indispensable. And according to Wilson we still are not past the stages of exploration. But Wilson also believes that science should move beyond exploration. Science is and should be more ambitious than that.

Some Qualifications and Refinements

Wilson believes total consilience is an oversimplification. It is an oversimplification mainly because it now seems – given what we currently think we know – that, at least from the level of the cell on, levels of organization display emergent properties. Emergent properties are properties we cannot predict on the basis of what we (think we) know about underlying constituent units and processes alone (ibid., pp. 93, 119). To describe these, new laws are needed that cannot be predicted from those at more fundamental levels (ibid., p. 59). This, Wilson argues, is the kernel of truth in holism (ibid., p. 91). Knowledge about units and processes at lower, fundamental levels do not suffice to predict what happens at higher levels of organization. There are two reasons for this (ibid., p. 73). There is too much idiosyncrasy in the arrangement of constituent units in individual units at higher levels. And ongoing interaction with environmental factors also affect what happens at higher levels.

This explains why Wilson thinks that bottom-up synthesis is not just top-down reduction (or analysis) executed in reverse direction. In fact, he emphasizes that the two are distinct. Analysing elements of behaviour in terms of biology and psychology – a species of what Wilson calls consilience by reduction (ibid., p. 73) – is the easy part of the consilience project, relatively speaking. The 'tough part' is bottom-up synthesis, or consilience by synthesis (as Wilson also calls it). Wilson argues that 'predictive synthesis' – predicting what happens at higher levels of organization from assembled knowledge about units and processes at lower levels of organization – is formidably difficult. But exactly herein lies the greatest challenge for scientists. Wilson considers consilience by synthesis to be the ultimate goal of science (ibid., p. 234). Wilson does not rule out the possibility that at some time we may be able to achieve consilience by synthesis. But at present we seem to be pretty far away from it (ibid., p. 170).

In sum, what Wilson believes should be done ideally is not only making the full traverse demanded by total consilience: from the social sciences to psychology and thence from the brain sciences and genetics (ibid., p. 226). Ideally, this should be followed up by bottom-up synthesis: 'The full understanding of utility will come from biology and psychology by reduction to the elements of human behaviour followed by bottom-up synthesis' (ibid., p. 228). This 'prophecy' can also be interpreted as a methodological task to be fulfilled.[20] As we have seen it is based on an epistemological view, which in turn is buttressed by Wilson's grand metaphysical (or ontological) view.

How Agreeable is Wilson's 'Consilience' to Economists?

We have seen that Wilson's selection of biology and psychology, and EP as serious biology and psychology, as *the* disciplines for economists to turn to is grounded in his notion of total consilience. Thus *if* 'total consilience' is accepted, the implication seems to be that EP is the discipline for economists to learn from.[21]

But how acceptable is 'total consilience' for economists? As Wilson himself notes, total consilience has its adversaries (all its nuances notwithstanding). They are to be found not only in postmodernism and deconstruction (ibid., pp. 43–5) and cultural relativism and political multiculturalism (or identity politics) (ibid., p. 204). There are also less radical thinkers challenging unification (understood as Hacking's singleness) as some sort of an ideal within and across disciplines (see, for example, Dupré, 1993; Galison and Stump, 1996; Morrison, 2000). Some advocate disunity and enduring pluralism both within and between disciplines.[22] Seen in this perspective, Wilson's total consilience entails controversial ontological and epistemological preconceptions.[23] Wilson's total consilience will not be acceptable for heterodox economists, for example, favouring non-reductionistic, non-mechanistic and non-individualistic approaches not just within economics, but also within other disciplines and across disciplines. Geoff Hodgson, for example, seems to be just such an economist. Wilson's total consilience can be called a prior (or preconceived) meta-belief about ideal or desirable relations and connections between disciplines that is as controversial, it seems, as the economists' prior beliefs about their own discipline.[24]

Neither the arguments that Wilson gives for the desirability and feasibility of total consilience, nor his qualifications and refinements of it, seem to be compelling enough to convert devoted anti-reductionists.

What about Wilson's 'moderate consilience'? Moderate consilience seems to be agreeable to many economists of different stripes and persuasions. But this is so, it seems, because it does not prescribe what discipline(s) economists should learn from. Moderate consilience prescribes that economists should connect and conform with solidly verified knowledge obtained in other disciplines. Without any further specification of what can qualify as 'solidly verified knowledge', however, it seems that an economist can still go his own way in freely picking out the discipline(s) of his own liking.

Thus neither of Wilson's two notions of consilience seem to be able to convince economists of all stripes and persuasions that EP is the discipline to turn to in cross-disciplinary learning. Moderate consilience is probably acceptable to many economists. But it is not at all clear that acceptance of moderate consilience should lead economists in the direction of EP. Total consilience seems to have to face the opposite problem. Acceptance of total consilience points in the direction of EP, but many economists, especially heterodox ones, will find total consilience hard to swallow, if not to be wholly mistaken.

The interesting thing, however, is that although many heterodox economists have a strong disposition to dismiss Wilson's total consilience and EP out of hand, they will find the implications for economics that Wilson derives from them much more congenial. Though much less hostile against total consilience and EP, it will be orthodox economists who will be inclined to resist the implications that Wilson derives from them. Or so I will argue in the next section.

WHAT IMPLICATIONS DOES EP HAVE FOR ECONOMICS?

What lessons do Wilson's discussion of epigenetic rules entail for economics? The first lesson is a general one. As Wilson sees it, all social sciences are wedded to folk psychology and SSSM. They all suffer from 'biophobia' (ibid., p. 206). They all are reluctant to take insights of EP and biology into account. Economics is no exception in this regard. So the lesson to be learned for economists is that they should take 'serious biology and psychology' seriously. But what particular insights of EP and biology are especially significant for economists? Wilson does not seem to have terribly much to offer here. What Wilson has to say pertains to the 'micro-phenomena' of (rational) choice and utility. One of the implications of EP and biology is that 'decision-making' and 'rational choice' get a different meaning. To the extent that humans choose rationally, they do this not because they are endowed with some sort of an intelligent general-purpose device, but because they avail themselves of a multitude of special-purpose modules (ibid., p. 126, 199). How humans behave is more a matter of what emotion-guided epigenetic rules are strongest in a given context than of what cool, correct calculation would prescribe.

But this still does not tell us what particular epigenetic rules are significant for the issues economists are interested in. The closest Wilson comes to this is in presenting a list of '. . . certain generalizations about utility' suggested by scattered studies in psychology and biology. One generalization is that some needs and opportunities are epistatic: '. . . needs and opportunities in one category alter the strength of others' (ibid., p. 226). Another is that needs and opportunities (such as drug addiction) are pre-emptive. Yet another is that incest avoidance is based on a strong hereditary epigenetic rule. Furthermore, the choices people make are often led by unselfish motives (such as patriotism and altruism) and are group-dependent. As Wilson himself indicates, however, a lot still is unclear. First of all, it is not clear whether (and if so, to what extent) the examples given bear on the things economists are interested in. For example, what is the relevance of incest avoidance for economics? Second, it is not at all clear whether the generalizations themselves are well-established in psychology and biology. And third, it is not yet established that all generalizations are due to underlying epigenetic rules.

It all looks very premature and programmatic. The last item on Wilson's list reveals the 'hard core' of the research program that Wilson wants psychologists and biologists to embark on: 'Decision-making is shaped category by category by epigenetic rules, which are the innate propensities to learn certain options in the first place and then to select particular ones among them. On average many of the propensities differ according to age and gender' (ibid., p. 227). But this only reinforces the overall impression that a lot of work still has to be done before we can tell what specific implications EP has for 'economic phenomena'.

In more general terms, however, the contours of Wilson's view on the implications EP should have for economics can be outlined. Economists should allow for more assumptions at the micro-level. To be more precise, further reliance on just one assumption, to wit that individuals always choose rationally given their preferences and expectations, should be given up. We have already seen that Wilson argues that economics is too Newtonian (or too parsimonious). Economists mistakenly believe that they can cover many disparate phenomena with a minimal set of general assumptions about the rationality of the behaviour of individuals. Wilson argues that 'serious biology and psychology', and EP in particular, point out that individual human behaviour is much more diverse than as depicted in rational choice theory. Only sometimes is what economists call rational choice probable or even possible (ibid., p. 218). Instead, economists should realise that human decision-making cannot be understood without having a prior knowledge of epigenetic rules.

There are economists who believe that the insights of EP can be neatly accommodated in standard economic theory, leaving the latter's framework largely intact (see, for example, Ben-Ner and Putterman, 1998 and 2000; Zywicki, 2000). They argue that the main contribution of EP to economic theory lies in its ability to identify actual preference patterns of people in a non-arbitrary, empirically informed way. It is not questioned here that the preference patterns that EP will identify can be homogenized into one comprehensive preference ordering. Equipped with such insights provided by EP, these economists argue, economists can then apply standard economic theory.

Although they do not refer to EP explicitly, proponents of the so-called 'indirect evolutionary approach' (Güth and Yaari, 1991; Güth and Kliemt, 1998) in economics similarly maintain that evolutionary theory can help economists identify the basic preferences that people actually have. What makes this approach indirect rather than direct is that evolutionary forces and pressures are assumed to affect our behaviour indirectly. Evolutionary game theory assumes that selection pressures mould (or, rather, moulded) our behaviour or our behavioural strategies directly. By contrast, the indirect evolutionary approach assumes that selection pressures in ancient times have shaped our present basic preferences. In doing so these selection pressures affect our current behaviour indirectly because the ways in which we currently behave, proponents of the indirect evolutionary approach hold, do not depend only on our evolved basic preferences. They also depend on our capacity for acting rationally on the basis of these preferences. Güth and Yaari explicitly state that '. . . we assume individual rationality for given preferences' (Güth and Yaari, 1991, p. 23).[25] And what is the rational thing to do depends not just on prevailing preference profiles, but also on prevailing constraints and opportunities. Even though the indirect evolutionary approach portrays us as prisoners of our own preferences, it '. . . does not neglect an individual's ability to adjust their behaviour in different environments when studying a selection process' (Huck, 1997, p. 777).

Note that the underlying idea here too is that EP (and evolutionary theory in general) does not contradict standard economic theory's assumption that people choose rationally on the basis of their preferences. It is sometimes acknowledged that in a comprehensive evolutionary account the capacity to behave rationally must itself be understood as a product of evolution (Güth and Kliemt, 1998). But the possibility that the rationality evolution has endowed us with may not be the perfect or full rationality that standard economic theory assumes is ignored. It is taken for granted that individuals make fully rational forward-looking choices (Güth and Kliemt, 1998, p. 390). Note also that it is assumed here that people's preference patterns are invariant across different types of conditions. No matter what conditions may prevail, it is assumed that the preference patterns that people have remain the same. This too, of course, is in line with standard economic theory.

Thus the economists discussed above apparently believe that basic tenets of standard economic theory can be retained when taking insights from EP (and evolutionary theory in general) on board. EP is believed to be compatible with a neat separation between affective and cognitive components of human decision-making. EP is believed to bear only on the affective component (preferences), leaving the cognitive component (full rationality) unimpaired. Furthermore these economists hold that individuals not only behave fully rationally in all conceivable circumstances and under all conditions, but also that for each individual the same preference ordering is displayed in all circumstances and under all conditions.

All this is quite different from Wilson's depiction of epigenetic rules and of their impact on human behaviour. Wilson's remarks clearly suggest that not all epigenetic rules are activated in all conceivable circumstances and under certain conditions. The general idea here rather is that different epigenetic rules are triggered in different circumstances and under different conditions. Under the one set of conditions the one epigenetic rule may be triggered, while under a seemingly only slightly different set of conditions an altogether different rule may be triggered. A seemingly small perturbation of conditions may thus lead to the activation of another epigenetic rule. This may have dramatic behavioural consequences.[26]

The economists discussed previously also acknowledge that changes in conditions can lead to different (kinds of) behaviour. But the channel through which changes in conditions lead to changes in behaviour does not involve changes in how individuals rank their basic preferences, let alone that it involves changes in the degree to which individuals behave rationally. It is assumed that both their capacity to act fully rationally and their ordering of basic preferences remain unaltered. What changes are only the parameters of the situation (such as relative prices) that individuals are in. Rational individuals endowed with a stable ordering of basic preferences, it is assumed, take notice of such changes in parameters and change their behaviour accordingly.

By contrast, Wilson's notion that different conditions can trigger different epigenetic rules suggests a different channel through which changes in conditions lead to changes in behaviour. If we insist on a translation of this into the familiar terms for economists, we may say that if a different epigenetic rule is triggered, this may bring along a different preference ordering and a different degree to which the individual can be said to act rationally. In some situations individuals may act in a better than rational way (Cosmides and Tooby, 1994). In such situations individuals immediately do the optimal thing without having to spend any energy on deliberation and calculation. In other situations individuals learn to do the optimal thing only after laborious search, if at all. In the one social setting a disposition to cooperate almost unconditionally may be triggered in individuals, whereas in another social setting a proclivity can be activated in the same individuals to improve or at least secure their relative position in a group's pecking order. EP may indeed be able to shed more light on the hitherto somewhat mysterious experimental phenomenon of preference reversals (Slovic and Lichtenstein, 1983).

Wilson's reading of epigenetic rules and of their impact on human behaviour may have even more profound implications for the standard way in which economists look at human behaviour. EP may undermine the neat analytic picture of human behaviour that economists are so accustomed to: the one in which the affective and cognitive components of decision-making are distinguished sharply. It can be argued that in the notion of an epigenetic rule affective and cognitive elements are inextricably intertwined. As we have seen, Wilson argues that human perception, learning and decision-making, for example (phenomena that economists would argue belong to the cognitive component), are always coloured and laden by emotions. Conversely, since especially our primary emotions arguably evolved to cope with acute selection pressures (such as instinctive fear of snakes), they can be said to store vital information.

Does More Consilience Between the Sciences Call for a Less Parsimonious Economic Theory?

What Wilson's view suggests is that the 'constrained maximization' framework cannot accommodate the rich variety in human behavioural patterns that EP depicts. 'Microfoundations' compatible with EP are likely to be less parsimonious than that. This 'result' can rightly be called ironical. Several economists have cherished the unifying power of the 'constrained maximization' framework (Aumann, 1985, for example). Some have even argued that the framework can be fruitfully and successfully applied to social phenomena that are generally understood to be beyond the scope of economic theory. Now here comes an outsider who in the name of unity among the great branches of learning argues for dethroning this alleged unifying framework! If Wilson is right, economists have to broaden the behavioural basis of their discipline even within their own home field. A wider array of different behavioural dispositions has to be assumed to account for the messy and rich variety of human behavioural patterns.[27]

Thus the lessons Wilson believes EP entails for economics are of an onto-logical kind. They pertain to essential properties of human beings at the micro-level of economic analysis. The main implication EP has for eco-nomics, Wilson argues, is that its 'microfoundations' should be less parsi-monious than they currently are. This message will be more congenial to many 'heterodox' economists than it is to many 'orthodox' economists. Many 'heterodox' economists can welcome Wilson's message as a support for their own prior or preconceived ideas. What is interesting is that this may also hold for economists who are sceptical of, if not hostile to, Wilson's notion of total consilience. Quite a few economists who are not attracted to evolutionary theory and evolutionary theorizing at all (or who are at any rate not attracted to the type of evolutionary theory Wilson is advocating) may think that Wilson is right here for the wrong reasons. Vice versa, it is likely that the opposite holds for some 'orthodox' economists who, like Krugman and Becker, are much more attracted to the type of evolutionary theory that Wilson is advocating. They may well find that Wilson draws wrong conclusions for economic theory from otherwise 'right' sources of knowledge.

CONCLUDING REMARKS

Wilson's interpretation of EP's implications for economic theory surely is disconcerting to staunch defenders of standard economic theory. For it challenges essential, if not defining, characteristics of standard economic theory. Not only does EP suggest that preference orderings may vary from the one context to the other, it also indicates that the degree to which indi-viduals can be called rational may vary from the one context to the other. What is more, EP also seems to imply that the neat analytical distinction between affective and cognitive components of individual decision-making is untenable.

Economists with different preconceived beliefs are likely to react differently to this. While staunch defenders of standard economic theory can be expected to take a protective posture, declared critics of it can be expected to be more open to it. However, as we saw, the situation seems to be a bit more complicated than this. Many critics of standard economic theory will be charmed neither by Wilson's notion of total consilience nor by his singling out of EP as *the* discipline economists should learn from.

Vice versa, several advocates of standard economic theory might agree with Wilson that economics should reconnect with (or should emulate) the natural sciences. Thus the whole package that Wilson presents – from his grand metaphysical view to the implications for economics that he draws on the basis of this – does not sit easily with any of these opposing camps. This may be one of the reasons why Wilson's cure for the present shortcomings of economics will in the end fail to resonate in any camp within the economics profession.

Wilson's contention that human behaviour is too diverse and varied to be captured in the constrained maximization framework may be grain on the mill for many heterodox economists. But when it comes to enhancing the credibility of their own preconceived belief it is hard to see how they could take Wilson to task unless they also accept Wilson's underlying reasons. If they reject both Wilson's notion of total consilience and EP as a useful source of insights for economics, it seems that calling upon Wilson's contention cannot strengthen their case. To argue here that the alleged 'fact' that Wilson arrives at the right conclusion even after fallacious reasoning only proves their point would amount to theoretical opportunism. Conversely, both Wilson's plea for reconnecting economics with the natural sciences and his selection of EP as the discipline economics can learn most from may be applauded by proponents of standard economic theory. But they will be inclined to prefer the reconciliatory connection made by the economists that were discussed in the previous section to the connection forged by Wilson. Here the problem lurking in the background is not so much theoretical opportunism as dilettantism. For although Wilson may be an outsider to economics, as a forerunner of EP he seems to be far more competent to judge what implications EP has for the study of human behaviour than economists.

Perhaps it should not come as a surprise that economists hold dearly to their preconceived beliefs. As experimental studies in the Heuristics and Biases program in psychology have demonstrated convincingly, people tend to be inattentive to new information contradicting their prior beliefs. Learning processes appear to exhibit a strong confirmatory bias (also called belief perseverance and anchoring). Cross-disciplinary learning does not seem to be exempted from this bias. It may even be that EP could help to explain this. Perhaps there are epigenetic rules responsible for the tenacity with which these beliefs are held and the hostile ways in which other beliefs are combated. As Wilson observes, participants in a debate or controversy all too easily slide back into 'archaic defensive postures' (ibid., p. 208). Such postures disable, or at least debilitate, reasonable discourse.

All this may be true. Yet we should be able to do better than this. Even if it were the case that there are ingrained epigenetic rules responsible for the tenacity with which we cling to our preconceived beliefs, this does not give us an excuse to take our preconceived beliefs for granted. We are not the slaves or puppets of our epigenetic rules. EP contends that different epigenetic rules are activated under different conditions, as we saw, and changing conditions is not beyond our control. Once we have identified the conditions under which we tend to fall back on archaic defensive postures, we may try to avoid such conditions. Instead, if we succeed in identifying the conditions under which people display a greater willingness to revise their preconceived beliefs when confronted with disconfirming evidence, and to rethink their beliefs when confronted with people with different beliefs, then we may try to promote these conditions.

NOTES

1. Yet Krugman also argues that some standard economists tend to forget that 'maximization' and 'equilibrium' are (and cannot be but) fictions. Krugman confesses that he sometimes is envious of evolutionary theorists using myopic, disequilibrium dynamics without apology (ibid., p. 28). See also Vromen (1995) and (2001a).
2. Smith suggests that this is due to differences in institutional circumstances. The findings need not tell us much about the inherent cognitive capabilities of agents.
3. See for example Cullenberg and Amariglio (2001) and Ruccio (1999).
4. Needless to say, those economists may err in believing this.
5. It is also possible, for example, that prior beliefs are of a political, ideological or moral kind.
6. I take it that all, except perhaps for a few radical social constructionists (for whom a quark is as unnatural a kind as child abuse; see Hacking, 1999), agree that physics ranks higher in this hierarchy than, for example, sociology. But this implicit hierarchy may also help to explain why many economists do not believe that 'solidly verified knowledge' is to be found in, for example, psychology.
7. The following economists have been reading (parts of) Wilson's manuscript: Gary S. Becker, Terence C. Burnham and Martin L. Weitzman.
8. Unless stated otherwise, page references in this section relate to Wilson (1998).
9. The history of the relation between economics and biology is an altogether different story. It seems that biology's impact on economics never was profound (see Rosenberg, 2000, but from the 1980s on this may have changed somewhat, see Vromen, 2001a). But it also seems that the turmoil caused by social Darwinism, and later on sociobiology, made economists shy away from biology (see Hodgson, 1999).
10. Excellent introductions into evolutionary psychology are Cosmides and Tooby (1992) and Buss (1999). See also Vromen (2000).
11. Dawkins (1976) coined the notion meme to denote the elementary unit of cultural evolution. A meme can be an idea, for example, or some tune.
12. What actually happened was the following. The rats were given some food and a few hours later they were given a dose of radiation that made them sick. (A similar arrangement was deviced for the buzzers and light flashes.) So the food did not actually cause the nausea. But this only shows the importance of prepared learning: apparently rats are preprogrammed to associate nausea with food (rather than other possible causes such as buzzers, light flashes or radiation). The Garcia experiments contributed to the demise of behaviourism.
13. Consider for example the so-called Sauce Béarnaise phenomenon. It turns out that people also tend to associate feeling ill with things they have eaten. One experience of

feeling ill after having eaten a meal with a Sauce Béarnaise can be enough for the person not to be able to eat it ever again (even though the actual cause for feeling ill might have been a stomach flu).

14. Wilson does not make clear what parts (or how much) of folk psychology (if any) could be maintained after the findings of serious biology and psychology were to find their ways into it.

15. Wilson adds to this that he has never met a biologist who really believed in genetic determinism (ibid., p. 208). The popularity of evolutionary economics in economics arguably suffered from evolutionary economics' reputation that it is wedded to some sort of 'genetic determinism'. See Vromen (2001b) for an argument that evolutionary economics need not be, and should not be wedded to anything of the sort.

16. I assume that Wilson writes about 'units' and 'processes' as they figure in explanations of some science.

17. For Wilson, reductionism is the cutting edge of science per se (ibid., p. 58).

18. Sometimes Wilson seems to suggest that disciplines can be distinguished according to the level of organization addressed. But he also notes there are quite a few disciplines addressing phenomena at several levels of organization.

19. Wilson seems to have proximate causes in mind here. But, in general, Wilson does not seem to distinguish sharply between proximate and ultimate causes, or between phylogenesis and ontogenesis. He does not distinguish between nomological and causal explanation either.

20. Seen in this light, exploring what lessons EP holds for economics is only some sort of a halfway construction.

21. Of course, advocacy of EP as the discipline economists should turn to does not presuppose the correctness of 'total consilience'. Advocacy of EP can also be based on other considerations.

22. Limited space prevents me from discussing this debate in more detail here. I plan to write another paper about Wilson's stance in this debate.

23. Postmodernists and social constructionists will find no problem in unmasking Wilson's grand narrative as 'just' some opinion or phantasy of a stubborn scientistic devotee. In a sense, social constructionism is as universal an acid as Dennett's (1995) 'Darwin's dangerous idea'.

24. Needless to say, I hope, the fact that Wilson's total consilience is controversial does not by itself make it suspect (and the same holds, of course, for the prior beliefs of economists).

25. Witness also Bolton's characterization of the approach: '. . . conceptualizing evolution as working on preferences, and then applying rational choice to explain actual decision making' (Bolton, 2000, p. 286). In Vromen (2000) I discuss the indirect evolutionary approach in more depth and detail. I also argue there that this approach is reminiscent of Becker (1976).

26. Conversely, it is also possible that a seemingly large change in conditions may lead to no change in behaviour. For example, in some social settings a disposition to cooperate may still be operative even if the rewards for cheating are raised considerably. The general point here is that what may be a large change in conditions seen from the perspective of standard economic theory (in terms of changes in opportunities) may amount to a small change in conditions seen from the perspective of EP (in terms of changes in the epigenetic rules and dispositions triggered).

27. As Morrison (2000) argues, Whewell, who coined the term 'consilience', held that consilience only is to be striven at within some discipline (and not among disciplines).

REFERENCES

Aumann, Robert (1985), 'What is game theory trying to accomplish?', in K.J. Arrow and S. Honkapohja (eds), *Frontiers of Economics*, Oxford: Basil Blackwell, pp. 28–76.

Backhouse, Roger (2000), 'Reaffirming the enlightenment vision' (Review of Edward O. Wilson's *Consilience*), *Journal of Economic Methodology*, **7**, 153–6.

Becker, Gary S. (1976), 'Altruism, egoism and genetic fitness: economics and sociobiology', *Journal of Economic Literature*, **14**, 817–26.

Ben-Ner, A. and L. Putterman (1998), 'Values and institutions in economic analysis', in A. Ben-Ner and L. Putterman (eds), *Economics, Values and Organization*, Cambridge: Cambridge University Press, pp. 3–69.

Ben-Ner, A. and L. Putterman (2000), 'On some implications of evolutionary psychology for the study of preferences and institutions', *Journal of Economic Behavior and Organization*, **43**, pp. 91–9.

Binmore, Ken (1999), 'Why experiment in economics?', *Economic Journal*, **109**, F16–F24.

Bolton, Gary E. (2000), 'Motivation and the games people play', in Leonard D. Katz (ed.), *Evolutionary Origins of Morality*, Thorverston, UK: Imprint Academics.

Brown, Andrew (2000), *The Darwin Wars*, London: Pocket Book Paperback.

Buss, David M. (1999), *Evolutionary Psychology*, Boston: Allyn and Bacon.

Coase, Ronald H. (1976), 'Adam Smith's view of man', *Journal of Law and Economics*, **19**, 529–46.

Coase, Ronald H. (1978), 'Discussion', *American Economic Review (Papers and Proceedings)*, **68**, 244–5.

Coase, Ronald H. (1993), 'The institutional structure of production', *American Economic Review*, **82**. Reprinted in Oliver E. Williamson and Sidney G. Winter (eds), *The Nature of the Firm. Origins, Evolution and Development*, Oxford: Oxford University Press, pp. 227–35.

Cosmides, L. and J. Tooby (1992), 'Cognitive adaptations for social exchange', in J.H. Barkow, L. Cosmides and J. Tooby (eds), *The Adapted Mind*, Oxford: Oxford University Press, pp. 163–228.

Cosmides, L. and J. Tooby (1994), 'Better than rational: evolutionary psychology and the invisible hand', *American Economic Review*, **84**, pp. 327–32.

Cullenberg, S. and J. Amariglio (2001), *Postmodernism, Economics and Knowledge*, London: Routledge.

Dawkins, Richard (1976), *The Selfish Gene*, Oxford: Oxford University Press.

Dennett, D. (1995), *Darwin's Dangerous Idea*, London: Penguin Press.

Dupré, John (1993), *The Disorder of Things: Metaphysical Foundations of the Disunity of Science*, Cambridge, MA: Harvard University Press.

Frey, Bruno S. (1992), *Economics as a Science of Human Behaviour: Towards a New Social Science Paradigm*, Boston: Kluwer Academic Publishers.

Galison, Peter and David J. Stump (eds) (1996), *The Disunity of Science*, Stanford, CA: Stanford University Press.

Granovetter, Marc (1985), 'Economic action and social structures', *American Journal of Sociology*, **91**, 481–510.

Güth, W. and M.E. Yaari (1991), 'Explaining reciprocal behavior in simple strategic games: an evolutionary approach', in U. Witt, *Explaining Process and Change: Approaches to Evolutionary Economics*, Ann Arbor: University of Michigan, pp. 23–34.

Güth, W. and H. Kliemt (1998), 'The indirect evolutionary approach: bridging the gap between rationality and adaptation', *Rationality and Society*, **10** (3), 377.

Hacking, Ian (1996), 'The disunities of the sciences', in Galison and Stump (eds), pp. 37–74.

Hacking, Ian (1999), *The Social Construction of What?*, Cambridge, MA: Harvard University Press.

Hausman, Daniel M. (1992), *The Inexact and Separate Science of Economics*, Cambridge: Cambridge University Press.

Hirshleifer, Jack (1977) 'Economics from a biological viewpoint', *Journal of Law and Economics*, **20**, 1–52.

Hodgson, G.M. (1999), *Evolution and Institutions: On Evolutionary Economics and the Evolution of Economics*, Cheltenham, UK and Northampton, MA, USA: Edward Elgar.

Hogarth, R.M. and Melvin W. Reder (eds) (1987), *Rational Choice: The Contrast between Eonomics and Psychology*, Chicago: University of Chicago Press.

Huck, S. (1997), 'Institutions and preferences: an evolutionary perspective', *Journal of Institutional and Theoretical Economics*, **153** (4), 771–9.

Krugman, P. (1999), 'What economists can learn from evolutionary theorists – and vice versa', in J. Groenewegen and J.J. Vromen, *Institutions and the Evolution of Capitalism: Implications of Evolutionary Economics*, Cheltenham, UK and Northampton, MA, USA: Edward Elgar, pp. 17–29.

Lewin, S. (1996), 'Economics and psychology: lessons for our own day from the early twentieth century', *Journal of Economic Literature*, **XXXIV** (September), 1293–1323.

McCloskey, D.N. (1994), *Knowledge and Persuasion in Economics*, Cambridge: Cambridge University Press.

Mill, John Stuart (1967), 'On the definition of political economy; and on the method of investigation proper to it', in *Essays on Economics and Society*, London: Routledge and Kegan Paul, originally published in 1836.

Morrison, Margaret (2000), *Unifying Scientific Theories: Physical Concepts and Mathematical Structures*, Cambridge: Cambridge University Press.

Nelson, Richard and Sidney Winter (1982), *An Evolutionary Theory of Economic Change*, Cambridge, MA: Harvard University Press.

Rabin, Michael (1998), 'Psychology and economics', *Journal of Economic Literature*, **36**, 11–46.

Robbins, L. (1932, 1936), *An Essay on the Nature and Significance of Economic Science*, London: Macmillan.

Rosenberg, Alexander (1992), *Economics – Mathematical Politics or Science of Diminishing Returns*, Chicago: University of Chicago Press.

Rosenberg, Alexander (2000), *Darwinism in Philosophy, Social Science and Policy*, Cambridge: Cambridge University Press.

Ruccio, D. (1999), 'The end of capitalism: queer identity, political affect, and non-capitalist economies – towards an anthropology of class discourses', *Rethinking Marxism: A Journal of Economics, Culture, and Society*, **11** (2), 53–7.

Samuelson, Paul A. (1938), 'Note on the pure theory of consumer's behaviour', *Economica*, **V**, 61–71, 353–4.

Savage, Leonard (1951), *The Foundations of Statistics*, New York: Wiley.

Slovic, P. and S. Lichtenstein (1983), 'Preference reversals: a broader perspective', *American Economic Review*, **73**, 596–605.

Smith, Vernon L. (1991), 'Rational choice: the contrast between economics and psychology', *Journal of Political Economy*, **99** (4), 877–97.

Vromen, Jack J. (1995), *Economic Evolution: An Enquiry into the Foundations of New Institutional Economics*, London: Routledge.

Vromen, Jack J. (2000), 'Cognitive science meets evolutionary theory: what promise (if any) does evolutionary psychology hold out for economics?', paper presented at Workshop on Cognitive Economics, Alessandria-Torino, 15–18 November.

Vromen, Jack J. (2001a), 'Ontological commitments of evolutionary economics', in U. Mäki (ed.), *The Economic World View*, Cambridge: Cambridge University Press.

Vromen, Jack J. (2001b), 'The human agent in evolutionary economics', in John Laurent and John Nightingale (eds), *Darwinism and Evolutionary Economics*, Cheltenham, UK and Northampton, MA, USA: Edward Elgar.

Wilson, E.O. (1998), *Consilience: The Unity of Knowledge*, New York: Alfred A. Knopf.

Zywicki, T. (2000), 'Evolutionary biology and the social sciences', *Human Studies Review*, **13** (1).

3. Economics and sociology in the transition from industrial to post-industrial capitalism

George Liagouras[1]

Over the two last decades the boundaries between economics and sociology have become increasingly blurred. On the one hand, proponents of 'economic imperialism' argue that the model of *homo oeconomicus* should be exported to all social sciences in order to provide them with the scientific rigor of neoclassical reasoning. On the other hand, proponents of 'economic sociology' argue that economic action is always embedded in social relations, and the neoclassical postulate of atomized and asocial individuals is not able to explain economic phenomena adequately. The above methodological debate corresponds to a shift in the subjects studied by each discipline. Economics of the last two decades has become aware of the importance for economic efficiency of knowledge, trust, norms, institutions, values, culture, and so on. Sociology in turn has discovered that the abstraction from economic concerns is a serious missing link in its analysis. As M. Zald has remarked in his review essay on the new institutional economics of O. Williamson, it is 'extraordinary how sociologists manage to ignore issues of profit and efficiency in their thinking about capitalism' (Zald, 1987, p. 705).

In this intellectual context the past relations between economics and sociology have come under scrutiny, especially from authors belonging to the strand of 'economic sociology' (Swedberg, 1987; Granovetter, 1990; Gislain and Steiner, 1995). Thanks to these works we have today a comprehensive view of the history of 'economic sociology' and indirectly of the past relations between economics and sociology. However, the already existing historical studies pay little attention to the role of the broader social and ideological context in the evolution of economic sociology. Consequently, many interesting questions remain insufficiently answered: why was the period 1890–1920 so fruitful for economic sociology? What happened during the period 1920–80, when the idea of an economic sociology was marginalized? And, most importantly, why has a new economic sociology been emerging during the last two decades? And, how can we explain the fact that, at the same time, economic imperialism finds considerable support within sociology?

In what follows this chapter attempts to provide a rough interpretative framework, aiming to analyse the different phases of the relations between economics and sociology in comparison with the social and economic context that prevailed in each phase. As the main concern is the links between the pre-theoretical assumptions (or the social ontology) of the different theories and their corresponding socioeconomic conditions, little reference will be made to purely analytical and methodological problems. The discussion is organized in two parts. Part I analyses the relations between economic and sociological disciplines during the phase of industrial capitalism. Part II presents the hypothesis of a post-industrial capitalism and examines the consequences for both economics and sociology.

ECONOMICS AND SOCIOLOGY IN INDUSTRIAL CAPITALISM

Regarding the question of social order, modern thought has produced three basic solutions until now, namely social contract (Hobbes, Locke), market (Smith) and shared representations or beliefs (Durkheim, Weber). The two last solutions, the economic and sociological conception of modern society, are proper to the era of industrial capitalism. The purpose of this first part of the chapter is to analyse how the economic and sociological disciplines have been founded as opposite conceptions of the civil society in different periods of industrial capitalism. The interpretative framework that is proposed follows the major structural changes in the history of the two disciplines. First is presented the rise of the economic conception of civil society in classical political economy and the dissolution of the latter into two opposite currents, namely marginalism and Marxism. The whole evolution is linked to the liberal phase of industrial capitalism. Then, the breakthrough of Durkheim and Weber in social theory is analysed in relation to the broader social context of the transitory period 1890–1920, that is with the questioning of the role of markets to guarantee the social order of industrial societies. Finally, the success of the division of labour between economics and sociology proposed by Robbins and Parsons in the 1930s is linked to some basic features of late industrial capitalism (Keynesian policies and welfare state).

The Rise and Fall of the Economic Utopia

The economic conception of civil society can be found in the work of
Adam Smith. Smith's notion of the market as a source of social order
builds clearly on the notion of the self-interested individual, first introduced by Hobbes. But at the same time Smith introduced three important
novelties. The first one is that the source of social order is now located
outside the state, and more precisely in the economic sphere. In other
words, the idea of civil society is based on self-regulating markets rather
than coercive authority. The second novelty is that economic society is
conceived by Smith in a dynamic sense. The market is not a one-off solution to the problem of social order but rather a principle of continuous
transformation. The interplay between the expansion of markets and the
deepening of the division of labour leads to economic progress that benefits
all members of society: in the short run by offering to the consumers goods
at lower prices; in the long run by creating the conditions of 'universal opulence' (Smith, 1776, book I [1966], p. 13). So, Smith's civil society is open
to all members of the nation and not only to the citizens that are pro-
prietors, as was the case with the seventeenth century's political philosophy.
That is because Smith seeks to conceal neither the antagonisms between the
different classes of capitalist society nor the disadvantageous position of
the working class. All these 'effets pervers' can be overcome as the continuously increasing wealth of nations transforms them into affluent societies.

The third novelty of Smith concerns the relations between nation-states.
Smith's thought on this point goes far beyond his criticisms against mer-
cantilist theories of international trade as a zero-sum game. Once the
market economy is conceived as the essence of society, all forms of antag-
onism between states – as, for example, the struggle to conquer colonies –
becomes absurd. In Smith's cosmopolitan and pacifistic utopia the individual and social benefits stemming from free trade make the conquest of
foreign lands completely useless.

It must be obvious that Smith's liberal utopia is more a plea for a transition to a market economy than an apology for an already existing market
economy and society. Furthermore, it is well known that Smith wrote just
before the rise of industrial capitalism. He, certainly, understood the wealth
of nations as an accumulation of goods that are commodities, and linked
the differences in the wealth of nations to the productivity of (manual)
labour and then to the sequence of specialization–mechanization in the
production process. However, due to the period in which Smith wrote he
could not but miss other important features of industrial capitalism that
would be analysed later by thinkers like Ricardo, Babbage, Ure and Marx.
More precisely, the 'machines' or tools observed by Smith in his famous

manufacture of pins remain too far from the steam engines of industrial revolution. So, the energy-intensive character of technologies in industrial capitalism was not taken into account. Additionally, even if the importance of the deepening of mechanization is more or less recognized, it lacks the other 'natural technological trajectory' (to use the terms of Nelson and Winter (1982)), the exploitation of latent economies of scale. Finally, the lack of a clear distinction regarding the division of labour inside the firm and between autonomous producers signifies that the centrality of the labour–capital relation in industrial capitalism was not fully recognized by Smith.

What is however more important for the purpose of this study is that the moral and political premises of Smith's conception of economic society have been challenged even from the earlier stages of industrial capitalism. The idea of a natural harmony between conflicting interests has been damaged by recurrent economic crises and by rising social disorder. During the first decades of industrialization, the promise of economic (or social) progress for the whole of society was far from achieved. Even inside the first industrial power of the world, the virtuous cycle between the expansion of markets and the deepening of the division of labour led to economic growth but did not ameliorate the fortune of the first generations of the working class (Braudel, 1985). And when, in the second half of the nineteenth century, the promise of economic growth that benefits also the inferior classes begins to seem realizable, industrial capitalism has been shaken by the claims and the struggles of the labour movements. Finally, the idea of the liberalization of international trade, which was a relative success during the nineteenth century, has been denounced by other countries as an instrument in the service of British world domination.

The above 'market failures' had provoked a serious crisis not merely in Western societies but also in classical political economy.[2] After a transitory period of gestation and turmoil, two basic solutions have been offered: Marxian political economy and neoclassical economics.

With the marginalist (neoclassical) revolution (Jevons, Edgeworth, Marshall, Walras) in the late nineteenth century, economic theory lost definitively both its moral and political character, as well as its privilege to be the principal science of modern society.[3] Furthermore, neoclassical economics has retreated not only from political and moral questions but also from purely economic issues. Marginalism offers a new explanation of the formation of prices and the functioning of the market, which draws upon the scientific rigor of mechanics. From this standpoint it continues the tradition of economic liberalism with other (more scientific) means, as denoted by the term 'neoclassical economics'. However, besides (or thanks to) the rigor of a mathematical apparatus that is getting more and more complex, a threefold reduction of the subject of economic science takes place.

First, the substitution of a pure theory of exchange for the labour theory of value put out of the scope of economic theory the technological and organizational aspects of production. Second, the adoption of mechanics as a normative model of science leads to a static representation of economic phenomena, which by no means can grasp the dynamics of capitalist economy. From the above two reductions results a new kind of economic theory that leaves out Smith's central question about 'the nature and the causes of the wealth of nations'. What was evil for classical economists, the stationary state or the end of development becomes now the normal situation of economic analysis. Finally, power relations between social classes are transformed to exogenously given technical relations between 'factors of production'. This is why, instead of the term 'political economy', the technical term 'economics' expresses much better the content of neoclassical theory.

Whereas neoclassical economists were destroying the corpus of classical political economy in order to retain its laissez-faire message, Marx had already opted for the opposite solution. Thus, despite his virulent attack on capitalism, Marx appears from a philosophical and theoretical point of view as the more faithful follower of Smith. This is not only because he retains all the basic questions that the marginalists exclude from economic theory (namely the analysis of production, the dynamics of capitalist development and the power relations between social classes). In my view, above all it is as a moral and political philosopher that Marx continues Smith's heritage. Marx is perhaps the last great thinker who takes seriously the economic conception of civil society. As he writes in the Preface of his *Contribution to the Critique of Political Economy*:

> My inquiry led me to the conclusion that neither legal relations nor political forms could be comprehended whether by themselves or on the basis of a so-called general development of the human mind, but that on the contrary they originate in the material conditions of life, the totality of which Hegel, following the example of English and French thinkers of the eighteenth century, embraces within the term 'civil society'; that the anatomy of civil society, however, has to be sought in political economy. (Marx, 1859, p. 262)

Furthermore, Marx's messianism preserves and develops further some of the most fundamental features of the liberal utopia: the coming of a self-regulating (transparent) and cosmopolitan society, the extinction of the state and of political power in general and the achievement of universal opulence. In other words, even though Marx praises the destruction of capitalist society, concerning his pre-theoretical assumptions he remains firmly rooted in the economic utopia founded by Smith.

A New Revolution in the Social Thought: Durkheim's and Weber's Social Ontology (1890–1920)

Durkheim's and Weber's works appear during the transitory period 1890–1920, when liberal capitalism is in retreat and its successor is far from obvious. The 1890–1920 era is mainly marked by the rise of protectionism, nationalism and imperialism, the demise of the liberal state and the market economy (at the national and world level), the deepening of class struggles and the implementation of the first social reforms. As Polanyi (1944) suggested in the *The Great Transformation*, the above changes can be interpreted as the reaction (or the self-protection) of societies against the disruptive consequences of the self-regulating market. Certainly, the questioning of the market economy as to its ability to guarantee the social order had never stopped during the liberal phase of industrial capitalism. For example in 1839, Comte, who first introduced the term 'sociology', accused political economy of promoting industrial anarchy and social disorder (Swedberg, 1987). Nevertheless, in the 1890–1920 period the reaction against the 'Manchester System' was much broader and deeper, and alternatives to the materialist and individualist premises of the liberal economic ontology became dominant.

The most prominent figures of classical sociology, Durkheim and Weber, apart from their differences, clearly participate in this new zeitgeist. According to them the ultimate source of social order, but also of societies' evolution, is to be found in the sphere of social representations or beliefs. And inside this sphere, values or morals held the most important role. Certainly, classical sociology addressed the question of institutions, social structures and collective action. But these three topics were overdetermined by the evolution of social representations, or of values. Thus, although the sociological tradition shared with political economy the idea of the primacy of civil society over the state, it introduced at the same time a major breakthrough against the 'possessive individualism' of contract and market theorists. The starting point of the analysis was not any more the 'materialist' notion of self-interested individuals but the 'idealist' notions of representations or of values. Man was viewed as a social animal, whose social determination is not based on the sphere of material reproduction but on the one of symbolic reproduction.

This also implies a rejection of cosmopolitanism, which is inherent in liberal and Marxist thought (Durkheim, 1887; Weber, 1898). Though material interests of individuals or of classes are rather spaceless, moral and intellectual life takes place inside national societies. Therefore for the emerging science of sociology, nations and their political expression, that is, nation-states, are not simple epiphenomena doomed to melt into the air by the dynamics of the world market. As Touraine (1981) argues, when classical sociology claims to be the science of modern society in its totality, modern society is identified with national society. This is not mere coincidence. Indeed, the rise of classical sociology goes together with what Balibar (1990) calls the 'delayed nationalisation of modern societies'. That is, even if the word 'nation' is not new – Smith speaks about the wealth of nations; French revolutionaries were referring to the nation – the notion of nation as employed today is rather new: it goes back to the late nineteenth century. More precisely, always according to Balibar, the delayed nationalization of modern societies has taken place through a threefold process: the development of transports and communications, the generalization of compulsory education and the progressive institutionalization of the welfare state.

The importance of national society in turn offers the geographical, moral and political foundations for implementing social reforms. And Durkheim and Weber, as many other sociologists of their generation, were convinced social reformers.[4] In fact, large-scale social reforms are hardly conceivable in the spaceless universe of individual or class interests. This could be one possible reason why Marx, who was so courteous with many great authors, was at the same time so unfair with the first generation of the German historical school. For him, their attachment to the moral and intellectual foundations of societies and to social reforms was the proof that they have understood nothing about the inner logic of the capitalist system.[5]

It must be noted however that the elements of the triangle 'idealist social ontology–national society–social reforms' existed already before the work of Durkheim and Weber, especially in continental Europe (French positivism, German romanticism, socialist-reformist movements, and so on). Furthermore, all the three above elements can be found in the German historical school, which influenced considerably Weber (Weber, 1898; Hennis, 1987) and Durkheim (1887). So, one can ask, what is so new in the contribution of classical sociology or what justifies its success in the social thought of the twentieth century? Certainly, from an analytical point of view, classical sociology displays much more rigor than its predecessors. But, above all, I think that the novelty of classical sociology lies in its pragmatic liberalism. Thus, even though Durkheim and Weber clearly participate in a social and intellectual context of reaction against the destabilizing effects of the market (Nisbet, 1970), they reject restoration conservatism (Comte), authoritarian reformism (German historical school) and revolutionary messianism (communist and anarchist movements). In a continental Europe where liberalism has never been influential (and at the end of nineteenth century it was too late for that) Weber's and Durkheim's positions constituted the only intellectual movement that was able to combine the triangle idealist social ontology–national society–social reforms) with liberalism.

Table 3.1   The origins of the economic and sociological conceptions of (civil) society in industrial capitalism

	Main social sphere	Source of social order	Relation to space	Policy framework
Classical political economy	Material reproduction	Markets	Cosmopolitanism	Liberalism
Classical sociology	Intellectual and moral reproduction	Beliefs, values	National societies	Social reforms (pragmatic liberalism)

Weber's fear of the tendencial bureaucratization of modern societies, and Durkheim's proposition to reconstruct the medieval guilds as intermediate occupational associations in order to avoid the 'sociological monstrosity' of a new Leviathan (Durkheim, 1893 [1902]), are good examples of this. It was left to Parsons to give a definite liberal twist in Weber's and Durkheim's theories in order to import them into the USA and to export them later to post-war Europe.[6] Table 3.1 summarizes the above discussion on the differences between the economic and the sociological conceptions of society. There remains the question of the relationships of sociology with the other social sciences, which were or came to be institutionalized in the same period.

The originality of Weber and Durkheim is that they have translated the idea of a unified social science (Comte, German historical school) into more reasonable terms. Roughly speaking, while classical sociology doesn't contest the *raison d'être* of the other social sciences, the latter are seen as technical investigations of limited social spheres whose meaning can be fully articulated only by sociology. As a consequence, for each of the other social sciences there is a corresponding sociological sub-field: political sociology for politics, sociology of law for law, economic sociology for economics, and so on.

The most delicate relation was the one with political economy, the ex-principal science of the social being. Durkheim in his early masterpiece on *The Division of Social Labour* (Durkheim, 1893) sought to show that the very nature of economic phenomena should be analysed only from a sociological perspective. In this context, it seems that there remains a place for an economic science, which is limited however to the technical or superficial aspects of economic phenomena. Meanwhile, in the middle of his career Durkheim was tempted by the idea of replacing the existing economic science by a new one based on his own methodology (Durkheim, 1894, 1900). But later he seems to abandon this 'radical' position and to come back to his early ideas (Durkheim, 1908).

As Weber followed developments in economic science much better than Durkheim, he developed a more elaborated and stable position concerning the boundaries between the two disciplines. In sum, Weber (1904, 1908) argues that economics is well positioned to study the 'commercial calculus' of everyday life, but it is unable to grasp the meaning of economic phenomena. Therefore, Weber accords to the abstract, formal, cosmopolitan economic theory the right to study questions like 'Why the price of pork is *x* pfennigs today in Berlin'. However, according to him, economic activity is characterized by the heteronomy of its ends (or aims or ideals). The ends of economic activity concern ethical and political questions, and consequently they stand outside the economic sphere. In other words, economics as a moral and political science now becomes a question for sociology. The same applies for the study of institutions, social structures, collective action, which are crystallizations of the value-oriented actions of social agents, and are considered as given by economic analysis.[7]

Economics and Sociology in Late Industrial Capitalism (1920s–1970s)

With the end of classical sociology, sociological imperialism in economics (or economic sociology) becomes progressively a research program of diminishing returns. This implies the end of a long period of hostilities between economics and sociology inaugurated by Comte's attack against political economy. As Swedberg (1987) has already pointed out, the period from the 1920s to the 1970s is characterized by the peaceful coexistence, or the mutual ignorance, of the two disciplines.

The origins of the peaceful coexistence between economics and sociology go back to the 'gentlemen's agreement' (Ingham, 1996) between Robbins and Parsons in the 1930s. Robbins proposes a methodology-based definition of economics as 'the science which studies human behaviour as a relationship between ends and scarce means which have alternative uses' (Robbins, 1932[1984], p. 15). Robbins's proposition finds its counterpart some years later in Parsons's definition of sociology as the social science that studies the values and norms that lead human action and that are considered as given (ends or means) by economists (see Camic, 1991, especially Chapters 8, 16, 17 and 18).

Still, the success of the agreement between Robbins and Parsons needs to be explained. A first explanation is that the above agreement had been already prepared by the evolution of the two sciences during the preceding decades. From the side of economics, the marginalist revolution, by emptying economic relations from their social content, created the conditions for a 'fruitful' division of labour between economics and sociology (Clarke, 1982). Significantly, almost all the founders of neoclassical economics rejected the 'imperialism' of classical political economy and recognized the need of other social disciplines as 'sociology' or 'social economics'. And if it is right that Robbins's definition of economics was narrower than that of Marshall and the Austrians (Hodgson, 2001), this was already implied in the work of more formal marginalists like Jevons, Edgeworth, Walras and Pareto. From the side of sociology, the essential of Parsons's definition can be found already in Weber's attitude towards abstract economics. What is new in Parson's is that he did not claim explicitly for sociology the right to be the principal social science, and by consequence he considered the two disciplines as equal partners working inside a mutually beneficial division of labour.

A second explanation refers to the coming of the Keynesian revolution in economic theory. As Swedberg argues:

> during the years of depression, when classical economics seemed to have lost contact with reality, the economists very quickly produced new and sophis-ticated theories to account for what was going on. From one point of view, one can say that Keynes and the Stockholm School pre-empted the need for eco-nomic sociology. (Swedberg, 1987, pp. 42–3)

In fact, Keynes's *General Theory* restored the lost prestige of the 'dismal science'. After the first successes of Keynesian policies it was difficult to pretend that economics is a science distanced from reality, or a science of industrial anarchy. Significantly, Keynes (1936) at the end of his *General Theory* (Chapter 24) ignored the elegant distinctions of his predecessors between facts and values and put forth the social philosophy underpin-ning his economic system. In his view social justice, instead of being an obstacle to capitalist expansion, is on the contrary a sine qua non con-dition for it.

Thus, appropriate state intervention suffices to transform what was con-sidered an insolvable trade-off into a virtuous cycle. The idea of an existing compatibility between economic efficiency and social order offers also the pre-theoretical foundations for the peaceful coexistence (or the mutual ignorance) between economics and sociology. If there is no contradiction between the economic and the social reproduction of late capitalist soci-eties, each discipline can address its own segment of reality with its own analytical tools and methods. It remains that Keynes's conception of eco-nomics as a moral science was not akin to the neoclassical framework set up by Robbins and his followers. But here lies the seminal achievement of Samuelson in his *Foundations of Economic Analysis*. Inspired by the already suggested interpretations of Keynes (such as by Hicks or Hansen), Samuelson transformed Keynes's thought into an organic part of main-stream economics.

The crisis of the Fordist economy and society in the late 1960s and in the 1970s brought about serious crises inside both disciplines. In economics, Keynesianism was challenged by monetarists and later by new classical economics. In sociology, Parsonian structural-functionalism was displaced by alternative methodological investigations (ethnomethodology, interactionism, hermeneutics) and by critical sociologies (see for example the work of Marcuse, Habermas, Bourdieu, Foucault and Gouldner). However, the above turbulences were confined inside the boundaries of each discipline and had little impact on their relations.

ECONOMICS AND SOCIOLOGY IN POST-INDUSTRIAL CAPITALISM

The basic idea of this second part of the chapter is that the dawning of post-industrial capitalism poses a challenge without precedent for the boundaries between economics and sociology. After reiterating some 'stylized facts' concerning the relations of the two disciplines during the last decades, I present briefly the hypothesis of the arrival of post-industrial capitalism and I argue why and how such a hypothesis matters for the shifting landscape in economics and sociology.

The Blurred Boundaries between Economics and Sociology in the Last Two Decades: an Overview

One can observe major changes that have been taking place within economics since the 1980s; from economics towards sociology, and from sociology towards economics. Inside economics a new scientific revolution takes place. As has already been argued, the marginalist revolution had left out of economic theory not only all social but even some of the economic issues that had been addressed by classical economists. During the last two decades economists seem to have reclaimed the maximum of issues they had left to other social sciences, and especially to sociology. The most representative example of this movement is 'human capital' theories and the so-called 'New Institutional Economics'. In the human capital approach (Becker, 1964), the neoclassical man, unaware of questions of identity, makes his choice about education in the same manner he would make a decision on alternative investment projects. So, what is a complex social process is reduced to an individual maximization problem. New Institutional Economics (mainly transaction costs, but also property rights and principal-agent approaches) follow the opposite direction. Instead of reducing the social to the individual, they start from the inefficiencies of coordination between agents (asymmetries and imperfections in the information held by agents, opportunism, uncertainty, and so on) in order to justify the functional need for economic or social institutions other than the market. In this case the limits of individual rationality, and the market failures in which they lead, account for the existence of alternative institutional frameworks. In other words, from the two fundamental notions of neoclassical theory, the individual and the market, the latter tends to be replaced by the concepts of institutions or of contracts. Thus, the market appears as a spot contract or as a special institutional framework.

Of course, it is well known that the above advancements of neoclassical economics have been seriously challenged by modern evolutionary and non-mainstream institutional economics. Moreover, from an analytical point of view, modern evolutionary and institutional economics realize an important breakthrough in the history of economic thought by offering alternative conceptions of knowledge, rationality, and institutions that are much more appealing than those of neoclassical economics proper (Nelson and Winter, 1982; Dosi et al., 1988; Hodgson 1993, 1999). Nonetheless, regarding the main subjects they focus on, they are part of the more general movement towards a reconquest by economic science of realms left a century ago to sociology and other social sciences.

In the 1990s a new concept, that of social capital, became very popular with sociologists, economists and other social scientists. Even though the uses of this notion vary, most of them aim to understand all the informal aspects of social life (habits, beliefs, norms, values, customs, trust, culture, and so on) as a form of individual capital, or of a public good. Social capital permits to revisit most sociological theories and to interpret them under the light of a unique economic metaphor. Thus, Woolcock, in his survey on social capital, refers to Swedberg (1987) in order to argue that 'the Durkheimian, Weberian, and Marxist traditions within classical sociology were all heavily influenced by the economic debates and issues of that period, and much of what we now refer to as "social capital" lay at the heart of these concerns' (1998, p. 160). This is true in the sense that the concept of social capital is merely 'relabelling' (Portes, 1998) of diverse informal aspects of social life studied separately until now by sociologists. But, at the same time, the concept of social capital (usually) analyses informal institutions from a perspective that is foreign to classical sociology, as it focuses on how functional or dysfunctional they are in order to achieve economic efficiency.[8]

In sum, if one combines the notions of human capital, social capital and transaction costs, then the major preoccupations of sociology (education, morals and institutions) could be analysed within economic theory.[9] The same applies for the question of collective action, reduced already by Olson (1965) to a free-riding problem. Compared to the acceptance by social scientists of the above economy-driven notions, more aggressive forms of 'economic imperialism' (concerning the economic analysis of family, crime, religion, marriage, and so on) are important only to the extent that they pave the way for less reductionist accounts of these issues.

In such an intellectual landscape the adoption of 'rational choice' approaches by eminent sociologists as Coleman (1994) is not surprising. However, the colonization of sociology by economics encounters serious reactions from sociologists. Apart from criticisms raised against the short-comings of rational choice sociology, there are also serious efforts to go further and challenge economic theory inside its own field; that is the current of 'New Economic Sociology' (Granovetter and Swedberg, 1992; Smelser and Swedberg, 1994). The latter distinguishes itself from the 'old' one on two points. First, as Granovetter argues, Durkheim and Weber 'though somewhat disdainful toward pure economic theory, neither attacked it directly; both were more interested in those sociological elements that formed the preconditions for markets and capitalist organization than in the every-day workings of the economy' (Granovetter, 1990, p. 90). By contrast, new economic sociology focuses on the everyday workings of the economy, and especially in the functioning of markets and organizations. However, and this is the second difference, new economic sociology is specialized in middle-range theories and not, as Weber and Durkheim did, in comprehensive accounts of the past and the future of modern societies (Ingham, 1996). The methodological impact of the above change is that New Economic Sociology does not pay much attention to the historical approach of social phenomena practised by Weber and Durkheim, and other famous scholars as Marx, Schumpeter and Polanyi (Piore, 1996). The objective is rather to start with middle-range theories of separate institutions in order to end up with 'one general theory of social institutions' (Granovetter, 1990, p. 106).[10]

It is rather obvious that sociological imperialism (New Economic Sociology) is less strong than the economic one. However, both seem to have good future prospects. It remains a question how one can explain the ongoing (con)fusion between the economic and sociological spheres in the last two decades.

The Hypothesis of the Transition to Post-Industrial Capitalism

My basic hypothesis is that industrial capitalism, as it has been conceptualized by a series of authors from Smith and Marx to Weber and Sombart, and then to Galbraith and Chandler, is already outdated. We are entering a new era, which I call by default 'post-industrial capitalism'. The most characteristic features of this new type of capitalism are the following:

A new technical system

The transition from an energy-intensive to an information-intensive technical system is well demonstrated by many authors. As Charles Jonscher argues:

> Electronics is almost synonymous, in today's economies, with information technology. This is what distinguishes electronics from other forms of technology, such as steam, diesel, nuclear, or electrical power machinery. In those latter systems the power levels present in the machinery are sufficiently high to enable useful physical work to be performed, work that before the Industrial Revolution would have been done manually. An electronic system is a particular case of an electrical system in which power levels are so low that substantial physical objects cannot be manipulated – only symbols can. The power in an electronic circuit is sufficient to represent a character of information, but not to operate an elevator or turn a lathe. Insofar as it replicates human effort, electronic power performs functions requiring intellectual rather than manual labour. (Jonscher, 1994, p. 8)

Still, even though the importance of technical change is well documented, sometimes it is underestimated by theories talking about a 'third industrial revolution' or a 'fifth Kondratieff wave'. The problem with these theories is that they presuppose, implicitly or explicitly, a continuity of paradigm between industrial and information revolution.

A new time–space equation

The information revolution, by enforcing an amazing 'compression of the time–space equation', which by no means could be realized from the energy-based technical paradigm, opens radically new perspectives of economic integration. As Manuel Castells writes:

> The informational economy is global. A global economy is a historically new reality, distinct from a world economy. A world economy, that is an economy in which capital accumulation proceeds throughout the world, has existed in the West at least since the sixteenth century, as Fernard Braudel and Immanuel Wallerstein have taught us. *A global economy is something different: it is an economy with the capacity to work as a unit in real time on a planetary scale.* (Castells, 1996, p. 92)

So, even though the ratios of external trade and capital flows to gross domestic product (GDP) are not higher today than they were during the Gold Standard era (c.1870–1914) (Hirst and Thompson, 1996), the resulted economic integration is without precedent in the history of capitalism (Baldwin and Martin, 1999; Bordo et al., 1999; Perraton, 2001).

A transformation of the nature of commodities

In the post-industrial economy the dominant form of wealth is no longer the accumulation of goods but the proliferation and the amelioration of symbolic and relational systems. In other words, the 'dematerialization' tendency (Roobeek, 1987) in modern economy is characterized by the increasing importance of software (including 'human capital') over hardware and of service relations over material components of commodities. For some, the dematerialization tendency is evidenced in the ongoing de-industrialization of advanced economies during the last three decades. Post-industrial capitalism is then understood as a service economy and society, according to an evolutionist schema presuming the transition from agricultural to industrial and then to service societies. The main problem in this approach is that it tries to define post-industrial capitalism by means of a statistical categorization that reflects the Weltanschuung of industrial society. Certainly, the very fact that the heterogeneous service sector gets more than two-thirds of the GDP in advanced economies constitutes major empirical evidence for the end of the industrial capitalism. However, by no means does it say anything about the logic of this new era of capitalism that is emerging. This is the reason why post-industrial capitalism is understood here not as the victory of services over manufacturing (Bell, 1973) but as the blurring of their boundaries, caused by the domination of cognitive, communicative and aesthetic components of commodities over physical ones.

A new paradigm in business organization
The essentials of business organization in industrial capitalism can already be found in the writings of classical economists: the long-term performance of the enterprise is identified with productivity. And productivity is obtained in three correlated ways: the deepening of the (technical) division of labour; the mechanization of the labour process; and the economies of scale. Today, the above model of business organization is in crisis. The notion of productivity no longer makes sense in an economic context, where quality and variety take precedence over quantity. Investment in intangible capital (research and development (R&D), training, software, long-term marketing positioning, and so on) becomes more important than the mechanization of labour processes. Last but not least, the secular tendencies towards specialization-deskilling of labour and vertical–horizontal expansion of the firm are clearly reversed. As a consequence, the centre of the business organization moves from the shop floor to the interfaces between the members of a network of enterprises and organisms, and between the network and its clients. The firm is better conceptualized as a 'knowledge-creating' than a 'materials-processing' company (Simon, 1966; Zuboff, 1988; Nonaka and Takeuchi, 1995). And, even if physical labour is far from being eliminated, the heart of the capitalist valorization process is situated now in the 'symbols manipulating' workers. By this term I am referring not only to the intensified use of cognitive resources in economic

activity, but also of communicative and aesthetic ones (Piore et al., 1994; Sternberg, 1998).

A new type of *possible* development
One of the main features of industrial capitalism was the tangible capital-deepening growth. The dangers of the continuous substitution of machines for labour were brought into light by Marx's analysis about the tendency of the organic composition of capital to rise, and thus of the rate of profit to fall. However, the coming of mass production inaugurated a new era, where investment in intangible capital (and especially in human capital) starts to have increasing importance over investment in a conventional one. For example, according to the estimations of Kendrick, in the US economy the ratio of intangible to tangible capital stock has grown from 0.535 in 1939 to 1.150 in 1990 (Kendrick, 1994; Abramovitz and David, 1996). This secular transformation of the nature of capital entails serious problems for our conception of development. Investment in intangible capital implies a much higher degree of uncertainty and complexity than investment in tangible capital. The same can be said about the depreciation of intangible capital. But, perhaps the most serious difficulty is to find convenient indicators in order to measure what is intangible or invisible. It is a more general problem, which concerns not only investment but also all basic concepts such as product, productivity, consumer surplus, and so on, which we inherited from the industrial era. In sum, we are supposed to enter a post-industrial economy, but we still don't know how to measure the performance of such an economy.[11] Note, however, that the coming of a new 'golden' era of development is understood here as a mere possibility and not as a matter of fact. *Pace* to some 'new economy' theories, which declared among others the end of business cycles (!!!), it is maintained that a durable phase of prosperity cannot be sustained without a new institutional framework of macroeconomic and social stabilization (Petit and Soete, 1999; Michie and Smith, 1998).[12]

In sum, according to the social sphere that serves as privileged support for the valorization of capital, one can distinguish among three main periods in the history of capitalism. The first period is merchant capitalism, and occurs when capital occupies the sphere of exchange. Industrial capitalism, the second major period, arises when the 'rationalization' of manual labour (or of the exchange between man and nature) becomes the main source of capital valorization. Finally, the third period, which is described here as post-industrial capitalism, is characterized by the subordination of societal and individual symbolic resources (cognitive, communicative and aesthetic) into the movement of capital.

From the 'Intellectual and Moral Reform of the Nation' to 'Public Investment in Human and Social Capital', or Why Post-Industrial Capitalism Matters

The main consequence the coming of a post-industrial economy and society implies for sociology is the undermining of its autonomy. At first glance, post-industrial capitalism questions the sociological conception of civil society as far as it implies the deconstruction of the national society, which constitutes the paradigmatic society of sociological inquiry. As it has been argued above, the nationalization of modern societies has been realized progressively through a threefold process: the (national) development of transports and communication, of education and of welfare state. Today all the three constitutive features of national societies are undergoing deep changes. First, financial or economic globalization makes the (national) social solidarity dysfunctional from a competitiveness point of view. At the same time, information and communication technologies enable the creation of new services in the education, medical and welfare sectors (Kodama, 2000) and offer lucrative perspectives for new markets. Second, education mechanisms no longer seek to produce good and instructed citizens (or patriots), but knowledge and skills appreciated by markets. Thus, the ongoing domination of the 'correspondence principle' between schooling and work tends to transform the educational system into a training institution (Luke, 1998). Finally, deregulation and privatization in transport and communication industries challenges the national borders in the same manner that the development of the national transport and communications networks challenged the regional ones a century ago.

Certainly, the decomposition of the national society does not imply necessarily the impossibility of a new type of sociology, or a 'sociology without society' (Touraine, 1981). However, the structural changes brought about by the rise of post-industrial capitalism go far beyond its negative effects on national society. *Above all, post-industrial capitalism undermines the sociological conception of (civil) society to the extent that the cognitive, moral and aesthetic reproduction of individuals and societies becomes the main input or output of economic activity.*

In a dematerialized economy, investment in 'human' and 'social' capital becomes the most strategic source of economic efficiency (Nahapiet and Ghosal, 1998; Lundvall, 1999). Consequently, cognitive and moral (re)production of social reality is no more seen on its own but as a strategic input for enhancing competitiveness in the micro-, meso- and macro-levels (of firms, regions and nations). That is why the career of concepts such as 'human capital' or 'social capital' among sociologists and other social scientists is considered here as characteristic of the coming of a new era in the history of capitalism. From this standpoint even what appears today as 'sociological imperialism', that is, contemporary sociological accounts of entrepreneurship, markets, economic networks and organizations, development and so on, expresses the decomposition of the sociological conception of civil society rather than an extension of sociology's conceptual framework.[13]

At the same time, information, knowledge, communication and culture appear in the everyday life of post-industrial capitalism not only as strategic inputs but also as high value-added consumption commodities (outputs). The social consequences of the postmodern condition of human knowledge and culture are sketched in apocalyptic terms by Bauman:

> It was the intellectuals who impressed upon the once incredulous population the need for education and the value of information. Here as well their success turns into their downfall. The market is only too eager to satisfy the need and to supply the value. With the new DIY (electronic) technology to offer, the market will reap the rich crop of the popular belief that education is human duty and (any) information is useful. The market will thereby achieve what the intellectual educators struggled to attain in vain: it will turn the consumption of information into a pleasurable, entertaining pastime. Education will become just one of the many variants of self-amusement. It will reach the peak of its popularity and the bottom of its value as measured by original intellectual-made standards. (Bauman, 1988, p. 225)

Even if one finds the above account too pessimistic, it is rather difficult to deny the importance of information, knowledge, communication, entertainment and culture – industries for the future of capitalism.

As the aforementioned problems of today's sociology have their common source in the pervasive action of economic imperatives one could anticipate a new golden era for economic science. However, this is not as evident as it seems.

First of all, the extension of economic discourse in new spheres of social life makes economic analysis even more irrelevant than it was until now. Already during the industrial era, neoclassical analysis reduced production and development dynamics to a form of exchange between different factors of production, mainly (physical) capital and labour. Nothing expresses better the failure of this attempt than the notions of 'x-efficiency' at the micro-level and of 'exogenous technical progress' at the macro-level. What these concepts amount to is a diplomatic admission that what was important to explain was beyond the analytical tools of the conventional theory. But if the ontology of possessive individualism, implied by a 'pure exchange theory', was already at odds with the technological and organizational dynamics of industrial production and growth, it becomes totally irrelevant in the context of an immaterial economy. As Piore put it in the early 1980s:

The critique of liberalism is that it views information and thought, more or less as it views society, as consisting of discrete individual elements, which produce through aggregation the continuous homogeneous phenomena of social life. It fails to recognize that those discrete elements are processed in terms of some model, framework or 'structure' of thought, and the same discrete 'bits' lead to very different outcomes, depending upon what the interpreting framework turns out to be. Society, social groups and institutions are part of the process through which that framework is generated. (Piore, 1983, p. 253)

From this standpoint, the efforts of mainstream theorists to analyse the economic importance of learning add new shortcomings to the old ones. Reducing knowledge to a piece of an already given information seems even more irrelevant than reducing the labour process to a certain amount of working hours. Trying to analyse educational achievements of individuals as investment in human capital sounds much more unrealistic than the conventional treatment of physical capital. Hence, even in the so-called 'endogenous growth theories', growth remains exogenous as far as no insights are offered about learning processes and appropriate institutional arrangements (except the old market–state dichotomy) (Dosi, 1992; Nelson, 1998; Fine, 2000).

Certainly, the question of institutions and organizations constitutes the main concern of the new institutional economics. However the latter, by opening the black box of the firm and of business organization in general, became more and more vulnerable to the criticisms of non-mainstream economists (Putterman, 1984; Teece, 1988; Winter, 1988; Dugger, 1990; Simon, 1991; Lazonick, 1991; Foss, 1993; Hodgson, 1999). Furthermore, by seeking to study subjects as institutions, modern neo-classical economics is undertaking a dangerous adventure in fields that conventional economic theory had ceded to sociology and other social sciences a century ago. If combining maximization behaviour of individuals with the market seemed reasonable, founding the existence of institutions on the maximizing action of individuals is much less so. Therefore, economics is exposed to competition by alternative theories of institutions, put forth by other social scientists. For example, the proponents of New Economic Sociology challenge economic analysis regarding not only institutions but also markets. Certainly the common conceptual framework of the middle-range sociological investigations of economic life is too thin to offer for the moment a theoretical alternative to mainstream economics. The unifying concepts of 'embeddedness' (social, cultural or political) and of 'social construction of economic reality' (Swedberg, 1997) do not yield a theoretical framework. But, how secure could the position of mainstream economics be if organizations or policy-makers started to be interested in more realistic (and less theoretical) accounts of economic life, as the World Bank already did with 'social capital'?[14]

Finally, if today mainstream economics addresses a series of topics that were considered to lie outside the scope of economic inquiry two decades ago, this is not due to their excessive 'self-confidence' or their desire to 'colonize' the other social sciences (Fine, 1999). As far as post-industrial capitalism shifts the centre of economic activity outside the sphere of 'material civilization', economists have no other choice but to explore areas of social life that were completely foreign to their interests. For example, conventional economics had no other choice but to address the question of 'economic institutions of capitalism' (Williamson, 1985). As argued here, in post-industrial business organization there is a shift of importance from the markets–hierarchies dichotomy to intermediate or hybrid organizational forms. In order to study the latter the market, which constituted the quintessence of economic reasoning, had to be sacrificed to the 'network effect'. The same token applies for the major part of economic imperialism.

CONCLUDING REMARKS

The economic and sociological disciplines have been founded as distinctive conceptions of civil society in different periods of industrial capitalism. The economic conception of civil society was put forward by the classical political economy in the beginnings of industrial capitalism. It presupposed that the sphere of material reproduction forms the base of the whole society and that the market is the ultimate source of social order (and economic development). The appearance of economic crisis, workers' struggles and the national antagonisms in the second half of the nineteenth century provoked the dissolution of the economic utopia of the classical tradition into two opposite currents. This produced the marginalists, who reduced drastically the scope of classical political economy to a static theory of exchange in order to preserve its laissez-faire message, and the Marxists, who developed further the corpus of classical political economy in order to praise the coming of a new self-regulating and cosmopolitan society through the destruction of the capitalist system.

The sociological conception of civil society was founded by social thinkers such as Durkheim and Weber during the transitory period of 1890–1920, that is, at the turning point from the early (liberal) to the late industrial capitalism. The ontology of classical sociologists postulated that the sphere of intellectual and moral reproduction overdetermined the rest of social reality and thus that the shared beliefs and values were the main source of social order. The rise of what we call today 'old economic sociology' in the work of Durkheim, Weber and others was the immediate consequence of the claim of classical sociology to be the principal science of the social being. Later however, the sociologists, following Parsons's agreement with Robbins, have moderated their claims over economics and have retreated from economic questions. The integration of the Keynesian revolution in neoclassical economics and the post-war economic and social success of interventionist economic policies restored the lost prestige of the 'dismal science' and eliminated the need for economic sociology.

Over the two last decades, however, the division of labour between economics and sociology we inherited from Parsons and Robbins becomes more and more obsolete. The main argument of this chapter is that the above change in the boundaries between the two disciplines should be understood in relation to the rise of post-industrial capitalism. Whereas the valorization of capital in industrial capitalism was anchored in the sphere of material reproduction, in post-industrial capitalism the valorization of capital depends primarily on the intellectual, moral and aesthetic resources of individuals and societies. To the extent that the latter become inputs or outputs of economic activity, the autonomy of the sociological conception of (civil) society is put into question. At the same time, as the centre of economic activities shifts from the material to the symbolic reproduction of human beings, economics is doomed to conquer the territories of the other social sciences, and above all, of sociology. However, by this method mainstream economics are also condemned to become more and more irrelevant because their pre-analytical assumptions and analytical tools stand at odds with the new subjects they seek to study.

Hence, from the perspective outlined here, the methodological opposition between '*homo oeconomicus*' and '*homo sociologicus*' is only the tip of the iceberg. The crisis of modern economics and sociology can be overcome neither by methodological innovations, nor by new middle-range and hybrid insights. What is at issue is a 'crisis of vision', as Heilbroner and Milberg (1995) diagnose for modern economic thought, or, in the words of this chapter, 'a vacuum in our representation of civil society'. Such lack of vision can be overcome only by a reflection on the major social problems that arise from the advent of post-industrial capitalism. In this respect, economic reductionism would be far more dangerous as an anticipation of a new form of life than as an academic mode. For example, perhaps what Arendt once said about behaviourism applies to today's economic imperialism: 'The trouble with modern theories of behaviourism is not that they are wrong but that they could become true' (Arendt, 1969, p. 322).

A last remark concerning the current of evolutionary and institutionalist economics, of which I am part. As I said earlier, they participate, although without any declared intention, in the broader tendency of today's economics to study a series of topics that were left by marginalists to sociology a century ago. Most importantly, in doing so their main inspiration outside economics has come rather from biology and cognitive psychology than from sociology and related social sciences. Obviously, there is a serious missing link here and a critical challenge for evolutionary and institutional economics. Thus, it is very encouraging to find recent contributions, besides these of this book, that address the question of the relations with sociology and related social sciences either directly (Hodgson, 2001), or indirectly, through the study of institutionalist approaches in the social sciences (Théret, 2001; Nielsen, 2001). Perhaps these contributions will constitute the starting point for a generalized dialogue among evolutionary and institutionalist scholars.

NOTES

1. The author gratefully acknowledges the very helpful comments he received from the two editors and the participants in the session 'Economics and Social Sciences' of the EAPE Conference 2000 in Berlin. Of course, the usual disclaimers apply.
2. 'During the 1870s English political economy suffered a considerable loss of public prestige. [. . .] On the occasion of a dinner given by the Political Economy Club of London to mark the centenary of the Wealth of Nations it was suggested that economists "had better be celebrating the obsequies of their science than its jubilee". The nadir of the movement was reached in 1877, when it was formally proposed that Section F of the British Association, dealing with Economics and Statistics, should be dropped because its proceedings and its subject-matter were unscientific' (Coats, 1954, p. 143).
3. The moral and political character of political economy has been already contested by J.S. Mill, who clearly distinguishes between positive (scientific) and normative statements in a way that reminds us of contemporary textbooks of (mainstream) economics (see also Swedberg, 1987, p. 22).
4. The social reformism of Durkheim and Weber is well documented. Weber was an active member of the 'Verein fur Sozialpolitik', a political-academic association struggling for social reforms (see Krüger, 1987). Durkheim's commitment to 'social justice' and 'national solidarity' is also well known. Mauss, in his Preface of Durkheim's book on 'Socialism' (Durkheim, 1895–6), reports that Durkheim's intention was to participate and motivate the French socialist party. Nevertheless, Durkheim rejected the materialist philosophy that inspired socialist claims for social justice and reforms. According to him, social problems are rather a 'question of morals' than a 'question of money'. Given that human nature is characterized by unbound desires, the objective should be rather to assuage these desires than to fully gratify them. In this sense, the 'moral and intellectual reform of the nation' takes precedence over the economic reforms. Or, put in an another way, the latter are justified only as means for achieving the former (Durkheim, 1895–6).
5. From this point of view, Gramsci (1971) can be considered as the most charismatic figure within the followers of Marx. Gramsci's Marxism, thanks to the notions of civil society and hegemony, and to the importance accorded to the formation of modern nations, is very close to the preoccupations of classical sociology. For an interesting comparison between Gramsci and Weber, see Levy (1987).
6. Thanks to the work of Mommsen (1984) we now have a comprehensive account of Weber's political 'preferences' that contradicts the more liberal interpretations of Weber

in post-war mainstream sociology. Nevertheless, Weber's ambivalence about liberalism must be situated in its historical context. As Krüger suggests, Weber and his brother were the more consequent liberal figures of the Verein fur Sozialpolitik. Furthermore, it seems that there is a close affinity between Weber's epistemology and his liberal positions in the debates inside the Verein:

> Weber's demand for scientific statements and conceptions free from value judgement was probably led by the intention (strictly speaking, in itself *also* political) to strip the aura of scientific objectivity from the demand for the preservation and support of the bureaucratic authoritarian state (if necessary at the expense of economic efficiency). To this extent, the conflicting situation in the Verein may have pushed Weber to formulate clearly his ideas on bureaucracy and on methodology of the social sciences. (Krüger, 1987, p. 80)

7. This argument can be seen as a more elaborated form of the early Durkheim's position. But Weber went much further. Instead of rejecting the methodology based on *homo oeconomicus*, he made an important contribution concerning the status of marginalist theory. He argued (Weber, 1908) that marginal utility theory does not rest on any psychological assumptions, and therefore that it could not be falsified by the findings of empirical psychology. *Homo oeconomicus* constitutes an ideal type, a theoretical and historically bound fiction, representing the instrumental rationality of economic action in capitalist societies. In this way, the *homo oeconomicus* of the marginalists corresponds to a special form of rationality and social action in Weber's general (and interpretative) sociology (Weber, 1922).

8. It must be noted that the meaning of the concept of 'social capital' has been subject to successive transformations. In the critical sociology of Bourdieu (1980), social capital was a constitutive part of new forms of domination, situated beyond the economic aspects of power studied by Marx. In its first English-speaking uses (Coleman, 1988), social capital served as a link between individual strategies and their micro-social environment. Finally, in the main bulk of recent research (Woolcock, 1998), social capital is seen as a strategic asset of firms, regions and nations in their struggle for competitiveness. For a critique of the passage from the second stage to the third one, see Portes (1998).

9. As Ingham reports: 'A colleague recently suggested to me that we probably no longer needed sociological theories of bureaucracy in an undergraduate interdisciplinary course because "it's all explained by transaction costs" ' (1996, p. 262, footnote). See also Baron and Hannan who, having ascertained the recent emergence of 'a plethora of capitals', declare being 'somewhat baffled that sociologists have begun referring to virtually every feature of social life as a form of capital' (Baron and Hannan, 1994, p. 1124).

10. Granovetter is very clear on the a-historical and positivist assumptions of his work: 'Though critical of neoclassical economic theory, I share with its proponents the positivist quest for general, universal explanations. In this respect, my position is close to Hempel's whose student I was' (Granovetter, 1990, p. 106).

11. For some, the position that the national accounts system tends to be obsolete is associated with conservative economists, like the participants in the Boskin report (Boskin et al., 1998). I think however that the existing mismatch between our accounting apparatus and today's economic reality goes far beyond the political intentions of conservative economists. The best example for this is the pioneering article of Block (1985).

12. For a detailed account on the contradictions of post-industrial capitalism, see Liagouras (2003).

13. The work of Beckert (1996) on the analytical foundations of the (new) economic sociology reflects very well in the theoretical level the recent tendency to reinterpret the sociological features of civil society from an economic point of view. If the existence of routines, habits, norms, institutions, organizational structures, power and so on within modern economic life is explained by their functional role in reducing the (radical) uncertainty faced by economic agents, then the very idea of social embeddedness of economic processes can be reduced to a more realistic account of *homo oeconomicus*.

By this way, what has been initially understood as a revival of 'sociological imperialism' could be transformed to an application field of the microeconomics of complexity and uncertainty.

14. The fact that proponents of the new economic sociology, but also heretic economists, find a hospitable climate in Business Schools is not a mere coincidence. Such departments are more interested in relevance than in theoretical elegance or mathematical rigor.

REFERENCES

Abramovitz, M. and P. David (1996), 'Technological change and the rise of intangible investments. The US economy's growth path in the twentieth century', in D. Foray and B.A. Lundvall (eds), *Employment and Growth in the Knowledge-Based Economy*, Paris: OECD, pp. 35–61.

Arendt, H. (1969), *The Human Condition*, Chicago: University of Chicago Press.

Baldwin, R. and P. Martin (1999), 'Two waves of globalisation: superficial similarities, fundamental differences', *NBER Working Paper*, No. 6904.

Balibar, E. (1990), 'La forme nation. Histoire et idéologie', in E. Balibar and I. Wallerstein (eds), *Race, Nation, Classe. Les Identités Ambiguës*, Paris: La Découverte.

Baron, J.N. and M.T. Hannan (1994), 'The impact of economics on contemporary sociology', *Journal of Economic Literature*, **XXXII**(3), 1111–46.

Bauman, Z. (1988), 'Is there a postmodern sociology?', *Theory, Culture and Society*, **5**(2–3), 217–37.

Becker, G. (1964), *Human Capital* [1975], New York: Columbia University Press.

Beckert, J. (1996), 'What is sociological about economic sociology? Uncertainty and the embeddedness of economic action', *Theory and Society*, **25**(6), 803–40.

Bell, D. (1973), *The Coming Post-Industrial Society*, New York: Basic Books.

Block, F. (1985), 'Post-industrial development and the obsolescence of economic categories', *Politics and Society*, **14**(1), 71–104.

Bordo, M., B. Eichengreen and D. Irwin, (1999), 'Is globalisation today really different than globalisation a hundred years ago?', *NBER Working Paper*, No. 7195.

Boskin, M., E. Dulberger, R. Gordon, Z. Grilisches and D. Jorgenson (1998), 'Consumer prices, the Consumer Price Index, and the cost of living', *Journal of Economic Perspectives*, **12**(1), 3–26.

Bourdieu, P. (1980), 'Le capital social: Notes provisoires', *Actes de la Recherche en Sciences Sociales*, **31**, 2–3.

Braudel, F. (1985), *Material Civilization and Capitalism, 15th–18th Century, (Vol. 3), The Perspective of the World*, London: Fontana Press.

Camic, C. (ed.) (1991), *Talcott Parsons: The Early Essays*, Chicago: University of Chicago Press.

Castells, M. (1996), *The Rise of the Network Society*, Oxford: Blackwell.

Clarke, S. (1982), *Marx, Marginalism and Modern Sociology. From Adam Smith to Max Weber*, London: Macmillan.

Coats, A.W. (1954), 'The historical reaction in English political economy, 1870–90', *Economica*, **XXI**(2), 143–53.

Coleman, J. (1988), 'Social capital in the creation of human capital', *American Journal of Sociology*, **94**, supplement, 95–120.

Coleman, J. (1994), 'A rational choice perspective on economic sociology', in N.J. Smelser and R. Swedberg (eds), *The Handbook of Economic Sociology*, Princeton, NJ: Princeton University Press, pp. 166–80.

Dosi, G. (1992), 'Industrial organisation, competitiveness and growth', *Revue d'Economie Industrielle*, (59), 27–45.

Dosi, G., C. Freeman, R. Nelson, G. Silverberg and L. Soete (eds) (1988), *Technical Change and Economic Theory*, London: Pinter.

Dugger, W. (1990), 'The new institutionalism. New but not institutionalism', *Journal of Economic Issues*, **XXIV**(2), 423–31.

Durkheim, E. (1887), 'La science positive de la morale en Allemagne', in E. Durkheim (ed.) (1975), *Textes*, Vol. 2, Paris: Minuit.

Durkheim, E. (1893), *De la Division du Travail Social* [1986], 2nd edition 1902, Paris: Presses Universitaires de France.

Durkheim, E. (1894), *Règles de la Méthode Sociologique* [1977], Paris: Presses Universitaires de France.

Durkheim, E. (1895–96), *Le socialisme* [1971], Paris: Presses Universitaires de France.

Durkheim, E., (1900), 'La sociologie et son domaine scientifique', in E. Durkheim (ed.) [1975], *Textes*, Vol. 2, Paris: Minuit.

Durkheim, E. (1908), 'Economie politique et sociologie', in E. Durkheim (ed.) [1975], *Textes*, Vol. 2, Paris: Minuit.

Fine, B. (1999), 'A question of economics: is it colonising the social sciences?', *Economy and Society*, **28**(3), 403–25.

Fine, B. (2000), 'Endogenous growth theory: a critical assessment', *Cambridge Journal of Economics*, **24**(2), 245–65.

Foss, N. (1993), 'Theories of the firm: contractual and competence perspectives', *Journal of Evolutionary Economics*, **3**(2), 127–44.

Gislain, J.J. and P. Steiner (1995), *La Sociologie Economique, 1890–1920: Durkheim, Pareto, Schumpeter, Simiand, Veblen et Weber*, Paris: Presses Universitaires de France.

Gramsci, A. (1971), *Selections from the Prison Notebooks*, London: Lawrence and Wishart.

Granovetter, M. (1985), 'Economic action and social structure: The problem of embeddedness', *American Journal of Sociology*, **91**(3).

Granovetter, M. (1990), 'The old and the new economic sociology: A history and an agenda', in R. Friedland and A.F. Robertson (eds), *Beyond the Marketplace. Rethinking Economy and Society*, New York: Aldive de Gruyter, pp. 89–112.

Granovetter, M. and R. Swedberg (eds) (1992), *The Sociology of Economic Life*, Boulder: Westview Press.

Heilbroner, R. and W. Milberg, 1995, *The Crisis of Vision in Modern Economic Thought*, Cambridge, MA: Cambridge University Press.

Hennis, W. (1987), 'A science of man: Max Weber and the political economy of the German Historical School', in W.J. Mommsen and J. Osterhammel (eds), *Max Weber and his Contemporaries*, London: Allen & Unwin, pp. 25–58.

Hirst, P. and G. Thompson (1996), *Globalization in Question*, Cambridge: Polity Press.

Hodgson, G. (1993), *Economics and Evolution: Bringing Life Back into Economics*, Cambridge: Polity Press.

Hodgson, G. (1999), *Evolution and Institutions: On Evolutionary Economics and the Evolution of Economics*, Cheltenham, UK and Northampton, MA, USA: Edward Elgar.

Hodgson, G. (2001), *How Economics Forgot History. The Problem of Historical Specificity in Social Sciences*, London and New York: Routledge.

Ingham, G. (1996), 'Some recent changes in the relationship between economics and sociology', *Cambridge Journal of Economics*, **20**(2), 243–75.

Jonscher, C. (1994), 'An economic study of information technology revolution', in T.J. Allen and M.S. Scott Morton (eds), *Information Technologies and the Corporation of the 1990s*, Oxford: Oxford University Press, pp. 5–42.

Keynes, J.M. (1936), *General Theory of Employment, Interest and Money* [1973], London: Macmillan.

Kendrick, J.W. (1994), 'Total capital and economic growth', *Atlantic Economic Journal*, **22**(1), 1–18.

Kodama, M. (2000), 'New multimedia services in the education, medical and welfare services', *Technovation*, **20**(6), 321–31.

Krüger, D. (1987), 'Max Weber and the younger generation in the Verein für Sozialpolitik', in W.J. Mommsen and J. Osterhammel (eds), *Max Weber and his Contemporaries*, London: Allen & Unwin, pp. 71–87.

Lazonick, W. (1991), *Business Organisation and the Myth of the Market Economy*, Cambridge: Cambridge University Press.

Levy, C. (1987), 'Max Weber and Antonio Gramsci', in W.J. Mommsen and J. Osterhammel (eds), *Max Weber and his Contemporaries*, London, Allen & Unwin, pp. 382–402.

Liagouras, G. (2005), 'The political economy of post-industrial capitalism', *Thesis Eleven*, (81), 20–35.

Luke, T. (1998), 'Miscast canons? The future of universities in an era of flexible specialisation', *Telos*, (111), 15–31.

Lundvall, B.A. (1999), 'Nation states, social capital and economic development', Working paper, Department of Business Studies, Aalborg University.

Marx, K. (1859), 'A Contribution to the Critique of Political Economy', in K. Marx and F. Engels (eds), *Collected Works* [1987], Vol. 29, Moscow: Progress.

Michie, J. and J.G. Smith (eds) (1999), *Global Instability. The Political Economy of World Economy Governance*, London: Routledge.

Mommsen, W.J. and J. Osterhammel (eds) (1987), *Max Weber and his Contemporaries*, London: Allen & Unwin.

Mommsen, W.J. (1984), *Max Weber and German Politics, 1890–1920*, Chicago: Chicago University Press.

Nahapiet, J. and S. Ghoshal (1998), 'Social capital, intellectual capital and the organisational advantage', *Academy of Management Review*, **23**(2), 242–66.

Nelson, R. (1998), 'The agenda for growth theory: a different point of view', *Cambridge Journal of Economics,* **22**(4), 497–520.

Nelson, R. and S. Winter (1982), *An Evolutionary Theory of Economic Change*, Cambridge, MA: Harvard University Press.

Nielsen, K. (2001), 'Institutionalist approaches in the social sciences: Typology, dialogue and future challenges', *Journal of Economic Issues*, **XXXV**(2), 505–16.

Nisbet, R. (1970), *The Sociological Tradition*, London: Heinemann.

Nonaka, I. and H. Takeuchi (1995), *The Knowledge-Creating Company*, Oxford: Oxford University Press.

Olson, M. (1965), *The Logic of Collective Action*, Cambrigde, MA: Harvard University Press.

Perraton, J. (2001), 'The global economy – myths and realities', *Cambridge Journal of Economics*, **25**(5), 669–84.

Petit, P. and L. Soete (1998), 'Is a biased technological change fuelling dualism?', paper presented at the meeting of American Economic Association, Chicago.

Piore, M. (1983), 'Labor market segmentation: To what paradigm does it belong?', *American Economic Review*, **73**(2), 249–53.

Piore, M. (1996), 'Review of the *Handbook of Economic Sociology*', *Journal of Economic Literature*, **XXXIV**(2), 741–51.

Piore, M., R. Lester, F. Kofman and K. Malek (1994), 'The organization of product development', *Industrial and Corporate Change*, **3**(2), 405–34.

Polanyi, K. (1944), *The Great Transformation. The Political and Economic Origins of our Time* [1957], Boston: Beacon Press.

Portes, A. (1998), 'Social capital: its origins and applications in modern sociology', *Annual Review of Sociology*, **24**, 1–24.

Putterman, L. (1984), 'On some recent explanations of why capital hires labor', *Economic Inquiry*, **22**(1), 171–87.

Robbins, L. (1932), *An Essay on the Nature and Significance of Economic Science* [1984], New York: New York University Press.

Roobeek, A. (1987), 'The crisis in fordism and the rise of a new technological paradigm', *Futures*, **19**(2), 129–54.

Samuelson, P.A. (1947), *Foundations of Economic Analysis*, Cambridge, MA: Harvard University Press.

Simon, H.A. (1966), 'The impact of new information-processing technology', Toronto: Canadian Imperial Bank of Commerce, republished in Simon, H.A. (1982), *Models of Bounded Rationality*, Vol. 2, Boston: MIT Press.

Simon, H.A. (1991), 'Organisations and markets', *Journal of Economic Perspectives*, **5**(2), 25–44.

Smelser, N. and R. Swedberg (eds) (1994), *The Handbook of Economic Sociology*, Princeton, NJ: Princeton University Press.

Smith, A. (1776), *An Inquiry into the Nature and Causes of the Wealth of Nations* [1966], New York: A.W. Kelley.

Sternberg, E. (1998), 'Phantasmagoric labor. The new economics of self-presentation', *Futures*, **30**(1), 3–21.

Swedberg, R. (1987), 'Economic sociology. Past and present', *Current Sociology*, **35**(1), 1–215.

Swedberg, R. (1997), 'New economic sociology: What has been accomplished, what is ahead?', *Acta Sociologica*, **40**(2), 161–82.

Teece, D.J. (1988), 'The nature of the firm and technological change', in Dosi et al. (eds) (1988).

Théret, B. (2001), 'Nouvelle économie institutionnelle, économie des conventions et théorie de la régulation: Vers une synthèse instituitionnaliste?', *La Lettre de la Régulation*, No 35.

Touraine, A. (1981), 'Une sociologie sans société', *Revue Française de Sociologie*, **XXII**(1), 3–13.

Weber, M. (1898), 'The national state and economic policy (Freiburg address)', in *Economy and Society* (1980), **9**(4), 428–39.

Weber, M. (1904), ' "Objectivity" in social sciences and social policy', in E.A. Shils and H.A. Finch (eds) (1949), *Max Weber on the Methodology of the Social Sciences*, New York: The Free Press.

Weber, M. (1908), 'Marginal utility and the fundamental law of psychophysics', in *Social Science Quarterly* (1975), **56**(1), 21–36.

Weber, M. (1922), *Economy and Society. An Outline of Interpretative Sociology* [1978], 2 vols., Berkeley: University of California Press.

Williamson, O. (1985), *The Economic Institutions of Capitalism: Firms, Markets, Relational Contracting*, New York: Free Press.

Winter, S. (1988), 'On Coase, competence, and the corporation', *Journal of Law, Economics and Organization*, **4**(1), 179–95.

Woolcock, M. (1998), 'Social capital and economic development: Toward a theoretical synthesis and policy framework', *Theory and Society*, **27**(2), 151–208.

Zald, M. (1987), 'Review essay: The new institutional economics', *American Journal of Sociology*, **93**(1), 701–8.

Zuboff, S. (1988), *In the Age of the New Machine*, New York: Basic Books.

4. The 'institutional turn' in the social sciences: a review of approaches and a future research agenda

Klaus Nielsen

THE BURGEONING FIELD OF INSTITUTIONALISM

Recent trends in the social sciences have been termed 'the cultural turn' (Ray and Sayer, 1999) and 'the cognitive turn' (Fuller et al., 1989). Although these terms capture important trends it is even more appropriate to portray the past quarter-century as 'the age of institutionalism' (Di Maggio, 1998, p. 696). We have certainly experienced an 'institutional turn' (Jessop, 2001). Currently, a multitude of institutional approaches are flourishing in the social sciences. New species crop up beside revitalized older brands. It is hard to distinguish new species from relabelled well-known types, and the terms being used to distinguish the various species suffer from myopia and often confuse instead of clarify. For instance, new institutional economics has not much in common with new institutionalism in political science and organization theory, which, however, share many characteristics with old institutional economics.

Many attempts have been made to survey the field but most stay within the boundaries of disciplines. Economists have distinguished between new and old institutional economics (Rutherford, 1994; Hodgson, 1989; Langlois, 1989) or outlined different approaches within either new institutional economics (Langlois, 1986) or old institutional economics (Hodgson, 1998; Coriat and Dosi, 1998). Sociologists have outlined the core characteristics of new institutionalism by means of comparisons with stylized versions of the 'old' institutionalism in sociology (Brinton and Nee, 1998), organization theory (Powell and DiMaggio, 1991) and economic sociology (Swedberg, 1991). Three forms of institutionalism have been distinguished in political science: rational choice institutionalism, historical institutionalism and new institutionalism (Hall and Taylor, 1996; Campbell, 1997). Campbell and Pedersen (2001) identify four different types. In addition to rational choice and historical institutionalism they mention organizational institutionalism and discursive institutionalism. Bogason distinguishes between individualist and collective approaches that give priority to actors and structures, respectively, and contributions focusing on processes between actors and structures (Bogason, 2000). Another contribution outlines seven different approaches in political science (Peters, 1999).

Only a few contributions cover trends in the social sciences in general. The surveys by Hall and Taylor (1996) and Campbell (1997) cover not only institutional approaches in political science but also at least some institutionalisms in other social sciences. Scott (1996) provides a generally applicable typology of contemporary institutional theory with his distinctions between the regulative, normative and cognitive pillars of institutions, and the three different carriers of institutions: culture, social structures and routines. Furthermore, Mayhew (1989) relates the distinction between new and old institutionalisms in economics to general trends in the social sciences.

This chapter takes as its point of departure the introductory article in a special issue of the *Journal of Institutional and Theoretical Economics* (DiMaggio, 1998). The special issue is meant to stimulate a dialogue between new institutional economists and institutionalists in other social sciences. The introduction is an attempt to survey the field of (new) institutionalisms in the social sciences. In the article, Paul J. DiMaggio also outlines an agenda for future cooperation between institutional approaches.

The article highlights important issues and develops a typology that covers all social science disciplines. Its agenda for future cooperation is pluralist and contains important insights and promising prospects. The article is stimulating but also has weaknesses. It is reductionist in its image of the contemporary variety of institutional thought and, consequently, blind to some of the most interesting and advanced endeavours to develop institutional approaches within a broadly common methodological framework and with broadly similar theoretical assumptions.

Another recent contribution by Bruno Théret (2000a; 2000b) can be read as an elaboration of DiMaggio's typology. Théret also identifies convergent trends in different institutionalisms. The typology is in several ways more developed and less problematic than the one presented by DiMaggio and the convergence identified in his contribution no doubt represents important current trends. Here I shall relate to the paper of Théret when it provides important supplements or corrections to the contribution by DiMaggio.

The next two sections give a summary of DiMaggio's article. This is followed by a critique and an alternative account of the current state of institutionalism. Among the many institutional approaches, six of them are identified as promising candidates for collaborative future research. The prospects for future joint endeavours among different strands of institutionalism are discussed in the next two sections focusing on methodological and theoretical foundations, respectively, followed by a conclusion.

THREE INSTITUTIONALISMS?

DiMaggio distinguishes three new institutionalisms: rational-action institutionalism,[1] social-constructivist institutionalism, and mediated-conflict institutionalism. The typology transcends the disciplinary boundaries although the three institutionalisms are seen as originating from economics, sociology and political science, respectively.

Table 4.1   Stylized comparison of three institutionalisms

	Action	Interests	Institutions	Change mechanisms
RAI	Individual action	Exogenous	Primarily formal	Strategic action/selection
SCI	Constructed/ weak agency	Endogenous	Primarily informal/ schemata	Diffusion/ contagion
MCI	Groups	Exogenous	Formal/informal organizational forms	Political conflict

Source: DiMaggio, 1998, p. 698.

Rational-action institutionalism (RAI) emphasizes the way in which individual rational action is channelled by the 'rules of the game', including laws, inherited organizational forms, and norms. Actors are seen as stable and exogenous. All kinds of institutions are studied within this framework but most of the focus is on economic rules or formal political institutions. Institutional change is conceived as an effect of the strategic action of individuals or as a result of (invisible or visible) selection mechanisms.

Social-constructivist institutionalism[2] (SCI) argues that all elements of rational-action models – actors, interests and preferences – are 'socially constructed' and therefore endogenous. Research is focused on informal institutions such as schemata, roles and scripts, or – in general – all that is

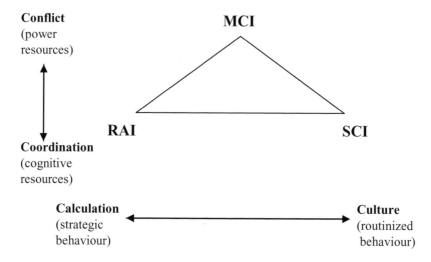

Source: The figure is a modified version of a figure presented in Théret (2000a).

*Figure 4.1   Three institutionalisms: conflict versus coordination;
                      calculation versus culture*

'taken for granted'. Institutional change is seen as a process of isomorphism or diffusion through mechanisms such as legitimacy pressures and normative schemes embedded in training and practice.

   Mediated-conflict institutionalism (MCI) focuses on how states and other
institutions structure and mediate conflict among groups with distinctive
interests. They study stability and change of the institutional set-up (formal
and informal organizational forms) in various contexts as a result of institutionally mediated political conflicts. Table 4.1 shows the distinctive
differences between the three different approaches.

   Another way of summarizing the differences and similarities of the three
main types of institutionalism is presented in Figure 4.1. The three institutionalisms are positioned in a diagram composed of two dimensions. The
horizontal dimension illustrates different conceptions of the relationship
between institutions and individual behaviour: calculus versus culture. The
vertical dimension illustrates how genesis and change of institutions is
conceptualized: coordination versus conflict. In relation to the first dimension, rational-action institutionalism stresses calculus, that is, behaviour is
seen as instrumental or strategic within institutionally defined constraints,
whereas social-constructivist institutionalism sees behaviour as routinized
and stresses the role of interpretation of the decision-making situations as
a function of the outlook of the institutionalized individual. In this respect,

mediated-conflict institutionalism is in an intermediate position. It sees individuals and groups as actors who are self-seeking and calculating based on their interests. However, these interests are seen as partly constituted by institutions.

In relation to the second dimension, both rational-action institutionalism and social-constructivist institutionalism emphasize the role of institutions in relation to problems of coordinating economic action, but they differ in their conceptions of the cognitive repertoire of individuals. Mediated-conflict institutionalism, on the other hand, stresses conflicts of interests rather than coordination problems as the ultimate cause of institutionaliz-ation and institutional change. In addition, power resources rather than cognitive resources are seen as important in explaining how institutions are generated and how they change.

DiMaggio is not explicit about which institutional approaches are covered by the typology, but it is not difficult to deduce. He describes rational-action institutionalism as an approach which 'started in economics . . . (but) many political scientists and a few sociologists as well as econo-mists are proponents of this view' (DiMaggio, 1998, p. 698). He obviously refers to new institutional economics but also to rational choice political institutionalism (for example, public choice theory and Ostrom, 1991) and rational choice sociology (Coleman, 1990). According to DiMaggio, social-constructivist institutionalism 'originated in sociology, although it too gained adherence among political scientists'. Apparently, he refers to the 'new institutionalism in organization theory', a term coined by himself and W.W. Powell (DiMaggio and Powell, 1991, p. 698) and to 'new institution-alism in political science' (March and Olsen, 1989).[3] Finally, he writes about mediated-conflict institutionalism that it is 'most closely identified with political science, although sociologists also contributed to its development' (DiMaggio and Powell, p. 698). He seems to refer to 'historical institution-alism' in political science (Thelen and Steinmo, 1992), 'historical and com-parative sociology' (Skocpol, 1985), and maybe also contemporary proponents of what DiMaggio himself designates 'old institutionalism in sociology' (DiMaggio and Powell, 1991).

A more elaborate image is presented in Théret (2000a, 2000b). He identifies contributions from all three social sciences within each of the three main types of institutionalism. Figure 4.2 is a modified version of the survey presented by Théret.[4] The approaches included in this model but implicitly ignored in the work of DiMaggio are in bold typeface. The main difference is that Théret includes more approaches from economics under the banner of contemporary institutionalisms. Also, the variety of socio-logical institutionalism is larger in his interpretation.

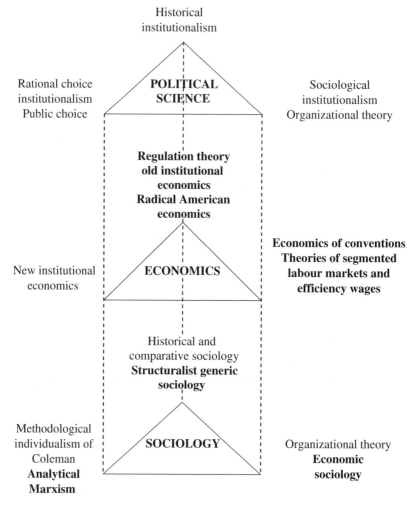

Source: Théret, 2000a, p. 13.

Figure 4.2   Institutionalisms in political science, economics and sociology

RELATIONSHIPS IN THREE STAGES, CONVERGENCE AND HYBRIDS

DiMaggio (1998) distinguishes three stages in the relationships among the three new institutionalisms. In the early stage of 'constructive disengagement', they concentrated on the opposition to the common enemy, methodological individualism. Then, a phase of 'mutual criticism' developed, leading to the third and present stage, where scholars are finding common interests around shared explanatory dilemmas. He outlines three such common challenges for future joint endeavours: how to develop an evolutionary approach; how to conceptualize rationality as 'constructed'; and how to take account of various types of networks and their relations to (other) institutions.

He identifies commonalities among the various institutionalisms as well as emerging hybrids. Mediated-conflict institutionalism shares with rational-choice institutionalism a realist conception of actors and a view of interests as flowing relatively straightforwardly from identities and structural positions. Social-constructivist and mediated-conflict institutionalism find common ground in their concern with informal institutions and cognitive repertoires. Social-constructivist institutionalism typically distances itself from the rational-action model of institutionalism. However, even here a rapprochement is seen following the shift of focus within social-constructivist institutionalism from demonstrating that actors behave irrationally to depicting and explaining different conceptions of rationality in different contexts. Hybrids are seen to have emerged as well, for instance, in economic history with the contributions of Avner Greif and Douglass C. North.

Likewise, Théret sees clear trends of convergence among the different institutionalisms (Théret, 2000a, 2000b). He identifies such developments in all three new institutionalisms. In economics, sociology, and political science, the various examples of rational-action institutionalism have begun to integrate the role of ideas and different perceptions of a given reality. Social-constructivist institutionalism in all three disciplines has become more aware of the role of interests, power and perceptions of institutions as not only taken-for-granted constraints but also as products of purposeful human behaviour. Finally, mediated-conflict institutionalism in its various forms has begun to put more emphasis on interpretation and the role of institutions as scripts and templates.

Théret also sketches the broad outlines of a future synthesis of the various institutionalisms and attributes a central role to American institutionalism in this respect, in particular, the contribution of John R. Commons. He considers Commons's concept of 'working rules' a particularly fruitful reference point for future endeavours to understand institutions as the mediators between social structures and individual behaviour. Working rules stabilize the contradictions between the two fundamental dimensions in all transactions: conflict and cooperation. In general, American institutionalism represents an early case of 'holindividualism', which is Théret's term for the emerging synthesis of the three different institutionalisms that not only integrates calculus and culture in its perception of the relationship between institutions and individual behaviour but also integrates conflict and coordination in its perception of the cause for institutionalization and institutional change.

HOW DOES THE TYPOLOGY FIT?

DiMaggio's article is in many ways a step forward. It is stimulating in its much-needed attempt to develop conceptual tools to cut through the confusion and myopia among observers of the burgeoning field of institutional thought, and it is constructive in its suggestion for an agenda for future dialogue and joint work among different institutionalisms. However, there are also good reasons for disagreement. DiMaggio's article is reductionist in its image of contemporary institutional approaches within the social sciences. Unfortunately, the most promising institutionalisms, in my view, either are not included, are misrepresented, or fit uneasily into the typology. In addition, the bold agenda for future cooperation underemphasizes the methodological barriers to joint work, and other promising areas of potential collaboration are ignored. The contribution of Théret provides helpful supplement and correction, but he likewise underemphasizes the methodological barriers to cross-fertilization, joint work and the road toward a synthesis.

What is not included in these accounts of contemporary institutionalisms? First, DiMaggio ignores economic approaches that do not fit into the category of rational-action institutionalism. According to DiMaggio, new institutional economics is apparently the only candidate within economics for inclusion among the 'neoinstitutionalisms'. In other words, contemporary American institutionalism is not included.[5] Neither is contemporary European institutional economics in the tradition of old institutional economics (Hodgson, 1988). Théret's work is much more useful in this respect, as he includes American institutionalism and the French regulation school. However, his image of contemporary European institutional and evolutionary economics is unsatisfactory. This strand of theoretical approaches is less coherent than its American counterpart. It can be seen as a mixture of inspiration from John Maynard Keynes, Karl Marx and Joseph Schumpeter, as well as from old institutional economics. In this context, I shall call this approach institutional-evolutionary economics. It is inspired by the heritage of Thorstein Veblen and John R. Commons, but it subscribes neither to the pragmatist philosophical underpinnings of American institutionalism, nor to the influence of Clarence Ayres in this tradition (Hodgson, 1998). At least three other approaches can be seen as part of, or strongly affiliated to, institutional-evolutionary economics: post-Keynesian economics, the French regulation school, and Schumpeterian evolutionary economics.[6] Although each of these institutionalisms is a coherent approach in its own right – and even if both post-Keynesian and Schumpeterian evolutionary economics include contributions that are hard to integrate with the other elements of institutional-evolutionary economics – they also represent the contemporary heritage of Keynes, Marx[7] and Schumpeter respectively, in forms open to dialogue and integration with other forms of institutionalism.

Second, DiMaggio misrepresents new economic sociology.[8] The studies by Mark Granovetter (1985) of the effects of networks on labour market outcomes are referred to as an example of studies within rational-action institutionalism; that is, networks are interpreted as constraints of action (DiMaggio, 1998). This is not an appropriate classification of new economic sociology, and it is also contradictory.[9] New economic sociology originates in explicit opposition to rational-action institutionalism in the form of new institutional economics. It stresses how economic transactions are necessarily embedded in social relations in general and in networks in particular. It also stresses how the efforts of economic actors to cope with (radical) uncertainty necessitate interpretation and, accordingly, social interaction (Beckert, 1996). In new economic sociology actors are not seen as irrational; they are perceived as rational in the sense that they attempt to act in a rational way, but rationality is 'intended' and operates in an embedded or interpreted – that is, 'constructed' – context. New economic sociology combines elements of rational-action, social-constructivist, and mediated-conflict institutionalism. It does not fit neatly into the typology. Théret locates new economic sociology as part of social-constructivist institutionalism. This is not as problematic as the treatment of new economic sociology in DiMaggio's article. However, Théret likewise ignores how new economic sociology does not really fit into the typology.

Third, other institutional traditions also fit uneasily with the typology. This is the case with both new institutionalism in political science and historical institutionalism. March and Olsen (1989) focus on the complex relationship between what they called 'logic of consequentiality' and 'logic of appropriateness'. Even if their work emphasizes the 'constructed' rationality of 'appropriateness', which may justify its inclusion in social-constructivist institutionalism, it encompasses elements from rational-action and mediated-conflict institutionalism as well, in a stimulating although sometimes confusing way. There are even more serious difficulties involved in fitting historical institutionalism into the typology. Historical institutionalism is the core example of mediated conflict institutionalism, but it has increasingly become a hybrid combining all three institutionalisms. Campbell (1997, 1998) provides a good example. His earlier studies (for example, Campbell et al., 1991) were on changing forms of economic governance as a result of rational responses to external pressures (such as changes in technology or power resources). Recently he has recognized that this line of study neglects how problems are defined and how possible solutions are identified and he has now redirected his studies toward the analysis of the role of ideas and the relationship between ideas and interaction. From an original basis in mediated-conflict institutionalism with much in common with rational-action institutionalism, he has now integrated elements of social-constructivist institutionalism as well (Campbell, 2004).

Fourth, North has outlined the rough contours of a cognitive-institutional approach (Denzau and North, 1994; North, 1998). The approach focuses on the central role of cognition and the processes of developing shared mental models. It does not fit into the typology, either. It has emerged from within new institutional economics, but the relaxation of the assumption of shared perceptions of a given reality has made it necessary to integrate the role of cognition with the wider implication of partly breaking away from the approach of rational-action institutionalism.

AN ALTERNATIVE ACCOUNT

Unfortunately, the typological deficiencies make it difficult to identify the most promising avenues of future development within institutional theory. The following institutional approaches are ignored, are misrepresented, or fit uneasily with the typology. They all attempt to integrate elements from rational-action, social-constructivist and mediated-conflict institutionalism in forms that cannot be understood by means of the typology:

- institutional-evolutionary economics;
- American institutionalism;
- new economic sociology;
- new institutionalism in political science;
- historical institutionalism; and
- the cognitive-institutional approach.

There are deep-seated methodological differences between the various institutional approaches. Three distinctions are relevant in this context: (1) the distinction between open system and closed system methodology; (2) the distinction between positivist and post-positivist approaches; and

(3) within post-positivist approaches, the distinction between realist and idealist ontologies. The listed six institutional approaches all share an open system, post-positivist and realist methodology, which makes collaboration, joint work, and even mergers, potentially fruitful. They also share a set of common theoretical assumptions:

- human agency is seen as purposeful, or intended rational;
- the constitutive importance of the cultural and cognitive framework is emphasized;
- the central and pervasive role of power and conflict is recognized; and
- path-dependent habits, routines and norms are crucial in the coordination of behaviour.

These common methodological and theoretical characteristics differentiate the above-mentioned approaches from other approaches and, consequently, make collaboration between these approaches obvious whereas collaboration with other approaches is far more difficult.

Pluralism is a virtue, but it is not one without limits. There may well be an optimum level of plurality below the maximum level. Not all institutionalisms can learn from each other. Some are methodologically and theoretically incompatible. According to Hay and Wincott, 'rational choice and sociological institutionalisms are based on mutually incompatible premises, or "social ontologies"' (Hay and Wincott, 1998, p. 951). In this context, these two institutionalisms are not only seen as mutually incompatible; both of them are also seen as incompatible with the six institutionalisms mentioned previously. Whereas this may be rather obvious in the case of rational-action institutionalism, it is less evident in relation to the new institutionalism in sociology and organizational theory that overlaps, to a large extent, with the above-mentioned approaches. Mutual inspiration between the new institutionalism in sociology and organization theory and the six institutionalisms listed above is certainly possible. However, some of the core methodological commonalities and theoretical assumptions of most contributions to the new institutionalism in sociology and organization theory are incompatible with the other six, and it is therefore not included in the list.

Next, I briefly outline how the different institutional approaches share such methodological and theoretical similarities. This is not a straightforward exercise. All six institutional approaches listed previously are internally ambiguous in relation to either the dimension of calculus and culture, or the dimension of coordination and culture, or both. American institutionalism includes contributions inspired by the heritage of Veblen as well as that of Commons, which are in several respects contradictory. The so-called institutional-evolutionary approach is a construct composed of several different traditions, and is in some respects even more difficult to characterize in the singular than American institutionalism. Likewise, new economic sociology, new institutionalism in political science and historical institutionalism consist of different components that are hardly unambiguous in relation to the methodological and theoretical dimensions discussed below. Furthermore, the cognitive-institutional approach is rather undeveloped and its methodological foundations and the theoretical implications are not at all clear. Such ambiguities are ignored in the following sections, which merely outline the argument based on an implicit interpretation of each of the six approaches. It is not elaborated in detail how these approaches can be seen as sharing core methodological commonalities and theoretical assumptions. The presentation is merely indicative. It does not always explicitly refer to the six institutional approaches in relation to each of the methodological and theoretical dimensions. However, the references to authors and contributions indicate how each of the different approaches can be seen as sharing the same core commonalities and assumptions.

METHODOLOGICAL COMMONALITIES AS A PREMISE FOR COLLABORATION

Most rational-action models operate within a closed system methodology. The interaction between the economy and the wider social system is trivialized into a set of 'given' preferences, beliefs, resources, technology, and so on. The economic system is closed in order to make possible a particular mode of explanation, namely deductivism, and the formulation of laws or law-like statements that express constant event conjunctures. An open system methodology recognizes the limitations of deductivism and law-like statements. It must be 'recognized that such a conception can be of only limited use in the fundamentally open social world in which we live, one that seems hardly susceptible to local and regional closure, pure theorizing as traditionally understood' (Lawson, 1997, p. 107).

Positivism is defined by an empiricist epistemology. Social reality is perceived as immediately observable and it is taken that nothing exists beyond the positively identifiable reality. Post-positivism, with its non-empiricist epistemology, opens up for cognition, constructed reality and underlying structures. Positivism does not recognize the existence of unobservable, underlying layers of reality and operates with more simplified perceptions of information and knowledge. Post-positivists share the assumption of non-empiricist epistemology but are divided as far as ontology is concerned. Some are (transcendental) realists, others idealists. The defining distinction is not whether language is a prison from which we are unable to escape as social actors. Today, few would argue that it is not, and that it is rather, for instance, a mere medium of communication. Instead the distinction is whether language or discourse is the only thing, or if a transcendental reality is presumed to exist. The issue is controversial but it is probably fair to say that dedicated postmodernists are part of the first group, whereas critical realists are in the second group. The distinction is clear in extreme cases but is otherwise often fuzzy. The strong common emphasis on epistemology among social constructivists tends to conceal the fact that some social constructivists are ontological idealists whereas others are ontological realists.

It appears that the above-mentioned six institutional approaches broadly share an open system, post-positivist and realist methodology, which makes collaboration, joint work, and even mergers potentially fruitful, whereas collaboration with approaches that do not share these characteristics have limited potential apart from exchange of information on empirical regularities, whether in the form of quantitative data or discourse analyses. All six institutionalisms are characterized by ontological realism, epistemological relativism (which says that evidence is not clear-cut, but rather in need of interpretation) and subscribe to an open system methodology as a result of their ontology.

Whereas it appears as relatively straightforward that all six institutionalisms are characterized by epistemological relativism and are in agreement in their critical stance towards the empiricist epistemology of rational-action institutionalism, it is perhaps less evident that all six approaches represent ontological realism. There are social-constructivist sources of inspiration within several of the traditions and it is not fully clear if this implies a realist or idealist ontological stance. Similarly, open systems methodology does not unambiguously characterize all the approaches. For instance, what is here called institutional-evolutionary economics includes the Sraffian part of post-Keynesian economics that applies closed system methodology (see Dunn, 2000). Likewise, some contributions to Schumpeterian evolutionary economics use closed models of agency in their pursuit of formal rigour. However, I believe that the core methodological characteristics of the six different approaches are similar, and that these characteristics clearly distinguish these approaches from, for instance, rational-action institutionalism with its positivist epistemology and closed system modelling, and (at least major segments of) new institutionalism in sociology and organizational theory which are characterized by ontological idealism.

COMMON THEORETICAL ASSUMPTIONS

The six institutionalisms not only share these methodological commonalities but they also have four central theoretical assumptions in common. These assumptions are outlined as responses to the two central explanatory problems of institutional theory outlined above: how the relationship between institutions and human agency is perceived, and how institutionalization and institutional change are explained. The four central theoretical assumptions represent attempts to confront the two central problems by combining, on the one hand, the dimensions of calculus and culture (with an emphasis on culture) and, on the other hand, the dimensions of conflict and coordination (with an emphasis on conflict). In this section I shall indicate how the six institutional approaches can be seen as sharing four central theoretical assumptions.

First, human agency is seen as intended rational, or purposeful, in the sense that actors attempt to make sense of the situations they are confronted with and act reasonably; that is, they are neither perceived as rational in the sense of rational choice theory, nor as irrational (that is, as automatic followers of tradition or as totally encapsulated in an externally defined role). They are seen as agents with a certain freedom to deliberate and to choose in accordance with individual psychology. They are culturally formed but not totally socialized (Hodgson, 1988). They are to a certain extent 'cultural puppets but like Pinocchio they can break away from the strings' (Mayhew, 1989). On the other hand, they are not rational in the sense of the isolated, maximizing 'economic man'. They are not prisoners of their utility functions (Hodgson, 1988). Historical institutionalism and the cognitive-institutional approach both emphasize rationality, in collective and individual behaviour respectively. However, this is different from individual optimization. Increasingly, historical institutionalism stresses how group identity and (perceived) group preferences do not automatically spring from objective interests. Furthermore, norms such as solidarity as well as group pressure and other collective phenomena are seen to influence the relationship between individual and group behaviour. The cognitive-institutional approach modifies its original assumption of rational choice as a result of the lack of an objective basis for rational behaviour in situations of uncertainty and the crucial influence of shared mental models.

New economic sociology is not based on a rejection of the rationality assumption, contrary to much sociological thought hitherto (Granovetter, 1985). Rather, behaviour is assumed to be rational but rationality is seen as contextual and formed by social interaction. Most interesting economic decision-making situations are characterized by uncertainty, which makes it impossible to base decisions on rational calculations of costs and benefits (Beckert, 1996). Consequently, social interaction is necessary to make sense of the uncertain future and to develop reasonable expectations. Rationality is, not only in these situations but generally, seen as neither objective nor independent of the specific situational context. The (formal and informal) institutions of the economy are seen as defining a rationality context; that is, economic actors attempt to act reasonably, sensibly, or in other words, they intend to behave rationally within the parameters of the institutional context, which does not constitute mere constraints but fundamentally defines what is rational, and, consequently, enables behaviour.

Rationality and norms are, by some scholars, seen as two distinctly different sources of human behaviour (Elster, 1989). However, acting in accordance with social norms, or pursuing a 'logic of appropriateness' (March and Olsen, 1989), can also be seen as a reasonable, and in a sense, rational, response to specific situational traits. Legitimacy is not an 'irrational' concern. In some contexts, it is perfectly 'rational' to act in a way to secure legitimacy, and at the same time it is 'rational' to legitimize past behaviour as guided by a 'logic of consequentiality', even if it actually follows a 'logic of appropriateness' instead. Likewise, norm-following can be seen as rational, if rationality is defined in a broader manner than in rational choice theory.

Second, the constitutive role of culture and cognition is stressed by all of the six related institutionalisms. Although behaviour can certainly be seen as calculating in the sense outlined in the previous section, it is in its very constitutive aspects formed by enculturation and cognitive framing and filtering. The constitutive role in relation to rationality contexts has already been mentioned. 'Enculturation' has once again moved into centre place after decades of individualism (Hodgson, 1988). Human beings can break free but they are also 'cultural puppets' (Mayhew, 1989). Cognitive psychology has documented how 'culture is fragmented: Individuals experience culture as disparate bits of information and as schematic structures that organize that information. Culture carried by institutions, networks, and social movements diffuses, activates, and selects among available schemata' (DiMaggio, 1997, p. 263). The simplistic image of information as readily accessible bits of information, and knowledge as the accumulated sum of such bits, is discarded in favour of an image of two processes of transformation mediated by cognitive filters: first, from sense data to information, and second, from information to knowledge. Cognitive filters make it possible to distinguish (meaningful) information from noise, and to make sense of bits of information by means of conceptual frameworks and theories of relationships.

Likewise, the simplistic image of learning as net increases in the stock of knowledge is rejected, and learning is (also) seen as restructuring of concepts and theories. According to Scott, culture is one of the carriers of institutions (Scott, 1995). Like social structures and routines, culture is a carrier of institutions, or, put otherwise, institutions are embedded in the cultural heritage. According to the new institutionalism in political science, behaviour reflects to a large extent a 'logic of appropriateness' that is constituted by cultural framing and cognitive filtering. Culturally embedded institutions provide frames of meaning that determine how problems are defined and how possible solutions are identified and evaluated. The relations between ideas and forms of interaction are of interest in this context. Ideas of problems and solutions actually change regularly in spite of strong 'enculturation'. Such processes of ideational change are explained, at least partly, by changes in forms of interaction among the relevant social actors (Sabel, 1992; Campbell, 1997; Campbell, 1998). Of particular interest in this context are the recent contributions by North outlining the cognitive-institutional approach as a new research programme. This is not much more than a broad agenda of research but it is interesting because it takes seriously the challenge of cognitive psychology, even to the extent of destroying the foundation of North's own earlier theories.

Third, power and conflict are seen as important and pervasive phenomena, although they are often hidden and ignored by both participants and observers. Whereas basic coordination problems are also seen as important, institutions exist and change mainly as a result of power and conflicts of interests in path-dependent processes of cumulative causation. This is seen as an intrinsic quality of economic and political systems rather than a systemic failure. Of course, this is in stark contrast to rational choice theory where power and conflict is attached only to deviations from the perfect market, such as monopoly power, or more generally, rent-seeking. It is also different from the position in this respect of the new institutionalism in organizational theory. As part of its foundational self-identity it distanced itself from old institutionalism, which is seen as focused on vested interests, conflicts and interest aggregation (DiMaggio and Powell, 1991), whereas new institutionalism in organization theory rather stresses 'taken-for-grantedness', 'logic of orthodoxy', and the unconsciousness in processes of adoption and imitation. New institutionalism in organization theory downplays the importance of explicit conflicts but it is compatible with a Foucauldian concept of power as an all-encompassing social reality.

Contrary to rational-action institutionalism and new institutionalism in organizational theory, the six related institutionalisms all see economic and political power as subject to conflicts and mediated by formal and informal institutions. Conflict-mediation is the defining characteristic of historical institutionalism but it also characterizes the other approaches. The cognitive-institutional approach stresses path-dependent patterns of political institutions and, accordingly, path-dependent forms of allocation of power that persist irrespective of efficiency concerns. American institutionalism focuses on the linkages and cumulativeness of economic and political power. The ceremonial role of institutions is seen as strengthening the status quo, which is another way of expressing the fact that institutions have a fundamental agenda-setting role. Power is similarly ever present in institutional-evolutionary economics. What may appear as power-free interactions based on the free will of individuals are seen as embedded in power relations that structure the relationships directly but, most importantly, indirectly, in forms that are often invisible to the participants. Structural and agenda-setting forms of power (Lukes, 1974) are also in focus in new economic sociology and new institutionalism in political science.

Fourth, individual behaviour is seen as most often habitual and routinized but occasionally punctuated by novelty and creativity. Habits and institutions as routines, customs and conventions are seen as crucial instruments for solving problems of coordination of behaviour. Such institutions stabilize behaviour, make it to some extent predictable how others will act, and thereby make behaviour possible. In this sense, institutions are formed as a response to basic coordination problems, and they change as a means to improve coordination. However, this takes place in a context that is fundamentally constituted by power relations. Both the habitual and the creative parts of behaviour are seen as reasonable, and in a sense rational actors follow habits and rules not because of calculated costs and benefits but because it is sensible and necessary to do so because of the existence of either extensive information, and/or complexity and uncertainty, and because of the fundamental role of cognition, learning and the necessity of communication, and consequently, language in economic interaction (Hodgson, 1998). Human beings are also inventive and regularly discover new ways of doing things, whether as a result of 'idle curiosity' – one of Veblen's basic 'instincts' – or other individual dispositions, or as an effect of social mechanisms such as innovation systems.

American institutionalism and institutional-evolutionary economics explicitly interpret behaviour as mostly habitual and routinized, and occasionally creative and innovative. Veblen stresses habituation, and a core concept in the institutional-evolutionary approach such as routine originates from Nelson and Winter (1982). The role of habitual and routinized behaviour, punctuated by acts of novelty, is a defining characteristic of these approaches that clearly distinguishes them from rational choice-based approaches that perceive of habits and routines as more sophisticated forms of optimization and have no room for genuine novelty as endogenous factors in an economic system. The four other institutional approaches do not explicitly relate to the role of habits, routines and creativity in the coordination of behaviour. However, they are compatible with this position in their emphasis on path-dependency, behavioural regularities, standard operating procedures and occasional path-shaping conjectures.

CONCLUSION

DiMaggio is both too optimistic and too pessimistic in his view of future joint cooperation between different institutionalisms. He underestimates the serious methodological and theoretical barriers against cooperation among some approaches, and, accordingly, the profound basis of the 'mutual criticism', which is for good reasons not only a phase of the past. On the other hand, he ignores the explicit 'constructive engagement' as well as the implicit, actual co-development of some institutional approaches as a consequence of their common methodologies and common theoretical assumptions. There are indeed common challenges to the different theoretical positions, and these challenges may inspire or force different approaches to adapt and change, such as has happened with the emergence of cognitive-institutional approach from within new insti-tutional economics. The challenges include how to come to terms with the evolutionary dimension and the 'constructed reality' of society, as well as the pervasiveness of networks, as outlined by DiMaggio. Other important common challenges are: (1) how to take account of radical uncertainty and ambiguity, which characterizes central areas of decision-making; (2) how to conceptualize trust and, more generally, social capital as the invisible glue that holds societies together; and (3) how to develop a proper under-standing of the role of knowledge and learning in both codified and tacit forms, and their interaction.

Widely unrecognized parallel work on both (1)–(3) and within the three areas of potential convergence mentioned by DiMaggio takes place within the above-mentioned six approaches. Of course, there is always a trade-off between internal development within more or less coherent frameworks, on the one side, and cooperation between different approaches, however close they may be, on the other. Anyway, currently there seems to be much to say in favour of pluralist cross-fertilization, joint work and even mergers of the approaches listed above, whereas incompatible methodological and theoretical assumptions strongly limit the prospects of pluralist engagement with other approaches, such as rational choice-based approaches, as well as some of the approaches based on social-constructivist foundations.

NOTES

1. DiMaggio applies the term 'neoinstitutionalism' for all three institutionalisms. In this chapter reference is made to 'institutionalism' instead.
2. Following Campbell and Pedersen (2001) it may be argued that this category consists of components that are so diverse that it is better to divide it into two categories: organizational institutionalism and discursive institutionalism. Both categories are social-constructivist but they emphasize culture and discourse respectively. Organizational institutionalism focuses on cultural embeddedness in a specific context that constitutes, rationalizes and legitimizes institutions, whereas discursive institutionalism emphasizes how institutions become constituted, framed and transformed through discourse. This reflects an important distinction within social-constructivist approaches. Some of them stress how cultural norms socialize and make individuals relatively passive, whereas others focus on the creative mobilization of scripts and templates by actors in processes of discursive rearticulation.
3. It is questionable whether it is reasonable to distinguish between new institutionalism in political science and new institutionalism in sociology and organization theory. They overlap in the sense that both can be seen as a dominant trend within contemporary organization theory and that James G. Marsh is a central figure. Indeed, Bruno Théret operates with only one category, that of sociological institutionalism (2000a, 2000b). However, March and Olsen – and their many followers within political science – relate particularly to the traditional objects of political science, whereas Powell and DiMaggio and others, within what I term 'new institutionalism in sociology and organization theory', relate to other fields of study. Consequently, even if the theories developed in new institutionalism in political science and new institutionalism in sociology overlap to a large extent, March and Olsen (1989) and other scholars within the former have also developed some concepts and theories that are specific to their chosen object of study. Therefore, in this context I shall distinguish between two different approaches.
4. The references to some sociological traditions that are largely unknown outside of France are not included here.
5. The omission of American institutionalism in the survey in the *Journal of Institutional and Theoretical Economy* is more a reflection of the context of the article – that is probably, the major new institutional economics journal – than representative of the views of the author. Or, maybe this tradition does not qualify as 'new' institutionalism.
6. The adjective Schumpeterian is meant to distinguish it from the other evolutionary economics, that is the Veblenian one.
7. It would be wrong to represent the French regulation school as only 'post-Marxist'. It is also strongly influenced by Keynes and Michal Kalecki as well as the Annales tradition of study of the longue duree.
8. The inclusion of economic sociology in this context follows the distinction made by Schumpeter between economic theory (about economic mechanisms) and economic sociology (about economic institutions).
9. This can be illustrated by the fact that whereas Granovetter is apparently seen as a representative of rational-action neoinstitutionalism, the contribution of another of the leading scholars within new economic sociology, Jens Beckert, is rather seen as contrary to rational-action neoinstitutionalism (DiMaggio, 1998, p. 701).

REFERENCES

Beckert, J. (1996), 'What is sociological about economic sociology: uncertainty and embeddedness of economic action', *Theory and Society*, **25**, 803–41.

Bogason, P. (2000), *Public Policy and Local Governance. Institutions in Postmodern Society*. Cheltenham, UK and Northampton, MA, USA: Edward Elgar.

Brinton, M.C. and V. Nee (1998), *The New Institutionalism in Sociology*. New York: Russell Sage Foundation.

Campbell, J.L. (1997), 'Mechanisms of evolutionary change in economic governance: interaction, interpretation and bricolage', in L. Magnusson and J. Ottoson (eds), *Evolutionary Economics and Path Dependency*. Cheltenham, UK and Northampton, MA, USA: Edward Elgar, pp. 10–32.

Campbell, J.L. (1998), 'Institutional analysis and the role of ideas in political economy', *Theory and Society*, **27**, 377–400.

Campbell, J.L., J.R. Hollingsworth and L.N. Lindberg (eds) (1991), *Governance of the American Economy*. New York: Cambridge University Press.

Campbell, J.L. and O.K. Pedersen (eds) (2001), *The Rise of Neoliberalism and Institutional Analysis*. Princeton, NJ: Princeton University Press.

Campbell, J.L. (2004), *Institutional Change and Globalization*. Princeton: Princeton University Press.

Coleman, J.S. (1990), *Foundations of Social Theory*. Cambridge MA: Harvard University Press.

Coriat, B. and G. Dosi (1998), 'The institutional embeddedness of economic change: an appraisal of the "evolutionary" and "regulationist" research programs', in K. Nielsen and B. Johnson (eds), *Institutions and Economic Change. Markets, Technology and Firms*. Cheltenham, UK and Northampton, MA, USA: Edward Elgar, pp. 3–32.

Denzau, A.T. and D.C. North (1994), 'Shared mental models: ideologies and institutions', *Journal of Institutional and Theoretical Economics*, **47** (1), 3–31.

Di Maggio, P.J. (1997), 'Culture and cognition', in *American Review of Sociology*, **23**, 263–87.

DiMaggio, P.J. (1998), 'The new institutionalisms: avenues of collaboration', *Journal of Institutional and Theoretical Economics*, **154** (4), 696–705.

DiMaggio, P.J. and W.W. Powell (1991), 'Introduction', in W.W. Powell and P.J. DiMaggio (eds), *The New Institutionalism in Organizational Analysis*. Chicago: University of Chicago Press, pp. 1–38.

Dunn, S. (2000), 'Wither Post Keynesianism', *Journal of Post Keynesian Economics*, **23** (3), 343–64.

Elster, J. (1989), 'Social norms and economic theory', *Journal of Economic Perspectives*, **3** (4), 99–117.

Fuller, S., M. De May and T. Shinn (eds) (1989), *The Cognitive Turn. Sociological and Psychological Perspectives on Science*. Amsterdam: Kluwer.

Granovetter, M. (1985), 'Economic action and social structure. The problem of embeddedness', *American Journal of Sociology*, **91**, 481–501.

Hall, P.A. and R.C.R. Taylor (1996), 'Political science and the three new institutionalisms', *Political Studies*, **44**, 936–57.

Hay, C. and D. Wincott (1998), 'Structure, agency and historical institutionalism', *Political Studies*, **46** (5), 951–7.

Hodgson, G.M. (1988), *Economics and Institutions. A Manifesto for a Modern Institutional Economics.* Cambridge: Polity Press.

Hodgson, G.M. (1989), 'Institutional economic theory: the old versus the new', *Review of Political Economy*, **1** (3), 249–69.

Hodgson, G.M. (1997), 'The ubiquity of habits and rules', *Cambridge Journal of Economics*, **21** (6), 663–84.

Hodgson, G.M. (1998), 'Some possible differences between American and European institutionalism', in D.D. James and J.W. Mogab (eds), *Technology,*

Innovation and Industrial Economics: Institutional Perspectives. Essays in Honor of William E. Cole, Boston, Dordrecht, London: Kluwer, pp. 127–46.

Jessop, B. (2001), 'Institutional re(turns) and the strategic-relational approach', *Environment and Planning A*, **33**, 1213–35.

Langlois, R. (1986), *Economics as a Process. Essays in the New Institutional Economics*. Cambridge: Cambridge University Press.

Langlois, R. (1989), 'What was wrong with the old institutionalism (and what is still wrong with the new)?', *Review of Political Economy*, **1** (3), 270–98.

Lawson, T. (1997), *Economics and Reality*. London: Routledge.

Lukes, S. (1974), *Power: A Radical View*. London: Macmillan.

March, J.G. and J.P. Olsen (1989), *Rediscovering Institutions*. New York: Free Press.

Mayhew, A. (1989), 'Contrasting origins of the two institutionalisms: the social sciences context', *Review of Political Economy*, **1** (3), 319–34.

North, D.C. (1998), 'Economic performance through time', in M.C. Brinton and V. Nee (eds), *The New Institutionalism in Sociology*, New York: Russell Sage Foundation, pp. 247–57.

Ostrom, E. (1991), 'Rational choice theory and economic analysis. Towards complementarity', *American Political Science Review*, **85** (1), 238–43.

Peters, G. (1999), *Institutional Theory in Political Science. The 'New Institutionalism'*. New York and London: Continuum.

Powell, W.W. and P.J. DiMaggio (1991), *The New Institutionalism in Organizational Analysis*. Chicago: University of Chicago Press.

Ray, L. and A. Sayer (eds) (1999), *Culture and Economy after the Cultural Turn*. London: Sage.

Rutherford, M. (1994), *Institutions in Economics. The Old and the New Institutionalism*. Cambridge: Cambridge University Press.

Sabel, C.F. (1992), 'Studied trust: Building new forms of cooperation in a volatile economy', in R. Swedberg (ed.), *Explorations in Economic Sociology*. New York: Russell Sage Foundation, pp. 104–40.

Scott, W.R. (1995), *Institutions and Organizations*. London: Sage.

Skocpol, T. (1985), 'Bringing the state back in', in P. Evans, D. Rueschemeyer and T. Skocpol (eds), *Bringing the State Back In*. New York: Cambridge University Press, pp. 3–37.

Swedberg, R. (1991), 'Major traditions in economic sociology', *Annual Review of Sociology*, **17**, 251–76.

Thelen, K. and S. Steinmo (1992), 'Historical institutionalism in comparative politics', in S. Steinmo, K. Thelen and F. Longstreth (eds), *Structuring Politics: Historical Institutionalism in Comparative Politics*. New York: Cambridge University Press, pp. 1–32.

Théret, B. (2000a), 'Institutions et institutionalismes. Vers une convergence intra et interdisciplinaires des conceptions de l'institution?', in B. Theret, M. Tallard and D. Uri (eds), *Innovations, institutionnelles et territoires*. Paris: L'Harmattan.

Théret, B. (2000b), 'Nouvelle economie institutionelle, economie des conventions et theorie de la regulation: vers une synthese institutionaliste', in *La Lettre de la Régulation*, **35** (December), 1–4, www.upmf-grenoble.fr/irepd/regulation/Lettre_regulation/index.html.

5. The problem of historical specificity

Geoffrey M. Hodgson[1]

INTRODUCTION

History is important, partly because every complex organism, every human being and every society carries the baggage of its past. As Charles Darwin and others have noted, evolution builds on past survivals that encumber actions in the present. Choices made by our ancestors can be difficult to undo. For example, the standard railway gauge used by modern high-speed trains has its origins in the axle dimensions of the horse-drawn carts of over two thousand years ago. We travel on railways that were designed with some dimensions inherited from an ancient and inappropriate means of transport. Other examples of lock-in and path dependence in the evolution of technology and conventions are well known in the social sciences.[2]

If history matters – at least in the sense of social development being path dependent – then our analyses must explore the particularities of the past. While we may retain general principles or guidelines, detailed analyses of particular events, structures and circumstances are required. If history matters in this sense then general theories have their limits. Explanations will depend on particular instances and configurations, and not merely general principles.

For centuries, scientists have admired general theories. Science rightly tries to unify; it strives for generality. The goal of unification has endured in the history of science and has inspired many of its achievements. Much innovation in science comes from combining different phenomena in a more general scientific framework. Philosophers of science have rightly identified the power and value of explanatory unification (Thagard, 1978; Glymour, 1980; Kitcher, 1981, 1989). The importance and possible value of explanatory unifications should not be underestimated.

However, the pursuit of a general theory should not lead to over-simplification and thus undermine the power of generality. Furthermore, the quest for explanatory unification should not be pushed to the neglect of the nature and value of the particular explanation adopted. Some explanations may unify, but be of little worth. A theory that every event is caused by the gods is an explanatory unification, but it is of no scientific significance. Likewise, a non-falsifiable general theory such as 'everyone is a utility maximizer' is at best of little explanatory value.

Some claims of explanatory unification are defective in their failure to consider their ontological presuppositions. Others fail, similarly, to question what is meant by 'explanation', being merely satisfied to point to a theory that seemingly 'fits' every eventuality. The ideas that everyone maximizes their utility, or that every event is caused by the gods, come into this category. However, once we attempt to build more careful and meaningful explanations, then we are faced with the problem that economic reality changes in a way that physical reality does not. Yet the lure of a general theory has often overcome such critical reflections.

The lure of a general theory pervades the social as well as the natural sciences. Again, it is believed that a general theory is always better than one with a narrower domain of analysis. Consequently it is upheld that to become respectable, economics, sociology and anthropology must also uncover general principles or laws – much in the manner of the natural sciences. The pervasive aim is for one theory that fits all circumstances.

This notion emerged in the heyday of classical economics. While Adam Smith attempted judiciously to blend induction with deduction, at the same time he sought general principles and laws. However, his successors such as David Ricardo and Nassau Senior went much further. They pursued an axiomatic and deductivist method, attempting to derive universal conclusions from a few professedly general and fundamental propositions. Ranged against this Ricardian tendency was Thomas Robert Malthus. Malthus criticized the overemphasis on deduction and generalization. He wrote in 1819: 'The principal cause of error, and of the differences which prevail at present among the scientific writers on political economy, appears to me to be a precipitate attempt to simplify and generalize' (Malthus, 1836, p. 4).

The goal of a general theory has been pursued to the greatest extent in the type of general equilibrium theory developed by Léon Walras, Kenneth Arrow, Gerard Debreu and others. For much of the post-war period, 'general equilibrium analysis' has been in vogue in economics. It has attempted to elaborate the general conditions for the existence and stability of market equilibria. This work was at the cutting edge of theoretical economics until it run into analytical difficulties in the 1970s. It was eclipsed by the rising interest in game theory in the 1980s.

Of course, the word 'general' in 'general equilibrium theory' applies to the word 'equilibrium' rather than 'theory'. General equilibrium is thereby distinguished from partial equilibrium. Nevertheless, general equilibrium theorists have used the rhetoric and appeal of general theorizing. Attempts have been made to apply this general equilibrium approach to feudalism and socialism, as well as to capitalism (Lange and Taylor, 1938; Rader, 1971). In particular, both Oskar Lange (1938) and Joseph Schumpeter (1954) lauded Walras as the architect of a 'truly general theory' in economics.

Likewise in sociology, there has been a similar reverence for general theory of social action, interaction and structure.[3] Overall, general theories have pervaded economics and sociology for the second half of the twentieth century. General principles are assumed and their logical consequences are explored. In this respect at least, the social sciences look to physics and other natural sciences as their role models. The more general and inclusive the theory, the greater its prestige. Universalizations take the accolade.

What characterizes a general theory in the social sciences? We may take the term 'general theory' to mean the following: it is any substantial explanation or model of the principal characteristics and behaviour of human economies or societies, *largely or wholly in terms of features that are assumed to be common to most conceivable social or economic systems.*

It is true that modern mainstream economists attempt to tailor their theories to specific situations. There are theories of perfect competition, theories of monopoly, theories of oligopoly, theories of labour markets, and so on. Such theories may claim to apply to a specific set of circumstances. Nevertheless, some presumptions – such as rationality, scarcity and fixed preferences – are common to all these theories. These core assumptions are held to apply to all socioeconomic systems. It is rarely claimed that the theory involved applies to a specific type of socioeconomic system or a limited historical period. In these two senses, ahistorical and acultural generalities pervade even specific modes of theorizing in modern mainstream economics.

Abstraction and simplification are necessary for any theory. General theorists, however, build upon features that are taken as common or universal, rather than historically or culturally specific. Their guiding examples in this respect are the successful explanatory unifications and general theories that are found in the natural sciences. In economics, for example, general equilibrium theorists have made ostensibly general assumptions concerning human agents, their endowments and their interactions. With these they attempt to deduce some general results concerning economic equilibria. Likewise, in social theory, general assumptions are made about social agents, their 'exchanges' and the social structures that they inhabit.

THE LIMITS TO EXPLANATORY UNIFICATION

By its nature, a general theory achieves some explanatory unification. However, as Uskali Mäki (1990a, 1990b, 2001) has shown, there are explanatory unifications of different types. First, logical or derivational unification means that 'more and more statements within a discipline become derivable from the same set of axioms, or when the same set of statements becomes derivable from a smaller set of axioms' (Mäki, 1990b, p. 331). This notion of unification involves purely deductive connections between axioms and derived statements. Many of the claims of explanatory unification within economics are of this derivational type. They are deductive accomplishments without ontological grounding.

While derivational unification is based on the inferential capabilities of theories, the contrasting idea of ontological unification is based on their referential and representational capabilities. If an ontological explanatory unification is possible, then it must be based on some underlying, ontological unity among a set of phenomena; they must share some substantial ontic foundations. Any explanatory unity among phenomena must result from investigation and discovery, rather than the mere imposition of assumptions. Priority is given to entities rather than propositions.

Accordingly, the nature and location of the limits of general theorizing vary in each case. The limits of general theorizing by derivational unification result from the lack of ontological grounding to its claims. These limits concern neither the boundaries of unification nor the number of items that can be unified, but the adequacy of the explanation. A derivational unification may be achieved, but on its own it cannot constitute a causal explanation of real phenomena.

On the other hand, the limits of ontological explanatory unification depend upon the existence or otherwise of underlying unities among the phenomena under investigation. While the search for underlying unities behind the diverse appearances of real phenomena is rightly a central aim of science, any absence of recurring elements or similarities poses limits to ontological unification. Ontological explanatory unification requires the identification of similar structures or causal mechanisms. The capacity of a theory to unify in this ontological sense depends not on its axioms or propositions but on the degree of real, underlying unity or similarity in its domain of application. It is primarily these possible limits to ontological explanatory unification that concern us in the present work.

Reality consists of different ontological levels. There is a level relating to matter addressed by physics, a level relating to molecules addressed by chemistry, a level relating to living organisms addressed by biology, and so on. These levels may themselves be subdivided. Within physics, for example, quantum physics and mechanics address different levels. Accordingly, different scientific theories may relate to different levels of reality.

Although universal laws have both scientific appeal and some explanatory power, they are often of limited use when it comes to the detail of specific contexts and situations operating at a different ontological level.

Einstein's theory of relativity may rule the universe, and its domain of application applies to all physical phenomena, but it tells us little of tomorrow's weather or of the carrying capacity of the Golden Gate suspension bridge. In achieving unification, general theories have an awesome appeal. But neither unification nor generality mean that the theory is sufficient for particular, contingent circumstances at a different ontological level.

Arguably, within the social sciences there are differences among the real items to be explained that place limits on the scope for any general theory. In 1904, Max Weber (1949, pp. 72–80) wrote that 'the most general laws' are 'the least valuable' because 'the more comprehensive their scope' the more they 'lead away' from the task of explaining the particular phenomenon in question. This argument is similar to Ernest Nagel's (1961, p. 575) 'principle of the inverse variation of extension with intension'. This principle alleges that there is a trade-off between the generality and the informative content of a theory. This argument, developed further by Lars Udéhn (1992), has some force against the claimed universality of some of the assumptions of modern mainstream economics.

Another set of problems arise with some types of general theory in the social sciences. The general theory that individual behaviour results from the maximization of individual utility is a case in point. Partly because utility is unobservable, this theory is non-falsifiable and it can apply, in principle, to any behaviour, including the behaviour of non-human organisms. If this argument is valid then there is a crucial difference between theories like Newton's or Einstein's, on the one hand, and the theory of utility maximization on the other. The difference is that the laws of physics impose restrictions on the type of supplementary theory that can be accommodated. This is not the case with utility maximization: *any* behaviour is compatible with it, even if utility-based explanations are sometimes tortuous. The reckless pursuit of generality in the social sciences has created theories that are compatible with *any* possible real behaviour by *any* possible organism. The same cannot be said for prominent theories in the natural sciences.

Accordingly, much explanatory unification in the social sciences is achieved without a search for recurring elements or similarities in reality. The theory of utility maximization is again a case in point. Instead of the successful identification of similar, underlying causal mechanisms and structures, its proponents simply manipulate this theory to fit any phenomenon. Hence, this theory achieves derivational unification but not ontological unification. In contrast, the Newtonian and Einsteinian theories achieved a high degree of ontological unification.

All sciences have to deal with both sameness and difference. General theorists sometimes overemphasize the similarities, neglecting the differences. These problems are particularly acute in the social sciences. A general theory can clumsily obscure all historical and geographical differences between different socioeconomic systems.

Nevertheless, there are some important examples of successful general theories concerning complex systems. Charles Darwin's theory of evolution is the most important. However, without diminishing the importance of this great achievement, biology does not confine itself to such generalities. Evolutionary biology has a few laws or general principles by which origin and development can be explained. Analysis of the evolution of a specific organism requires detailed data concerning the organism and its environment, and also specific explanations relevant to the species under consideration. Evolutionary biology requires theories that have both specific and general domains. As Richard Lewontin (1991, pp. 142–3) has argued, the notion that 'science consists of universal claims as opposed to mere historical statements is rubbish' and 'a great deal of the body of biological research and knowledge consists of narrative statements'. Likewise in economics and the other social sciences, there is a place for both.

GENERAL THEORIZING IN ECONOMICS

A central problem with all models in the social sciences is that they have to consider not only the structured relations between agents, but also the computations of the agents themselves, as they react to their changing circumstances. Both the system and the agents must be modelled, where the model of the agent includes its perception of the system. This is a level of tangled complexity that is difficult to put in a general model, at least without the imposition of severe simplifying assumptions.

For example, how does the individual agent deal with multiple markets in a general equilibrium model? Roy Radner (1968) has considered the computational problems involved. The general equilibrium models of the type of Kenneth Arrow and Gerard Debreu assumed that a 'market' existed for the exchange of every possible commodity, on every possible date, in every possible state of nature. Hence if there are a thousand types of commodity, a thousand possible 'dates' and a thousand possible 'states' then there will be a billion different markets. Assuming all possibilities and connections, the number of markets explodes beyond the calculating engagement of any human agent. Radner (1968, p. 32) concluded that 'there is a basic difficulty in incorporating computational limitations in . . . equilibrium theory based on optimizing behaviour'.

Overall, general equilibrium theorists have had great difficulty deriving general explanatory principles. As Arrow (1986, p. S388) declared, 'In the aggregate, the hypothesis of rational behaviour has in general no implications.' Within general equilibrium theory, the aggregated excess demand functions can take almost any form.[4]

Facing such problems, Alan Kirman (1992, p. 118) wrote that 'there is no plausible formal justification for the assumption that the aggregate of individuals, even maximizers, acts itself like an individual maximizer.' Research into the problems of the uniqueness and stability of general equilibria has shown that they may be indeterminate and unstable unless very strong assumptions are made, such as the supposition that society as a whole behaves as if it were a single individual (Arrow, 1986; Coricelli and Dosi, 1988). Not only is it assumed that preference functions are exogenously given, it is also assumed that all of these preference functions are exactly the same.

Because general theories become overwhelmed by explosive complexity, all attempts at general theorizing ultimately have to abandon many generalities. They simplify, declaring that 'more work remains to be done' to generalize the model. The principal theoretical results of general equilibrium theory have depended on such restrictive assumptions. Truly general theorizing has proved to be difficult, if not impossible. It is widely accepted that the only truly general explanatory principle that has been derived from general equilibrium theory is 'everything depends on everything else'. The weakness of the theory derives in part from its wanton pursuit of universality, as well as from the limitations of its basic axioms.[5]

In practice, all attempts to erect an all-embracing general theory in economics have been highly limited or have led to failure. Leading general equilibrium theorists have latterly accepted the limitations of their project. For example, Frank Hahn (1980) has candidly admitted that the typical Walrasian type of theory excludes time, because it collapses the future into the present. It also excludes money, which is essentially a means of dealing with an uncertain future (Hahn, 1988). Robert Clower (1994, 1999) passed a similarly negative verdict. He argued, on similar lines, that the Walrasian theory actually excludes production, markets, competition and real trade. Crucially, Walrasian theory concentrates on the logical existence of equilibrium states, at the expense of the mechanisms of market operation (Costa, 1998). Overall, theories of complex phenomena that aim to be general typically turn out to be very narrow in their scope.

In practice, attempts at general theorizing in economics, and in other sciences dealing with complex phenomena, turn out to be restricted in their sweep and thereby fail to be truly general. Although general principles or laws may exist, general theories are either not so general, or of very limited explanatory value. The elaboration of a truly general theory of complex phenomena can be confounded by severe problems of computation and tractability.

WHY A GENERAL THEORY OF BARTER WOULD LOSE MONEY

To recapitulate: it has been argued above that there are several problems with general theorizing in the social sciences. One is of analytical and computational intractability. Facing such computational limits, general theorists typically simplify their models, thus abandoning the generality of the theory. Another related problem with a general theory is that we are confined to broad principles governing all possible structures within its domain of analysis. In practice, a manageable theory has to confine itself to a relatively tiny subset of all possible structures. Furthermore, the cost of excessive generality is to miss out on key features common to a subset of phenomena.

To illustrate the latter argument we shall consider two very simple 'models' of, respectively, a barter and a monetary economy, and consider which involves fewer assumptions and which is more general. Robert Clower's (1967) theoretical framework is the starting point. In a barter economy, every commodity can in principle be traded for every other commodity. By contrast, in a money economy without barter, commodities are traded for money only. Hence, for Clower in a monetary economy: 'the peculiar feature of money as contrasted with a barter economy is precisely that *some* commodities in a money economy *cannot* be traded directly for all other commodities. . . . *Money buys goods and goods buy money; but goods do not buy goods*' (1967, pp. 5–7).

Figure 5.1 – taken and amended slightly from Clower (1967) – represents these two contrasting arrangements:

In Figure 5.1, C_1, C_2, C_3 and C_4 each represent commodities. M is money. The presence of symbol '×' indicates that an exchange between two commodities is possible; a '0' indicates that no such exchange normally

	C_1	C_2	C_3	C_4
C_1	×	×	×	×
C_2	×	×	×	×
C_3	×	×	×	×
C_4	×	×	×	×

Exchange relations in a barter economy

	M	C_2	C_3	C_4
M	×	×	×	×
C_2	×	×	0	0
C_3	×	0	×	0
C_4	×	0	0	×

Exchange relations in a monetary economy

Figure 5.1 Exchange relations under money and barter

takes place. This restrictive structure of an exchange economy is a necessary, but not sufficient, condition for the existence of money. In addition, money has other special attributes – such as a store of value and means of dealing with an uncertain future – that are not represented here.

At least at first sight, a barter economy model in which all exchanges are possible involves fewer restrictive assumptions than a model in which there is money. A model of a monetary economy must include *additional* restrictive assumptions in order to obtain the special structure of a monetary economy as in Figure 5.1. The theoretical representation of a monetary economy requires *more* rather than *fewer* restrictive assumptions.

Which model is 'more general'? Of the two models in Figure 5.1, the barter economy model is more general in a sense. The presence of an '×' in any cell in a matrix in Figure 5.1 indicates that an exchange is possible, not that the exchange has to take place. In this sense, therefore, a monetary economy is a special case of a barter economy: the barter economy model is more general. However, this gives us a partial and potentially misleading picture and the statement needs to be qualified.

Crucially, the very process of apparent 'generalization' – from a monetary to a barter model – means that some essential features of a monetary economy are lost. Because everything in a barter economy has the money-like property of being able to exchange with everything else, then nothing has the property of money. If all men are kings then there are no kings, because kingship implies the existence of non-regal inferiors.

Money exists only because some exchanges are admitted and some are excluded. If *all* exchanges are admitted then money is excluded. In this sense the barter model is not general: it excludes money. Hence, from this point of view, neither a barter model nor Walrasian-type theory (which excludes money) is an adequate representation of a monetary economy. For a theory to accommodate money, it has to incorporate the special qualities of money, with some forms of exchange being excluded.

This example shows that, while seeming more general in scope, the barter economy model loses key features of the monetary economy. A general theory of barter would not include money. Greater generality in some respects can be gained at the cost of an ability to discriminate between and explain concrete particulars.

GAME THEORY AND THE ESCAPE FROM GENERALITIES

Without much discussion, mainstream economics quietly dropped the search for a general theory in the 1980s. The general equilibrium theory project had broken down (Kirman, 1989; Rizvi, 1994a, 1994b). Game theory had originally been developed and applied to economics by John von Neumann and Oskar Morgenstern in 1944. But it did not become popular until after the general equilibrium project had stumbled upon intractable problems in the 1970s. The eventual turn to game theory was an abandonment of a general theory of market behaviour.

In game theory there are few general results. Outcomes depend on the assumed structure and parameters of the game itself. Such theoretical constructions exemplify rather than generalize. However, most game theorists retain ahistorical models of human motivation and agency. The individual remains a pay-off or utility maximizer. Pay-off maximization is a general theory of individual behaviour but it does not constitute a complete theory of socioeconomic dynamics. Game theory mixes pay-off or utility maximization with specific game structures. Many other generalities have disappeared.

With the exception of Franklin Fisher (1989), the abandonment by game theorists of the historical quest for a comprehensive general theory has occurred with remarkably little comment or reflection by mainstream economists. Nevertheless, the big message behind the abandonment of general equilibrium theory should not be overlooked. The true achievement of all the efforts behind the development of the Walrasian and Arrow-Debreu models is to show the severe limits of general theorizing in economics. In addition, developments in computability theory in the 1980s and 1990s have shown that optimization problems typically involve difficulties not only of specification but also of computability.[6]

Perhaps the greatest overall achievement of mainstream economic theory in the last half of the twentieth century has been to confirm the suspicion that substantive general theorizing in economics will always bring highly limited and inadequate results. All substantive general theories in complex systems are characterized by shortcomings.

THE PROBLEM OF HISTORICAL SPECIFICITY

Emphatically, the argument in this chapter is not against the power or value of generalization. While general theorizing can never be enough, general statements are not only necessary but also unavoidable. Neither should we underestimate the value of empirical work. The concern, however, is that both empiricism and deductive generalization have their flaws, and some faulty presumptions are shared in common. Accordingly, any attempt to steer a middle way between these poles is likely to share the limitations of each. A more sophisticated position has to be found, recognizing a significant role for general theories but also their limitations. Some kind of middle-range theorizing – to use Robert Merton's (1949) famous term – is required to bridge the general with the empirical. Much valuable work in the modern social sciences is broadly of this kind. The problem, however, is that the methodological underpinnings and meta-theoretical justifications are relatively unexplored.

We have set the stage for a methodological problem of vital significance for the social sciences. As noted below, economists were concerned with this central theoretical and methodological problem for much of the nineteenth century. It continued to be discussed by leading economists up until the outbreak of the Second World War.

Today, however, the problem is largely ignored. Most social scientists are unaware of it. It is absent from the popular textbooks. Neither neoclassical economists nor post-Keynesians seem conscious of the problem. Although earlier theorists such as Karl Marx and John Commons addressed it, contemporary Marxists and institutionalists give it little attention. Although Max Weber was preoccupied with the problem, it is absent within much of modern theoretical sociology, except in the shadow play of the modern discourse on ideal types. Yet for about one hundred years this issue preoccupied some of the greatest minds in the social sciences and was central to much social and economic analysis.

I call it 'the problem of historical specificity'. It first acknowledges the fact that there are different types of socioeconomic system, in historical time and geographic space. The problem of historical specificity addresses the limits of explanatory unification in social science: substantially different socioeconomic phenomena may require theories that are in some respects different. If different socioeconomic systems have features in common then, to some extent, the different theories required to analyse different systems might reasonably share some common characteristics. But sometimes there will be important differences as well. Concepts and theoretical frameworks appropriate for one real object may not be best suited for another. The problem of historical specificity starts from a recognition of significant underlying differences between different objects of analysis. One theory may not fit all.

For instance, the socioeconomic system of today is very different from the systems of five hundred, one thousand or two thousand years ago. Even today, despite having some important features in common, existing socioeconomic systems in different countries are substantially different from each other in key particulars. There are important variations in the structures, rules and mechanisms of production and allocation. Individual purposes and social norms also vary, relating to differences in culture. These differences may be so substantial that they place limits on ontological explanatory unification. As a result, to some degree, different types of socioeconomic system may require different conceptual and theoretical tools. A fundamentally different object of analysis may require a different theory.

To repeat: any common aspects of these different theories might reasonably reflect common features of the systems involved. Historically common phenomena – such as the scarcity of physical resources – may exist. However, when we compare socioeconomic systems, there are important differences as well as similarities. Arguably, the theories used to analyse them may also have to be different to a significant degree.

Many such differences cannot be captured by mere differences in parameter values. The complexity of economic phenomena suggests that much more than particular applications of a single, general theory would be required. The problem of historical specificity is concerned with the development of distinctive, particularistic theories, each applicable to a particular kind of socioeconomic system. An adequate theory of (say) feudalism may not be completely adequate for (say) capitalism as well. An essentially different reality may require a substantially different theory.

An adequate theory of capitalism must address the pervasiveness of markets and employment contracts, and explain the behaviour of market-oriented, profit-seeking firms. However, markets and market-engaged corporations had a much less significant role under feudalism. Accordingly, concepts that relate exclusively to the market – such as market supply, market demand and market competition – would have much less relevance for a theory of feudalism. Instead, a theory of feudalism would have to be centred on another set of essential phenomena. Other concepts, concerning the nature of feudal hierarchy and power, would assume greater relevance. Of course, there is the possibility that a theory of feudalism and a theory of capitalism may share common features and an underlying theoretical framework (Hodgson, 2001). But it would be mistaken to assume that the common underlying framework would necessarily constitute an adequate or complete theory. The essential differences between capitalism and feudalism place limits on the scope of explanatory unifications that embrace them both.

Note that there is a great deal of openness and flexibility here as to what, for example, may constitute an 'essential' difference between one reality and another, or in what ways a theory may 'differ' from another. There may be different understandings of the ways in which systems 'vary in essence', or of what constitutes a 'core concept' of a theory. These questions cannot be answered without some elaboration of a methodology and a social ontology. But it is neither possible nor necessary at this initial stage to achieve absolute precision in these terms. The point being made is that there is a prima facie case to answer, covering a wide range of meanings of phrases such as 'reality may differ in essential respects' and 'core concepts and categories of a theory may have to differ'. Acceptance of the prima facie case then requires us, necessarily, to try to be more precise about these statements. Indeed, much of the important detail of the debate concerns these very questions of further examination and precision.

As noted above, there are problems of complexity and tractability involved in formulating any general model, spanning complex and very different cases. The problem of tractability forces many theorists to make specific assumptions. As a consequence, most theorizing that claims to be general is in fact specific in its scope. Furthermore, as the comparison of a barter and a monetary economy shows, a move towards seemingly greater generality can sometimes lose the emphasis on the specific connections and linkages that are important features of specific socioeconomic structures. Any attempted resolution of the problem of historical specificity should address this possible trade-off between generality and engagement with specific detail.

However, the problem could be rephrased more accurately as 'the problem of historical and geographical specificity', as there are differences in socioeconomic systems across space as well as time. Particular kinds are not in principle restricted in space or time. It is possible – but unlikely in the social context – that two instances of one kind of socioeconomic system could appear in different times or places. Hence it could be rephrased as 'the problem of specificity'. However, the phrase 'problem of historical specificity' is retained here because, in the historical discussions of the problem over more than a century, the consideration of differences of type has been placed principally – but not entirely – in a historical context. Nevertheless, geographical differences are as important as historical ones and the discussion here applies to all variations, ranged across terrain as well as time.

Recognition of the problem of historical specificity involves asking such questions. In part, the problem of historical specificity helps to demarcate the social from the physical sciences. Socioeconomic systems have changed markedly in the last few thousand years, whereas the essential properties and laws of the physical world have not altered since the 'Big Bang'. Accordingly, the methods and procedures of the social sciences must alter to follow the changing subject of analysis. This is not so in the physical sciences.

A partial exception is biology. In the biotic world, as in the social world, new species and phenomena arise, and others pass away. Accordingly, biology combines general principles (for example: taxonomy, the laws of evolution) with particular studies of specific mechanisms and phenomena. This is one reason why the social sciences should be closer to biology than to physics: biology has the problem of historical (or evolutionary) specificity.

PAST ENCOUNTERS

Today, it is remarkable that this vital methodological problem is rarely if ever posed in all the modern mainstream economics textbooks, at any level, and is discussed infrequently even in the dissenting or methodologically informed literatures in economics. By contrast, the problem of historical specificity was raised clearly by Marx and his followers, and was explored by the German historical school from the 1840s to the 1930s. Leading names such as Gustav Schmoller and Werner Sombart addressed this problem. In Britain, Alfred Marshall took the problem on board and acknowledged the contribution of the German historical school. The problem was also addressed by American institutionalism. But in theoretical terms – with notable exceptions such as John Commons and Frank Knight – there was a failure in America to develop the topic much further than the earlier, German-speaking economic theorists.

In sum, the problem of historical specificity was clearly addressed by German-speaking economists in the nineteenth century, but it never appeared as a major issue in the English language literature in economics. However, it shall be argued here that the issue must be central, at least to any broadly realist approach to the subject. Indeed, the problem is one of the most crucial in economic and social science, and it is not belittled in stature by its neglect.

If this assessment is correct then the virtual absence of any discussion of the problem in modern economics has itself to be explained. In part, the explanation lies in the persecution and wartime destruction of the Nazi period – from 1933 to 1945 – and their negative effects on German philosophy and social science. The fact that trained economists are no longer required to read German must also be taken into account.

However, there is more to it than that. Despite raising the problem clearly, both Marx and the German historical school had methodological frameworks that were inadequate to deal with the problem. In particular, the successes of their 'Austrian' opponents, in the controversies of the Methodenstreit of the 1880s and thereafter, were partly due to these weaknesses. The first methodological counter-attack by the historically inclined economists was flawed, and even with Schmoller an adequate methodological response did not emerge. A principal weakness in the earlier historical school tradition was an excessive faith in empiricism and inductive methods.

The later historical school, including Sombart, recognized this weakness but had inadequate time to develop an alternative. Nazism and the Second World War intervened. By 1945 the problem was buried under the rubble of destruction. The conventional wisdom emerged that the German historical school had lost out in the Methodenstreit, and the argument was closed.

It shall be argued here that this assessment is wrong, that the problem of historical specificity cannot legitimately be ignored, and that there were serious methodological and theoretical defects on all sides of the debate: in the positions of Marx, the historical school, and their 'Austrian' critics.

It may seem remarkable that it was in economics that this problem was discussed and widely debated for about one hundred years. Sociology did not fully establish itself in Western academia until the early part of the twentieth century. Both economics and sociology went through a methodological transformation in the 1930s, involving a redefinition of the nature and subject matter of these disciplines. These transformations further explain the dereliction of the problem of historical specificity.

The principal architects of this reconstruction were Lionel Robbins (1932) in economics and Talcott Parsons (1937) in sociology. Although their stances differed, they reached a territorial agreement concerning the domain of analysis of each discipline. In their accounts, economics would be devoted to 'choice' and sociology to 'action'. What they also did in common was to attempt to bury the problem of historical specificity. With the collapse of German academia in the Second World War, and the defeat of institutionalism in the USA in the 1940s, post-war economics left the problem of historical specificity behind.

General theorists do not recognize the problem of historical specificity because they believe that economics can proceed entirely on the basis of universal and historically unspecific assumptions. In the past some empiricists have reacted against general theorists, emphasizing the specificity of each case. But by failing to establish a prior theoretical framework, empiricists are lost without a system of categorization. In extreme cases, general theorists see only the similarities – empiricists see only the differences. The problem is about the establishment of appropriate categories and assumptions upon which both empirical and theoretical work must proceed. It is impossible in principle to resolve the problem simply by delving into facts. Neither general theorizing nor empiricism can do adequate credit to the problem of historical specificity.

SOME WAYS OF AVOIDING THE PROBLEM

Consider some ways in which the problem of historical specificity has been evaded or ignored.

Evasion 1

The affirmation of overwhelming common features or pervasive problematics.
It is sometimes claimed that all viable socioeconomic systems have
common attributes. As it stands, it is reasonable to suggest that they may
have something in common. It is reasonable to uphold a restricted version
of this postulate. However, the mistake is to concentrate entirely on the
commonalities, and forget the differences. The existence of common characteristics in all socioeconomic systems does not imply that the particular,
different characteristics are of little or no importance. It is necessary to
focus on both the particular and the general. The error is to assume that all
that matters is that which is general or common to socioeconomic systems.

Dismissals of the problem of historical specificity typically exclude the
particulars. They assume that the allegedly common attributes of all socioeconomic systems (for example, markets, exchange, choice) are the key
phenomena of economic analysis to the exclusion of other, historically
contingent, features. Economics becomes ahistorical by focusing solely on
what is presumed to be common to all systems.

The one-sided emphasis on commonalities is related to the particular
conception of economics as the universal 'science of choice'. Menger,
Robbins and others argued that economics should address the common
problematic of individual choice under scarcity and trace out the consequences of multiple, individual 'rational' choices in terms of their intended
or unintended outcomes. Whatever the value of this choice–theoretic
approach to economics, it leaves much out of the picture. Insufficient stress
is placed on the unique historical circumstances in which individual decisions always take place. The ways in which institutions or cultures may
mould individual preferences are neglected.

On the contrary, it is argued here that all socioeconomic systems are
necessarily combinations of dissimilar elements. These combinations will
in turn depend on historical and local circumstances. Once we recognize the
unavoidability and importance of additional and non-universal phenomena, then a new set of theoretical problems emerge concerning the assumptions that are appropriate in a given context. How do we ground such
assumptions in an appropriate methodology? This is part of the problem
of historical specificity.

Evasion 2

The doctrine of a natural type of socioeconomic system. Another way of
avoiding the problem of historical specificity is to assume that one system
is 'natural' and all other systems are 'unnatural'. This idea is deeply rooted

in the more general view that the uniformities and regularities of economic life are determined by nature.

Once any given type of socioeconomic system is regarded as 'natural' then all deviations are regarded as aberrations to be corrected by an appeal to the singular brute facts or natural laws of economic life. This ancient idea has often been used in attempts to give scientific justification to the status quo. Moreover, it encourages the social scientist to focus on one type of system only.

One of the problems in this doctrine is that it takes the concept of the 'natural' for granted. In both society and nature, what is and what is not 'natural' is far from straightforward. Evolution has many examples of quirks and path-dependent outcomes. Are extinct species 'unnatural'? Is all that survives and endures 'natural'? Although the Soviet-type economies have collapsed, does that mean that they were 'unnatural'? If it is argued that the Soviet-type economies were unnatural because they were short-lived, then we are drawn to the conclusion that the slave societies of antiquity are more natural than modern industrial capitalism: antiquity lasted for thousands of years whereas capitalism has existed for little more than two centuries. Despite the long-lasting persistence of the doctrine of natural types in the social sciences, the criteria for bestowing the term 'natural' on one system rather than another have remained elusive.

Evasion 3

The view of economics as an expression of human nature or psychology.   A common variant of the former doctrine is the idea that the chosen system is an expression of 'human nature'. Many Enlightenment thinkers upheld the view that 'human nature' was constant and universal. In the *Wealth of Nations* Adam Smith wrote of the universal 'propensity in human nature to . . . truck, barter and exchange one thing for another' (Smith, 1976, p. 17). Smith assumed that the predilection to make contracts was not historically and culturally created but it was 'a propensity in human nature'. To sustain this 'natural' view of contract and exchange, they have to be regarded as something separate from specific and historically created institutions, such as property, law and courts. By making it universal and 'natural', Smith was thus inclined to see exchange simply as a flow of goods, services or money between persons. However, when exchange occurs in market economies, it is not simply things that are exchanged, but also property rights. Furthermore, contracts are made in the context of the laws and potential sanctions of the legal system. By seeing exchange and contract as essentially manifestations of 'human nature', Smith downplayed the historically contingent institutions upon which these activities depend. As will be shown later, Carl Menger and members of the Austrian school of economics made a similar error.

This idea that economics is founded largely on 'human nature' or psychology is remarkably persistent. It is not argued here that these factors are irrelevant to the understanding of human societies. The problem arises when it is believed that social and economic analysis stem largely from an understanding of human nature or psychology alone.

Remarkably, the Enlightenment notion of an individual, with given purposes or preference functions, still pervades modern mainstream economic thought. With the spread of modern rational choice theory to other disciplines, it is also making an appearance in sociology and political science. The research agenda often involves a search for the optimal economic, social or political arrangement on the basis of the assumption that society is a collection of fixed, ahistorical individuals. History is then admitted only insofar as it involves comparisons with a single, optimal system. By making the individual ahistorical, the real history of socioeconomic systems is lost.

On the contrary, if we regarded the individual as partially constituted by society and its institutions, then history can be readmitted into the story. The individual and society are mutually constitutive; each forms and reforms the other in an ongoing process. Neither society nor the individual is fixed. Human nature has real effects but it is not static. Neither is there a single, natural order. Accordingly, recognition of the problem of historical specificity is allied to a view of human nature as moulded and reconstituted by social institutions.

Evasion 4

The affirmation of the free market as the ideal.   Dismissals of the problem of historical specificity often involve a heavy dose of free market ideology. In the history of the subject since Adam Smith, many economists have attempted to use alleged 'economic laws' to attempt to justify free market policies. Those that advocate free and unfettered markets typically hold them up as a pure and ideal standard by which to judge reality. Of course, they observe many cases of inflexible, regulated, fettered, or even missing, markets in the real world. These are denounced as deviations from the pure and perfect norm.

It has been said that economic theory demonstrates that free markets are optimal. But any competent economic theorist knows that this claim is based on restrictive and challengeable assumptions. Nevertheless, the belief in optimality persists. By believing that markets are the solution, and that markets will work well if only they are free and unfettered, the cases of imperfect or missing markets are then ignored. If the theory does not fit reality, then reality must be made to fit the theory. Imperfections and restraints in existing markets must be removed, and new markets must be set up in places where they are missing.

Leaving the ideological issues on one side, there are important theoretical implications of this commonplace gambit. In short, economics becomes the study of one ideal, pure market system. It is held that no other system, past or present, needs to be studied because it is deemed to be an aberration from the ideal norm. Economic history becomes the story of the development of all economies towards this ideal. Any impurities or 'imperfections' in existing market systems are regarded as unfortunate hangovers from the past. The theoretical discourse focuses on a single model of an allegedly pure market system.

Of course, not all mainstream economists take this extreme view. Many find good reasons for the survival of market imperfections in the system – such as public goods, externalities and transaction costs – and advocate some government intervention and some non-market forms of organization. However, the view previously described is sufficiently powerful to constrain the analysis of non-market forms of allocation. Deviations from the pure market ideal are often addressed largely in terms of the central concepts (exchange, prices, costs, supply, demand) of the market system. They are not treated as separate entities, requiring additional theoretical and conceptual frameworks.

A particular version of this free-market ideology is to assume that the ensemble of institutions in American capitalism is the ideal. When economies elsewhere experience recession, such as in Japan and East Asia, it is then exclaimed that the reason for this suboptimal performance is that the free and competitive economic institutions of American capitalism are not adequately replicated in these economies. Again, this gives an excuse for ignoring the specific institutions and structures involved. The possibility that their development may be path-dependent, or that they may be capable of consistently outperforming American capitalism in other circumstances, does not appear on the agenda.

A theory of the ideal economy is likely to emerge in periods dominated by a single, successful type of system. Opposition to this ideal is most likely to emerge in contexts where it is deemed imperfect or inappropriate. In the nineteenth century, when British capitalism was the engine of its global power, recognition of the problem of historical specificity was notable in Germany and Ireland. German and Irish economists opposed British economic policies, seeing them as a brake on their own national development. They also developed a distinctive theoretical outlook. These dissenting ideas were imported into the USA and influenced American institutionalism.

However, by 1945 Britain was no longer the leading world power, and America saw itself as the model for the world. America had emerged from its isolationism and saw its own institutional structures as models for others to follow. This American intellectual domination endured for the remainder of the twentieth century, except for a brief period in the 1980s when Japan was seen as a rival model in terms of economic growth. Accordingly, the notion of a single, ideal system persists.

REALISM MEANS THE PROBLEM REAPPEARS

Despite the evasion of the problem of historical specificity, we are used to terms such as 'capitalism', 'feudalism' and 'socialism' in the discourse of economics and other social sciences. The merits of one type of system over another are proclaimed. In many ways, leading economists allude to some taxonomic classification of different types of economic system. If these differences are to be meaningful, there must be an assumption that different systems behave in different ways. In other words, different systems are subject to 'laws' or principles of operation that differ from one system to another. Even if it is accepted that all socioeconomic systems are subject to common 'laws' or principles then such differences are being accepted as well. Otherwise we would have no basis to suggest that one system functioned in a different way from another.

Yet, strikingly, there is little discussion throughout modern economics of the underlying methodological problems in making such comparisons. Today, the subdiscipline of 'comparative economic systems' is relatively neglected. The relevant methodological issues and problems are rarely taught on the economics degree programmes of leading universities. In-depth taxonomic discussions of different types of socioeconomic system, or of different types of firm or market are all notable by their rarity.

In contrast, modern mainstream economics defines itself as the science of choice under scarcity, alleging that its principles can apply to all economies where choice and scarcity exist (Robbins, 1932). Real differences between socioeconomic systems are either downplayed or ignored at this conceptual level.

How do we establish a typology of different types of socioeconomic system? What criteria do we use to distinguish one system from another, and how are these criteria derived? How do we identify incisive principles of operation of specific socioeconomic systems, alongside principles or 'laws' that may be common to a larger set of such systems?

Arguably the role of any science is to address a particular segment or level of objective reality and to attempt to understand and explain the phenomena in that domain. Every science, in this view, has a real domain of analysis to which it is related. Hence, physics is about the nature and properties of matter and energy, chemistry is about substances, astronomy about heavenly bodies, biology about living things, psychology about the human psyche and so on.

This is a realist view of science, which would be accepted quite widely, but not universally, among philosophers. To deny that the sciences have a real object is tantamount to a denial of the existence of an objective reality. With the current crisis in the theoretical foundations of the social sciences, it is necessary to defend the existence of such a reality and its place in scientific discourse. It would not have been necessary at the time of Marshall or Marx: they took its existence for granted.

Although philosophical realists know of no royal road to truth, they claim that truth, nevertheless, is a primary objective for science. Even if all science is provisional and an infallible methodology is always beyond our grasp, this does not mean that we may abandon the search for truth. This search may reveal multiple and contradictory truth claims. Science should not simply rest there, but it should investigate reality and create dialogue between researchers so that error can be removed and the more viable claims advanced. The central task of science is to advance the understanding of how the real world actually works.[7]

Philosophical realism is based on the claim that the acceptance of the existence of a real world beyond our senses makes intelligible such essential scientific concepts as explanation and truth. Science, to be science, must be *about* something; it must have a real object of enquiry.

The question is basically this: are the core assumptions of economic science appropriate for *all* types and forms of economy, since the dawn of human history, or appropriate for a (temporal or geographical) subset of them only? For example, are the assumptions of economics appropriate for modern market systems only, or for all types of socioeconomic system? Do some assumptions have general and transhistorical applicability, while others are historically specific? If so, how do we establish concepts at each level of generality? This, with all its attendant questions, is the problem of historical specificity.

CONCLUDING REMARKS

Discussions of several of the key problems raised here are relatively sparse in the recent literature in social science. Accordingly, for purposes of clarification and to avoid misunderstandings, some propositions are listed below. They constitute the standpoint of this work, concerning questions of generality and specificity in economic and social theory. The following propositions are upheld here:

1. Science cannot be merely the analysis or description of empirical particulars. Descriptions themselves always rely on prior theories and concepts, either explicit or tacit.
2. Science cannot proceed without some general or universal statements and principles. Explanatory unifications and generalizations that explain real causal mechanisms are worthy goals of science.
3. However, general theories of complex phenomena are always highly limited simplifications, largely because of the complexities and computational limitations involved in attempting any truly general theory.
4. Unifications and generalizations in social science provide powerful conceptual frameworks, but they often lack the ability to discriminate between and adequately explain concrete particulars.
5. Purportedly general theories have explanatory power in the social sciences only when additional, confining and particular, assumptions are made.
6. In dealing with complex (socioeconomic) systems, we require a combination of general concepts, statements and theories, with particular concepts, statements and theories relating to particular types of system or subsystem.
7. The most powerful and informative statements and theories in the social sciences are those that emanate from particular theorizing that is targeted at a specific domain of analysis and also guided by general frameworks and principles.
8. The social sciences must thus combine general principles with theorizing that is aimed at specific domains. These operate on different levels of abstraction. A philosophically informed meta-theory must address the relationship between these levels.

An overemphasis on general theory stems from an endorsement of the first two propositions but from a neglect of the other six. Many past attempts to deal with the problem of historical specificity have failed because of a denial of the second proposition and a failure to understand the first. The thrust of the argument here is to establish and accept the first two propositions but also to move on to enforce the other six. It is in this latter zone that the historical argument has been relatively impoverished.

To some, the above propositions may be relatively uncontroversial. It is openly accepted here that the best of modern social science involves theorizing that combines some general principles with a specific domain of analysis. The trouble, however, is that typically the meta-theoretical bases for such combinations are inadequately articulated. Furthermore, many social scientists make unwarranted and exaggerated claims for general theory alone. To address the problem of historical specificity we require, simultaneously, more modest claims for general theorizing and a more sophisticated and illuminating meta-theoretical framework. This is the pressing theoretical agenda for economists and sociologists alike.

NOTES

1. This chapter is based on the author's plenary lecture in Berlin in 2000 and makes extensive use of material from Hodgson (2001). The author is very grateful to many people for discussions on its central theme. They are acknowledged more fully in the monograph, but particular mention should be made here of Uskali Mäki, who was an invaluable critic and discussant on the methodological theme of this essay. Hodgson (2001) is followed by a second companion volume, centring on the problem of agency and structure (Hodgson, 2004).
2. See, for example, David (1985, 1994), Dosi et al. (1988), Arthur (1989, 1994), North (1990), Hodgson (1993), Young (1996) and Garrouste and Ioannides (2001).
3. Twentieth century milestones in sociological theory – such as Talcott Parsons (1937), Robert Merton (1949), George Homans (1961), Peter Blau (1964), Jeffrey Alexander (1982–83), Anthony Giddens (1984), James Coleman (1990), Harrison White (1992) and Niklas Luhmann (1995) – are all general attempts to understand 'society', largely unconfined to any historically specific epoch or type of social structure.
4. See Sonnenschein (1972, 1973a, 1973b), Debreu (1974), Mantel (1974) and the discussions in Lavoie (1992, pp. 36–41), Rizvi (1994a) and Screpanti and Zamagni (1993, pp. 344–53).
5. Mirowski (1989) and Potts (2000) have characterised general equilibrium analysis as a mathematical 'field theory' where every point in space is connected with every other. Potts argued that, on the contrary, economic reality is characterised by limited interconnectedness, as in a lattice or network. Following the precedents of Kirman (1983, 1987), Bush (1983), Ellerman (1984) and Mirowski (1991), Potts saw mathematical techniques such as graph theory as an appropriate formalisation of the limited interconnectedness of this reality.
6. See, for example, Cutland (1980), Bennett and Landauer (1985) and Velupillai (1996, 2000).
7. For versions of philosophical realism in the social sciences see Archer (1995), Bhaskar (1979), Lawson (1997), Mäki (1989, 1990b, 1997, 1998, 2001) and Searle (1995).

REFERENCES

Alexander, Jeffrey C. (1982–3), *Theoretical Logic in Sociology*, 4 Vols. Berkeley, CA and London: University of California Press, Routledge and Kegan Paul.

Archer, Margaret S. (1995), *Realist Social Theory: The Morphogenetic Approach*, Cambridge: Cambridge University Press.

Arrow, Kenneth J. (1986), 'Rationality of self and others in an economic system', *Journal of Business*, **59** (4.2), October, S385–S399. Reprinted in John Eatwell, Murray Milgate and Peter Newman (eds) (1987), *The New Palgrave Dictionary of Economics*, Vol. 2, London: Macmillan.

Arthur, W. Brian (1989), 'Competing technologies, increasing returns, and lock-in by historical events', *Economic Journal*, **99** (1), March, 116–31.

Arthur, W. Brian (1994), *Increasing Returns and Path Dependence in the Economy*, Ann Arbor, MI: University of Michigan Press.

Bennett, Charles and Rolf Landauer (1985), 'The fundamental physical limits of computation', *Scientific American*, **253**, July, 48–56.

Bhaskar, Roy (1979), *The Possibility of Naturalism: A Philosophic Critique of the Contemporary Human Sciences*, 1st edn, Brighton: Harvester.

Blau, Peter (1964), *Exchange and Power in Social Life*, New York: Wiley.

Bush, Paul Dale (1983), 'An exploration of the structural characteristics of a Veblen-Ayres-Foster defined institutional domain', *Journal of Economic Issues*, **17** (1), March, 35–66.

Clower, Robert W. (1967), 'A reconsideration of the microfoundations of monetary theory', *Western Economic Journal*, **6**, 1–9. Reprinted in Robert W. Clower (ed.) (1969), *Monetary Theory*, Harmondsworth: Penguin.

Clower, Robert W. (1994), 'Economics as an inductive science', *Southern Economic Journal*, **60** (4), April, 805–14.

Clower, Robert W. (1999), 'Post-Keynes monetary and financial theory', *Journal of Post Keynesian Economics*, **21** (3), Spring, 399–414.

Coleman, James S. (1990), *Foundations of Social Theory*, Cambridge, MA: Harvard University Press.

Coricelli, Fabrizio and Giovanni Dosi (1988), 'Coordination and order in economic change and the interpretative power of economic theory', in Giovanni Dosi, Christopher Freeman, Richard Nelson, Gerald Silverberg and Luc L.G. Soete (eds) (1988), *Technical Change and Economic Theory*, London: Pinter, pp. 124–47.

Costa, Manuel Luis (1998), *General Equilibrium Analysis and the Theory of Markets*, Cheltenham, UK and Lyme, USA: Edward Elgar.

Cutland, Nigel J. (1980), *Computability: An Introduction to Recursive Function Theory*, Cambridge: Cambridge University Press.

David, Paul A. (1985), 'Clio and the economics of QWERTY', *American Economic Review (Papers and Proceedings)*, **75** (2), May, 332–7.

David, Paul A. (1994), 'Why are institutions the "Carriers of History"? Path dependence and the evolution of conventions, organizations and institutions', *Structural Change and Economic Dynamics*, **5** (2), 205–20.

Debreu, Gerard (1974), 'Excess Demand Functions', *Journal of Mathematical Economics*, **1** (1), March, 15–21.

Dosi, Giovanni, Christopher Freeman, Richard Nelson, Gerald Silverberg and Luc L.G. Soete (eds) (1988), *Technical Change and Economic Theory*, London: Pinter.

Ellerman, David P. (1984), 'Arbitrage theory: a mathematical introduction', *SIAM Review*, **26**, 241–61.

Fisher, Franklin M. (1989), 'Games economists play: a noncooperative view', *Rand Journal of Economics*, **20**, 113–24.

Garrouste, Pierre and Stavros Ioannides (eds) (2001), *Evolution and Path Dependence in Economic Ideas: Past and Present*, Cheltenham, UK and Northampton, MA, USA: Edward Elgar.

Giddens, Anthony (1984), *The Constitution of Society: Outline of the Theory of Structuration*, Cambridge: Polity Press.

Glymour, Clark (1980), 'Explanations, tests, unity and necessity', *Noûs*, **14** (1), March, 31–50.

Hahn, Frank H. (1980), 'General equilibrium theory', *The Public Interest*, special issue, 123–38. Reprinted in Frank H. Hahn (1984), *Equilibrium and Macroeconomics*, Oxford: Basil Blackwell.

Hahn, Frank H. (1988), 'On monetary theory', *Economic Journal*, **98** (4), December, 957–73.

Hodgson, Geoffrey M. (1993), *Economics and Evolution: Bringing Life Back Into Economics*, Cambridge, UK and Ann Arbor, MI: Polity Press and University of Michigan Press.

Hodgson, Geoffrey M. (2001), *How Economics Forgot History: The Problem of Historical Specificity in Social Science*, London and New York: Routledge.

Hodgson, Geoffrey M. (2004), *The Evolution of Institutional Economics: Agency, Structure and Darwinism in American Institutionalism*, London and New York: Routledge.

Homans, George C. (1961), *Social Behaviour: Its Elementary Form*, London: Routledge and Kegan Paul.

Kirman, Alan P. (1983), 'Communication in markets: a suggested approach', *Economics Letters*, **12**, 101–8.

Kirman, Alan P. (1987), 'Graph theory' in John Eatwell, Murray Milgate and Peter Newman (eds) (1987), *The New Palgrave Dictionary of Economics*, Vol. 2, London: Macmillan, 558–9.

Kirman, Alan P. (1989), 'The intrinsic limits of modern economic theory: the emperor has no clothes', *Economic Journal (Conference Papers)*, **99**, 126–39.

Kirman, Alan P. (1992), 'Whom or what does the representative individual represent?', *Journal of Economic Perspectives*, **6** (2), Spring, 117–36.

Kitcher, Philip (1981), 'Explanatory unification', *Philosophy of Science*, **48**, 507–31.

Kitcher, Philip (1989), 'Explanatory Unification and the Causal Structure of the World', *Minnesota Studies in the Philosophy of Science*, **13**, 410–505.

Lange, Oskar R. (1938), 'The rate of interest and the optimum propensity to consume', *Economica*, **5** (1), February, 12–32.

Lange, Oskar R. and Frederick M. Taylor (1938), *On the Economic Theory of Socialism*, Minneapolis: University of Minnesota Press.

Lavoie, Marc (1992), *Foundations of Post-Keynesian Economic Analysis*, Aldershot, UK and Brookfield, USA: Edward Elgar.

Lawson, Tony (1997), *Economics and Reality*, London: Routledge.

Lewontin, Richard C. (1991), 'Facts and the factitious in natural science', *Critical Inquiry*, **18** (1), 140–53.

Luhmann, Niklas (1995), *Social Systems*, translated from the German edition of 1984 by John Bednarz with a foreword by Eva M. Knodt, Stanford: Stanford University Press.

Mäki, Uskali (1989), 'On the problem of realism in economics', *Ricerche Economiche*, **43** (1–2), 176–98.

Mäki, Uskali (1990a), 'Mengerian economics in realist perspective', *History of Political Economy*, **22** (5), Annual Supplement on *Carl Menger and his Legacy in Economics*, 289–310.

Mäki, Uskali (1990b), 'Scientific realism and Austrian explanation', *Review of Political Economy*, **2** (3), November, 310–44.

Mäki, Uskali (1997), 'The one world and many theories', in Andrea Salanti and Ernesto Screpanti (eds) (1997), *Pluralism in Economics: New Perspectives in History and Methodology*, Cheltenham, UK and Lyme, USA: Edward Elgar, pp. 37–47.

Mäki, Uskali (1998), 'Aspects of realism about economics', *Theoria*, **13** (2), 301–19.

Mäki, Uskali (2001), 'Explanatory unification: double and doubtful', *Philosophy of the Social Sciences*, **31** (4), December, 488–506.

Malthus, Thomas Robert (1836), *Principles of Political Economy*, 2nd edn, London: Pickering. Reprinted 1986 (New York: Augustus Kelley).

Mantel, Rolf R. (1974), 'On the characterization of aggregate excess demand', *Journal of Economic Theory*, **12** (2), 348–53.

Merton, Robert K. (1949), *Social Theory and Social Structure*, 1st edn, Glencoe, IL: Free Press.

Mirowski, Philip (1989), *More Heat Than Light: Economics as Social Physics, Physics as Nature's Economics*, Cambridge: Cambridge University Press.

Mirowski, Philip (1991), 'Postmodernism and the social theory of value', *Journal of Post Keynesian Economics*, **13** (4), Summer, 565–82.

Nagel, Ernest (1961), *The Structure of Science*, London and Indianapolis: Routledge and Hackett Publishing.

North, Douglass C. (1990), *Institutions, Institutional Change and Economic Performance*, Cambridge: Cambridge University Press.

Parsons, Talcott (1937), *The Structure of Social Action*, 2 vols, New York: McGraw-Hill.

Potts, Jason (2000), *The New Evolutionary Microeconomics: Complexity, Competence and Adaptive Behaviour*, Cheltenham, UK and Northampton, MA, USA: Edward Elgar.

Rader, John Trout (1971), *The Economics of Feudalism*, New York: Gordon and Breach.

Radner, Roy (1968), 'Competitive equilibrium under uncertainty', *Econometrica*, **36** (1), January, 31–58.

Rizvi, S. Abu Turab (1994a), 'The microfoundations project in general equilibrium theory', *Cambridge Journal of Economics*, **18** (4), August, 357–77.

Rizvi, S. Abu Turab (1994b), 'Game theory to the rescue?', *Contributions to Political Economy*, **13**, 1–28.

Robbins, Lionel (1932), *An Essay on the Nature and Significance of Economic Science*, 1st edn, London: Macmillan.

Schumpeter, Joseph A. (1954), *History of Economic Analysis*, New York: Oxford University Press.

Screpanti, Ernesto and Stefano Zamagni (1993), *An Outline of the History of Economic Thought*, Oxford: Clarendon Press.

Searle, John R. (1995), *The Construction of Social Reality*, London: Allen Lane.

Smith, Adam (1976), *An Inquiry into the Nature and Causes of the Wealth of Nations*, originally published in 1776, edited by Roy H. Campbell and Andrew S. Skinner, London: Methuen.

Sonnenschein, Hugo F. (1972), 'Market excess demand functions', *Econometrica*, **40** (3), 549–63.

Sonnenschein, Hugo F. (1973a), 'Do Walras's identity and continuity characterize the class of community excess demand functions?', *Journal of Economic Theory*, **6** (4), 345–54.

Sonnenschein, Hugo F. (1973b), 'The utility hypothesis and market demand theory', *Western Economic Journal*, **11** (4), 404–10.

Thagard, Paul (1978), 'The best explanation: criteria for theory choice', *Journal of Philosophy*, **75**, 76–92.

Udéhn, Lars (1992), 'The limits of economic imperialism', in Ulf Himmelstrand (ed.) (1992), *Interfaces in Economic and Social Analysis*, London: Routledge, pp. 239–80.

Velupillai, Kumaraswamy (1996), 'The computable alternative in the formalization of economics: a counterfactual essay', *Kyklos*, **49**, Fasc. 3, 251–72.

Velupillai, Kumaraswamy (2000), *Computable Economics*, Oxford: Oxford University Press.

Weber, Max (1949), *Max Weber on the Methodology of the Social Sciences*, trans. and ed. by Edward A. Shils and Henry A. Finch, Glencoe, IL: Free Press.

White, Harrison C. (1992), *Identity and Control: A Structural Theory of Social Action*, Princeton: Princeton University Press.

Young, H. Peyton (1996), 'The economics of convention', *Journal of Economic Perspectives*, **10** (2), Spring, 105–22.

PART II

New light on rationality, social relations and
the environment

6. The irrationality of utility maximization or the *Death of a Salesman*

Irene van Staveren[1]

THE DEATH OF A SALESMAN

This chapter begins by analysing the rationality concept of neoclassical economics in terms of its implications for actual individual behaviour. The focus is on the characterization of rationality as utility maximization. If people would behave like 'rational economic man', maximizing their utility, would they lead a successful economic life (or even become happy as Bentham suggested)? Then the chapter suggests an alternative characterization of rationality, which would be more realistic – that is, ontologically founded in human behaviour – as well as more rational – that is, more coherent or consistent in its actual behavioural implications (for a set of interesting contributions to the ontology of rationality see also Uskali Mäki, 2001).

In addressing these questions about the irrationality of utility maximization, I have chosen an unusual methodology: a literary metaphor. A literary metaphor has the advantage of providing a character interacting with a social context in some coherent way (Kenneth Burke, 1945; Charles Taylor, 1992; Linda Alcoff, 1996), whereas the commonly used method to test behavioural assumptions in economics seems to be game theory, which often explicitly excludes social context, or even communication, from its experiments. Moreover, literary imagination has epistemological value, as Martha Nussbaum (1995a: xiii) has argued: 'story telling and literary imagining are not opposed to rational argument, but can provide essential ingredients in a rational argument'. Of course, there is a well-known use of literary metaphor in economics, with Daniel Defoe's novel *Robinson Crusoe* often employed to illustrate gains from trade.

The literary metaphor that I will use here is also about a lone man – not literally alone as was Robinson on his island, but alone in his dream of becoming a successful businessman. Our man here is Willy Loman, a salesman, trying to make his life on a smile and a shoeshine. He features in the theatre play *Death of a Salesman*, written by Arthur Miller and first performed in 1949. Willy is determined to maximize his utility through selling. Gradually, however, Willy finds himself failing in his tradings, without understanding what happens nor knowing how to get back into business again. He just holds on to his belief of ending up one day in 'big business', together with his sons. The harder he tries to increase his sales, the worse things get. The more ruthlessly he tries to maximize his utility, the unhappier he becomes. He tries everything to keep his contract, even betraying friendship and family life, until in the end life itself. Willy had only one role in life, which was selling: he derived all his self-esteem, pride and dreams from being a salesman. All other values in life were made subordinate to this ideal, traded off against expected business success. His preferences therefore can, in the neoclassical world, be represented by a smooth, concave, complete and transitive utility function.

Dreaming about the old days when his sons Biff and Happy were still small, Willy remembers how he used to come home from trips, telling his sons stories about his travels to New England (where he appears to have a mistress too – but that part he does not tell of course).

Willy instructs his boys to become businessmen, like himself, and shares his dreams with them.

> *Willy*: Because the man who makes an appearance in the business world, the man who creates personal interest, is the man who gets ahead. Be liked and you will never want. You take me for instance. I never have to wait in line to see a buyer. 'Willy Loman is here!' That's all they have to know, and I go right through.
> *Biff*: Did you knock them dead, Pop?
> *Willy*: Knocked 'em cold in Providence, slaughtered 'em in Boston.
> (Miller, 1949 [1976], p. 33).

Then Linda, Willy's wife, appears on the stage, inquiring about his earnings on the trip.

> *Willy*: I'm telling you, I was sellin' thousands and thousands, but I had to come home . . . I did five hundred gross in Providence and seven hundred gross in Boston.
> *Linda*: No! Wait a minute, I've got a pencil. That makes your commission . . . Two hundred – my God! Two hundred and twelve dollars!
> *Willy*: Well, I didn't figure it yet, but . . .
> *Linda*: How much did you do?
> *Willy*: Well, I – I did – about a hundred and eighty gross in Providence. Well, no – it came to – roughly two hundred gross on the whole trip.
> (Miller, 1949 [1976], pp. 34–5).

His friend Charley, aware of Willy's decreasing sales, takes pity on Willy. He walks in one night to play cards with him, offering not only his friendship but also a decent job to Willy. But Willy keeps turning down Charley's job offer. He does not want to admit that he failed. And worse, it would imply admitting that he never was a good salesman, hardly earning enough to make a modest living. All consumer goods they have are paid on credit, even the repairs are. Rather, Willy prefers to keep up appearances: 'Business is bad, it's murderous. But not for me, of course.' (Miller, 1949 [1976], p. 51). Meanwhile, Willy is borrowing money from his friend.

> *Charley*: How much do you need, Willy?
> *Willy*: Charley, I'm strapped, I'm strapped. I don't know what to do. I was just fired.
> *Charley*: Howard fired you?
> *Willy*: That snotnose. Imagine that? I named him. I named him Howard.
> *Charley*: Willy, when're you gonna realize that them things don't mean anything? You named him Howard, but you can't sell that. The only thing you got in this world is what you can sell. And the funny thing is that you're a salesman, and you don't know that.
>
> (Miller, 1949 [1976], p. 97).

Charley takes out more notes and gives them to Willy. On the verge of tears, Willy exclaims: 'Charley, you're the only friend I got. Isn't that a remarkable thing?' (Miller, 1949 [1976], p. 98). But he will never admit that his one-dimensional salesman dream is misleading. He simply cannot, because throughout his life he finds meaning in only this dream. Admitting the shallowness of it would come down to accepting the meaningless of his entire life. Even in the relationship with his wife, the education of his sons and his attitude toward his friend, he plays the role of the salesman, it makes up his identity. Willy is a salesman through and through, maximizing his utility through maximizing his (dreamed) trades. Not however, as a ruthless, self-interested profit maximizer, trying to mislead customers. Not at all: Willy's dream is to be liked as a salesman, to be respected as a salesman. Or, in Aristotelian terms: to be a *good* salesman in the ethical sense of the word. But in making everything else instrumental to this end, regarding every action as a trade, he did not realize that he became a tragic hero, pitiful rather than respectful, an unreliable personality to deal with. One by one, his customers turned their back on him.

Willy did not realize that in selling, you cannot demand respect from your clients when you do not respect others; you cannot expect people to become friends with you merely because you sell them stockings; you cannot expect to be liked merely because of your business success. The story of Willy Loman shows that these values simply *cannot* be realized through exchange. More importantly, the story reveals that these values are preconditions for being a good businessman, rather than tradables. Willy

Loman's unsuccessful career reveals that one cannot be a good salesman when one does not know how to respect people, how to make friends and how to smile genuinely to people, rather than merely for instrumental reasons. Values like respect, friendship and generosity cannot be traded but rather seem necessary conditions for success in trade. It seems, from the theatre play, that these values need to be generated and cherished intrinsically, for their own sake, before they will have a beneficial impact on exchange. But Willy's utilitarian reasoning does not allow for such values. Nor does his preference ordering allow him to admit his failure as a salesman. Instead he prefers to die, imagining the crowd of former business partners that would come to his funeral (but none of them came). Over his grave, Charley tried to make Willy's dream understandable:

> Nobody dast blame this man. You don't understand: Willy was a salesman. And for a salesman, there is no rock bottom to the life. He don't put a bolt to a nut, he don't tell you the law or give you medicine. He's a man way out there in the blue, riding on a smile and a shoeshine. And when they start not smiling back – that's an earthquake. And then you get yourself a couple of spots on your hat, and you're finished. Nobody dast blame this man. A salesman is got to dream, boy. It comes with the territory. (Miller, 1949 [1976], p. 138)

THE IRRATIONALITY OF UTILITY MAXIMIZATION

The salesman in Miller's play appears a remarkable embodiment of neoclassical economic man. He is way out there, alone, maximizing his individual utility in the market place just like 'rational economic man' is assumed to do (Martin Hollis and Edward Nell, 1975). 'Rational economic man', as well as Willy the salesman, has given ends and tries to maximize his utility by trading off different ends (material as well as moral ends such as friendship, respect, fatherhood and being a good husband) in his pursuit of becoming big in business. He does so even when the price of maximizing his preferences eventually becomes infinitely large – life itself. Within the neoclassical framework there seems nothing irrational about Willy's behaviour. He uses the scarce resources available (that is, his time, his smile and shoeshine) to maximize his sales. He does not or cannot adapt his preferences, even when his wife and his friend point out to him that it would be for the better. Arthur Miller's tragic embodiment of neoclassical economic man just set out to maximize his given preferences until the final end, comparing the marginal utility of life with the marginal utility of holding onto his dream of business success.

But all the people who watched the play over the past half century will not have escaped the impression that Willy's behaviour cannot be labelled as rational. Arthur Miller's masterful description of Willy's utilitarian behaviour and feelings makes his behaviour understandable, but not rational. It is not rational to choose death over a job offer. Nor is it rational to make important human values instrumental to selling, whereas at the same time expecting these values to continue to hold. It is not rational to raise your sons in a way that makes them unfit for the labour market when at the same time one wishes them to earn their own income. Nor is it rational to reject friendship when you need it most and to betray your wife when you claim to value faithfulness and respect.

The utilitarian foundation of neoclassical economics appears unable to detect rational from irrational behaviour, and to distinguish between a successful pursuit of an economic actor's ends and a failure to do so. How meaningful is a theory that explains the suicide of a salesman as rational behaviour? Utilitarianism, and its formalization in modern economics since the marginal revolution, assumes that at the margin all ends can be traded off against each other, because they are all measured on the single scale of utility. Choices may be difficult, yes, but thanks to a well-defined utility function they would always be optimal, given prevailing constraints.

Moral Preferences?

A neoclassical response to the critique of the utilitarian approach to rationality tries to integrate moral values into utility functions to account for immaterial ends. Gary Becker, for example, has taken up the idea of moral preferences in his *Accounting for Tastes* (1996). He accepts that such ends can no longer be assumed to be exogenous, as with preferences in standard neoclassical theory. At the same time, Becker holds onto the idea of individual utility maximization (1996, p. 4). In order to bring in endogenous ends in the utility function, reflecting moral preferences rather than preferences for material goods, he assumes that they are formed through past experience and the extent to which these values are shared by others, one's peer group. So, part of an individual utility function now becomes endogenous, depending on past behaviour and behaviour by others. Depending on time constraints, budget, and prices, a particular set of exogenous and endogenous preferences will be satisfied. The outcome will only be optimal over time when one chooses at time $t = 0$ the set of moral values that will provide maximum utility. If not, Becker argues, the choice would be irrational. So, the implication of Becker's extension of utility with moral preferences is that economic actors are assumed to calculate expected costs and benefits of moral values to select the morality that will maximize their individual utility. People would select those families, peer groups and neighbourhoods at birth, and hence, their moral preferences, that will generate the highest material and immaterial benefit over their lifetime. In other words, Becker turns moral values into an instrument for utility maximization, thereby destroying the very meaning of moral value.

I do not find this amended utilitarian explanation of human behaviour very persuasive. It is not convincing to assume that people acquire and write off moral values as they would do with goods and services such as shoes or insurances. We do not choose our parents, our peer group and our social class, or even our whole moral world view, as a means to maximize our utility – we simply find ourselves placed in these contexts and acquire, challenge and adapt our moral views in relation to this context. Apart from the practical limitations implied by his assumptions, Becker's proposal is theoretically inconsistent. It is incoherent to define moral and socially influenced values as intrinsic while at the same time treating them as instrumental.

It is no surprise to find that Becker's examples that should support his analysis are not convincing. He writes, for example, that 'people would not attend churches where they acquire norms that lower their utility unless they are compensated with sufficient benefits' (1996, p. 227). So, would people go to church because it delivers more utility than not going? And, if this utility is not enjoyed on earth, would their motive to go to church lie in the promise of a place in heaven? Becker ignores here the more obvious and well-researched reasons that people have to attend churches, namely habit, upbringing and a deep sense of religious belief. Human values are acquired in historical time and through social interaction, and are often experienced as self-evident, being part of one's identity. Human values are essentially ethical in nature and lose their meaning when they become instrumental to a higher end, even when this is loosely defined as 'utility'. Respect can only be attained through deserving it, not through buying it. Friendship can only be developed by trying to be a good friend, not for the expected utility to be derived from a friendship, as Aristotle explained so well. Recognizing the intrinsic ends implied in human values, utility functions no longer serve to explain economic behaviour. Utilitarianism seems no longer helpful for the explanation of individual behaviour, nor for the explanation of aggregate behaviour, as Amartya Sen (1999) argued so well in his Nobel Lecture. So, we have an answer to the question posed in the introduction: the utilitarian rationality concept does not seem to guide economic actors to economic success, let alone happiness. In fact, it does not appear rational at all.

The remainder of the chapter will be concerned with an alternative approach to rationality. I will start with a brief exploration in the next section (not doing justice to the richness of each of these contributions) of some responses that have been provided outside of neoclassical economics, and I will discuss a few problems with these approaches.

ECONOMIC ENDS, MORAL ENDS AND COMMITMENTS

Moral Ends Versus Economic Ends

One approach that has been proposed as an alternative to the uniform utilitarian perspective is founded upon a conceptual separation of moral motives from economic motives. Whereas utilitarian calculation is deemed valid for economic decisions, other decisions should be explained in a different manner, proponents of this approach argue. In *The Moral Dimension* Amitai Etzioni (1988) distinguishes two types of ends in human behaviour: moral ends and economic ends. Only the pursuit of economic ends can be analysed in a conventional utilitarian framework, he holds, since their objective is to generate pleasure. Moral ends should be analysed in a deontological framework of moral duty rather than utility maximization: they stem from people's moral principles, Etzioni argues (1988, pp. 41–2). Human behaviour consists of both types of motives, he asserts: pleasure and moral duty. But he does not explain how individuals decide between activities to pursue the one or the other type of ends. They are posed as a dualism, as two mutually exclusive categories. The question remains then how utility maximization relates to moral duty. Are moral principles to be understood as constraints on utility maximization, as in the new institutional economics (see for example Douglass North, 1990)? Or do moral principles define people's preferences, which thereby may become endogenous, as with Becker? Moreover, Etzioni ignores different types of moral values and restricts morality to rules and duties. Unfortunately, Etzioni does not go into these problems. Elizabeth Anderson (1993) follows with a similar approach in *Value in Ethics and Economics* but stresses that the moral ends that people pursue are diverse and hence, incommensurable.

The approach followed by Etzioni, Anderson and others is insightful and important, but also a bit misleading. First, it does not challenge utilitarianism in economics: it only limits it to less cases than the economics profession has become used to do. It limits economics to the study of people's material choices while leaving the study of non-material choices to philosophy. Second, and more fundamental, the approach rests on the crucial assumption that economic motives and moral motives, and economic ends and moral ends, are separate and can be analysed as separate forms of human behaviour. As if moral decisions do not apply to the allocation of scarce resources. And, as if economic decisions do not refer to the under-lying values that economic actors hold. Again, the play is illustrative. Charley offers his friend a job and Willy refuses, out of pride:

> *Charley*: You want a job?
> *Willy*: I got a job, I told you that. What the hell are you offering me a job for?
> *Charley*: Don't get insulted.
> *Willy*: Don't insult me.
> *Charley*: I don't see no sense in it. You don't have to go on this way.
> *Willy*: I got a good job. What do you keep comin' in here for?
> *Charley*: You want me to go?
>
> (Miller, 1949 [1976], p. 43).

> *Willy*: I – I just can't work for you, Charley.
> *Charley*: What're you, jealous of me?
> *Willy*: I can't work for you, that's all, don't ask me why.
>
> (Miller, 1949 [1976], pp. 97–8).

Mary Douglas and Baron Isherwood (1996) have shown the inadequacy of the dualistic assumption about economic motives and moral motives. Economic decisions often imply moral values, just like moral decisions cannot escape scarcity. Moral decisions involve the allocation of scarce resources as soon as these decisions are implemented in the real world. No one's time extends beyond 24 hours a day, which limits one's efforts to sustain friendships, to care for ill family members or to live up to one's prin-ciples of fairness. No tax revenue is high enough to do justice to all social needs that remain unfulfilled through the market process.

> Goods that minister to physical needs – food or drink – are no less carriers of meaning than ballet or poetry. Let us put an end to the widespread and misleading distinction between goods that sustain life and health and others that service mind and heart – spiritual goods. (Douglas and Isherwood, 1996, p. 49)

Commitment

In economics, this conclusion was drawn already by the Dutch welfare economist Pieter Hennipman in 1945. Economic ends and moral ends cannot be separated: they are closely intertwined. Moreover, as Anderson has pointed out for moral ends only, the ends that actors pursue in economic life are equally likely to encompass a wide diversity of moral con-siderations. They range from feeding one's family to creating new styles in modern dance, or from developing self-respect through financial independ-ence to the accumulation of scientific knowledge. Because of this diversity, stemming from different moral considerations, the ends that economic actors pursue cannot easily be assumed to be commensurable. The ends that actors pursue have value in themselves, they are pursued because they feel right, because they express the person one is or wants to become, as has been understood by some important contributors to economic methodology (Jon Elster, 1983; Nelson Goodman, 1983; Martin Hollis, 1987). If the ends were not intrinsically important, but preferences that can be traded off and among which one is indifferent, why would people try to satisfy a set of preferences that might require enormous efforts and resources? If it is just any set of given preferences they are happy to fulfil, 'rational economic men' would then go for the easiest set of preferences: they don't care *what* they maximize, as long as they maximize the set of preferences given to them. It may be much easier to satisfy preferences for potatoes than for caviar, or for a bicycle than for a Mercedes. If one would not value the ends themselves, why bother satisfying a given set of 'expensive' preferences whereas a different set of 'cheap' preferences might be easier to satisfy?

However in reality, as well as in Arthur Miller's play, people often feel attached to the ends they pursue; the ends are important to them and they care about their goals, which will often form part of their identity. The ends, in other words, reflect people's commitments. They are not instrumental to a commensurable higher goal as preferences are in a utility function. They cannot be traded off smoothly at the margin where one is assumed to be indifferent between one's ends.[2] Commitments are ends in themselves, each valued in their own right and in their own terms, not commensurable on a single, overall scale. Hence the pursuit of one's commitments involves a human will, a moral judgement in order to 'reconcile alternative points of view and different weighting of values', as Herbert Simon (1983, p. 85) has formulated it so well. Behaviour that is motivated by commitment thus implies deliberate choosing, rather than following fixed-decision rules as in rational choice theory. In fact rational choice theory, focusing on utility maximization, comes down to the calculation of a determinate outcome, excluding a human will (Thorstein Veblen, 1919; James Buchanan, 1969; Geoffrey Hodgson, 1988; Sen, 1995). An explanation of economic behaviour that relies on the notion of commitment, however, needs to address the human will and actors' capability to make real choices in an imperfect, uncertain world, rather than 'menu dependent' decisions (Sen, 1995, p. 385).

An important conclusion from these contributions to the literature on motivation and decision-making in economics is that economic interaction presupposes actors' adherence to human values. Without a commitment to human values, an economic actor will not be able to generate trust, nor will he be able to develop a reputation necessary for continued sales, for example, according to Robert Frank (1988). In the short run, without a commitment to human values an economic actor will not even be able to persuade someone else to engage in an exchange with him or her (Deirdre McCloskey, 1994a). Indeed, commitment and its intrinsic motivation has been suggested as a relevant concept for the explanation of economic behaviour by various economists, such as Amartya Sen (1977 and 1992), Jon Elster (1983 and 1992), Martin Hollis (1987), Robert Frank (1988), Richard Langlois and Lásló Csontos (1993), Bruno Frey (1997) and Lanse Minkler (1999).

In these and other writings about the role of commitment in economic behaviour, it is important to distinguish commitment from moral principles on the one hand, and from altruism on the other hand. Commitment is the valuation of an end for the end itself, like one values honesty for the sake of honesty or friendship for the sake of friendship, or courage for the sake of courage. Moral principles (referred to by Etzioni) are a particular kind of commitment, namely a commitment that can be characterized as a duty, a general rule one has to follow, no matter one's own costs and benefits (see also Lanse Minkler, 1999 who skilfully applies a Kantian interpretation to commitment in a formal utility/commitment function). There are however other types of commitment than those of moral duty, that are either of a more individualistic character, or responsive to particular others.

Another distinction that is important to make is between commitment and altruism. It is a common misunderstanding to assume commitment to be the same thing as altruism. But commitment is not altruism, or indeed the opposite of egoism. It does not follow the assumed dualism that economists have constructed between the two motives (see for critiques of such dualism Sheila Dow, 1990; Philip Mirowski, 1989; Julie Nelson, 1993 and 1996). Instead, commitment refers to the valuation of ends in themselves, not for one's own benefit (self-interest), nor for the exclusive benefit of someone else (altruism), but simply to further the value one is committed to. Acting upon one's commitments may be the most rational option to choose, even when one's self-interest or the interests of a beloved one are compromised (Amartya Sen, 1977 and 1992; Richard Langlois and Lásló Csontos, 1993). Just as we value honesty for the sake of honesty, not because it benefits us (sometimes it pays more to lie) or because it benefits a particular other (people who value honesty tend also to be honest towards persons they dislike or whom they simply do not know). An example provided by Amartya Sen (1992) may clarify the idea of commitment. His example is about a man who wants to stop a fight he sees on the street and gets hurt in the action. His jumping between the fighters is difficult to explain from self-interest: he will get hurt and will probably not leave behind the number of his bank account to receive a reward. He might feel embarrassed when people thank him afterwards. Nor can his behaviour be explained easily as stemming from altruism: it is not the fighters or one of them whom he intended to benefit. He probably does not know either of them and is probably not interested in getting to know them. Still, he is committed to stopping the fight. His decision stems not from self-interested preferences, nor from altruistic preferences, but from a commitment to values such as human integrity, justice or respect.

Intrinsic Motivation as Commitment

Bruno Frey (1997) develops the idea of commitment a bit further and elaborates its intrinsic motivation that derives from the end itself, not from outside. He argues that 'it is inconceivable that people are motivated solely or even mainly by external incentives' (p. ix), such as prices. In the real world, people are often motivated to do things because of the meaning it provides, that is, an intrinsic value. He gives examples about the labour market, arguing that it is not only wages that motivate workers to produce, but also intrinsic motivation that determines labour productivity. A major example that he does not mention lies however in unpaid labour: that clearly has no extrinsic motivation, at least not of a monetary kind (Nancy Folbre, 1995; Marga Bruyn-Hundt, 1996; Marilyn Waring, 1988). When economic actors are committed to the work they do, they will be motivated to do the job well, no matter whether one is a housewife, an account manager, an artist or a scientist.

> This, presumably, is why artists are artists, scientists scientists, and so on. They do not engage in art or science to get a thrill, but to 'get it right', and yet the thrill they get when they get it right strengthens their motivation to do this kind of work. (Elster, 1983, p. 107)

So, if commitment is what is needed to explain rational economic behaviour, how then can we explain the choices that economic actors make between different commitments, if they cannot be traded off along a single scale? Friendship and honesty, for example, are not valued along the same scale, nor are the love for one's son and the love for one's daughter.[3] So a proposal to substitute utility for commitment without explaining how choices among different commitments are made would be inadequate, since in a world of scarcity people have to make choices and these involve opportunity costs. In the next section I will suggest a direction in which an answer to this problem may be found. It is a first step that needs a lot more elaboration, both theoretically and empirically, so my suggestion should be interpreted as only tentative and exploratory, and not beyond.[4]

THE RATIONALITY OF THE MEAN: AN ARISTOTELIAN PERSPECTIVE

Aristotle's Virtue Ethics

How can incommensurable, intrinsic ends be furthered within the limits of scarcity and uncertainty? A possible answer should search for an ethical perspective that entails exactly these elements: incommensurability, intrinsic ends, scarcity and uncertainty. Aristotle's ethical theory provides such a perspective. In his theory developed in the *Nichomachean Ethics*, Aristotle defines valuable ends as virtues, as the good in life that is valuable in itself, which is of necessity plural, not commensurable. Contrary to utilitarianism, virtue ethics holds that ends are valuable in themselves and incommensurable, rather than contributing to a higher goal called utility. Aristotle mentions a list of virtues, such as courage, liberality, patience, pride, justice, equitability, friendliness and truthfulness (*Nichomachean Ethics* [1980], IV, pp. 1–9 and V, pp. 1–10). Virtue, Aristotle explains, implies decisions that are deliberate and voluntary, involving a human will within an uncertain context. The good is not a matter of maximization according to a fixed menu. Aristotle instead argues that the good is a mean between extremes, between excess and deficiency. This mean can be found only through careful deliberation and skilful interpretation of an uncertain context, in close interaction with others who are placed in a similar situation. So, rational decision-making in an Aristotelian sense is about finding a mean and not a maximum. Therefore, Aristotle admits, it is not easy to be virtuous, it implies a process of trial and error: 'So much then is plain, that the intermediate state is in all things to be praised, but that we must incline sometimes towards the excess, sometimes towards the deficiency; for so shall we most easily hit the mean and what is right' (*Nichomachean Ethics* [1980], p. 47).

A soldier is courageous, he explains, when he is neither a coward, trembling with fear, nor rash, running foolishly into the arms of the enemy. With this example Aristotle shows how virtue strikes a mean between too much and too little of a particular human value in relation to other human values. In this case, the mean of courage is found in relation to values such as respect, responsibility and self-esteem. Aristotle's definition of virtue seems to reflect what Sen, Elster, Frank and others have described as commitment: an end that is valuable in itself, not instrumental, and which cannot be traded off. Therefore, I suggest that commitment might be interpreted as virtue, in the Aristotelian sense (see also McCloskey, 1994b, on bourgeois virtue).

Aristotle admitted that there are numerous virtues, but mentioned only some that he considered to be most important in his days. Today, some philosophers try to list those virtues that are considered to be relevant in modern times. There are also attempts at developing an exhaustive, cross-cultural list of virtues (see, for example, Martha Nussbaum, 1995b). I will not go into these delicate issues, because it is not my purpose to define people's ends (the idea of a black box in economics has its attractions).

Three Economic Commitments

My intention is to analyse how commitments can be conceptualized in economic theory. What is the relationship between commitment and the allocation of scarce resources under uncertainty? Or what type of commitments, and the capabilities that belong to these, do actors in economic life need in order to allocate, in a rational manner, scarce resources over alternative uses? This is a question that requires an understanding of the possible types of allocation mechanisms that would help realize particular commitments. This is exactly what Adam Smith seemed to imply in his *Theory of Moral Sentiments.* He suggested that in social/economic life there are three major types of virtue that guide people's decisions: liberty (or prudence), justice (or propriety) and benevolence (or beneficence): 'Concern with our happiness recommends to us the virtue of prudence; concern for that of other people, the virtues of justice and beneficence; of which, the latter one retains us from hurting, the other prompts us to promote that happiness' (Adam Smith, 1759 [1984] Part VI, II, Conclusion, p. 262).

Smith implied in this book, but also in *The Wealth of Nations,* that an economy needs not only the virtues of the market (virtues belonging to liberty), but also the virtues of the state (virtues of justice) and the virtues of the 'moral sentiments' among the population (virtues of benevolence). According to Smith, these are the three types of virtue that guide behaviour in the economy: 'If virtue, therefore, does not consist in propriety, it must consist either in prudence or benevolence. Besides these three, it is scarce possible to imagine that any other account can be given of the nature of virtue' (ibid., p. 267).

Smith's ideas were repeated and elaborated by later economists and other social scientists, like Karl Polanyi (1944), Albert Hirschman (1970) and Kenneth Boulding (1970 and 1985). Each of the three types of commitment (or virtue) put forward as having economic relevance by these authors, belongs to one particular allocation mechanism (see Figure 6.1). Throughout economics, exchange is closely connected with liberty, expressed beautifully by Milton and Rose Friedman (1980) in their book *Free to Choose.* The relationship between distribution and justice has been analysed extensively in welfare economics and public finance, whereas the relationship between gift-giving and benevolence has hardly been analysed at all by

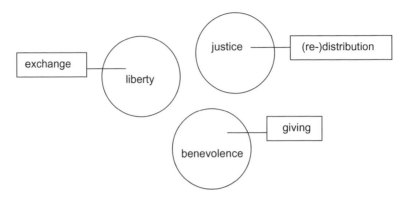

Figure 6.1   Commitments and allocation mechanisms

economists. Nevertheless, also on this relationship some writings can be found, both empirical studies (Richard Titmuss, 1970, on blood donation is a good example, Marilyn Waring, 1988, on women's unpaid household labour another one), and theoretical research with, again, Adam Smith's *Theory of Moral Sentiments* as a good starting point. From the literature after Adam Smith it appears that the relationship between commitments and allocation mechanisms is of a two-way kind. A commitment is expressed through an allocation mechanism, and at the same time a commitment brings about and supports a particular form of allocation. So liberty is furthered through free exchange, while at the same time free exchange furthers liberty, and similar for the other two commitments and respective allocation mechanisms. Justice is furthered through (re-)distribution of resources, whereas a (re-)distribution of resources will only develop when a society has a shared commitment to justice. Benevolence is furthered through gifts of time, energy and other resources among people, whereas such gifts will only prevail in a society that cherishes values of benevolence.

Commitment Balancing Rather than Utility Maximization

Yet the relationship between types of commitment and allocation mechanisms is more complex. The salesman was committed to liberty and sought to realize virtues that belong to liberty, such as pride, self-esteem and personal freedom. Nevertheless, he was not successful in market exchange. The problem was not that he was not committed enough to the virtues of the market. Rather, he was committed too much to liberty and too little to values of justice and benevolence. Or, in Aristotelian terms, he behaved in excess in trying to maximize his liberty, whereas he was deficient on the other values. He did not strike a mean between different values, but maximized only one, making respect, friendship and generosity instrumental to his single commitment to liberty. But locating all one's economic activities only in the market place results in behavioural deficiencies and, as a consequence, is not rational. One day, Willy's eldest son Biff realizes this bias in his father's dream and blames his father for having given him a wrong picture of economic life. Although in his thirties, Biff and his brother still depend on Willy, unable to keep a job and to earn themselves a living.

> *Biff*: And I never got anywhere because you blew me so full of hot air I could never stand taking orders from anybody! That's whose fault it is! . . . It's goddam time you heard that! I had to be boss big shot in two weeks, and I'm through with it!
>
> (Miller, 1949 [1976], p. 104).

So, the Aristotelian mean consists of a balance between deficiency and excess, in each set of commitments to liberty, justice, and benevolence. In order to know how to balance one's commitments, it is important to know what the deficiencies (and as a mirror image, the excesses) consist of. The deficiencies of one-dimensional behaviour are of two kinds. First, market failures necessitate that some ends are only to be attained when resources are allocated in a different way than through exchange; either through state redistribution or through care giving. Public goods and merit goods are well-known examples of state redistribution being preferable over market exchange, whereas raising one's children or the accumulation of social capital are generally better done through unpaid gifts of time and energy rather than through the market or the state. So the first type of deficiency is ignoring certain ends by ignoring the fact that they cannot be brought about by a single allocation mechanism. The second type of deficiency that arises from dealing exclusively with one type of commitment is that the ends represented by a commitment do need inputs from other types of commitment in order to come about. In the case of a single commitment to liberty values, market exchange cannot do without some redistribution and gifts. Without a minimum guarantee of justice, economic actors would not be willing to engage in an uncertain exchange (David Gauthier, 1977). And without any benevolence, leading to trust between economic actors, they will not be able to persuade each other into an exchange (Frank, 1988; McCloskey, 1994a). In other words, there will not be much exchange without some distribution and some benevolence around, even though economic actors, like Willy Loman, are strongly committed to the liberty values of the market.[5]

As a consequence, the existence of these two deficiencies of holding a single commitment and using a single allocation mechanism in the economy to further this commitment induce economic actors to compensate for these deficiencies. It is only rational to diversify one's activities over different commitments and allocation mechanisms given the inherent deficiencies of a single commitment and allocation mechanism. Rational economic actors will generally try to engage with a variety of commitments, and experience and learn their value, depending on the problems they see themselves confronted with. This experience will help them to develop some intrinsic motivation for each type of commitment, as in learning by doing, which will strengthen their commitment even further. In fact rational actors in real economic life, making their decisions in an imperfect world of uncertainty and interdependence with others, do look for compensations of the deficiencies of a one-dimensional set of goals. They learn to hold onto a diversity of commitments, addressing a wide variety of human needs, and they engage in other allocation mechanisms next to exchange: redistribution and giving. The implication is that the three economic domains distinguished by Adam Smith are to be regarded as complementary as well as interdependent (see Figure 6.2).

Now it becomes possible to explain why the salesman failed. He did not recognize this interdependence between types of commitments in the economy. He acted as if all of economic life is exchange, and as if the other values that he cherished (friendship, respect and generosity) could be realized through exchange as well. This misunderstanding reflects the irrationality of the salesman and is the source of his tragedy. It is also the irrationality of utility maximizing 'rational economic man'. Rational behaviour in a context of scarcity and uncertainty implies that individual economic actors choose for each end that they are committed to the allocation mechanism that will employ the least amount of scarce resources and at the same time will contribute most to the end one is committed to. So in order to find a job in the labour market it is not rational to write an

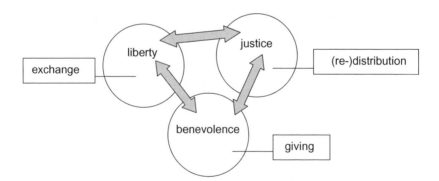

Figure 6.2   Interdependence between different commitments and allocation mechanisms

application letter arguing that one is entitled to this job based on some criterion of justice, rather than sending a CV. Or, to be taken care of in old age in a developing country without pension schemes, it is not rational to try to compete with younger and healthier workers in the labour market – one will certainly lose in the competition. More rational is to build and trust on one's lifelong relationships with one's family or local community, however meagre these may be.

Also, from a dynamic perspective, it is rational to develop capabilities in each area of allocation and commitment, rather than to specialize in only one, since circumstances as well as value commitments may change over time. A variety of capabilities will ensure that economic actors can deliberate over appropriate actions to be taken in each context and that they are able to interact with each other on the terms that are required by each type of commitment and allocation mechanism.

The Aristotelian Mean as Balancing Commitments

In the previous section, it was shown how economic actors will choose among different commitments, by referring to the deficiencies of holding onto a single commitment. First, not all ends that one may have can be satisfied through a single allocation mechanism, since each allocation mechanism has its limitations. Second, even when only one type of commitment is sought, this set cannot be satisfied because satisfaction of each type of commitment requires input from other commitments.

But there is a third, supportive 'mechanism' (in the Elsterian sense of a social mechanism) that contributes to the Aristotelian mean. This third mechanism does not operate at the individual level but at the aggregate level, as a 'synthetic aggregate' (Kevin Hoover, 2001, p. 230) connecting the different types of commitment. The mutually beneficial relations between each domain, filling mutual deficiencies (as illustrated in Figure 6.2) help to balance activities between the three complementary domains. The relations occur as unintended consequences of acting in one domain on the functioning of another domain. The diversity of capabilities that economic actors acquire helps them in their functioning in each domain. For such unintended beneficial effects, economics has a relevant concept: positive externalities. The positive effects of the respective domains of liberty/exchange, justice/redistribution and benevolence/giving on each other can be explained in terms of externalities since they do not occur intentionally but as a consequence of economic actors' multiple commitments, leading to the generation of a variety of capabilities. They are positive because they help to reduce the deficiencies inherent in each domain, while at the same time they help to limit possible excesses arising from a dominant domain.

The positive externalities from liberty/exchange on the other two domains are, for example, self-esteem and personal freedom.

These positive spillovers from liberal market exchange are important conditions for fair state distributions and for sustaining relationships between people in an economy. Without personal freedom, actors can only be forced to contribute to redistribution, making the costs of control very high. Without self-esteem, giving may easily lead to being exploited, affecting the quality of the care given. The positive externalities from justice/redistribution on the other two domains are, for example, rights and respect. Without property rights exchange will not be able to occur, since there is fundamental uncertainty over what can be exchanged by whom. Without respect, caring for others will soon be undermined, since the intrinsic motivation of caring for others will suffer. Finally, the positive externalities from benevolence/giving on the other two domains are, for example, trust and social capital. Without trust, transaction costs of exchange will be extremely high. Without social capital, government will not be deemed reliable for the provision of goods and services. So the positive spillovers between the three types of commitments and allocation mechanisms are an extra help for individual actors to find a balance between their commitments.

This idea of positive externalities of individual economic behaviour is similar to but not the same as Elster's idea of 'by-products', and Frey's idea of 'motivational spillovers'. Elster did not explain why a by-product occurs in the first place, and of what it is a side effect. Frey limits the concept of spillovers to motivation, arguing that motives for doing one thing may extend to doing (or not doing) other things. This is indeed how I have analysed the salesman's failure to commit himself to justice and to benevolence: he held on to motives and ends exclusively belonging to the domain of liberty/exchange. In an Aristotelian approach, the idea of externalities is extended to the mutually supportive effects of holding onto different commitments and acting through different allocation mechanisms, developing a range of capabilities in economic life. The balance that occurs between the different domains of economic interaction thus occurs endogenously, depending on the context in which individual actors are placed. This is a very different idea of equilibrium than Pareto optimality that follows from utilitarianism. An Aristotelian understanding of equilibrium as a mean rather than as an optimum is more complex, but at the same time more embedded in the type of economic processes that characterize an economy comprising markets, states and caring relations. The Aristotelian approach requires economists to understand the meaning of allocation mechanisms rather than only the mechanics of them.

CONCLUSION

The play *Death of a Salesman* has illustrated that the neoclassical notion of rationality is not likely to lead to rational behaviour by actors in economic life. The main character of the play did try to maximize his utility but his choices turned out to be unfortunate. The main obstacles in his psyche seemed to lie in the fixedness of his preferences, the belief in the market as the only suitable allocation mechanism in economic life, a deep faith in the values of the market at the cost of a commitment to other values, the illusion that all ends in life can be traded off at the margin, and a stubborn denial of uncertainty. These psychic characteristics of the salesman, however, happen to coincide with the character of 'rational economic man': exogenously given preferences, a belief in the free market as the major mechanism generating utility, a lack of human will but menu-dependent maximization, independent utility functions and perfect information. The tragic fate of the salesman has expressed the irrationality of these behavioural characteristics in a metaphorical way.

In a brief discussion about alternative formulations for the utilitarian characterization of rationality, the idea of moral preferences was rejected, as these are still subordinate to utility maximization. Another suggestion was found in the literature, on separating moral motives from economic motives, but here the problem appeared to be the artificial separation. In economic life many decisions are guided by the values that economic actors adhere to, while moral decisions cannot escape the world of scarcity. A third alternative was found in the notion of commitment, that is, the valuing of an end in itself rather than for instrumental reasons. Commitments escape the utilitarian framework, since they are by definition incommensurable; they cannot be traded off against each other. This idea was elaborated with the help of Aristotle's virtue ethics, since commitments and virtues appeared to be similar concepts. From Aristotle, the idea was borrowed that virtue is a contextual value, a mean between deficiency and excess, determined in a process of trial and error. For economic life, economists since Adam Smith have recognized three major commitments that guide economic behaviour: liberty, justice and benevolence. Regarding these as three distinct, incommensurable types of commitments that economic actors have, rational behaviour may be characterized as the trial- and error-process of finding a balance among these three commitments.

The idea of the Aristotelian mean between these three commitments suggests three mechanisms for finding a balance. First, each type of commitment and the allocation mechanism belonging to each type of commitment (market, state, gift) is deficient. Not all ends that actors pursue in life can be reached by a single allocation mechanism: they are complementary.

Second, even if only one type of commitment is chosen to be pursued in life, the other commitments need to be involved as well, since they are interdependent: they address the deficiencies in each other. Third, this balancing process benefits from external effects, through the spilling over of values from one domain to the others. It is these spillovers that help individual actors to find a balance and to adjust to changes.

Just before his father hangs himself, Biff realizes that if he wants to be happy and earn himself a decent living he has to break with his father's fantasy: 'Will you let me go, for Christ's sake? Will you take that phony dream and burn it before something happens?' (Miller, 1949 [1976], p. 133). Economists might want to take this metaphorical warning to heart: take the phony dream of 'rational economic man' and burn it . . .

NOTES

1. This chapter could not have been written without the wise advise, stimulating discussions and careful comments that I have received during the research for my PhD at Erasmus University Rotterdam in the period 1996–8. It is impossible to thank everyone involved, but here I do want to mention my thesis supervisor Arjo Klamer and special member of the committee Deirdre McCloskey, who have ensured the academic environment that I needed to develop my ideas. I also want to thank Diane Elson, Nancy Folbre, Fieke van der Lecq and Julie Nelson, who have supported my research in various ways. Last but not least, thanks go to the editors of this book for their helpful comments.
2. This characteristic of commitment shows why commitments cannot be turned into moral preferences, as Becker tried to do in his utilitarian approach.
3. Parents will recognize how difficult it is to answer one's children's question about whom of them is loved most. An answer that assumes that such a choice can be made is inevitably painful and generally not deemed to reflect good parenthood.
4. See also van Staveren, 2001.
5. Even economists like Milton Friedman and Friedrich Hayek acknowledge this (see van Staveren, 2001, pp. 27–32).

REFERENCES

Alcoff, Linda (1996), *Real Knowing. New Versions of the Coherence Theory*, Ithaca, NY: Cornell University Press.
Anderson, Elizabeth (1993), *Value in Ethics and Economics*, Cambridge, MA: Harvard University Press.
Aristotle [1980] *Nichomachean Ethics*, Oxford: Oxford University Press. Trans. by David Ross, revised by J.L. Ackrill and J.O. Urmson.
Becker, Gary (1996), *Accounting for Tastes*, Cambridge, MA: Harvard University Press.
Boulding, Kenneth (1970), *A Primer on Social Dynamics. History of Dialectics and Development*, New York: Free Press.
Boulding, Kenneth (1985), *The World as a Total System*, Beverly Hills, CA: Sage.

Bruyn-Hundt, Marga (1996), *The Economics of Unpaid Work*, Amsterdam: Thesis Publishers.

Buchanan, James (1969), 'Is economics the science of choice?', in Erich Streissler (ed.), *Roads to Freedom. Essays in Honour of Friedrich A. von Hayek*, London: Routledge, pp. 47–64.

Burke, Kenneth (1945), *A Grammar of Motives*, New York: Prentice-Hall.

Douglas, May and Baron Isherwood (1996), *The World of Goods. Towards an Anthropology of Consumption* [1979], London: Routledge.

Dow, Sheila (1990), 'Beyond dualism', *Cambridge Journal of Economics*, **14**, 143–57.

Elster, Jon (1983), *Sour Grapes. Studies in the Subversion of Rationality*, Cambridge: Cambridge University Press.

Elster, Jon (1992), *Local Justice: How Institutions Allocate Scarce Goods and Necessary Burdens*, Cambridge: Cambridge University Press.

Etzioni, Amitai (1988), *The Moral Dimension. Toward a New Economics*, New York: The Free Press.

Folbre, Nancy (1995), 'Holding hands at midnight: the paradox of caring labour', *Feminist Economics*, **1**, 73–92.

Frank, Robert (1988), *Passions within Reason. The Strategic Role of the Emotions*, New York: W.W. Norton.

Frey, Bruno (1997), *Not Just for the Money. An Economic Theory of Personal Motivation*, Cheltenham, UK and Lyme, USA: Edward Elgar.

Friedman, Milton and Rose (1980), *Free to Choose. A Personal Statement*, New York: Harcourt Brace Jovanovich.

Gauthier, David (1977), 'The social contract as ideology', *Philosophy and Public Affairs*, **2**, 130–64.

Goodman, Nelson (1983), 'Notes on the well-made world', *Erkenntnis*, **19**, 99–107.

Hennipman, Pieter (1945), *Economisch Motief en Economisch Principe*, Amsterdam: Noord-Hollandse Uitgevers Maatschappij.

Hirschman, Albert (1970), *Exit, Voice, and Loyalty: Responses to Decline in Firms, Organisations, and States*, Cambridge, MA: Harvard University Press.

Hodgson, Geoffrey (1988), *Economics and Institutions. A Manifesto for a Modern Institutional Economics*, Cambridge: Polity Press.

Hollis, Martin (1987), *The Cunning of Reason*, Cambridge: Cambridge University Press.

Hollis, Martin and Edward Nell (1975), *Rational Economic Man*, Cambridge: Cambridge University Press.

Hoover, Kevin (2001), 'Is macroeconomcis for real?', in Uskali Mäki (ed.), *The Economic World View. Studies in the Ontology of Economics*, Cambridge: Cambridge University Press, pp. 225–45.

Langlois, Richard and Lásló Csontos (1993), 'Optimisation, rule-following, and the methodology of situational analysis', in Uskali Mäki, Bo Gustafsson and Christian Knudsen (eds), *Rationality, Institutions, and Economic Methodology*, London: Routledge, pp. 113–32.

Mäki, Uskali (ed.) (2001), *The Economic World View. Studies in the Ontology of Economics*, Cambridge: Cambridge University Press.

McCloskey, Deirdre (1994a), *Knowledge and Persuasion*, Cambridge: Cambridge University Press.

McCloskey, Deirdre (1994b), 'Bourgeois virtue', *American Scholar*, **63**, 177–91.

Miller, Arthur (1949), *Death of a Salesman* [1976], London: Penguin Books.
Minkler, Lanse (1999), 'The problem with utility: toward a non-consequentialist theory synthesis', *Review of Social Economy*, **57**, 4–24.
Mirowski, Philip (1989), *More Heat than Light. Economics as Social Physics: Physics as Nature's Economics*, Cambridge: Cambridge University Press.
Nelson, Julie (1993), 'Value-free or valueless? Notes on the pursuit of detachment in economics', *History of Political Economy*, **25**, 121–45.
Nelson, Julie (1996), *Feminism, Objectivity, and Economics*, London: Routledge.
North, Douglass (1990), *Institutions, Institutional Change and Economic Performance*, Cambridge: Cambridge University Press.
Nussbaum, Martha (1995a), *Poetic Justice. The Literary Imagination and Public Life*, Boston: Beacon Press.
Nussbaum, Martha (1995b), 'Human capabilities, female human beings', in Jonathan Glover and Martha Nussbaum (eds), *Women, Culture, and Development. A Study of Human Capabilities*, Oxford: Clarendon Press, pp. 61–104.
Polanyi, Karl (1944), *The Great Transformation*, New York: Rhinehart.
Sen, Amartya (1977), 'Rational fools: a critique of the behavioural foundations of economic theory', *Philosophy and Public Affairs*, **6**, 317–44.
Sen, Amartya (1992), *Inequality Re-examined*, Oxford: Clarendon Press.
Sen, Amartya (1995), 'The formulation of rational choice', *American Economic Review*, **84**, 385–90.
Sen, Amartya (1999), 'The possibility of social choice', *American Economic Review*, **89**, 349–78.
Simon, Herbert (1983), *Reason in Human Affairs*, Oxford: Basil Blackwell.
Smith, Adam (1759), *The Theory of Moral Sentiments* [1984], Indianapolis: Liberty Fund.
Staveren, Irene van (2001), *The Values of Economics. An Aristotelian Perspective*, London, Routledge.
Taylor, Charles (1992), *Philosophy and the Human Sciences* (Philosophical Papers 2), Cambridge: Cambridge University Press.
Titmuss, Richard (1970), *The Gift Relationship – From Human Blood to Social Policy*, London: Allen & Unwin.
Veblen, Thorstein (1919), *The Place of Science in Modern Civilisation. And Other Essays* [1961], New York: Rusell & Rusell.
Waring, Marilyn (1988), *If Women Counted*, New York: Harper Collins.

7. Social capital or sociality? Methodological contrasts between economics and other social sciences

Desmond McNeill

INTRODUCTION

By reference to the two concepts of 'social capital' and 'sociality', my purpose in this chapter is to explore the middle ground between economics and its polar opposite in the social sciences–anthropology. The longstanding methodological debate within the social sciences between what I shall for simplicity call the economic and the anthropological perspectives has been renewed in recent years by the concept of 'social capital' being actively taken up – by economists, political scientists and sociologists. This has focused attention again on the differences between alternative perspectives, and the prospects of finding a substantive synthesis, a coherent 'middle ground' between the two extremes. A common way of distinguishing these two extremes is between 'methodological individualism' and 'methodological holism'. I shall seek also to draw attention to other, related, distinctions: between entities and relations, and between alternative notions of rationality.

I begin by reviewing the methodological approach of economics. I then turn to the concept of social capital, and assess whether this concept – with its focus on networks and norms – represents progress in methodological terms. I conclude that on the evidence so far it does not. In the next two sections I explore two very different approaches, based on the concept of 'sociality', first as an empirical phenomenon (in child psychology) and then as an analytical concept (in anthropology), and indicate how these might provide more promising grounds for methodological innovation. First, I explore a reformist position, where the analytical focus remains on individuals but where their innate drive is not autonomous self-interest, but a drive to connect with other individuals. Second, I explore a radical position, where the analytical focus shifts from entities to relations. The latter is largely unexplored territory, and raises rather basic questions (for example, as to whether rules can constitute a fundamental motivating force). I conclude by considering, in broad terms, how the two approaches derived from 'sociality' compare with what might be called the middle ground of economic sociology, as summarized in terms of the concepts of the actor and rational action.

ECONOMICS AND THE SOCIAL SCIENCES

In the introduction to his book *Philosophy and the Human Sciences*, the philosopher Charles Taylor provides an excellent analysis of the state of the social sciences. He is critical of those theories that seek to emulate the natural sciences, for their reductive nature and their allegiance to what he calls 'naturalism':

> Because behind and supporting the impetus to naturalism . . . stands an attachment to a certain picture of the agent. This picture is deeply attractive to moderns, both flattering and inspiring. It shows us as capable of achieving a kind of disengagement from our world by objectifying it. . . . The ideal of disengagement defines a certain – typically modern – notion of freedom, as the ability to act on one's own, without interference or subordination to outside authority. . . . The great attraction of these ideals, all the more powerful in that this understanding of the agent is woven into a host of modern practices – economic, scientific, technological, psycho-therapeutic, and so on – lends great weight and credence to the disengaged image of the self. The liberation through objectification wrought by the seventeenth century has become for many the model of the agent's relation to the world, and hence sets the very definition of what is to be an agent. (Taylor, 1985, pp. 4–5)

This is the approach of economics that takes as its starting point *homo economicus*: rational, self-interested and autonomous.[1] Outside economics, but still within the individualistic mode, we find Jon Elster, another major contributor to the methodological debate in the social sciences. He too notes the 'persistent cleavage' in the social sciences between *homo economicus* and *homo sociologicus*: the former guided by instrumental rationality and the latter by social norms. But he argues that the distinction between rationality and social norms 'does not coincide . . . with the distinction between methodological individualism and a more holist approach', and he seeks to develop a theory of social norms within a wholly individualist framework. For him a norm is 'the propensity to feel shame and to anticipate sanctions by others at the thought of behaving in a certain, forbidden, way' (Elster, 1989, p. 105).

To develop this individualist approach to social norms has been a major project for Elster in the last ten years. Indeed, to judge from his recent book, his position is now more extreme than it was in 1989:

> I have argued elsewhere that social norms are an immensely powerful influence on behaviour. I now think, however, that I had the emphasis somewhat wrong. . . . Roughly, I now think that the emotion of shame is not only a support of social norms, but *the* support. (Elster, 1999, p. 145)

Thus, though emphasizing the importance of social norms and willing to abandon the rationality assumption, Elster nevertheless takes up a position which is individualistic/psychological.

Also, outside economics we find the philosopher Hollis: within the rationality mode, but open to a less individualistic approach. Hollis has 'a simple conviction that people act for the most part, rationally and that the social sciences depend on it' (Hollis, 1996, p. 1). But he does not favour an extreme economic position, based on rational choice theory, which 'bleaches out' not only the social but even psychology, replacing it by logic alone. He identifies three alternative ways to go:

> One is to restore some explicit psychology to flesh out the schematic character of preferences. The second is to restore instrumental rationality as the primary or only definition of rationality worth relying on. The third is to challenge the individualism which pervades the game-theoretic treatment of social interaction as a sum of strategic choices by rational individuals. (Hollis, 1996, p. 6)

In assessing the first alternative Hollis distinguishes between psychological and philosophical egoism. The former is that associated with economics.[2] Philosophical egoism, by contrast, 'has room for a more generous psychology which can credit us with less selfish passions, like sympathy for others, love of our fellows or altruistic concern' (ibid.).

Hollis's second alternative is to challenge the primacy of instrumental reason, allowing for a less stringent interpretation of rationality that is in keeping with Kant's idea that, at least in moral matters, it is rational to act on a relevant and universal maxim, like 'everyone should keep their promises'. Hollis's third alternative is to replace the atomic individuals of the standard model with agents who are essentially social: '*Homo sociologicus* takes the stage' (ibid, p. 8). He finds shortcomings in all three possible approaches but rejects combining them, arguing that they are incompatible – they pull in two directions:

> One (direction) is towards a universal standpoint from which to judge whether an agent had acted, prudently or morally, on rational preferences or as anyone so placed would rationally act. The other is towards recognizing that reasons for action are relative to roles and contexts, thus suggesting that rationality can be a matter of following a local rule in an appropriate way. (ibid., p. 13)

Thus Hollis, too, identifies a wide gap between two extreme approaches in the social sciences, which he refers to as 'the universal and the relative'. But he sees no place for a synthesis between them, even on the basis of modified versions of rational choice game theory.[3]

I agree with Hollis's criticism of the first approach (although I would note that rules concerning behaviour towards others need not necessarily be portrayed as altruism). I also agree with his doubts about the second approach (although the impetus toward 'moral' action, in a Kantian sense, need not be termed 'rationality'). I therefore build on his third approach, as I shall elaborate on here.

In rejecting an extreme reductionist approach and seeking a middle ground, it is important not to go too far the other way; as Taylor notes when he warns against the other extreme, of postmodernists such as Derrida:

> The kind of critique we need is one that can free it (the disengaged identity) of its illusory pretensions to define the totality of our lives as free agents, without attempting the futile and ultimately destructive task of rejecting it altogether. (Taylor, 1985, p. 7)

He identifies one of the most negative features of the modern identity as 'atomism', which conceals how an individual 'is constituted by the language and culture which can only be maintained and renewed in the communities he is part of' (Taylor, 1985, p. 8).

> The community is not simply an aggregate of individuals nor is there simply a causal interaction between the two. The community is also constitutive of the individual, in the sense that the self-interpretations which define him are drawn from the interchange which the community carries on. A human being alone is an impossibility, not just de facto, but as it were *de jure*. (Taylor, 1985, p. 8)

The challenge is to conceptualize this mutuality between the individual and the community. In recent years, there has been a sudden interest in this topic among political scientists and economists, drawing on the work of sociologists and focused on the new concept of social capital. One might hope that this would contribute to our understanding, and in the next section I shall briefly review the status of theory and methodology here.

ECONOMICS: SOCIAL CAPITAL

The last five to ten years have witnessed a very rapidly growing literature on social capital, thanks mainly to its being adopted by the political scientist Robert Putnam in his book *Making Democracy Work* (1993), a comparative study of Northern and Southern Italy. Among economists its appeal has been especially in the field of development studies, thanks largely to the efforts of the World Bank; but it has also been used in other fields such as management studies and social planning.

Its appeal may be explained in part by its fitting the prevalent concern, especially in USA, with 'loss of community'.[4] (Indeed, it was another article by Putnam, 'Bowling Alone' (Putnam, 1995), which hit the headlines in Washington.) Another reason for its appeal, at least in the World Bank, is that it appears to provide not only an analytical tool but also a concept that can be used directly in policymaking.[5]

Putnam takes the term from the sociologist James Coleman,[6] who, in his seminal paper from 1988, expressly adopts a methodological individualist perspective (Coleman, p. 20). His task, he says, is to make a revisionist analysis of the functioning of economic systems: 'to maintain the conception of rational action but to superimpose on it social and institutional organization – either endogenously generated, as in the functionalist explanations of some of the new institutional economics, or as exogenous factors, as in the more proximate-causally oriented work of some sociologists' (ibid, p. 15).

To assist in this purpose, he adopts the concept of social capital, which, unlike other forms of capital, 'inheres in the structure of relations between actors and among actors' (ibid, p. 16). 'The value of the concept of social capital lies first in the fact that it identifies certain aspects of social structure by their functions. . . . [namely] the value . . . to actors as resources that they can use to achieve their interest' (ibid, p. 19). 'Actors establish relations purposefully and continue them when they continue to provide benefits. . . . Norms arise as attempts to limit negative external effects or encourage positive ones' (ibid, p. 23).

From these few quotations it is clear that Coleman adopts a perspective closely akin to that of economics. Indeed, he concludes by saying that 'This [paper] is part of a theoretical strategy that involves the use of the paradigm of rational action but without the assumption of atomistic elements stripped of social relations' (ibid, p. 36). In other words, he seeks to retain the rationality paradigm, but without, perhaps, the assumption of autonomy. And he asserts the importance of relations. Yet his notion of social relations, and social norms, clearly derives from an individualistic and self-interested perspective.

There are other definitions of social capital, both narrower and broader. According to the World Bank, the most narrow one is associated with Putnam, and for analytical purposes I prefer to adopt this more narrow definition.[7] The appeal of Putnam's work, to economists, was that it seemed to provide a new explanatory factor in economic growth.[8] The main thesis of Putnam's book is that community, trust and shared values are 'a good thing' – as demonstrated by a comparison between the economic fortunes of Northern and Southern Italy. His book, he claims, 'helps explain why social capital, as embodied in horizontal networks of civic engagement, bolsters the performance of state and economy' (Putnam, 1993). Encapsulated in a single sentence, Putnam's thesis is: 'strong society, strong economy; strong society, strong state' (Putnam, 1993, p. 176). This position he contrasts with two others that have recently made some impact on the state–society–market debate. First, that of Mancur Olson: 'strong society, weak economy' and second, Joel Migdal: 'strong society, weak state'.

But what exactly does Putnam mean by social capital? He says that it 'refers to features of social organization, such as trust, norms and networks, that can improve the efficiency of society by facilitating coordinated action' (ibid, p. 167). He thus moves swiftly from social capital itself to trust, norms and networks, which he also refers to as 'forms', or 'stocks', or 'components' of social capital. Trust, he says, is an essential component of social capital. And he further distinguishes between 'thick' trust and 'thin' trust, by which he means personal trust, based on individual relations, and social trust, where individuals do not necessarily know each other. The second of these is especially important because he sees it as part of the key to 'community'; it is also, of course, more difficult to explain from an individualistic standpoint. How does such trust come to be and how can it persist over time? To explain this, he turns to the other two forms of social capital: 'Social trust in complex modern settings can arise from norms of reciprocity and networks of civic engagement' (ibid, p. 171).

Norms, in his words, undergird social trust; and the most important norm is reciprocity, which may be specific or generalized. Such norms are closely linked to networks of civic engagement or of commerce and exchange: 'An effective norm of generalized reciprocity is likely to be associated with dense networks of social exchange. . . . Conversely, repeated exchange over a period of time tends to encourage the development of a norm of generalized reciprocity' (ibid, p. 172). And networks are also of two kinds, horizontal or vertical ('weblike' or 'maypolelike'), 'bringing together agents of equivalent status and power, or unequal agents in asymmetric relations of hierarchy and dependence' (ibid, p. 173).

To summarize: Putnam argues the merits of social trust, based on norms of generalized reciprocity built up and maintained over time through numerous contacts among persons of equivalent status and power. So 'what is new?' one may ask – at least if one is a well-read student of social relations. Is this an advance in either methodological or empirical terms? The answer is likely to vary according to one's disciplinary perspective.

While being largely welcomed by many political scientists and sociologists,[9] the concept of social capital has found less favour in what I would call the extreme wings of the social sciences: anthropology and economics. Anthropologists outside the field of development studies have effectively ignored it (McNeill, 2006). Even within development studies, those that refer to it tend to see it as an unnecessary and even unwelcome concept, which at best presents well-established concepts in new (economic) garb, and at worst distorts such concepts, in a simplistic and reductionist manner (for example, Jul-Larsen, 1999).

Economists have been more active in their response; partly because they have been urged to do so thanks to the initiatives of the World Bank, which has in recent years undertaken two major research programmes, organized conferences and produced numerous publications on this topic. The criticisms levelled against the concept from economics are, of course, very different. Some of these are to be found in the World Bank volume *Social Capital: A Multifaceted Perspective* (Dasgupta and Serageldin, 1999), which arose out of an initiative by Ismail Serageldin, a Vice-President of the World Bank, to invite a number of prominent academics to give their views on the concept. The authors of the book note that 'it is difficult to think of an academic notion that has entered the common vocabulary of social discourse more quickly than the idea of social capital'. But they add that, 'while the term has gained wide currency, it has not found favour among economists' (ibid, p. x).

In his chapter of the book, the Nobel Prize winning economist Arrow recognizes the importance of social networks but rejects the term 'social capital', mainly because it fails to satisfy the requirement of capital of 'deliberate sacrifice in the present for future benefit' (Arrow 1999, p. 4). Another Nobel Prize winner, Solow, also doubts that social capital is the right term to describe the important phenomenon under discussion, namely 'behaviour patterns' such as 'trust, the willingness and capacity to cooperate and coordinate, the habit of contributing to a common effort even if no-one else is watching . . .' (Solow, 1999, p. 7). He notes that economists try but often fail to analyse everything in terms of rationality and individual greed, and adds: 'Patterns of behaviour, of acceptable and expectable behaviour, start off as social norms, enforced by parental pressure or peer pressure or religious instruction, or in some other way, and are eventually internalized' (ibid, p. 8).

The then Chief Economist of the World Bank, Stiglitz, is rather more positive about the concept, relating it to a hypothesized evolution (the process of modernization?): 'a change from a situation in which economic activity is embedded in social relations, to one in which social relations are embedded in the economic system' (Stiglitz, 1999, p. 65).

In the concluding chapter of the book (which contains contributions also from sociologists and political scientists), another reputed economist (and co-author of the book), Dasgupta, seeks to give a provisional verdict on the merits of the term. He concludes that Putnam's characterization of social capital suffers from a weakness: 'it encourages us to amalgamate incommensurable objects, namely (and in that order), beliefs, behavioural rules and such forms of capital assets as interpersonal networks . . . One of my intentions here is to show that they cannot be amalgamated' (Dasgupta, 1999, p. 327).

I agree that this is the challenge that Putnam faces, but I disagree with the way in which it is here formulated. By referring to 'beliefs, behavioural rules and interpersonal networks' as 'objects' Dasgupta, I suggest, exemplifies the limitations of an economic approach. He does, however, have interesting things to say about trust, which, like other dispositions, 'is to a greater or lesser extent formed through communal living, role modeling, education and receiving rewards and punishments. The process begins at the earliest stages of our lives' (ibid, p. 339). In a footnote he refers to literature in psychology which 'contain accounts of what is currently known of the development processes through which people from their infancy acquire prosocial dispositions – for example by learning to distinguish accidental effects from intentional effects of others' actions' (ibid, p. 339). I argue in this chapter that we may usefully draw on psychology for an understanding of the processes whereby such dispositions come about but I refer to different studies, which comes to rather different conclusions. The challenge, as I see it, is precisely to link norms and networks, which I see as mutually constitutive, in a process that – for the individual person – begins at birth.

In summary, the weakness of the concept of social capital, as judged by economists, seems to lie not so much in the 'social' as in the 'capital'. Commentators such as Arrow and Solow recognize that the phenomenon in question ('norms and networks') is important, not least because it has an impact on economic phenomena, such as an individual or group's material well-being. But they doubt whether our understanding of the phenomenon is enhanced by regarding it as capital. My own view is similar, and perhaps more critical. Economists may be able to improve our understanding of how social networks and norms contribute to economic well-being, but they have far less to offer when it comes to 'norms and networks' as such. The problem is that the economic perspective on this phenomenon – the rational, individualistic approach – does not add much to our understanding; indeed, it may even detract from it.

In his scathing study of the concept of social capital, Fine (2001) deals at some length with economists' usage of the term. Before social capital was invented, he asserts, 'it was necessary to take the social, institutions and customary behaviour as given, with the latter taken to be irrational. Now, even on the continuing basis of methodological individualism, this need no longer be the case' (Fine, 2001, p. 10). He sees the adoption of the term by economists as yet another example of its colonization of the social sciences, and draws some 'harsh and general' conclusions about how economics proceeds in such circumstances:

> First, it tends to be parasitical on the other social sciences, picking up ideas that have originated there and reworking them through the new economic principles. . . . Second, contributions are often profoundly ignorant of existing literature . . . From an analytical perspective, however, the most important feature of economics' incursion into other social sciences is its reductionism. (ibid, p. 11)

Although some of these comments are well placed, it is fair to lay blame also on sociologists, such as Coleman: and to note that some economists – such as Arrow and Solow – are sceptical, as shown here. The problem, I suggest, is that other economists have – thanks to the efforts of the World Bank – allowed themselves to be 'bumped' into this arena, leading to inadequately researched 'middle-level theorizing' of an a priori character. The urge to establish the credentials of the concept in economic terms, and to 'operationalize' it, have led to its being adopted before it has proved adequate to the task. Certainly one can find evidence here for Fine's claim that economists writing about social capital have tended to ignore the existing literature from other disciplines. In the World Bank publications there are very few references to anthropology, most are to sociology and political science; this despite a massive empirical literature in anthropology concerned with communities and a significant theoretical literature concerning social networks dating back to the 1970s.[10]

Whether or not one chooses to use the term social capital, the conceptual and methodological challenge that we face is to analyse a combination of 'norms and networks' (as Putnam defines it), or, even more abstractly, a combination of a set of relations and the set of beliefs/meanings about them. It is – I suggest – impossible to separate social relations from the beliefs/meanings about them; they have no independent existence (see discussion of Taylor in the previous section).[11] In this sense they are mutually constitutive. But that should not necessarily mean that they are impossible to conceptualize; merely that in our search for the tools we require we will need to look outside the 'reductionist' toolbox.

We may, I suggest, find inspiration for this task in two very different sources of literature (from child psychology and anthropology) and two closely linked concepts (intersubjectivity and sociality). It is to these that I now turn.

INTERSUBJECTIVITY: CHILD PSYCHOLOGY

In this section I wish to radically challenge the assumption of 'autonomy' in the model of *homo economicus*; not merely to deny that human beings are autonomous,[12] but to assert that they have an innate drive to connect. (Whether or not this also challenges the assumptions of rationality and self-interest I leave aside here.) And I put this forward as an empirical claim, based on the study of human behaviour. Here I draw on child psychology, and more specifically detailed studies by Trevarthen and others which, he claims, demonstrate that human beings have an innate predisposition to experience and act intersubjectively: 'In the past 25 years developmental psychologists . . . have uncovered motivations in infants that have revolutionary implications for the human sciences' (Trevarthen and Logotheti, 1989, p. 166). According to these authors, a newborn baby:

> makes orientations, expressions, and gestures and moves in concert with the sympathetic partner. . . . This is primary inter-subjectivity or basic person–person awareness. . . . The infant quickly identifies the most protective, most constant and most affectionate partner who is responded to preferentially . . . In contrast, unknown persons tend to be regarded with unsmiling suspicion and expressions of fear and withdrawal . . .' (ibid, p. 167).

The story continues in detail. At three months, babies have begun to imitate, and also to play: they 'assert increasing individuality of purpose within the companionship they experience through play'. At six to nine months: 'the child develops a mastery of intended activities that arise in independence of others' wills, but that acknowledge others' interests and approval or disapproval'. At about nine months there is 'a momentous change . . . that brings a capacity for co-operation in the performance of joint tasks and a new level of symbolic understanding. . . . The feelings that others have about objects or situations are taken up by the infant and projected on to the things to which they refer. . . . This we have called "secondary intersubjectivity" or person–person–object awareness.' At the same time, 'the 1-year old infant becomes capable of performing "acts of meaning" in protolanguage. . . . The baby is making the first step into culture itself. . . . Both the conventional uses of things and roles to be played become of consuming interest for the child' (ibid, p. 169).

> Desires and motives for reciprocity are not based upon optimization of individual benefits – they are of a structure that seeks joint engagement and cooperative achievement of experience and action. From the start of childhood to old age, . . . motives for mutual benefit are powerfully ascendent. Antagonistic motives gain the upper hand when the cooperative motives are deceived or frustrated. (ibid, p. 182)

In summary, there is good empirical evidence to suggest that far from being autonomous, individuals are the very opposite: they have a drive to connect – to communicate and relate to others. If there is such a thing as 'tabula rasa' for a person, as a new born baby it seems that it is first a connecting, communicating, trusting being, and only later discriminating and fearful. And a person, at a very young age, seeks meaning: to engage in shared activities and follow shared 'rules'.

> On the basis of these observations, the theory of innate intersubjectivity was proposed. The claim made, while not questioning that development involves learning or that infants depend on care, underlined that a child is born with motives to find and use the motives of other persons in 'conversational' negotiation of purposes, emotions, experiences and meaning. (Trevarthen, in Bråten, 1988, p. 16)

If one were to adopt this as the basic assumption of human behaviour it could have major theoretical consequences: to replace the assumed autonomous individual of mainstream economics by a very different sort of being. It might, nevertheless, be compatible with a modified version of *homo economicus*; the actor does not simply take account of the actions of others, but a powerful motivating force for the actor is to relate to and communicate with others.

SOCIALITY: ANTHROPOLOGY

The work to which I have just referred has been taken up also by anthropologists (Carrithers, 1992; Howell and Willis, 1989), who have used it in the context of a more theoretical debate about the relationship between the society and the individual. They use both the term intersubjectivity and sociality (and psychologists may sometimes use the term sociality), but for clarity I shall here use the term 'sociality' in reference to anthropology and intersubjectivity in reference to psychology.

What is, for my purposes, interesting is that the term 'sociality' is used in order to escape from an extreme anthropological perspective, in which 'culture' constitutes the basis for a 'holistic' approach, in order to come to grips with what Carrithers calls the 'mutualist ontology' of anthropology. He defines the term 'sociality'(provisionally) as a capacity for complex social behaviour, and uses this term in place of 'culture' in order to shift the emphasis to 'individuals in relationships, and the interactive character of social life' (Carrithers, 1992, p. 34). According to Carrithers:

> The significance of sociality stems partly from its ability to mend a failed aspiration carried within the idea of culture. On the one hand, anthropologists have

stressed from the beginning that culture is public, a shared and common resource. To that extent, culture has been recognized as a social matter. But in fact the recognition has tended to stop at an uneasy halfway mark, at a position that still fails to grasp the thoroughly social nature of humans as a species, fails fully to accept that humans, in the first instance, relate to each other, not to the abstraction of culture. (ibid, p. 35)

He quotes Geertz: 'Man's nervous system does not merely enable him to acquire culture, it positively demands that he do so if it is going to function at all' (Geertz, 1973, p. 73). But he notes the deficiencies of such an extreme position, in which the stress is laid upon 'the relationship between an abstracted, idealized individual and that other abstraction, culture. Nothing else, and no one else, intervenes' (Carrithers, 1992, p. 35). The same error, he suggests, is to be found in another of anthropology's dominant figures, Marcel Mauss, although Mauss (1979) uses the term 'collective representations' in place of culture. And for an extreme example of the same point, he quotes the Presidential Address by Leslie White to the American Anthropological Association in 1958. Carrithers argues that:

on this showing the only significant, the only really real features of the human species comprise 1) each individual alone, 2) the world of objects, and 3) that immaterial object, that veil between them, culture. . . . But if we restore what was abbreviated we see something much more intricate: humans living in a multitude of relationships with each other and managing jointly to understand and manipulate the physical world. In that perspective, culture, or what French sociologists have called collective representations, exists in and through such relationships, and the significance of the collective representations cannot be separated from the relationships. . . . Collective representations have significance in their use by people in relation to other people and none apart from these . . . (ibid, p. 36)[13]

It is here that Carrithers draws on child psychology, referring to the work of Trevarthen and Logotheti:

. . . the most general way of talking about sociality is as intersubjectivity, an innate human propensity for mutual engagement and mutual responsiveness. Some of this propensity is cognitive or intellectual, some of it emotional, but in any case human character and human experience exist only in and through people's relations with each other. (ibid, p. 55)

He contrasts this with an earlier view, in which what is real 'included individuals and their innate abilities to deal with the world of objects, including people. There was then culture, or what was learned on top of these basic existents' (Carrithers, 1992, p. 56). He attributes this outmoded view to both anthropologists and psychologists. The new approach that he advocates is one in which 'there are individuals, but they are only under-stood in relationships with other individuals' (Carrithers, 1992, p. 56).

I suggest that this approach may have much to offer in our search for methodological guidance. The problem is that anthropologists are notably reluctant to develop formalized models and tend to be critical of grand theory. While economics develops its methodologies from a theoretical rather than an empirical base, and with little critical concern for the valid-ity of its assumptions, anthropology is almost excessively 'reflexive', ques-tioning its theoretical foundations, emphasizing diversity rather than universals, and resisting rigorous formalisations.[14]

The research by Trevarthen and others is also referred to by Howell and Willis in their book *Societies at Peace*, where they use it to argue against claims of an a priori aggressive drive in humans. They suggest, instead, that 'the presence of innate sociality, on the other hand, has much evidence in its favour. Humans are a priori sociable beings; it is their cooperativeness that has enabled them to survive, not their aggressive impulses' (Howell and Willis, 1989, p. 2).[15]

It is important to note that a theory of innate human sociality is not a reductionist theory. As Carrithers puts it:

Unlike pop socio-biology which appeals to the gene as the ultimate and funda-mental causal factor in human evolution and behaviour, innate sociality sup-poses a predisposition in human beings towards the continual absorption of existing meanings and the creation of new meanings in local universes of thought that are constantly being discovered, destroyed, and negotiated anew in the process of social interaction. (Carrithers, 1992, p. 20)

This asserts a predisposition of humans to make meanings; a need to classify, connect, and relate to that with which they come into contact – not only things but also people, events and so on. People, in other words, are concerned with 'rules and meanings' (to cite the title of the book by the famous anthropologist Mary Douglas, 1973) or, in the broadest sense of the term, morality. And perhaps one can study this in comparative terms: 'The fact that few anthropologists have attempted the empirical study of different moral discourses does not mean that such studies should not, or could not, be undertaken' (Howell, 1997, p. 5). She argues that one may 'approach morality as a field of cultural predispositions informing and cre-ating, rather than supporting social relations between groups and persons' (ibid, pp. 5–6).

Thus, sociality might be used as an empirical as well as an analytical cat-egory, to refer also to a 'field of predispositions' varying somewhat over time and space – and is difficult to study.[16] With this, we have moved very far – from the economist's individual, atomistic approach, to the study of social phenomena, to the 'holistic' approach of the anthropologist – and the methodological challenges are daunting.[17]

METHODOLOGICAL IMPLICATIONS

What may be learnt, in methodological terms, from psychology or anthropology, from the concepts of intersubjectivity and sociality? I begin with the former. To posit the human person as innately intersubjective would, despite the focus on individuals, imply a very different assumption than that of *homo economicus*. The human person, in such a theory, is born with an innate drive to connect: 'A child is born with motives to find and use the motives of other persons in "conversational" negotiation of purposes, emotions, experiences and meaning' (Trevarthen, in Bråten, 1998).

If this is an accurate empirical description of why and how people behave, then in place of the rational, self-interested, autonomous person we have an 'other-oriented' person. This does not imply altruism, lack of self-interest, loss of rationality. It is, I suggest, a reformist rather than a radical alternative to *homo economicus*, implying a change primarily in the assumption of autonomy.

I call this a 'reformist' alternative because it goes only part of the way down the road from reductionism. A radical alternative, in methodological terms, would be to shift the focus from the person – even an innately interactive, social, person – to relations; relations between persons and the meanings associated with these.[18] (Norms and networks, if you will, but perceived from the opposite perspective. Relations – certainly social relations, and arguably all relations – exist only if there is an associated meaning.) What would this imply? In fact, what would it even mean?

To conceive of phenomena in terms of relations rather than entities requires a major shift in perspective, but one that is apparently possible in fields as varied as physics, anthropology and philosophy, as the following quotations indicate:

> But in quantum theory . . . an elementary particle is not an independently existing unanalyzable entity. It is, in essence, a set of relationships that reach outward to other things. (Stapp, 1971, p. 1310)

> The Kamo . . . knows himself only by the relationship he maintains with others. He exists only insofar as he acts his role in the course of his relationships. He is situated only with respect to them. If we try to draw this, we cannot use a dot marked 'self' (ego), but make a number of lines to mark relationships. (Leenhardt, 1979)

'2.14 What constitutes a picture is that its elements are related to one another in a determinate way.
"A picture is a fact."' (Wittgenstein, 1961)

Linguistics provides yet another example of how one may perceive a whole as a set of relations, rather than an aggregate of entities. And I have argued elsewhere that an economy is like a language; value is analogous to meaning, and coins to words.

> In linguistics, as Saussure says, value comes 'from the reciprocal situation of the pieces of the language'. Similarly, in a commodity system, there is a complex reciprocal situation obtaining between commodities, by virtue of the social context within which they are set; a context in which values are like meanings. (McNeill, 1988, p. 206)

And this approach can be extended also to people, not only commodities. I have argued for an interpretation of Aristotle's analysis of exchange in these terms (McNeill, 1990). And Polanyi, in commenting on Aristotle, shows how he emphasizes the links and the community rather than the individual:

> In mapping out a field of study he would relate all questions of institutional origin and function to the totality of society. Community, self-sufficiency and justice were the focal concepts. The group as a going concern forms a community (koinonia) the members of which are linked by the bond of good will (philia) . . . Philia expresses itself in a behaviour of reciprocity (anti-peponthos). (Polanyi, 1968, p. 97)

In brief, I am suggesting – in very abstract terms – an approach to the complex problem of conceptualizing social phenomena that may replace, or at least supplement, an exclusive focus on individual entities, by a focus on a system of relations. But I wish to suggest that these two contrasting paradigms – which I associate with economics and anthropology respectively – may be treated as complementary rather than contradictory. To illustrate how two apparently conflicting views can both be valid, consider the classic 'duck/rabbit illusion': the well-known silhouette that looks first like a duck and then, when perceived otherwise, as a rabbit. Or – to move nearer to the issue at hand, namely whether to focus on entities or relations – consider a triangle, which may be seen either as three points joined by lines, or three lines meeting in points: as a set of entitities or a set of relations. Could we consider society in the same way?

One problem with this approach is the dominance of reductionism – a focus on entities rather than relations – not only in our models, but in the very way we conceive of causality. So strong are the links between

Newtonian mechanics and our concepts of cause that it is hard for social scientists to get away from a billiard ball approach to causality, that is, to 'mechanisms'. Concepts such as 'force fields' may be helpful, but I suggest that we nevertheless find them less compelling (partly, perhaps, because we feel that we understand less how they work even in the physical world). What is at issue may thus be no less than the concept of causality itself. Is a causal explanation by definition reductionist; and does reduction necessarily imply reduction to single entities?

Can something other than entities – relations, for example – constitute a 'motive force'? I wish to suggest that they may. My hypothesis is that there is an innate propensity for interaction between human beings, and for them to create shared rules and meanings, and that this may be regarded as a 'motive force'.[19]

CONCLUSION

It is difficult to bring my argument to a conclusion, in view of the very speculative nature of the last section, and I prefer instead to summarize it and seek to locate the different methodological positions I have described in relation to what is the more well established 'middle ground' of economic sociology. This, as the name implies, is where one may find sociologists and economists seeking to better understand the workings of the economy, starting from premises other than crude methodological individualism. It is a large space, including (most relevant perhaps for our purposes) both the new and the old institutional economics. The former seeks to apply rational choice theory and other recent theoretical developments (concerning information and transaction costs) to our understanding of institutions. The latter – which has recently enjoyed a revival – draws on Veblen (1899), Polanyi (1957) and others, where the emphasis is on context and 'embeddedness'. There is an unresolved debate as to whether these two are reconcilable. My own view is that despite the apparent similarities between them, they nevertheless differ in fundamental ways. In brief, old institutional economics treats markets as institutions, while new institutional economics treats institutions as markets. The distance between the two positions may be small, but the chasm between them is deep – being, in effect, the same chasm that I have just referred to between economics and anthropology. But this may be too pessimistic.

A useful summary of the state of the art is found in Smelser and Swedberg (1994) who list seven respects in which economic sociology differs from mainstream economics: the concept of the actor, economic

Table 7.1   Contrasting economic sociology and mainstream economics (after Smelser and Swedberg, 1994)

	Economic sociology	Mainstream economics
Concept of the actor	The actor is influenced by other actors and is part of groups and society	The actor is uninfluenced by other actors ('methodological individualism')
Economic action	Many different types of economic action are used, including rational ones (rationality as variable)	All economic actions are assumed to be rational (rationality as assumption)
Constraints on the action	Economic actions are constrained by the scarcity of resources, by the social structure and by meaning structures	Economic actions are constrained by tastes and by the scarcity of resources, including technology

action, constraints on the action, the economy in relation to society, goal of the analysis, methods used and intellectual tradition.[20] In this chapter I have been concerned especially with the first, but also, to lesser extent, the next two (Table 7.1).

The 'reformist' alternative that I have proposed, deriving from psychology, is certainly different from mainstream economics; and also to some extent from economic sociology, for it assumes a pro-active engagement of the individual with others, rather than an actor that is simply 'influenced by other actors' or 'constrained by structures'.

The radical alternative that I have proposed is substantially different from both mainstream economics and economic sociology. Instead of the actor (see row 1 of Table 7.1) we have the relation. And the social structure (and 'meaning structure' with which it is intimately bound up) is not a constraint; indeed it is, in a sense, the motivating force. I say 'in a sense' for this alternative implies a 'social and meaning structure', which is more like a field: a totality of relations.

Perhaps in seeking a middle ground we do not have to adopt an either/or methodology: either universal or relativistic; either holistic or reductionist; either based on norms, structures and roles or rationality, atoms and autonomy. The concept of social capital might, in principle, have provided the starting point for making progress in methodological terms, but unfortunately it seems that this is not the case. It remains, however, an important task for social scientists to better understand 'norms and networks'. What is required for this purpose is a rigorous but not reductionist approach; here, I have argued, the concept of sociality may prove most useful.

NOTES

1. Hodgson (1988) provides a detailed critique of this approach, which more strictly one should refer to as neoclassical economics, for there exists a range of alternative approaches (to which Hodgson himself has made a substantial contribution) that contrast to varying extents with what has for some time been the 'mainstream'. Since my aim here is to contrast the extremes in social science I will, however, concentrate on the mainstream, and refer to it simply as 'the economic approach'.
2. He quotes Edgeworth: 'the first principle of economics is that every agent is actuated solely by self-interest' (Edgeworth, 1881, p. 16).
3. I shall not in this chapter try to include an evaluation of game-theoretical approaches, but a brief summary of the current state of the art may be in order. Most important, in the context of this chapter, are evolutionary game theory and bounded rationality. The former 'imagines that the game is played over and over again by biologically or socially conditioned players who are randomly drawn from large populations' (Binmore, 1997, p. xiii). This implies that historical and institutional factors cannot be ignored. 'But economists remain resistant to the idea that the same game might receive a different analysis if the players have a different history of experience, or live in different societies, or operate in different industries' (ibid, p. x).

    An alternative path, also derived from game theory, is to assume 'bounded rationality'. This implies models 'in which decision makers make *deliberate* decisions by applying procedures that guide their reasoning about 'what' to do, and probably also about 'how' to decide' (Rubinstein, 1998, p. 2). To put it another way, following Simon (1955): 'Boundedly rational behaviour is behaviour that is *intendedly rational, but limitedly so*. That is, the individual strives consciously to achieve some goals, but does so in a way that reflects cognitive and computational limitations' (Weibull, 1997, p. 151).

    The 'rules of the game' can matter enormously to the outcomes predicted by game-theoretic analysis, but: 'Game theoretic analyses in economics tend to take the rules of the game too much for granted, without asking where the rules come from' (ibid, p. 129). The challenge, in coming to grips with the behaviour of individual agents who are boundedly rational, is, according to Weibull, to take account of 'retrospective behaviour', that is, 'behaviour where the past influences current decisions' (ibid, p. 151) or, indeed, 'Whenever behaviour is governed by social convention' (ibid, p. 152).
4. See, for example, *Trust* by Fukuyama (1995).
5. I explore in some detail elsewhere (McNeill, 2004) why and how the World Bank became so committed to the concept.
6. In fact, the story is rather more complicated. Another sociologist, Bourdieu (1985), has also coined the term; but his usage is rather different (less individualistic) and it is Coleman and Putnam, not Bourdieu, that have shaped the subsequent debate. However Coleman himself states that he adopted the term from an economist, Lowry (1977), who in turn drew on sociological literature! For a fuller account see Portes (1998), Woolcock (1998) or McNeill (2006).
7. 'The most encompassing view of social capital includes the social and political environment that shapes social structure and enables norms to develop' (World Bank, 1997, p. 1). This definition is so broad that it includes almost anything whatever in the social and even political arena. Putnam's definition, in addition to being narrower, has the added merit that it has become the standard starting point for many commentators, thanks to Putnam's dominant position as the popularizer of the term.
8. Putnam also quotes numerous economists in his book, such as Dasgupta on 'trust' and North on 'path dependency'.

9. The concept is certainly not without its critics, even in political science and sociology. See, for example, Portes (1998) and Tarrow (1996).

10. A comprehensive overview is provided by Clyde Mitchell, in his 1974 paper 'Social Networks', who attributes the origin of the term to Barnes (1954).

11. The same may even apply to relations in general; but I leave that even more fundamental question aside.

12. A standard assumption of economics is that human beings are autonomous. This is associated with, but not the same as, methodological individualism, which Lukes defines as the view that 'Facts about society and social phenomena are to be explained solely in terms of facts about individuals' (Lukes, 1968, p. 120; see also Hodgson, 1988). To question the assumption of autonomy is not alien to economics. Clearly many economists would also recognize that this is an extreme assumption, and some readily concede that this is unrealistic. A few have even tried to rectify this, notably with regard to the study of consumption. It is unfortunately difficult to model interdependent preferences, and extremely difficult to collect the data necessary to test hypotheses empirically.

13. He adds: 'So long as we think of humans simply as individuals subjected to a collectivity . . . change . . . becomes . . . difficult to understand. A more thoroughly sociological view places change, not permanence, at the centre of our vision' (Carrithers, 1992, p. 36). I shall not explore this point further here, but this is an important issue in view of the frequent criticism that 'structural' theories are incapable of coping with change.

14. It is not a coincidence, however, that kinship is one area where anthropology has been formalized; for this is the study of relations, independent of actual persons. The contrast with social capital is interesting also: from kin to kith, from meaning to self-interest.

15. My concern in this chapter is not with peacefulness and aggression. For the purposes of my argument (and perhaps for theirs), I require only that humans are innately sociable, not innately cooperative.

16. 'Each person confronted with a system of ends and means . . . seems to face the order of nature objective and independent of human wants. But the moral order and the knowledge which sustains it are created by social conventions . . . [which] are not merely tacit but extremely inaccessible to investigation' (Douglas, 1973, p. 15).

17. Hollis is aware of the difficulties – as well as the danger – of substituting *homo economicus* by 'an equally mechanical *homo sociologicus*, who is a creature of determining social positions and roles' (Hollis, 1996, p. 10). He suggests that 'a fertile alternative might start from Wittgenstein's portrait of us as players of the "games" of social life . . . whose actions are moves in the game of the moment and whose reasons for action are internal to the games we play. Whereas game theory conceives games as sums of strategic choices by individuals, Wittgensteinian games have so different a character that it can seem idle to make comparisons. Yet, with all due caution, it is instructive to contrast their very different ideas of norms and reasons for action . . . The most obvious fact about games, in the everyday sense of the word, is that they have rules. The rules of chess, for example, . . . establish the construct and make chess possible. They constitute the game. . . . Chess thus illustrates an instructive distinction between constitutive rules, which are prior to a class of actions and make them possible, and regulative rules, which guide choices among possible actions' (Hollis, 1996, p. 10).

18. A more intermediate position, exemplified by Hollis, would replace a focus on autonomous persons by one on interrelated roles: 'Whereas homo economicus is an abstract, individual, yet universal, homunculus, homo sociologicus is a social being, essentially located in a scheme of positions and roles. . . . [Hence] presocial atoms are replaced *essentially* by role-bearers, *constituted* by the social positions to which the roles belong' (ibid, p. 24).

19. Whether this should be regarded as a 'property' of human beings as individuals, or of society as a set of relations, may be debated.

20. These contrasts, I suggest, are relatively moderate manifestations of the much more fundamental contrasts discussed previously, between economics and anthropology.

182   *New light on rationality, social relations and the environment*

REFERENCES

Arrow, K. (1999), 'Observations on social capital' in P. Dasgupta and I. Serageldin (eds) (1999), *Social Capital: A Multifaceted Perspective*, Washington, DC: The World Bank.
Barnes, J. (1954), 'Class and committees in a Norwegian island parish', *Human Relations* **7**, 39–58.
Binmore, K. (1997), 'Introduction' in Weibull (1997).
Bourdieu, P. (1985), 'The forms of capital', in J.G. Richardson (ed.), *Handbook of Theory and Research for the Sociology of Education*, New York: Greenwood, pp. 241–58.
Bråten, S. (ed.) (1998), *Intersubjective Communication and Emotion in Early Ontogeny*, Cambridge: Cambridge University Press.
Carrithers, M. (1992), *Why Humans Have Cultures: Explaining Anthropology and Social Diversity*, Oxford: Oxford University Press.
Coleman, J. (1988), 'Social capital in the creation of human capital', *American Journal of Sociology*, **94**, supplement s95–s120. Reprinted in P. Dasgupta and I. Serageldin (eds) (1999), *Social Capital: A Multifaceted Perspective*, Washington, DC: The World Bank.
Dasgupta, P. (1999), 'Economic Progress and the Idea of Social Capital' in Dasgupta and Serageldin (eds) (1988), *Social Capital: A Multifaceted Perspective*, Washington, DC: The World Bank.
Dasgupta, P. and I. Serageldin (eds) (1999), *Social Capital: A Multifaceted Perspective*, Washington, DC: The World Bank.
Douglas, M. (1973), *Rules and Meanings*, Harmondsworth: Penguin.
Edgeworth, F. (1881), *Mathematical Psychics*, London: Routledge and Kegan Paul.
Elster, J. (1989), *The Cement of Society: A Study of Social Order*, Cambridge: Cambridge University Press.
Elster, J. (1999), *Alchemies of the Mind: Rationality and the Emotions*, Cambridge: Cambridge University Press.
Fine, B. (2001), *Social Capital Versus Social Theory: Political Economy and Social Science at the Turn of the Millennium*, London: Routledge.
Fukuyama, F. (1995), *Trust: the Social Virtues and the Creation of Prosperity*, New York: The Free Press.
Geertz, C. (1973), *The Interpretation of Cultures*, New York: Basic Books.
Hodgson, G. (1988), *Economics and Institutions: A Manifesto for a Modern Institutional Economics*, Cambridge: Polity Press.
Hollis, M. (1996), *Reason in Action: Essays in the Philosophy of Social Science*, Cambridge: Cambridge University Press.
Howell, S. and R. Willis (eds) (1989), *Societies at Peace: Anthropological Perspectives*, London and New York: Routledge.
Howell, S. (ed.) (1997), *The Ethnography of Moralities*, London and New York: Routledge.
Jul-Larsen, E. (1999), 'Social capital: old wine in new bottles? An anthropological assessment', paper delivered at the Local Level Institutions Conference, CMI Bergen, 5–7 May.
Leenhardt, M. (1979), *Do Kamo: Person and Myth in the Melanesian World*, trans. by Basia Miller Gulati, Chicago: University of Chicago Press.
Lowry, G. (1977), 'A dynamic theory of racial income differences', in P. Wallace

and A. La Mond (eds), *Women, Minorities and Employment Discrimination.* Lexington, MA: Heath, pp. 153–86.

Lukes, S. (1968), 'Methodological individualism reconsidered', *British Journal of Sociology*, **19**, 119–29.

Mauss, M. (1979), *Sociology and Psychology*, London: Routledge and Kegan Paul.

McNeill, D. (1988), *Fetishism and the Value-form: Towards a General Theory of Value*, unpublished Ph.D thesis, University College London.

McNeill, D. (1990), 'Alternative interpretations of Aristotle on exchange and reciprocity', *Public Affairs Quarterly*, **4** (1), 55–68.

McNeill, D. (2004), 'Social capital and the World Bank', in M. Bøås and D. McNeill (eds), *Global Institutions and Development: Framing the World?*, London and New York: Routledge.

McNeill, D. (2006), 'The spread of ideas in development theory and policy: a bibliometric analysis', *Global Social Policy*, **6**(3).

Mitchell, C. (1974), 'Social networks', in *Annual Review of Anthropology*, **3**, 279–99.

Polanyi, K. (1957), *The Great Transformation*, Boston: Beacon Press.

Polanyi, K. (1968), 'Aristotle discovers the economy', in G. Dalton (ed.) *Primitive, Archaic and Modern Economies*, Boston: Beacon Press.

Portes, A. (1998), 'Social capital: its origins and applications in modern sociology', *Annual Review of Sociology*, **24**, 1–24.

Putnam, R. (1993), *Making Democracy Work: Civic Traditions in Modern Italy*, Princeton, NJ: Princeton University Press.

Putnam, R. (1995), 'Bowling alone: America's declining social capital', *Journal of Democracy*, **6**, 65–78.

Rubinstein, A. (1998), *Modeling Bounded Rationality*, Cambridge, MA: MIT Press.

Simon, H. (1955), 'A behavioral model of rational choice', *Quarterly Journal of Economics*, **69**, 9–118.

Smelser, N. and R. Swedberg (1994), *The Handbook of Economic Sociology*, Princeton, NJ: Princeton University Press.

Solow, R. (1999), 'Notes on social capital and economic performance', in P. Dasgupta and I. Serageldin (eds), *Social Capital: A Multifaceted Perspective*, Washington, DC: The World Bank.

Stapp, H. (1971), 'S-matrix interpretation of quantum theory', *Physical Review*, **3** (6).

Stiglitz, J. (1999), 'Formal and informal institutions', in P. Dasgupta and I. Serageldin (eds), *Social Capital: A Multifaceted Perspective*, Washington, DC: The World Bank.

Tarrow, S. (1996), 'Making social science work across space and time: a critical reflection on Robert Putnam's *Making Democracy Work*', *American Political Science Review*, **90** (2), 389–97.

Taylor, C. (1985), *Philosophy and the Human Sciences: Philosophical Papers 2*, Cambridge: Cambridge University Press.

Trevarthen, C. and K. Logotheti (1989), 'Child in society, and society in children: the nature of basic trust', in S. Howell and R. Willis (eds), *Societies at Peace: Anthropological Perspectives*, London and New York: Routledge, pp. 165–86.

Veblen, T. (1899), *The Theory of the Leisure Class: An Economic Study in the Evolution of Institutions*, New York: Macmillan.

Weibull, J. (1997), *Evolutionary Game Theory*, Cambridge, MA: MIT Press.

Wittgenstein, L. (1961), *Tractatus Logico-philosophicus*, London: Routledge and Kegan Paul.

Woolcock, Michael (1998), 'Social capital and economic development: toward a theoretical synthesis and policy framework', *Theory and Society*, **27**, 151–208.

World Bank (1997), *Expanding the Measure of Wealth: Indicators of Environmentally Sustainable Development*, Environmentally sustainable development studies and monograph series 17, Washington, DC: World Bank.

8. Where disciplinary boundaries blur: the environmental dimension of institutional economics

Eyüp Özveren[1]

And did the Countenance Divine
Shine forth upon our clouded hills?
And was Jerusalem builded here
Among these dark Satanic Mills?
(William Blake (2002), from 'Preface' to Milton, pp. 211–14)

The world is too much with us, late and soon,
Getting and spending, we lay waste our powers
Little we see in Nature that is ours;
We have given our hearts away, a sordid boon!
This Sea that bares her bosom to the moon,
The winds that will be howling at all hours,
And are up-gathered now like sleeping flowers,
For this, for everything, we are out of tune,
It moves us not.
(William Wordsworth (2000), from 'The World Is Too Much with Us', p. 270)

DISCIPLINARY BOUNDARIES AND RIVAL STRATEGIES

Very few would notice that in naming as 'Satanic Mill' the first half of the second and most original part of his book, Karl Polanyi sought safe harbour in William Blake's poetry. Written during the interwar period, this book borrowed not only this title from William Blake but also owed much of its spirit to the English Romantics who reacted to the so-called Industrial Revolution:

> In literary *romanticism* Nature had made its alliance with the Past; in the agrarian movement of the nineteenth century feudalism was trying not unsuccessfully to recover its past by presenting itself as the *guardian of man's natural habitat,*

the soil. If the danger had not been genuine, the stratagem could not have worked. (Polanyi, 1944, p. 186; emphases added).

It is a pity that more than half a century after its publication, this connection, of vital importance to Polanyi, seems to have been lost because of our blinding disciplinary specialization, and as such Polanyi's *The Great Transformation* remains less than fully appreciated. At a time when the Iron Curtain of disciplinary boundaries was about to be further consolidated, Polanyi himself insisted he would 'encroach upon the field of several disciplines in the pursuit of this single' overarching intellectual motive (Polanyi, 1944, p. 4).

If, as was apparent on the eve of the twenty-first century, our dissatisfaction with existing disciplinary boundaries has considerably increased, then it must be time to look at the process of the formation of these boundaries with a long view. The disciplinary boundaries as they exist today are a legacy of modernity in general, and of nineteenth-century intellectual heritage in particular. Whereas the division among the natural and the social sciences was incumbent upon the spread of Cartesian philosophy that separated the domain of the natural from that of the human condition, the differentiation among the social sciences came much later and rested on less philosophical and more practical foundations. Within the domain of the social sciences, disciplinary boundaries crystallized during the last quarter of the nineteenth and first quarter of the twentieth centuries. Having crystallized as such, they were diffused as much as possible over the globe under US hegemony as consolidated after the Second World War. US hegemony meant practically the worldwide dominance of Anglo-American social sciences.

The fracture of US hegemony came about first with the intellectual upsurge of 1968 and then with the 1973 economic crisis. As a consequence, a questioning of the existing academic structures of knowledge and intellectual paradigms gained legitimacy and momentum (Gulbenkian Commission, 1996). Today we stand at a major turning point along this process of unfolding dissatisfaction. There is a debate over where we go next. While some may think that it is time to bring down once and for all this last Berlin Wall that divides the disciplines, others may take a more moderate stand and content themselves with the greater liberty of travelling across the boundaries. It should be noted that virtually all parties to this debate, including those subscribing to neoclassical orthodoxy, agree that it is high time something should be done about existing disciplinary boundaries. The differences remain as to what exactly should be done.

There exist three rival strategies concerning what should be done. The first strategy belongs to the dominant neoclassical approach. Neoclassical economics considers itself as the logical culmination and perfection of a century-long tradition that has increasingly abstracted itself from time and space, thereby becoming a pure theory of choice under constraint with universal applicability. If neoclassical approach has become a truly pure theory of choice under constraint, then the choices in question do not necessarily have to be economic ones. This approach can now liberate itself from the restricting domain of economics and apply equally well to other domains of inquiry where choice-making under constraint is involved. This strategy can conveniently be dubbed the imperialism of economics. In tune with the more current fashion, we may well term it as the purported 'globalization' of the neoclassical approach to all fields of social inquiry.

According to neoclassics, there are right and wrong approaches in all distinct fields of inquiry. The notion of the neoclassical approach as being the right approach can be exported to other fields to the detriment of the supposedly inferior approaches that have until now found safe haven in those fields that were 'protected' from intrusion by disciplinary boundaries. The now classic work of Gary Becker that seeks to explain conventionally sociological subjects such as family, marriage and education by way of microeconomic tools is a good example (Becker, 1976). When the scope of some concepts is broadened beyond a certain point, they inevitably cast light on their own limitations (Foucault, 1977). In Foucault's terminology, such concepts have a trangressional attribute. Inspired by this, we might as well characterize the neoclassical attitude as transdisciplinary aggression.

In juxtaposition to the expansionist momentum of the neoclassical strategy that attempts to do away with all substantial differences, the other two strategies belong to the opposition. Of these, the currently more fashionable one is the second strategy. It is characteristic of the New Institutional Economics (hereafter NIE). At first glance it seems to be very cautious and as such, it is likely to exert a growing influence over the greater part of the academic audience. Nowadays one can find behind most contemporary interdisciplinary academic events a legitimization and reinforcement of this strategy. This strategy takes for granted existing disciplinary boundaries. Some economists venture into other domains, borrow ideas and/or tools, and bring them into the domain of economics and apply it for the study of relevant problems. By doing so, these economists (Williamson, 1985; North, 1990) have extra ideas and/or tools at their disposal in addition to those that they are as much equipped with as their rivals by their disciplinary training. As such, they have an advantage over their rivals within their own field, namely economics.

Metaphorically, in the shadow of such economists we can identify the image of the medieval or early-modern-period merchants of long-distance trade (Pirenne, 1936; Braudel, 1979). A typical medieval merchant would bring from far away lands a piece of valuable china or an exquisite spice and benefit from windfall profits due to prevalent market differentials based on risk, uncertainty and ignorance. In a similar vein practitioners of NIE bring piecemeal ideas and tools from neighbouring disciplines into the domain of economics, which has shut itself off from the social sciences. Within this kingdom of self-imposed ignorance, high returns for the otherwise fairly commonplace ideas and tools can be enjoyed. Obviously, this strategy is more prudent than its neoclassical rival. It does not ignore substantial differences, nor does it outright attack the disciplinary boundaries. Far from doing so, it is in the interest of these adherents of NIE that the disciplinary boundaries should remain as a Berlin Wall for all others but themselves. Were the Wall to be brought down, this strategy would become defunct as it is actually parasitic on the existence of the disciplinary boundaries.

In contradistinction to the second strategy identified with NIE, the third strategy seeks deliberately to challenge the very logic of disciplinary specialization. This strategy is a distinguishing attribute of the original institutional economics, oftentimes misleadingly referred to as the Old Institutional Economics (hereafter OIE). While in certain other respects original institutional economics and NIE can be reconciled and integrated within a broader research program, as far as this strategic attribute is concerned the two variants of institutionalism stand as poles apart. Whereas moderate scholarship has satisfied itself with occasional '*inter*disciplinary' or '*multi*disciplinary' ventures that take for granted the existing disciplines as building blocks of these temporary interdisciplinary or multidisciplinary projects, institutional economics has persistently defined itself as essentially '*trans*disciplinary'.

William Kapp, one of the two institutionalists we will study at great length in this chapter, in his work *Social Costs of Business Enterprise* (dating from 1963 and further revised in 1976), insisted on the transdisciplinary scope of institutional economics. These two dates deserve particular emphasis as shortly before and after the 1968–73 prolonged crisis. We have already seen how Karl Polanyi, the other institutionalist who will be evaluated in the rest of this study, in his book *The Great Transformation* (1944), had defined his motive as encroachment into the field of several disciplines. By doing so, at a time when the disciplinary boundaries were on the verge of consolidation *pace* the Iron Curtain, he chose to swim against the tide. Therefore, during the golden age of disciplinary boundaries, institutional economics remained at odds with this characteristic of the dominant structures of knowledge. In light of this fact we can conclude that of the two oppositions to mainstream neoclassical economics, as far as the attitude to disciplinary boundaries is concerned, we can label economists of NIE as the 'loyal opposition' – where the 'loyalty' component outweighs the 'oppositional' ingredient – and the institutionalist economists as the true rebels.

We have so far dwelled upon the nature of disciplinary boundaries within the social sciences and the attitudes of economists of different persuasion. It is no coincidence that much of the ongoing academic activities concentrate on the relationships among the social sciences. However, specialization within the social sciences is deeply entrenched within a broader division of labour that extends from humanities to the natural sciences. The intermediary position in this spectrum of sciences is occupied by the social sciences in general, and by economics in particular. It is also due time for addressing the problem of separation within this broader domain (Santos, 1995). We should remind ourselves that Polanyi's characterization of Satanic Mill, cited previously, covered an equally broad spectrum ranging from the English Romantic literature to the social sciences.

The study of environment is a field of inquiry that relates to the interface of the social and natural sciences.[2] As such, when addressing the study of environment, we should not narrowly concentrate on exchanges among the social sciences, but delve into the broader interaction taking place across the social and natural sciences. Furthermore, it should be noted that nowhere is the contrast between NIE and OIE more marked than in the study of environment. Whereas in other domains the two can be reconciled to some effect, within environmental studies NIE starts off from Coase (1960) and develops by recourse to the Property Rights School (Sagoff, 1998).[3] The underlying attitude of this approach is to elaborate, extend and hypothetically construct markets where there are none. Put differently, according to NIE environmental problems arise because, first, property rights are not properly defined and generalized, and second, markets are not as universalized as they ought to be. In juxtaposition, the institutional approach connects environmental problems to the logic and domination of the market system and seeks remedy at circumventing the market in accordance with the principle of social value that can be made operational by way of a participatory deliberation process.

The purpose of this study is twofold. First, I would like to demonstrate how institutional economics, as evidenced in the works of Polanyi and Kapp, was environmentally conscious from the very beginning. The study of nature was conceived as integral to the economic process in a systemic way with real temporal and spatial attributes. In juxtaposition to neoclassical environmental economics, which is the manifestation of the venture of microeconomic analysis after its maturation into a virgin domain, institutional economics was originally defined in such a way as to be simultaneously an institutional and an environmental economics. Second, institutional economics could not have been conceivable without an environmental dimension. It evolved together with the environmental metaphor, to which it owes much of its originality.

In contradistinction to this rich potential that has always been at the core of institutional economics, some recent contributions to the field lose sight of these two aspects and unintentionally betray the intellectual layout of the original institutional research program (Swaney, 1985 and 1987; Martinez-Alier and Schlupmann, 1987; Godard and Salles, 1991; Dietz and van der Straaten, 1992; Sachs, 1993; Söderbaum, 1994; Martinez-Alier, 1999). The vulnerability of such works of recent vintage arises from two reasons. They take for granted the existence of a subfield of specialization, namely 'environmental economics', that bears the heavy birthmark of neo-classical strategy for expansion.[4] Having taken these coordinates as given, they inevitably succumb to some extent to the underlying policy-oriented and pragmatic-minded philosophy of neoclassical environmental econom-ics. On the other side, when critical scholars reject to accept the subfield as such, they seek refuge under alternative labels such as 'ecological econom-ics' (Martinez-Alier, 1987; Costanza, 1997; Daly, 1999). Ecological eco-nomics is linked to the seminal work of Nicholas Georgescu-Roegen, by all accounts a vital link in the institutionalist chain. Within this literature, Kapp is cited from time to time, whereas, at best, infrequent lip service is paid to Polanyi. However, ecological economists have so far not established systematic connections with such important earlier links of the very same institutionalist chain. Furthermore, one crucial distinction among envir-onmental and ecological economists can be traced back to the contrast between market values as favoured by the former, and alternative values as elaborated by the latter. Some ecological economists incline towards a forum-like deliberative process for the determination of the alternative set of social values, whereas other ecological economists insist that we might as well to resort to some scale of physical value (van der Straaten, 1999).

A convenient point of departure to this end has been identified in Georgescu-Roegen's concept of energy (Georgescu-Roegen, 1976). Whether market prices can be used interchangeably or together with physical values refers us to the question of the social constitution of values of various kinds in a market society. Practical as it may seem, this is obviously a method-ological problem linked with the quest for ontological foundations. Therefore, as long as this alternative terrain of ecological economics is not linked with a strong ontological specification, it remains as shaky ground. In order to resist the temptation to succumb to neoclassicism directly or by way of NIE, a potentially institutionalist alternative has to be conscious of its own strategy. It is argued that a return to original sources such as, first, Polanyi's work (that provides us with an alternative ontological layout), and second, Kapp's work (which develops practical tools without betraying the underlying ontological premises), is of critical importance.[5] Last but not least, the institutional approach would not content itself with a one-way expansion from economics to environment but on a reciprocal relationship where the metaphorical deployment of environment would equally well open new vistas for the study of institutional economic phenomena. Therefore a return to original sources would in fact be a step forward to tackle the shortcomings and drawbacks inherent in some recent institutional environmental studies.

BRINGING NATURE BACK IN: THE DARK SIDE OF *THE GREAT TRANSFORMATION*

A creative reading of Polanyi's main theses through the lens of institutional economics would provide us with a set of valuable inferences for the kind of ontological foundation we are now in search of. The so-called Industrial Revolution that took place in England introduced an entirely new era in the history of human civilization. This era was a 'distinct stage', a 'singular departure' (Polanyi, 1944, p. 5, 71), and a 'parenthesis' that was bound to come to an end. What exactly was the character of this exceptional epoch, most manifest in the case of England but of worldwide significance?

According to Polanyi, the Industrial Revolution was of paramount importance as it raised the rate and scale of production, thereby massively expanding the scope of consumer markets, which would therefore impact back upon factor markets as the convention would call them:

> But how shall this Revolution itself be defined? What was its basic characteristic? Was it the rise of the factory towns, the emergence of slums, the long working hours of children, the low wages of certain categories of workers, the rise in the rate of population increase, or the concentration of industries? *We submit that all these were merely incidental to one basic change, the establishment of market economy, and that the nature of this institution cannot be fully grasped unless the impact of the machine on a commercial society is realized.* We do not intend to assert that the machine caused that which happened, but we insist that once elaborate machines and plant were used for production in a commercial society, the idea of a self-regulating market was bound to take shape. (Polanyi, 1944, p. 40; emphasis added)

Hence the synergetic combination of a commercial society with modern machinery is the key to the explanation of the achievements of the so-called Industrial Revolution. Had it not been for what the Industrial Revolution unintentionally achieved, the above presentation would fit well with any standard description of economic history. However, with the sudden lift it gave to production and consumer markets, the Industrial Revolution made insufficient and obsolete the type of institutional setup within which the pre-industrial economy was contained. Precisely because the existing institutional setup could no longer suffice to contain the dynamism of the nascent industrialism, economy was let loose, that is, paraphrasing Polanyi, 'disembedded' from social relations (Polanyi, 1944). We should re-emphasize that this disembeddedness was largely because the existing institutional setup was no match for the nascent economic system. Far from being able to regulate it, the institutional setup became an obstacle on its way. Under these circumstances, the most practical and ad hoc solution was to remove the obstacles on the way and leave the mechanism to its own, at least in the short term. Power and policy worked effectively to this end, and helped create the space within which the 'self-regulating market system' could then be left to its own in order to run its course: 'There was nothing natural about *laissez-faire*; free markets could never have come into being merely by allowing things to take their course' (Polanyi, 1944, p. 139). As such, the putting into effect of the market system was far from spontaneous, but once in effect, the system worked in its own spontaneously expansionist way.

When approached in this manner, the whole 'nineteenth-century civilization' becomes a period of permanent crisis where the whole thrust was to recreate an institutional setup that could measure up to the demands of the new economic way of life. The eventual creation of this institutional setup by a combination of spontaneous, self-protective and instinctive reactions together with human design, if and when accomplished, would serve to re-institute the market in the ensemble of social relations thereby bringing an end to the exceptional disembeddedness of the economy.

The impasse of market society was that it could not do without an integrated set of self-regulating markets – including those for 'fictitious commodities', namely land, labour and money – *pace* Léon Walras as the organizing principle of the whole social edifice, and yet not help cultivate various reactions in favour of self-protection, which, if put into effect, would inhibit the market. With respect to specific instances, Polanyi talked of 'the needs of an industrial civilization with which market methods were unable to cope' (Polanyi, 1944, p. 154). In fact, in conformity with the thrust of Polanyi's overall assessment, this message ought to be generalized to the relationship among the market on the one side and industrial civilization on the other. This is what Polanyi did in another context. As Polanyi put it, the challenge was to come up with a new way other than the self-regulating market for how the industrial system could be instituted: '*The congenital weakness of nineteenth century society was not that it was industrial but that it was a market society*. Industrial civilization will continue to exist when the utopian experiment of a self-regulating market will be no more than a memory' (Polanyi, 1944, p. 250, italics as original).

Market society had not measured up to the task of harnessing the full potential of an industrial system. It remains to be seen whether mankind is any better prepared now than it was at the dawn of the Industrial Revolution to come up with a solution to the problem of recreating the necessary institutional setup for this purpose.

We may now have serious misgivings about the exclusive timing and placing by Polanyi of the centre and scope of this self-regulating market system to nineteenth-century England. Nevertheless, the system that Polanyi constructed of the market society has much to offer for a proper understanding of the world in which we still live. Within the 'concepticon' of the Polanyi-esque approach, two terms stand out in terms of widest usage, namely 'embeddedness' and 'fictitious commodity'. We shall look at each of these terms in turn. We shall then proceed with linking them to one another. The nexus of these concepts will serve us to define the parameters within which we can bring nature back into the institutionalist analytical framework in light of the lessons of *The Great Transformation*.

The thesis concerning the embeddedness of the economy within the broader domain of the social has already been noted. For Polanyi, there exists a 'natural' counterpart to the 'social', implying that the economy under the normal state of things is embedded squarely in both the 'natural' and the 'social', and that it cannot be otherwise. As such, the natural and the social constitute the double pillars of the economy. When the economy assumes the form of a self-regulating market, both the 'natural' and the 'social' find themselves in an inevitable state of retrogression. The two supporting structures are by no means symmetrical. However badly violated, while the 'social' responds by way of a self-protective instinct seeking to restore its previous integrity, the 'natural' cannot react on its own behalf as if it were an active social agent such as labour. Polanyi notes that classes linked with the land, namely landowners and the peasantry, react in the name of the natural as a second best (Polanyi, 1944, p. 133). Consequently, nature, unlike the 'social', is less than fully represented in the struggle against the vagaries of the market mechanism.

This leads to a further implication: whereas the integrity of the 'social' could in principle be restored in the future, nature is subject to an irreversible process of deterioration. This difference boils down to a differential assessment of the 'time's arrow' with respect to the two foundations. In Polanyi's view, pre-market societies are a kind of 'paradise lost' when remembered in the light of the historical experience of the market society. One might be tempted to think that this characterization of the past as a paradise is exaggerated. Truly, the past was not an absolute paradise, but compared with the hell of satanic mills, it must have been a relative para-dise. Nevertheless, the possibilities of industrial society pave the way towards a resurrection of the 'social' from the disgrace it has been exposed to under the so-called 'nineteenth-century civilization'. However, 'paradise lost' cannot be a 'paradise regained', precisely because the effect of 'time's arrow' on nature, unlike its effect on the 'social', is irreversible.

We need further dwell upon the issue of 'time's arrow'. This metaphor is inevitably linked to the dark side of modernity, that is, the dogma of progress, of which Polanyi was loudly critical (Özveren, 1999). In his lengthy discussion of the historical antecedents of the market society in England, Polanyi approaches the question in a different light. He adopts a 'habitation-versus-improvement' perspective. On the whole, Polanyi's position can be summarized as essentially pro-habitation and anti-improvement. Polanyi justifies his claim on the basis of the argument that at certain critical junctures 'the rate of change' can be as important as the 'direction of change' and policies that remain incapable of reversing the direction may nevertheless suffice to alleviate the ills of rapid change:

> As to England, . . . facts suffice to identify the change from arable land to pasture and the accompanying enclosure movement as the *trend of economic progress*. Yet, but for the consistently maintained policy of the Tudor and early Stuart statesmen, the *rate of that progress might have been ruinous, and have turned the process itself into a degenerative instead of a constructive event*. For upon this rate, mainly, depended whether the dispossessed could *adjust* them-selves to changed conditions without fatally damaging their substance, human and economic, physical and moral. (Polanyi, 1944, p. 37; emphases added)

This position not only delineates Polanyi from his social scientist contem-poraries but also links us back to the 'embeddedness' thesis. It is our con-tention that this slowdown, so critically important for a readjustment, was the *only* way that an economy on the way to enter the orbit of a market would not be entirely disembedded and therefore derailed. In other words, by mon-itoring rate of change, additional time was provided for the existing insti-tutional frame to catch up with the demands of a nascent market economy, thereby avoiding a full rupture among the rapidly unfolding dynamic market system, on the one side, and the relatively change-resistant institutional setup on the other. It should be noted that for Polanyi, the preservation of the archaic institutional setup was seen as a positive, rather than a negative. Once the problematic is defined in this way, we see that Polanyi takes sides with Joseph A. Schumpeter, who also had a favourable opinion of the leftover of the *ancien régime* as providing the 'protecting strata' of the new economic order. There is therefore here an important rapprochement between the two founding fathers of institutional and evolutionary approaches. In Polanyi's analytical scheme, if the advent of market society could inflict such irreparable damage on nature, this has been so because of the dismantling of the institutional fetters that held it in check.

The disembedding of market economy from its social and natural crust amounted to no less than the invention of 'fictitious commodities'. In a market society, fictitious commodities were land, labour and money, which were not originally produced for sale with a gain but nevertheless treated as if they were commodities and produced as such; hence the fiction. While this may serve as a useful abstraction for the sake of theorizing, if in reality the market mechanism is made the 'sole director' of the 'natural environment' by way of the commodification of land, consequences would be far-reaching: 'Nature would be reduced to its elements, neighborhoods and landscapes defiled, rivers polluted, military safety jeopardized, the power to produce food and raw materials destroyed' (Polanyi, 1944, p. 73).

The detrimental effects of such a process were very clear to Polanyi, they would threaten man's 'natural habitat with annihilation' (Polanyi, 1944, p. 42). In fact, by replacing the Speenhamland mode of labour regulation, the genesis of the labour market had reversed an important aspect of embeddedness. Man was 'torn from his roots and all meaningful environment' (Polanyi, 1944, p. 83). The nascent working-class was provided with a new surrounding that amounted to much less than a 'meaningful environment':

> The industrial town of the Midlands and the North West was *a cultural wasteland*; its slums merely reflected its lack of tradition and civic self-respect. Dumped into this bleak slough of misery, the immigrant peasant, or even the former yeoman or copyholder was soon transformed into *a nondescript animal of the mire*. It was not that he was paid too little, or even that he labored too long – though either happened often to excess – but that *he was now existing under physical conditions which denied the human shape of life* (Polanyi, 1944, p. 99; emphases added).

If anything, the ongoing process was grinding the environment, in the broadest sense of the term, into a wasteland:

> the destruction of family life, the devastation of neighborhoods, the denudation of forests, the pollution of rivers, the deterioration of craft standards, the disruption of folkways, and the general degradation of existence including housing and arts, as well as the innumerable forms of private and public life. (Polanyi, 1944, p. 133)

Nature could thus make its debut after a very long interval precisely because Polanyi's mode of analysis departed radically from that of the classics. Classical political economy had emphasized the role of labour as the sole factor directly or indirectly responsible for economic growth. By this specification other factors were deprived of their distinguishing attributes. The ultimate formulation was that of Karl Marx himself, where the labour theory of value was almost fetishized to explain man's transformation of nature (Lippi, 1979) within the context of a productionist obsession. By contrast, Polanyi, writing after the Marginalist Revolution and fully aware of the Walrasian scheme of general equilibrium analysis, scaled down labour to being only one of the three fictitious commodities: 'Production is *interaction* of man and nature; if this process is to be organized through a self-regulating mechanism of barter and exchange, then *man and nature* must be brought to its orbit' (Polanyi, 1944, p. 130; emphases added). In this context, nature in the form of land, rather than being a passive recipient, could reassume a novel analytical role and engage with labour to determine the overall course of events within market society.

It was squarely unfortunate that whereas nature had experienced a profound change in status in the transition to the market society, this fact could so easily be overlooked just because the classical political economists set out to pursue a line of inquiry that privileged labour as the sole source of value or the major cost factor. The discounting of nature during the construction of One Big Market was at a parity with that of labour, and yet was so easily overlooked:

> The proposition is as utopian in respect to land as in respect to labor. The economic function is but one of many vital functions of land. It invests man's life with stability; it is the site of his habitation; it is a condition of his physical safety; *it is the landscape and the seasons.* We might as well imagine his being born without hands and feet as carrying on his life without land. And yet to separate land from man and organize society in such a way as to satisfy the requirements of *a real-estate market* was a vital part of the utopian concept of a market economy. (Polanyi, 1944, p. 178; emphases added)

We have thus seen how Polanyi brought nature back in as the partner to labour, as well as how the natural and the social are inextricably linked for Polanyi. However, to think that 'nature' is personified into a kind of 'social', or to put it differently, that 'nature' is entirely 'socially constructed' for Polanyi would be entirely misleading. Polanyi was vehemently critical of the 'natural' when it came to explaining human institutions such as the market. But this does not mean that he would disregard the attributes of the 'natural' when it came to understanding 'natural environment'. As a final note, we should remind ourselves that whereas Polanyi rejected 'scarcity' as *the* point of departure for a substantive science of economic activity, and preferred instead a focus on man's procurement of his livelihood – which brings with it an added emphasis on systemic self-reproduction – this does not mean that he rejected 'scarcity' either (Polanyi, 1957, pp. 246–7). In discussing nineteenth-century American exceptionalism, Polanyi underscored the role of free availability of land; in other words, as long as land had not become 'scarce', it could not function as a 'fictitious commodity' (Polanyi, 1944, p. 201). For a commodity to qualify as 'fictitious', it had to become squarely scarce; scarce as any other commodity and yet even scarcer as it could not be produced to demand. Without concepts such as 'scarcity', 'irreproducibility' and 'irreversibility', we could not possibly dwell upon the implications of 'time's arrow'.

A CONCEPTUAL CONTRIBUTION TO INSTITUTIONAL ENVIRONMENTALISM: 'SOCIAL COST'

There exists one concept in *The Great Transformation* that has so far not attracted much attention, despite the fact that it happens to be one of the very few concepts Polanyi himself placed in inverted commas! Had it not been for Kapp's independent placement of this concept at the centre of his own institutional analytical scheme, its presence in Polanyi's text would have gone entirely unnoticed. This is all the more paradoxical because the idea behind the concept plays a fundamental role in Polanyi's analysis, in fact more fundamental than either 'embeddedness' or 'fictitious commodity'. It was Kapp who characterized the dominant intellectual motive of *The Great Transformation* as the rewriting of economic history from a social costs perspective (Kapp, 1963, p. 45). The whole thrust of Polanyi's overall assessment is that the advent of market society, whatever purely economic improvements it may have brought with it, was bought at such a high social price that it was not actually worth it. However when it came to naming this idea, Polanyi was rather spendthrift. On only one occasion, when discussing the antecedents and consequences of Speenhamland, did he coin the two words 'social' and 'cost' together:

> The burden consisted mainly in two seemingly contradictory effects of manufactures, namely, the increase in pauperism and the rise in wages. But the two were contradictory only if the existence of a competitive labor market was assumed, which would, of course, have tended to diminish unemployment by reducing the wages of the employed. In the absence of such a market – and the Act of Settlement was still in force – pauperism and wages might rise simultaneously. Under such conditions the 'social cost' of urban unemployment was mainly borne by the home village to which the out-of-work would often repair. (Polanyi, 1944, p. 94)

This was a most unfortunate context to introduce the concept of 'social cost'. Whereas the idea behind the concept was virtually present in all of *The Great Transformation*, when introduced in this instance the concept was tied up with a very specific context that had dire implications for its general prospects as an analytical tool. The problem here is that the existence of a 'social cost' is traceable to the absence of a competitive labour market. Had there been a competitive labour market, as Polanyi admits, a reduction in wages would have served to reduce unemployment. One might be tempted to read into this a reduction of 'social cost'. Given the cost-reducing or economizing interpretations of the market process by the NIE adherents, such a misreading can be easily understood. The very idea of a 'social cost' reducing market is, however, against the very spirit of Polanyi-style institutional analysis.

Within the macro-structure of his argument, the very creation of a self-regulating market system was responsible for the enormous 'social cost' incurred. If so, how could the market alleviate social costs, as can by stretch of imagination be deduced from the one place in the text where social cost is explicitly cited? Of course, there is another dimension to the specific case under study. With a competitive labour market, 'social cost' would be placed elsewhere other than the rural community. Urban community would possibly undertake some of it while the rest would fall on the shoulders of the very workers who would be paid less in wages. In retrospect, if anything is involved here, it is not social cost-reducing, but instead 'cost-shifting' in contemporary neoinstitutionalist parlance (Swaney, 1987) – a theme we will return to when we discuss William Kapp's contribution. Be that as it may, given the ambiguity involved in the quoted passage, in order for 'social cost' to be uplifted to an analytically useful status one had to wait for another intervention.

The commonplace economic conception of cost is by definition private and individualistic, if not fully subjective in the Austrian sense. Conventional economic analysis works exclusively with this version of cost. The 'social' in Polanyi's sense defies conceptualization in a similar manner by way of induction. In other words, it is not reducible to the summation of individual 'private costs'. As such, it is also incommensurate, and therefore qualitatively different, from the cost concept of conventional economics that Polanyi knew very well. In this light, to Polanyi, coining 'social' and 'cost' together was an act of construing a contradiction in terms. However, the very concept of 'social cost' could be made analytically useful by recourse to the very distinction between the natures of the two constituent parts. This is precisely what William Kapp did in his *Social Costs of Business Enterprise*.

Whereas for Polanyi 'social cost' as a concept was of limited use except as a contradiction in terms, for Kapp it became the conceptual point of departure. Kapp was well aware of all the limitations inherent in such a concept. He acknowledged that the concept could be criticized for its lack of 'definiteness and precision' (Kapp, 1963, p. 20), and that 'quantification will always remain an important question' (Kapp, 1963, p. 21) as far as social costs are concerned. It is important to emphasize that for Kapp, 'social cost' covered a wide terrain extending from within the domain of the very 'economic' to that of the broadly 'social'. As such it was a concept that cut across conventional disciplinary boundaries and connected, rather than artificially separating:

> The fact that some of these social costs are ultimately reflected in private monetary losses and public expenditures emphasizes their 'economic' character even in the narrow sense in which the term is used in traditional economic analysis. Other social costs, as for example the detrimental effects on esthetic and recreational values and partly also the impairment of human health, are of a less tangible character and cannot be fully evaluated in monetary terms or market prices. (Kapp, 1963, p. 264)

Kapp's ingenious argument transformed step by step the seeming limitations of the concept into positive attributes. So much so, that by the end of this refinement process the concept became indispensable not only for the study of environmental problems in general but also for a devastating critique of neoclassical economics. Ever since the beginning of institutional economics, neoclassics had insisted that, irrespective of the methodological grain of truth they may display, institutional theoretical critiques were actually inferior in achievement to mainstream theory precisely because they could not come up with an alternative value theory. Therefore, according to neoclassical economists, as long as the institutionalists did not have a rival value theory that explained price formation, their criticisms would add up to little and eventually boil down to a kind of empiricism *pace* the German Historical School (Özveren, 1998). Setting aside the legitimacy of whether or not the formulation of a technical value theory in conformity with the metaphor of Newtonian physics constitutes the most important problem of economic inquiry, the fact remained that by the prevailing standards of economic science, there was one domain where institutional economics was outperformed by the dominant orthodoxy. Efforts to catch up with neoclassical theory in this domain so far have proven of limited success, if any:

> Even more significant was the fact that *pure* economic theory began to concern itself more and more with the analysis of an essentially stationary image or model of the market economy . . . Good illustrations of this procedure which tended to eliminate the dynamic and less congenial factors of reality from

economic analysis can be found in nearly every branch of economic investigation. But nowhere is this tendency more marked than in *the very core of economic analysis: namely, the theory of value and price. Here the concentration on
private costs and private wants has been almost complete. In fact, for all practical
purposes value theory considers it as axiomatic that entrepreneurial outlays and
private returns constitute a theoretically adequate measure of the costs and benefits
of productive activities.* (Kapp, 1963, pp. 5–6; emphasis added)

As Kapp demonstrates, the neoclassical practice is in fact erroneous and
therefore misleading in terms of its implications. The neoclassical conception
of cost is 'incomplete and apparently in need of correction' (Kapp, 1963,
p. xii). Mainstream economics works with an 'incomplete system of cost
accounting': 'Nothing is more irrational than an incomplete system of cost
accounting. An economic calculus that neglects one part of the costs of production can hardly claim to promote social efficiency' (Kapp, 1963, p. 17).

The very foundation of neoclassically idealized rational economic
behaviour as the sine qua non of social welfare and economic efficiency is
shaken to ground if what is at work is an incomplete cost–benefit analysis.
Furthermore: 'As long as it continues to confine itself to *market value* neoclassical economics will fail to assimilate to its reasoning and to its
conceptual system many of the costs (and returns) which cannot be
expressed in dollars and cents' (Kapp, 1963, p. 11; emphasis added).

Kapp's critique undermines the foundations of neoclassical superiority
in this regard. It is only with the way in which Kapp used the concept of
'social cost' that the tables have been definitively turned around. As of this
point, the issue is no longer whether or not institutional economics measures up to the standards set by the neoclassical mainstream in putting
forward a theory of value and price, but instead, whether or not the neoclassical theory in this respect is fundamentally flawed. Consequently, there
remains no standard reference, something that the institutionalists should
presumably try to catch up with.

Kapp's elaboration of the concept of 'social cost' requires further com-
mentary. First and foremost, he broadened the scope of the concept. This
can best be understood in comparison with Polanyi's use of the term. While
discussing the implicit antecedents of social cost analysis, Kapp referred to
the tacit presence of social costs in Simonde de Sismondi's and Karl Marx's
studies, among others. He situated such works within the 'period of transition following the introduction of the machine method of production'
(Kapp, 1963, p. 33); a characterization strongly reminiscent of Polanyi's
The Great Transformation. He further argued that the kind of social costs
that Sismondi brought to the foreground were specifically social costs of
technological change, which in turn should be seen as a 'special case of the
social costs of transition' (Kapp, 1963, p. 33).

In conformity with Kapp's reasoning, we should further add that 'social costs of transition' are a special case of social costs in general. Now, in this sense, whereas Polanyi concentrated exclusively on the 'social costs of transition', Kapp developed a much broader conception of social costs. This shift had one very important consequence. 'Social costs of transition' refer exclusively to the long term. In the long term, society as a whole faces these costs. There may even be rollovers at work from one generation to the next. However, when we broaden the scope of the concept of 'social costs' *pace* Kapp, not only long-term but also short- and medium-term considerations are introduced into the picture.[6] This makes a major difference. In many instances that Kapp studies in detail, social costs concern a situation where, albeit being members of the same society, some pay in the place of others. As such, social costs have a redistributive effect within the very society involved. It must be for this reason that Kapp insisted on including a 'third party' in his definition of social costs:

> In short, the term 'social costs' refers to all those harmful consequences and damages which other persons or the community sustain as a result of productive processes, and for which private entrepreneurs are not held accountable. This definition of the concept is comprehensive enough to include even certain 'social opportunity costs', which take the form of avoidable wastes and social inefficiencies of various kinds. (Kapp, 1963, p. 14)

According to Kapp, social costs, while possessing a common denominator that served to justify their characterization as a single category, were manifest in a wide range of fields. Furthermore, they were not incidental but systemic in nature:

> [I]t can be shown that the social costs which are shifted to other persons or to society as a whole are not only substantial but that such shifts are *typical and regular* occurrences which can be obviated, if at all, only by an elaborate system of technical regulations and social legislation. (Kapp, 1963, p. 271; emphasis added)

The fact that they were systemic occurrences in a market system where the profit motive dictated the logistic calculus of business enterprises led Kapp to a sweeping conclusion. While institutionalists like Veblen and Polanyi had expressed their discomfort with the Marxian idea of 'exploitation' as an analytical device, it was Kapp who once again came up with not only a critique but also an alternative:

> As soon as one passes beyond the traditional abstractions of neo-classical price analysis and begins to consider the neglected aspects of unpaid social costs it becomes evident that the social efficiency of private investment criteria, and

hence the alleged beneficial outcome of the allocation process under conditions of private enterprise, is largely an illusion. For, if entrepreneurial outlays fail to measure the actual total costs of production because part of the latter tend to be shifted to the shoulders of the others, then the traditional cost–benefit calculus is not simply misleading but actually serves as an institutionalized cloak for large-scale spoilation which exceeds everything which the early utopian socialists and even their Marxian successors had in mind when they denounced the exploitation of man by man under the emerging system of business enterprise. (Kapp, 1963, p. 271)

Irrespective of in which specific domain they manifested themselves, all social costs were traceable to the operation of the market economy as a whole where production was organized within private business enterprises. In fact, a careful scrutiny of Kapp's study of various types of social costs would indicate that while many of them originate from the market mechanism in a Polanyi-esque manner, others are more immediately connected with the notorious practices of business enterprise in a Veblenian sense. Kapp was well aware of Veblen's earlier statements concerning the 'wasteful' attributes of business enterprise and explicitly mentioned Veblen as a source of inspiration in his second revised edition of *Social Costs of Business Enterprise*. In fact, one of the revisions involved was to replace 'private enterprise' in the title of the first edition in order to affirm his lineage with the institutional analytical tradition (Kapp, 1963, p. x, 43). Kapp's insistence that 'what may be technologically wasteful might still be economical' bears the imprint of an important Veblenian theme (Kapp, 1963, p. 70). Kapp made only two references to works of Polanyi, which look more like last minute footnote insertions to emphasize parallels rather than thematic borrowing (see Kapp, 1963, p. 45, 288), but the strong parallelism among the two scholars is strikingly manifest (Heidenreich, 1998; Swaney and Evers, 1989). It would be appropriate to say that Kapp and Polanyi arrived at similar conclusions somewhat independently of each other. Even so, we should remind ourselves that Polanyi concluded his widely influential article with the following ambitious remark:

> Even in regard to the market system itself, the market as the sole frame of reference is somewhat out of date. Yet, as should be more clearly realized than it has been in the past, the market cannot be superseded as a general frame of reference *unless the social sciences succeed in developing a wider frame of reference to which the market itself is referable.* This indeed is our main intellectual task today in the field of economic studies. (Polanyi, 1957, p. 270; emphasis added)

In the very first chapter of his book, Kapp spelled out his overriding purpose in a way that should make us think that he conceived his own work as a follow up to Karl Polanyi's research agenda:

The present investigation must thus be understood *as part of a larger inquiry* the purpose of which is twofold: to measure the performance of the system of business enterprise *by yardsticks which transcend those of the market* and lay the foundation for a *reformulation of economic analysis* so as to include those omitted aspects of reality which many economists have been inclined to dismiss or neglect as 'noneconomic'. (Kapp, 1963, pp. 11–12; emphases added)

In short, Kapp provided an enviable early synthesis of the Polanyi and Veblen approaches in his landmark study of social costs.

Kapp probed further into the consequences of the functioning of a market economy. According to him, the market economy has a tendency to lead to spatial polarization by way of the concentration of industry and labour-force in certain localities. This is because the principle of external economies at work exerts a pulling effect. As a consequence, there emerges a cumulative process of environmental deterioration. In fact, Kapp stressed time and again 'the cumulative character and complexity of the causal sequence which gives rise to environmental disruption and social costs' (Kapp, 1970, p. 837), as he called it:

What appears to be profitable in terms of private costs and private returns is actually a wasteful agglomeration of industries without regard to the social costs caused thereby. Indeed if these industries had to pay the social costs caused by their concentrating in urban centers it might well turn out that at least some of the much-taken-for-granted economies would be partly if not wholly offset by the tangible and intangible diseconomies of over-concentration. (Kapp, 1963, p. 262)

While the spatial manifestation of the spontaneous working of a market economy takes the above form and leads necessarily to eventually rising social costs, further effects of the market process are readily identifiable. Particularly within the range of renewable resources, the price system fails because first, it cannot rationally identify the ideal output position, second, it cannot take into account the equation of social costs and benefits, and third, it has a tendency to accelerate the use of resources sooner rather than later because of the focus on here and now as befits the motive for private gain (Kapp, 1963). As for the utilization of non-renewable resources, competitive logic leads, first, to unnecessary duplication of capital outlays, second, to loss of reserves due to surplus capacity and depressed prices which induce private enterprises to use less efficient methods of production, and third, to premature depletion of resources with a further negative consequence on future generations (Kapp, 1963).

Although Kapp was concerned with the wasteful effects of the 'business enterprise and the competitive market calculus' (Kapp, 1963, p. 263) in

general, within this broad context, he did address the more specific question of the 'institutional approach to the study of resource depletion'
(Kapp, 1963, p. 114) and pursued a thorough investigation of the environmental question as it takes shape under the various 'institutional arrangements' (Kapp, 1963, p. 98) of an industrial civilization. He saw that 'man
must make the necessary adjustments if he is not to destroy the basis of
human survival' (Kapp, 1963, p. 73) and he was confident in the coming
assertion by man in the industrial world of his 'unalienable right' (Kapp,
1963, p. 72) to a clean environment. While Kapp concentrated his systemic
analysis on the role of social costs, he did see beyond the immediate horizon
of this relativistic logic and noted the absolute effects of the problem as per-
tinent to the environment:

> Water and air pollution do *much more than* shift some of the costs of pro-
> duction to people living outside of a given area. They create *a new physical
> environment* for man. Indeed, instead of the *natural environment* in which man
> has lived for centuries, the permanent revolution of technology has created *a
> man-made environment* the full implications of which, for human health
> and human survival, are far from being fully understood. We are only at the
> threshold of the realization that this man-made environment may be exceed-
> ingly detrimental to all life on this planet. (Kapp, 1963, p. 87; emphases
> added)

In addressing the environmental question, Kapp was well aware of the
inherent problems of using non-renewable resources. He also made use of
the concept of 'social limit', beyond which the use of renewable resources
would cause various social losses (Kapp, 1963, p. 93). He identified a 'critical zone' in the utilization of renewable resources. A rate of use exceeding
this limit would cause an 'economically irreversible depletion which is
associated with considerable social losses' (Kapp, 1963, p. 96). Furthermore, Kapp referred to 'ecological balance' as it concerns 'the delicate
system of interrelationships between the land and its vegetative cover'
(Kapp, 1963, p. 94). However, Kapp was no naive environmentalist, nor
was he a neoclassical economist who would uphold the principle of
reversibility – far from it. He was well aware of the irreversible time's arrow
at work:

> To define the ecological balance is not to suggest that its maintenance must
> become a norm. There is no need to point out that any *general advance of pop-
> ulation makes it increasingly difficult to maintain intact the ecological balance.*
> Even apart from the general increase of population there may be other overrul-
> ing reasons why this balance cannot be maintained – as for instance in periods
> of natural disaster or national emergencies. However, any such disturbance has
> long-term *cumulative consequences* which man can anticipate to a large extent

and which it is always imprudent to ignore in the interest of maximizing current returns or minimizing current costs. (Kapp, 1963, p. 95; emphases added)

In retrospect, whereas Polanyi's concept of 'embeddedness' did serve to bring nature back in, unless further elaborated this concept in itself possesses a dualistic quality. In other words, this concept in purely semantic terms relies on the distinction of the 'external' from the 'internal'. The 'external', while surrounding the content, continues to preserve its separate identity. With the concept of 'social costs' as refined by Kapp, we enter a new domain where processes that take place within the 'content' bear a traceable impact upon the 'embedding' container, in a way true to the spirit of Polanyi's work. However, a further step whereby the distinction between the content and the container is violated is now in order. The correct specification of the institutional approach to environment requires this step. Kapp was well aware of this necessity. In his reformulation of institutional economics he brought to the foreground the need to analyse the subject matter as an 'open system', working in conformity with the principle of 'circular and cumulative causation'. Kapp summarized his viewpoint in a way that would inevitably lead to the questioning of conventional disciplinary pigeonholes:

> The relevant boundaries of the limits of social inquiry differ depending upon the problems under discussion. In any event, in view of the cumulative circular interdependencies which link the economy to *the environment and the resource base* and hence to the interests of future generations economic processes cannot be adequately described without reference to a time horizon: that is to say, without reference to the time schedule of inputs in relation to scarce available resources, and the direction of the qualitative changes which *the use of energy and matter as well as the disposal of waste have upon the environment* and hence on economic processes and the well-being of future generations. It is this concern for a longer time horizon and the complex interdependencies of actual social phenomena and processes moving in a definite direction with possible *irreversible* qualitative changes and, last but not least, the rejection and the replacement of the mechanical analogy by the principle of circular causation which gives modern institutionalism, what I venture to call its modern character and its *transdisciplinary* scope. (Kapp, 1976, p. 230; emphases added)

Accordingly, processes characteristic of the content bear the input and therefore the imprint of the container, while the container itself changes shape with the transformations within its content. Put differently, in this mature state of institutional analysis, the 'internal–external' distinction is dissolved in order to make room for a conceptualization of the systemic evolution of the whole along the irreversible trajectory of 'time's arrow'.

ENVIRONMENT AS INSTITUTIONALISTS' FAVOURITE METAPHOR FOR THE SOCIAL

The relationship of the social sciences to the natural sciences has attracted much attention. It is commonplace knowledge that the dominant trend in economic science has aspired to Newtonian physics as its role model. Institutionalist critiques of mainstream economics have, since Veblen, attacked orthodoxy for this obsessive compulsion (Veblen, 1898; Georgescu-Roegen, 1971; Mirowski, 1989). Instead of physics, if economic science were to take Darwinian biology or the then anthropology as a role model, it would become an evolutionary science (Veblen, 1898). It goes without saying that what institutionalists had in common with their rivals was a shared belief in the superiority of the natural sciences to social sciences in general.

A further consequence of this long-held belief has been studies that trace the effects of natural metaphors on social, but especially on economic, thought. For example, one such study identifies in Schumpeter a leading example of how the 'natural' and the 'social' can be conceived as essentially identical in 'metaphorical structure' (Mirowski, 1994, p. 11). Another study that focuses on the theme of evolution in economics concludes that Schumpeter shied away from natural metaphors in general, and the kind of thinking he displayed was 'evolutionary' in a sense other than implied by the post-Darwinian biological metaphors (Hodgson, 1996). While there may be different assessments of his intellectual debt to natural metaphors, a discussion of Schumpeter is of great importance for us here. This is because Schumpeter is an influential evolutionary economist who gave as strong an emphasis, if not more, to institutional factors in his research program as the self-proclaimed institutionalists themselves. In his *Capitalism, Socialism and Democracy* we can identify some of the most mature formulations of otherwise institutional themes.

It is somewhat paradoxical that, of all the institutional or evolutionary economists, Schumpeter, noted for his less-than-average interest in using the explicit lessons of the natural sciences for his theorizing within the domain of economics, should display the most mature deployment of the natural metaphor for the conceptualization of the so-called 'non-economic' or 'social'. For this purpose, Schumpeter exploited the full potential of what we will, for the sake of convenience, name 'social environment'. Interestingly enough, 'social environment' in Schumpeter plays a role strongly reminiscent of the function of environment with respect to the economy as discussed in the institutionalist literature. Implicit in Schumpeter's discussion is a conception that qualifies 'social environment' as a non-renewable resource. It is something that has a given magnitude and is inherited from the pre-capitalist past, and furthermore is subject to depletion as capitalism as an evolutionary process moves ahead in conformity with time's irreversible arrow.

The whole point of Schumpeter's argument in *Capitalism, Socialism and Democracy* is that, while creative in many respects, capitalism is essentially uncreative, and actually destructive when it comes to its 'social environment'. It cannot replace the institutional framework that helps contain it, and furthermore, it fosters critical habits of mind and hostile attitudes. These 'environmental factors', in Schumpeter's terminology, serve to pollute the 'social atmosphere' from within (Schumpeter, 1942, p. 112, 143–55). In the Schumpeterian scenario, it is by destroying its historical heritage from the pre-capitalist era that the economic process undermines itself as a result of its very success. On this point we should note that there exists a strong parallel between Schumpeter and Polanyi. In Polanyi as well we have already encountered how the advent of market system was destructive of the 'social' that was characteristic of the pre-market era.[7] Where Schumpeter and Polanyi stand together, that is, on the conception of the 'social' in the broad sense of the 'non-economic' as subject to erosion, we have grounds for a general conclusion that should help characterize the institutional approach as a whole. Therefore, before making the specific contributions to the study of environment observed in the earlier parts of this work, institutional economics had already possessed a notion of environment as a metaphor it used for the study of the 'social'.

CONCLUSION

In the first part of this work we listed three rival strategies with respect to the existing disciplinary boundaries. The first of these was characteristic of the dominant neoclassical approach noted for its imperialistic transdisciplinary aggression. On the other side, that is on the terrain of opposition, there were two camps. We identified, first, the parasitic strategy of NIE that takes for granted existing disciplinary boundaries in order to traverse them selectively by way of interdisciplinary or multidisciplinary ventures only to score gains vis-à-vis its neoclassical rival. The second camp on the opposition side belonged to the true institutionalists who contested the very logic of specialization and opted instead for a singular transdisciplinary approach.

Of the two opposition strategies, in the short-to-medium term, the second strategy seems to be more rewarding as it can bring immediate benefits at a time when the 'wall' continues to exist. On the other hand, because this strategy occupies a middle ground by opportunistically combining some basic methodological attributes of neoclassical analysis with its periodic interdisciplinary assaults, it can always fall prey to the strength of the dominant neoclassical approach and lose its independence. To remain in place and preserve its autonomy, it needs as much the pulling-effect of a truly original institutionalist economics as it needs the repellent push of the mainstream. Be that as it may, in the medium-to-long term, if and as the 'wall' comes down, because the second strategy's parasitic position will be undermined, the third strategy has greater prospects thanks to its ontological soundness and logical consistency.

With respect to the above spectrum, rapidly increasing contemporary institutionalist contributions to environmental economics coincide with the second strategy. While far from readily embracing NIE, they nevertheless share with it a number of characteristics and their fortunes. First and foremost, these works take for granted the legitimacy of a subdiscipline of environmental economics and therefore succumb to the trappings of disciplinary specialization. Within the constituted domain of environmental economics as derivative of neoclassical economics, it is not surprising that measurement fetishism prevails. A major impasse of institutionalist environmental economists concerns the valuation process. As we have seen, the mainstream economists make a case for the effective valuation process of the market mechanism. Environmental institutional economists react by wavering between natural physical values on the one side, and social valuation by way of a forum-like deliberation process on the other. Either way, they take the centrality of neoclassical valuation by way of market pricing more seriously than they should. By doing so, they provide their rivals with ammunition because their proposed alternatives are not as practical. The whole critique of market valuation we find in Kapp and the concomitant phenomenon of 'exploitation' could provide them with much safer ground to turn the tables around.

To benefit from the support of original institutionalism, however, institutional environmental economists have first to develop a new sense of ontological foundations of the disciplinary ground under their feet. Instead of accomplishing this task, so far whereas neoclassical economists venture into the subdiscipline of environmental economics from one side, these institutionalists arrive from the opposite side in much the same way, yet with the baggage of different piecemeal tools and convictions. Irrespective of which direction they come from, both parties take for granted the constitution of the domain in question. In contrast, from the viewpoint of original institutionalists like Polanyi and Kapp, the very existence of such a separate domain needs to be contested. It should be emphasized here that the adoption of this latter position does not mean that all institutional economists have to study environment together with other strictly economic concerns. It is natural that different institutional economists should have different research foci. However, mere concentration of research foci should neither constitute nor legitimize a subdiscipline. In light of our above discussion of the works of Polanyi and Kapp, it has become obvious that the domain of original institutional economics was broadly defined so as to include at least not only the domain of neoclassical economics but also that of environmental economics.

A comparison of the size of the disciplinary domains of the neoclassical and institutional economics in the above sense would nevertheless not yield the whole truth. Long before environmental economics or the so-called environmental institutionalism were officially born, within its very structure the institutional approach possessed an implicit metaphor of environment that it deployed effectively for the characterization of the 'social', as the seminal works of Polanyi and Schumpeter attest. In this sense, environmental institutional economics should get rid of its self-image as being a simple extension of institutional analysis to just another field of inquiry. If anything it should stand as heir apparent to the heritage of one important tool in the original institutionalist way of thinking that had always been there. We are only now beginning to see what has for long been in front of our eyes. If we can now refer as we did earlier in this chapter to the discussion of the status of environment in Polanyi's work 'as bringing back in nature', this is because we have for a long time been blinded to seeing what has always been in those texts before our very eyes. This may well have to do with the fact that, with the ongoing challenge to the dogmatic practice of disciplinary boundaries, we are regaining our long-lost sight.

NOTES

1. I would like to thank Dr Fikret Adaman of Boğaziçi University and Dr Serap Türüt Aşık of the Middle East Technical University for their valuable comments. The suggestions of the editors of this volume gave this work a new turn for the better. I assume full responsibility for remaining errors.
2. The mainstream study of environment is primarily shared among an older natural resource economics and an environmental economics of more recent vintage. Whereas the former specializes on how nature provides inputs by way of factors into the economy the latter concentrates on the post-production and consumption effects, that is, the flow of waste materials and energy residuals, which bestow upon the environment a sink function (Kneese, 1995, pp. xiii–xv). Genealogically, the two fields of specialization come from different sources (agricultural economics and welfare economics respectively) and epochs (the first is as old as Malthusian classical economics, whereas the latter gained widespread currency as of the 1970s), but because both deal with the relationship of the economy and nature by recourse to similar research tools and techniques, for the sake of convenience they will be treated jointly under the rubric of environmental economics in this study.
3. An institutionalist interpretation of Coase on social costs in tune with the rest of his work

on transaction costs would resist the popular function of this seminal article as a basis for the Property Rights School. According to such an interpretation, Coase indulged himself in the study of a hypothetical special case, which was of little significance but to illustrate how radically the real world differed from this case. However, it so happened that the abstract specification of this special case overlapped with the neoclassical model, thereby serving interests other than its own (Mulberg, 1995, pp. 153–4).

4. This structural affinity of neoclassical and environmental economics is well noted even by adherents of the conventional approach (Pearce, 1998, p. 313).

5. A notable exception (Swaney and Evers, 1989), albeit with restricted focus, deserves mention as a precursor of this study.

6. This does not mean that Kapp overlooked the importance of the long-term. On the contrary, Kapp insisted that 'the time horizon of organized society in all matters related to the resource base must necessarily extend further than that of an individual or a private firm' (Kapp, 1963, p. 124).

7. If anything, the difference between the two leading theorists would boil down to the fact that unlike Schumpeter, who foresees a gradual evolution into socialism with virtually little positive role for 'movements' to play, Polanyi envisages the inevitable growth of a 'self-protective' reaction: a theme that should not concern us here.

REFERENCES

Becker, Gary (1976), *The Economic Approach to Human Behavior*, Chicago: The University of Chicago Press.

Blake, William (2002), 'Milton', in W.B. Yeats (ed.), *William Blake: Collected Poems* [1804–10], London: Routledge, pp. 211–14.

Braudel, Fernand (1979), *Les jeux de l'échange*, Paris: Armand Colin.

Coase, Ronald H. (1960), 'The problem of social cost', *Journal of Law and Economics*, **III**, 1–44.

Costanza, Robert (1997), *Frontiers in Ecological Economics*, Cheltenham, UK and Lyme, USA: Edward Elgar.

Daly, Herman E. (1999), *Ecological Economics and the Ecology of Economics*, Cheltenham, UK and Northampton, MA, USA: Edward Elgar.

Dietz, F.J. and Jan van der Straaten (1992), 'Rethinking environmental economics: missing links between economic theory and environmental policy', *Journal of Economic Issues*, **XXVI**, 27–51.

Foucault, Michel (1977), *Language, Counter-Memory, and Practice*, Ithaca, New York: Cornell University Press.

Georgescu-Roegen, Nicholas (1971), *The Entropy Law and the Economic Process*, Cambridge, MA: Harvard University Press.

Georgescu-Roegen, Nicholas (1976), *Energy and Economic Myths*, New York: Pergamon.

Godard, Olivier and Jean-Michel Salles (1991), 'Entre nature et société. Les jeux de l'irréversibilité dans la construction économique et sociale du champ de l'environnement', in Robert Boyer, Bernard Chavance and Olivier Godard (eds), *Les figures de l'irréversibilité en économie*, Paris: Éditions de l'École des Hautes Études en Sciences Sociales, pp. 233–72.

Gulbenkian Commission (1996), 'Open the social sciences', report of the Gulbenkian Commission on the restructuring of the social sciences, Stanford: Stanford University Press.

Heidenrich, Regine (1998), 'Economics and institutions: the socioeconomic approach of K. William Kapp', *Journal of Economic Issues*, **XXXII** (4), 965–84.

Hodgson, Geoffrey M. (1996), *Economics and Evolution*, Ann Arbor: The University of Michigan Press.

Kapp, K. William (1963), *Social Costs of Business Enterprise* [1950], Bombay, India: Asia Publishing House.

Kapp, K. William (1970), 'Environmental Disruption and Social Costs: A Challenge to Economics', *Kyklos*, **23** (4), 833–47.

Kapp, K. William (1976), 'The nature and significance of institutional economics', *Kyklos*, **29** (2), 209–32.

Kneese, Allen V. (1995), *Natural Resource Economics*, Aldershot, UK and Brookfield, US: Edward Elgar.

Lippi, Marco (1979), *Value and Naturalism in Marx*, London: New Left Books.

Martinez-Alier, Juan (1987), *Ecological Economics*, Oxford: Basil Blackwell.

Martinez-Alier, Joan and K. Sclupmann (1987), *Ecological Economics: Energy, Environment and Society*, Oxford: Basil Blackwell.

Martinez-Alier (1999), 'From political economy to political ecology', in Kozo Mayumi and John M. Gowdy (eds), *Bioeconomics and Sustainability*, Cheltenham, UK and Northampton, MA, USA: Edward Elgar, pp. 25–50.

Mirowski, Philip (1989), *More Heat than Light: Economics as Social Physics: Physics as Nature's Economics*, Cambridge: Cambridge University Press.

Mirowski, Philip (1994), *Natural Images in Economic Thought*, Cambridge: Cambridge University Press.

Mulberg, Jon (1995), *Social Limits to Economic Theory*, London: Routledge.

North, Douglass C. (1990), *Institutions, Institutional Change and Economic Performance*, Cambridge: Cambridge University Press.

Özveren, Eyüp (1998), 'An institutionalist alternative to neoclassical economics?', (Review), *A Journal of the Fernand Braudel Center*, **XXI** (3–4), 469–530.

Özveren, Eyüp (1999), 'Return of the "primitive" in modern social sciences: the institutionalist legacy of Karl Polanyi', paper presented at the Seventh International Karl Polanyi Conference, Centre Auguste et Léon Walras, Université Lumiere-Lyon II, 26–28 May, ERC Working Paper, no. 99/1, Middle East Technical University Economic Research Center.

Pearce, David (1998), *Economics and Environment*, Cheltenham, UK and Lyme, USA: Edward Elgar.

Pirenne, Henri (1936), *Economic and Social History of Medieval Europe*, New York: Harvest.

Polanyi, Karl (1944), *The Great Transformation: The Political and Economic Origins of Our Time*, Boston: Beacon Press.

Polanyi, Karl (1957), 'The economy as instituted process', in Karl Polanyi, Conrad M. Arensberg and Harry W. Pearson (eds), *Trade and Market in the Early Empires: Economies in History and Theory*, New York: Free Press, pp. 243–70.

Sachs, Ignacy (1993), *L'écodéveloppement*, Paris: Syros.

Sagoff, Mark (1998), *The Economy of the Earth*, Cambridge: Cambridge University Press.

Santos, Boaventura de Sousa (1995), *Towards a New Common Sense: Law, Science and Politics in the Paradigmatic Transition*, London: Routledge.

Schumpeter, Joseph A. (1942), *Capitalism, Socialism and Democracy*, New York: Harper.

Söderbaum, Peter (1994), 'Actors, ideology, markets: neoclassical and institutional perspectives on environmental policy', *Ecological Economics*, **10**, 47–60.

Straaten, Jan van der (1999), 'What type of economic theory dealing with the environment do we need?', in Jörg Köhn, John Gowdy, Friedrich Hinterberger and Jan van der Staaten (eds), *Sustainability in Question*, Cheltenham, UK and Northampton, MA, USA: Edward Elgar, 33–47.

Swaney, James A. (1985), 'Economics, Ecology, and Entropy', *Journal of Economic Issues*, **XIX**, 4, 853–65.

Swaney, James A. (1987), 'Elements of a neoinstitutional environmental economics', *Journal of Economic Issues*, **XXI**, 4, 1739–79.

Swaney, James A. and Martin A. Evers (1989), 'The social cost concepts of K. William Kapp and Karl Polanyi', *Journal of Economic Issues*, **XXIII** (1), 7–33.

Veblen, Thorstein (1898), 'Why is economics not an evolutionary science?', *The Quarterly Journal of Economics*, **12** (July),

Williamson, Oliver E. (1985), *The Economic Institutions of Capitalism: Firms, Markets, Relational Contracting*, New York: Free Press.

Wordsworth, William (2000), 'The world is too much with us', in his *The Major Works* [1807], Oxford: Oxford University Press, p. 270.

PART III

Flexibility, routines and production in
economics and social sciences

9. Economic flexibility: a structural analysis

William A. Jackson

INTRODUCTION

The idea of flexibility has become commonplace in economic discussion. Price flexibility has always been a focus of attention, but flexibility is now interpreted more widely and applied to areas such as employment and production. Interest in the topic has been aroused by the alleged global trend towards flexible specialization and post-Fordism.

Yet economic flexibility, despite its prominence in the academic literature, lacks a single definition and is construed in different ways by different authors. Neoclassical economists often view flexibility as the absence of social structures impeding free markets: flexibility is then a prerequisite for Pareto efficiency, and inflexible structures or institutions should, if possible, be removed. In the neoclassical ideal, a perfectly competitive economy would function as a complete, smoothly operating natural system where immediate price adjustments accommodate any changes in external circumstances.

From a non-neoclassical angle, this approach to economic flexibility is inadequate, since markets are unavoidably structural, based on role playing, and can never be structure-free. Flexibility does not require that economies somehow escape social structures and deliver an efficient natural order. The portrayal of flexibility should allow for social structures and institutions that in neoclassical parlance would be described as imperfections or rigidities. Paradoxically, economic flexibility will revolve around what neoclassical economists regard as inflexibility.

Recent work in sociology is relevant here, as it can provide an enhanced account of social structure. One strand of this work is the interdependence of social structure and human agency, so that structure may enable as well as constrain action. Another strand is the recognition of various types of social structure, for example, institutional structures founded on roles and figurational structures founded on personal relations. The interplay between structure and agency and among different types of social structure creates a broader analytical framework that can envisage many sources of flexibility.

This chapter draws from recent sociological theories to adopt an interdisciplinary approach to economic flexibility and argues that, contrary to the neoclassical view, flexibility is a structural property best understood through an augmented treatment of social structure.

THE MEANING OF FLEXIBILITY

The term 'flexibility' is more subtle than it appears at first sight and several of its connotations are passed over in much economic discussion. Before considering economic flexibility, it is worth looking at what 'flexibility' means.

To describe an object or institution as flexible suggests that it can bend or adapt to external pressures without breaking or losing its shape. Flexibility refers not just to a capacity to change, but to a capacity to change within a larger system or structure that itself remains unchanged. The outcome mixes adaptation and stability: some limited adaptation does occur, but the containing system or object stays intact. An example of this is the notion of the 'flexible firm', where various modes of adaptation are available but they are all confined within a given, unchanging firm (Atkinson and Meager, 1986; Pollert, 1988b). Aligning flexibility too closely with economic change may well be misleading. Although flexibility seems to imply dynamism and fluidity, it may entail the persistence of economic arrangements in the face of external challenges. Flexibility could be vital in reproducing and maintaining economic institutions.

A related point is that flexibility generally refers to short-term adaptations, as against long-term changes of economic institutions or technology. If economic changes went beyond minor adaptations and transformed the whole economic system, then they would no longer be classified under the heading of flexibility. Rather, they would be part of a more radical process of economic evolution or growth. Flexible institutions might seem conducive to economic progress, but this is not inevitably the case; short-term adaptations within a flexible system might stifle or delay fundamental reforms. Consequently, short-term flexibility should be distinguished from long-term evolution and growth.

Economic flexibility is anything but unidimensional, there being many dimensions in which adaptations take place. Flexible employment, for instance, can be subdivided among numerical flexibility (changing numbers of workers); functional flexibility (redeployment of workers to different tasks); financial flexibility (changes in wages and other payments);

working-time flexibility (changes in working hours); and labour-market flexibility (movements between different industrial and regional labour markets) (Rubery, 1989; Boje, 1991; Dex and McCulloch, 1997, Chapter 1). Production flexibility too appears in numerous guises and is not uniquely determined by technology (Morroni, 1991). Systemic adjustments can be made through any of the key economic variables in the formal economy, such as prices, employment and output. Because the formal economic accounts will record these variables, the adjustments will be visible and measurable. Other sources of flexibility are less obvious. Adjustments can be made informally, through changes in work intensity, variable working patterns, networking and so forth. Flexibility may be achieved by changes in several formal variables, alongside informal changes located beyond the formal economy or in the gaps left by formal arrangements. Some adjustments will be interrelated, and it would be short-sighted to consider only one dimension of flexibility in isolation from the others.

Sceptics of economic flexibility feel that the many types of adaptation have little in common and do not cohere into a recognizable trend towards increasing flexibility (Pollert, 1988a, 1991; Sayer, 1989; Clarke, 1992). For the sceptics, the apparent shift from inflexible Fordism to flexible post-Fordism has no real substance, and it would be better to discard blanket concepts such as economic flexibility. If the term 'flexibility' is used carefully, however, it need not imply universal trends or common patterns and is compatible with diverse forms of economic adjustment. Doubts over the post-Fordist and neoclassical analyses of recent economic experience can coexist with concepts of economic flexibility, as long as one accepts that flexibility exists in multiple, perhaps unrelated, varieties and does not have to follow any single path. It may, indeed, be wise to retain the idea of flexibility and aim for a more elaborate, heterodox interpretation, rather than abandon it to the restrictive neoclassical usage.

The characteristics of economic flexibility – its systemic nature, its short-run time scale and its diversity – all contribute to its being a complex and amorphous topic. Such topics are hard to deal with theoretically, and any attempt to do so will be prone to oversimplification. Flexibility is, nevertheless, an important issue that should be addressed in economic theory. The following discussion first considers neoclassical accounts of flexibility and then moves on to alternative views.

NEOCLASSICAL ACCOUNTS OF FLEXIBILITY

Neoclassical economists have portrayed flexibility as the means by which an economy attains equilibrium outcomes with desirable efficiency properties.

Flexibility, in neoclassical eyes, is characterized as a rapid and optimal adjustment process. By contrast, non-neoclassical views of flexibility dwell on how an imperfectly adjusted system can survive unforeseen external circumstances through partial adaptations with no efficiency properties and no continuous equilibrium.

A major trait of neoclassical approaches is the dominance of price and wage flexibility over other modes of adjustment. From the neoclassical standpoint, flexible economic arrangements must permit prices and wages to move freely to equate supply and demand, thereby generating allocative efficiency. Other economic variables, such as output and employment, may also be changing, but they change in response to relative price movements and play no independent part in economic flexibility. The dominance of price and wage movements means that neoclassical flexibility is less diverse than one might conclude from surface observation of economic variables. Other variables do change in neoclassical models, but they are subordinate to the prices and wages that guide economic behaviour; in neoclassical theory, economic flexibility is virtually synonymous with price and wage flexibility.

Neoclassical views of flexibility leave no room for slackness as a way of accommodating outside pressures and sustaining the economic system. On the contrary, slackness is dismissed as an allocative inefficiency caused by imperfections or rigidities. The faith in price adjustments assumes that the economy can function on a tight, allocatively efficient basis and that slackness and excess capacity must be harmful. When slackness does appear, neoclassical theory interprets it only as a symptom of inflexibility, not as a source of flexibility permitting short-run adjustment. The neglect of economic slackness prevents neoclassical theory from differentiating easily between the short run and the long run: all adjustments are accomplished through price variation, so flexibility cannot be set apart from longer-term processes of economic growth and structural change.

As is standard with neoclassical methods, the account of flexibility says nothing about roles or social structure. Economic agents have fixed preferences, whose origin goes unexplained, and act rationally in accordance with these preferences at all times. There are no roles defined in relation to other people (forming a social structure) and distinct from people's actual behaviour. The simplified, mechanical picture of human agency removes the flexibility made possible, for example, by the space left within formal roles. Neoclassical theory tolerates only a single kind of economic flexibility arising from the properties of perfectly equilibrating markets. This universal, individualistic, socially unspecific account denies that flexibility is an attribute of particular social and economic systems. Neoclassical flexibility comes from removing market imperfections and pushing for a universal market system on the lines of general equilibrium theory; a flexible economy should have little or no institutional baggage.

Flexibility in neoclassical theory normally refers to relations between individual agents. Far less attention is paid to flexibility within firms or other organizations, since neoclassical approaches generally treat firms as 'black boxes' that respond consistently to external stimuli and adhere to profit maximization. With all firms having fixed, well-defined preferences there is little need to delve into how firms are constituted and how they function; they are assumed to have found the best internal arrangements, otherwise they would not be reaching a true optimum. Any adjustments are made through revised, optimal decisions in response to changed external circumstances.

The way to encourage economic flexibility, for neoclassical economists, is to bring the economy closer to the neoclassical template by removing institutional or informational obstacles that might hamper free markets. Under these conditions it is unclear why institutions such as firms would exist, and the case for firms may require a breach of the ideal assumptions (Coase, 1937). If actual conditions ever matched the theoretical ideal, then firms would either be superfluous or have to reflect market principles, with the members of the firm transacting among themselves. Neoclassical conceptions of flexibility, when applied to policy issues, will justify pro-market measures stressing decentralization, privatization and curbs on trade union power. Advances in information technology might seem to chime with neoclassical flexibility, as transaction costs fall and improved communications offer smoother functioning of markets, yet none of these developments can ever go as far as to make a real economy coincide with the stylized and artificial neoclassical benchmark.

Orthodox policy discussions of economic flexibility have had an implicit neoclassical core, in the high profile given to wage flexibility and the assumption that increased flexibility must be desirable (OECD, 1986, 1987, 1994; IMF, 1994). Although orthodox studies have recognized other sources of flexibility, they have given a special status to wage flexibility and promoted it as the badge of a flexible economy. Any restrictions on wage movements have been characterized as rigidities that block the efficient functioning of markets and generate allocative inefficiencies, reduced investment and slower growth. Such reasoning is evident in the contrast frequently drawn between the dynamic, low-unemployment US economy and the more regulated, high-unemployment economies of the EU: the differences are routinely attributed to the greater flexibility of US labour markets, even though the importance of wage flexibility remains doubtful and the reasons for the US–EU contrast may lie elsewhere (Palley, 1998; Simonazzi and Villa, 1999). Implicit neoclassicism also underpins the assumption that flexibility is always beneficial, which allows policy analysts to recommend increased flexibility in all times and places. This stems from the use of perfect competition as the benchmark in studies that ostensibly take an institutionally specific form. The policy advice is governed by the theoretical presuppositions of the advisor, independently of the particular case being considered.

Neoclassical flexibility clashes with the characteristics of flexibility identified above: it neglects diversity and gives precedence to wage and price flexibility over other sources of variation; it does not treat flexibility as a short-run phenomenon and merges it with more fundamental, long-run change; and it refuses to see flexibility as contingent on particular social structures. The upshot is a narrow and tendentious account of economic flexibility – the rest of this chapter considers how structural approaches can provide an alternative account.

STRUCTURAL APPROACHES TO FLEXIBILITY

There is no official definition of social structure in sociology or elsewhere, but the commonest use of the term is based on a necessary or internal relationship among roles, where one role cannot exist without the other: cases from economics would be the roles of buyer and seller, creditor and debtor, and landlord and tenant. This usage, derived largely from Durkheim and Parsons, has come to be regarded as the traditional sociological view. The role-centred approach ensures that social structure, made up of interrelated roles, is distinct from the people who occupy the roles and would persist even if the entire cast of role occupants was changed.

The customary image of social structure is as something hard and solid like a building, which would seem to conflict with flexibility. Structural approaches, taken to an extreme, could deny human agency and uphold the primacy of social context in guiding human behaviour. Where 'hard' social structures prevail, the result might be a hierarchical, static, rule-based society with little leeway for change and few outlets for human agency. Structural arguments have mostly appeared in sociology and are often contrasted with the agency-led individualism of neoclassical economics. It is easy to depict structural methods as being too rigid to represent flexible markets, for which the individualism of neoclassical theory might seem better suited. This is misguided, as all markets and other economic relations (flexible or not) are structural and need a structural analysis. Markets do not arise naturally or spontaneously, as neoclassical theory implies, but are maintained and organized through formal institutions to yield a standardized, impersonal setting for economic exchange (Hodgson,

1988, Chapter 8; Fourie, 1991; Lazonick, 1991, Chapter 2; Rosenbaum, 2000). Since all markets have institutional content, one cannot legitimately equate economic flexibility with an absence of 'rigid' structures. Flexibility must occur within a broader social structure and can never stand alone.

Recent social theory has avoided a stark opposition of structure and agency and moved towards a closer interdependence, whereby social structure need not be at odds with human agency – prime examples are Giddens's structuration theory and Bhaskar's transformational model of social activity (Giddens, 1984; Bhaskar, 1979). Other authors have made similar arguments, expressed in different conceptual language (Bourdieu, 1977; Goffman, 1983; Alexander, 1985, 1998; Munch and Smelser, 1987; Elias, 1991). The drift of social theory in the last few decades has been away from an unbending social structure that dominates human behaviour. Instead, structures are seen as enabling as well as constraining action, with agents in part influenced by structure and structures reproduced through agency (Jackson, 1999, 2003). Because social structure and human agency cannot be separated, it is no longer valid to regard social structure as an external, removable constraint on behaviour. Structures are vital to all human activities, flexible as well as inflexible.

Another strand in the sociological literature has softened social structure in a different way, by recognizing a new, more fluid type of social structure, termed a figuration or figurational structure (Elias, 1978, 1991). In a figurational method, social structure and human agency are replaced by figurations, which consist of relations among people, not roles or positions. For any given society, figurations will be highly diverse, ranging from direct personal contacts to indirect dealings with representatives of government or business. Nobody can be isolated from figurations, and so individual agency becomes a redundant concept – all human action occurs in a social setting. Likewise, there is no longer any need for a concept of role playing, and the usual agency–structure distinctions can be depicted through the distance and degree of formality in personal relations. Face-to-face personal contact will permit informal relations ('human agency'), while indirect contacts will have to be formal and institutional ('role playing'). A figurational method hopes to transcend agency–structure dualism by replacing role-based social structures with people-based figurations that embody both structure and agency.

Critics of figurational sociology have argued that figurations on their own cannot resolve the problems of agency–structure dualism and that the neglect of roles may blur important theoretical distinctions (Layder, 1994, Chapter 7; Mouzelis, 1995, Chapter 4). To opt exclusively for figurational methods could oversimplify matters and provoke a collapse into structural or individualistic reductionism, depending on how personal relations are interpreted – a stress on indirect relations would downgrade human agency and free will; a stress on direct relations would imply a loose, unstructured aggregate of individual agents. Figurational methods, the critics claim, will undermine a genuinely structural approach.

Instead of replacing social structure, figurations could be viewed as augmenting the role-centred account of structure. One can, for example, distinguish institutional structures (based on roles) from figurational structures (based on personal relations) and allow for both in social theory (Mouzelis, 1995). Any social structure will have an institutional and figurational side, as it relies on role playing and on social interaction among the people involved. No role can cover every facet of the role occupant's behaviour, and even the most role-based human activities will have a residual, figurational component. Recognizing figurations will make social structure more pliable, diverse and responsive to external changes, so that it can no longer be just a barrier to human action.

The new approaches to social structure have significant implications for flexibility because they counteract the belief that social structures are fixed and an obstacle to change. With looser and plural social structures it becomes straightforward to accommodate a degree of flexibility. One possible approach is shown in Figure 9.1.

Diversity of social structure creates three interdependent layers (institutions, figurations and agents), none of which can exist without the others.

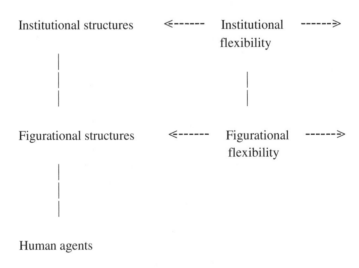

Figure 9.1   Institutional and figurational flexibility

Flexibility can arise in Figure 9.1 in two ways, either through institutions or through figurations. The first case – institutional flexibility – assumes that existing roles in production, employment and public policy can cope with external changes. Examples are where changes in demand can be met with variations in formal employment or where employment contracts sanction variable working practices. The second case – figurational flexibility – meets external changes through personal relations extending beyond economic roles and contracts. Even if institutions cannot in themselves cope with external changes, flexibility can still be attained through adjustments in figurational structures, particularly in the day-to-day working relationships among people well known to each other. Any such adjustments are likely to be specific to a single workplace and probably temporary – if they persist and become permanent, they may be converted into new roles. Generally speaking, more predictable changes will be met by institutional flexibility and less predictable changes by figurational flexibility.

A structural account of flexibility raises the issue of who gains and who loses. Neoclassical economics avoids this issue, as flexibility occurs through spontaneous price changes and the distribution of gains and losses depends on resource entitlements, assumed fixed from the outset. Distributive matters can then be hived off from flexibility and considered under a separate heading. With a structural account, flexibility does not come from an invisible hand process and can be obtained in various ways, which have their own distributive consequences. Some adjustments would place the cost primarily on workers, whereas others would penalize employers. A more socially specific approach can bring out the equity implications of flexibility often neglected in orthodox discussion.

MICRO- AND MACRO-FLEXIBILITY

Economic flexibility pertains to both the micro-level of small-scale activities and the macro-level of the whole economy. For a firm or other organization, flexibility will absorb unforeseen events that might otherwise threaten the organization's survival. For a whole economy, flexibility will aid the stability of the economic system: short-term variations, which might be perceived as instability, will protect the system from more severe upheavals. Micro- and macro-flexibility can each take an institutional or figurational form.

At the micro-level, a firm or other organization must respond to changes in economic conditions. One option is to rely on institutional flexibility expressible through impersonal roles, positions and contractual relations.

In labour markets a firm can respond to a change in the demand for its output by recruiting or laying off workers or by adjusting working hours. Both approaches are institutional in form; recruitment/lay offs will have a far less even impact on employees, causing hardship for those who lose their employment roles. Other economic events might call for employees to be redeployed to different tasks and thus switched between employment roles. Beyond labour markets, the adaptations made inside an organization will frequently be channelled through institutional structures. The idea of flexible specialization links increased adaptability to a shift towards greater decentralization and vertically disintegrated production (Piore and Sabel, 1984; Hirst and Zeitlin, 1997). Small, loosely connected production units would, it is claimed, be better placed to revise their own practices and their relations with other production units in the face of fragmentary and rapidly changing patterns of demand. Flexibility is here being fostered by new, supple institutional structures.

Another option is for a firm to exploit figurational flexibility, which goes beyond recognized economic roles and positions. In labour markets, employers could change the intensity of work within existing employment contracts or encourage their workforce to adopt new working methods compatible with current employment roles. The figurational dimension of production has long been discussed by heterodox economists, who have argued that employment contracts are incomplete and leave loopholes for flexible working practices. Firms do not have a single optimum production method in the neoclassical manner, but operate with variable productivity (Hodgson, 1982). Much the same will apply in other contractual relations outside of labour markets. The impossibility of pure contract, as a general principle, ensures that contractual and institutional relations will not cover every possible adaptation and that some flexibility will occur by non-contractual and non-institutional means.

At the macro-level, changes in economic activity can also be accommodated in several ways. Output and employment variations are backed by public welfare measures, notably unemployment benefits and social assistance, which alleviate the poverty associated with unemployment and act as automatic stabilizers, maintaining aggregate demand and reducing economic instability. Output and employment variation has become institutionalized as the main avenue for economic adjustment in modern capitalist economies. Within the present framework, the government can be seen as performing the economic role of supporting the unemployed. The receipt of welfare benefits offers a role or social position for jobless people – they have lost their employment roles but are afforded secondary roles as benefit recipients, so as to prevent their exclusion from institutional structures. Welfare policies, often portrayed as rigidities in neoclassical theory, will ease economic adjustment by offsetting the harsher consequences of unemployment and reducing the volatility of aggregate demand.

Other institutional structures at the macro-level are bound up with macro-economic policies. An activist macroeconomic policy on Keynesian lines entails a willingness to bolster and stabilize aggregate demand through fiscal and monetary measures. The government takes on a role as an economic manager and establishes the necessary institutional structures, which will usually have a formal, visible character. A laissez-faire policy stance might seem to reject an economic role for government, yet it results from a deliberate decision to withdraw from economic management and constitutes a (passive) role being consciously played by government. Hence laissez-faire is not an unstructured state but the outcome of formal rules precluding government intervention. Both activist macroeconomic policy and laissez-faire are the expression of institutional structures that guide policymaking.

Along with its institutional aspect, macroeconomic flexibility will also have a figurational aspect. Most people have negligible macroeconomic influence, as their economic behaviour is on too small a scale relative to the whole economy; they are micro-agents who belong to macroeconomic aggregates but play no significant part in macroeconomic affairs. A few people, by virtue of their privileged status in the social structure, do have enough influence for their decisions to make a difference at the macro-level: these macro-agents include government policymakers, senior business leaders and major participants in financial markets. The figurational aspect of macroeconomic flexibility will stem from the personal interactions among macro-agents. Sometimes the interactions may be direct and visible, as when politicians discuss coordinated economic policies or negotiate with the heads of multinational businesses about the location and extent of their investments; at other times the interactions may be less direct, as when participants in financial markets seek to anticipate the behaviour of government policymakers. Personal interactions among business leaders could generate explicit agreements, or much looser networks, or tacit understandings with little formal expression. The resulting figurational structures will stand beside institutional ones and may in some cases evolve into an institutional form – close cooperation between businesses can, for instance, culminate in a merger that replaces figurational with institutional structures.

SOURCES AND LEVELS OF ECONOMIC FLEXIBILITY

Institutional and figurational structures will normally coexist, but their relative importance will vary. If institutions are deeply entrenched and

people follow clearly defined roles, then social structure is apt to be dominated by institutions, even though social interaction will also have a
figurational element and role players may forge relations with other role
players and perform their roles in a personalized fashion. If, on the other
hand, institutions are ill defined and give only weak behavioural guidelines,
then figurations will assume a greater relative importance, as people will
have to develop their own styles of working and interacting with others.

The same can be said of institutional and figurational flexibility: they will
coexist but in some cases one will outweigh the other. There is little prior
reason to suppose that institutional and figurational flexibility are always
correlated, to yield a 'flexible' economy (with high levels of both) or an
'inflexible' one (with low levels of both). A more general view would let
them vary independently and open up the prospect of flexibility having an
asymmetrical quality. Economies might be more flexible in the figurational
domain than in the institutional domain, or vice versa, which makes it
harder to talk in simple, dualistic terms about flexible versus inflexible
economies. Adding figurations to the analysis helps to demonstrate the
diverse sources and levels of flexibility.

If institutional and figurational flexibility can each take high or low levels,
then there are four possible combinations, as shown in Figure 9.2. High
levels of institutional and figurational flexibility (top left of Figure 9.2)
implies an economy whose institutional and figurational structures display
a strong capacity for adaptation. Under these conditions, the economy can
accommodate short-term events and disturbances via regular adjustments
of both institutions and figurations. In the long run the economic system as
a whole ought to be durable, given that the regular adjustments should
prevent systemic breakdowns and remove the need for wholesale changes of
system. Short-run adjustments are coupled with long-run durability.

The opposite case is where institutional and figurational flexibility are at
low levels (bottom right of Figure 9.2). Here the economy possesses fixed
institutions and personal relations, which might be well matched with each
other but show little capacity for adaptation. The low flexibility should
yield limited economic change in the short run, but over a longer period the
economy would be susceptible to systemic failures and crises that might
bring a change of economic system. Short-run inertia is coupled with long-
run instability.

The top-right case in Figure 9.2 involves institutions that cannot readily
meet external changes, beside figurations that are malleable. Most variability will have to come from figurations and may create tensions between
changing figurations and invariant institutions: people's actual behaviour
and relationships may diverge from their roles and social positions. There
will be pressures for the invariant institutions to change as well, especially

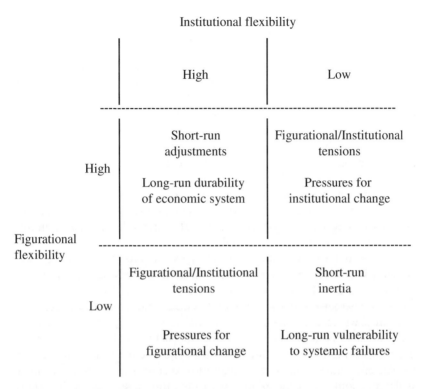

Figure 9.2   Sources and levels of economic flexibility

if the figurational adjustments prove to be more than merely temporary and persist over long periods. An example is where new technologies encourage new ways of working, expressed as figurational changes, which may clash with older roles and institutions.

The bottom-left case in Figure 9.2 combines variable institutions with unchanging figurations, so that institutions become the chief source of variability. With the previous case reversed, the pressure is now for personal relations to conform to new and unfamiliar roles and positions. An example is where managers of a firm introduce administrative reforms, setting up new roles that require changes in people's behaviour and personal relations. Whenever institutions and figurations are mismatched, there will be frictions or resistance to change within the social and economic system. Long-run change will take place only if the variable element dominates and the initial resistance is overcome.

Figure 9.2 conveys no normative message. In particular, it should not be taken for granted that the top-left, high flexibility case is better than the others. Whether flexibility is desirable or not depends on the nature of the adjustments and how they are being implemented. Flexible institutional and figurational structures may impose the heaviest adjustment costs upon the poorest and weakest groups in society, while protecting the interests of more privileged groups; on its own, flexibility cannot guarantee ethically appealing outcomes. Conversely, the low flexibility case at the bottom right of Figure 9.2 could denote a static but egalitarian society which, because of its inertia, gives rise to few adjustment costs – by some ethical criteria, this might be thought superior to more flexible alternatives. Normative assessments cannot therefore rely on the degree of flexibility alone, but need to ask how flexibility is accomplished and whose interest it serves. Within the scheme of Figure 9.2, each case can still embrace a wide range of adjustment methods with various social and distributive consequences. One should beware the oft-encountered but oversimplified conclusion that high flexibility is inherently desirable.

Institutional and figurational flexibility are related to the concepts of system integration and social integration used in the Marxian and socio-logical literature (Lockwood, 1964; Mouzelis, 1997). System integration refers to whether the parts of a social system hold together and function smoothly, where the parts are impersonal items such as institutions and roles. Social integration refers to whether the members of a society or group interact harmoniously and identify with collective goals and interests. In the present framework, system integration is concerned with institutional structures, and social integration with figurational structures (Mouzelis, 1995). A stable, well-ordered society will have high levels of system and social integration, although at times one or the other might be lost. In capit-alist economies, for example, mass unemployment apparently indicates system disintegration but does not as a rule prompt major social break-downs or unrest, which suggests that social integration has remained intact. Using the twin concepts of system and social integration shows that a full treatment of economic change should acknowledge the personal and impersonal sides of how an economy functions, along with the connections between them.

In the scheme of Figure 9.2, institutional flexibility broadly corresponds to system integration and figurational flexibility to social integration. An economy with institutional flexibility can make adjustments within the economic system itself, so the system should be stable and well integrated. Less flexible systems will have fewer outlets for short-term adjustments and be more prone to systemic difficulties. Likewise, an economy with figurational flexibility will have close, well-developed personal relation-ships that can accommodate social adjustments without undergoing a breakdown; this implies a high level of social integration. Inflexible figurations will involve more distant and less harmonious relations among members of society, together with an increased chance of frictions and resistance to change. Marxian and other heterodox economists, unlike their neoclassical counterparts, may sometimes be willing to see figurational inflexibility in a positive light: it could indicate class consciousness among workers who dispute arrangements biased in favour of employers and capital.

Economic flexibility, as defined here, will bring only limited changes that can be contained within a given economic system. Larger changes, over longer periods, will normally require a mismatch between institutional and figurational structures. If either institutions or figurations change independently, so as to create a mismatch, then there will be pressures for further, more fundamental social changes. Such arguments characterize the theories of long waves and structural change put forward by the Regulation School, neo-Schumpeterians and the social structures of accumulation approach (Boyer, 1988; Perez, 1983; Freeman and Perez, 1988; Tylecote, 1991; Freeman and Louca, 2001; Gordon, 1980). Adopting a materialist stance, these theories root economic development in a transformation of technology prior to later adjustments of institutions and social structures. Long-run changes will start with new methods of production and novel ways of working that clash with older institutions; as the new methods are diffused, they evoke increasing tensions and pressures for institutional change until new institutions are created, more in tune with the new technologies and working procedures. A wave of expansion will then ensue. The stimulus to long-term growth comes from the top-right case of Figure 9.2, where new ways of working appear first through figurational flexibility and institutional change lags behind. If institutions do eventually undergo fundamental reform, then the economy should tend back towards high institutional and figurational flexibility (top left of Figure 9.2). Long-run development will go through phases of institutional inflexibility until the resistance to change is broken down, institutions and figurations are rematched, and institutional flexibility is restored.

From this perspective, a growing economy cannot be lodged permanently in the 'ideal' top-left case of Figure 9.2 and must see periods of institutional/figurational mismatch when one source of change outstrips the other. It follows that flexibility should not be equated with growth, and inflexibility with stagnation. Economic growth takes place by a dialectical and historical process calling forth systemic tensions (inflexibilities) and, at certain times, crises and reformulations. Contrary to what one might think, a perfectly flexible world would experience only minor changes within a perennial, all-encompassing social and economic system.

CONCLUSION

Two features of economic flexibility have been emphasized in this chapter. The first is that flexibility is a structural property, specific to particular social structures, and not something that emerges spontaneously from an unstructured environment. If social structures are interdependent with human agency and multiple in form, as recent social theory has argued, it becomes clear that they may assist rather than restrict economic flexibility. Their original image of hardness and solidity has been replaced by a softer image more consistent with variable economic arrangements. Far from being an obstacle to economic flexibility, social structures provide the means by which flexibility is accomplished.

The second feature is that flexibility arises from diverse and open economic relations, as against a perfect, complete economic system. No economy can make instant and optimal adjustments to every external event. Actual economies accommodate outside disturbances by having diverse, plural arrangements that allow for varied responses. The diversity ensures that there is no unique, even-handed adjustment method; the outcomes of flexibility will be socially specific, giving rise to conflicting interests and an unequal distribution of gains and losses. One should not therefore assume that flexibility is always and everywhere desirable.

Both features are missing from neoclassical economics, whose mistrust of social structure and reliance on perfectly adjusted equilibria presents a false account of natural, unstructured and optimal flexibility. Neoclassical thought has overlooked important matters surrounding flexibility, including its structural basis, its short-run character and its uneven social consequences. A good starting point for examining these matters would be to learn from recent sociology and seek a richer understanding of how social structures underlie economic behaviour.

REFERENCES

Alexander, J. (ed.) (1985), *Neofunctionalism*, Beverly Hills: Sage.
Alexander, J. (1998), *Neofunctionalism and After*, Oxford: Blackwell.
Atkinson, J. and N. Meager (1986), *Changing Working Patterns: How Companies Achieve Flexibility to Meet New Needs*, London: National Economic Development Office.
Bhaskar, R. (1979), *The Possibility of Naturalism*, Brighton: Harvester Press.
Boje, T.P. (1991), 'Flexibility and fragmentation in the labour market', in A. Amin and M. Dietrich (eds), *Towards a New Europe? Structural Change in the European Economy*, Aldershot, UK and Brookfield, US: Edward Elgar, pp. 137–65.
Bourdieu, P. (1977), *Outline of a Theory of Practice*, Cambridge: Cambridge University Press.

Boyer, R. (1988), 'Technical change and the Theory of Regulation', in G. Dosi, C. Freeman, R. Nelson, G. Silverberg and L. Soete (eds), *Technical Change and Economic Theory*, London: Pinter, pp. 67–94.

Clarke, S. (1992), 'What in the F . . .'s name is Fordism?', in N. Gilbert, R. Burrows and A. Pollert (eds), *Fordism and Flexibility: Divisions and Change*, London: Macmillan, pp. 13–30.

Coase, R.H. (1937), 'The nature of the firm', *Economica*, **4**, 386–405.

Dex, S. and A. McCulloch (1997), *Flexible Employment: The Future of Britain's Jobs*, London: Macmillan.

Elias, N. (1978), *What is Sociology?*, London: Hutchinson.

Elias, N. (1991), *The Society of Individuals*, Oxford: Blackwell.

Fourie, F.C. v. N. (1991), 'The nature of the market: a structural analysis', in G.M. Hodgson and E. Screpanti (eds), *Rethinking Economics: Markets, Technology and Economic Evolution*, Aldershot, UK and Brookfield, US: Edward Elgar.

Freeman, C. and F. Louca (2001), *As Time Goes By: From the Industrial Revolutions to the Information Revolution*, Oxford: Oxford University Press.

Freeman, C. and C. Perez (1988), 'Structural crises of adjustment, business cycles and investment behaviour', in G. Dosi, C. Freeman, R. Nelson, G. Silverberg and L. Soete (eds), *Technical Change and Economic Theory*, London: Pinter, pp. 38–66.

Giddens, A. (1984), *The Constitution of Society: Outline of the Theory of Structuration*, Cambridge: Polity Press.

Goffman, E. (1983), 'The interaction order', *American Sociological Review*, **48**, 1–17.

Gordon, D. (1980), 'Stages of accumulation and long economic cycles', in T.K. Hopkins and I. Wallerstein (eds), *Processes of the World-System*, London: Sage, pp. 9–45.

Hirst, P. and J. Zeitlin (1997), 'Flexible specialization: theory and evidence in the analysis of industrial change', in J.R. Hollingsworth and R. Boyer (eds), *Contemporary Capitalism: The Embeddedness of Institutions*, Cambridge: Cambridge University Press, pp. 220–39.

Hodgson, G.M. (1982), 'Theoretical and policy implications of variable productivity', *Cambridge Journal of Economics*, **6**, 213–26.

Hodgson, G.M. (1988), *Economics and Institutions: A Manifesto for a Modern Institutional Economics*, Cambridge: Polity Press.

IMF (International Monetary Fund) (1994), *World Economic Outlook, May 1994*, Washington, DC: IMF.

Jackson, W.A. (1999), 'Dualism, duality and the complexity of economic institutions', *International Journal of Social Economics*, **26**, 545–58.

Jackson, W.A. (2003), 'Social structure in economic theory', *Journal of Economic Issues*, **37**, 727–46.

Layder, D. (1994), *Understanding Social Theory*, London: Sage.

Lazonick, W. (1991), *Business Organization and the Myth of the Market Economy*, Cambridge: Cambridge University Press.

Lockwood, D. (1964), 'Social integration and system integration', in G.K. Zollschan and W. Hirsch (eds), *Explorations in Social Change*, London: Routledge, pp. 244–57.

Morroni, M. (1991), 'Production flexibility', in G.M. Hodgson and E. Screpanti (eds), *Rethinking Economics: Markets, Technology and Economic Evolution*, Aldershot, UK and Brookfield, US: Edward Elgar, pp. 68–80.

Mouzelis, N. (1995), *Sociological Theory: What Went Wrong?*, London: Routledge.
Mouzelis, N. (1997), 'Social and system integration: Lockwood, Habermas, Giddens', *Sociology*, **31**, 111–19.
Munch, R. and N. Smelser (1987), 'Relating the micro and macro', in J. Alexander, B. Giesen, R. Munch and N. Smelser (eds), *The Micro–Macro Link*, Berkeley: University of California Press, pp. 356–87.
OECD (Organization for Economic Cooperation and Development) (1986), *Flexibility in the Labour Market: The Current Debate*, Paris: OECD.
OECD (1987), *Structural Adjustment and Economic Performance*, Paris: OECD.
OECD (1994), *The OECD Jobs Study: Facts, Analysis, Strategies*, Paris: OECD.
Palley, T.I. (1998), 'Restoring prosperity: why the US model is not the answer for the United States or Europe', *Journal of Post Keynesian Economics*, **20**, 337–53.
Perez, C. (1983), 'Structural change and the assimilation of new technologies in the economic and social system', *Futures*, **15**, 357–75.
Piore, M. and C.F. Sabel (1984), *The Second Industrial Divide: Possibilities for Prosperity*, New York: Basic Books.
Pollert, A. (1988a), 'Dismantling flexibility', *Capital and Class*, **34**, 42–75.
Pollert, A. (1988b), 'The "flexible firm": fixation or fact?', *Work, Employment and Society*, **2**, 281–316.
Pollert, A. (1991), 'The orthodoxy of flexibility', in A. Pollert (ed.), *Farewell to Flexibility?*, Oxford: Blackwell, pp. 3–31.
Rosenbaum, E.F. (2000), 'What is a market? On the methodology of a contested concept', *Review of Social Economy*, **58**, 455–82.
Rubery, J. (1989), 'Labour market flexibility in Britain', in F. Green (ed.), *The Restructuring of the UK Economy*, Hemel Hempstead: Harvester Wheatsheaf, pp. 155–76.
Sayer, A. (1989), 'Post-Fordism in question', *International Journal of Urban and Regional Research*, **13**, 666–95.
Simonazzi, A. and P. Villa (1999), 'Flexibility and growth', *International Review of Applied Economics*, **13**, 281–311.
Tylecote, A. (1991), *The Long Wave in the World Economy*, London: Routledge.

10. Routines: a brief history of the concept

Markus C. Becker[1]

It is a strange but indisputable fact that the commonality of a phenomenon – the circumstance that we are well acquainted with it in everyday life – neither facilitates nor speeds up its scientific explanation. . . . No science offers more examples for this than economics . . . (Schumpeter, 1911, p. 324)

INTRODUCTION

The concept of a routine is very prominent in the literatures on organizational and economic evolution (for example, Cohen et al., 1996; Dosi, 1988; Egidi, 1992, 1993; Hodgson, 1993a, 1998a, 1999a; Malerba and Orsenigo, 1996; Marengo, 1996; Nelson, 1995; Nelson and Winter, 1982; Rutherford, 1994; Winter, 1986, 1987, 1990, 1995), mainly due to the use of the concept by Nelson and Winter (1982). Nelson and Winter use 'routine' as a 'general term for all regular and predictable behavioral patterns of firms' (1982, p. 14), comprising 'most of what is regular and predictable about business behavior' (1982, p. 15). A routine is a repetitive pattern of activity, it can be likened to a computer program. The theoretical relevance of routines lies in the idea that routines play the role that genes play in biological evolutionary theory. The behaviour of firms can thus be explained by the routines they employ. Furthermore, organizational routines are seen as the analogue of individual skills, they are the organizational memory of the organization's specific operational knowledge. Nelson and Winter (1982) also consider motivational aspects of routines, pointing out that they embody a 'truce' among conflicting interests in the organization. Following Nelson and Winter (1982), routines are considered as very important in evolutionary accounts, not at least because they represent the units of selection, one of the three pillars of any evolutionary explanation.[2] For an overview of the literature on organization routines see Becker (2004).

Despite its importance and frequent use, the concept of a routine is, however, still somewhat ambiguous. Since Nelson and Winter (1982), many authors have picked up on the notion of routines. Many ambiguities and inconsistencies in the concept still prevail however. At the same time, conceptual contributions have been rare and their impact on open questions has been very limited, leading to the conclusions that 'a unified academic vision of the notion of routine does not exist' (Reynaud, 1998, p. 468). Although '"routine" seems to be a keyword in a very large number of papers appearing in the mid-1990s . . . there has been little progress so far in reaching agreement on what routines are . . .' (Cohen et al., 1996, p. 656). A history of the concept, still lacking, can provide a contribution to its understanding and to conceptual progress.

While no account of the history of the concept of routines yet exists, a history of the concept of habit – a close cousin of the concept of a routine – was published in 1986 (Camic, 1986). This lack is all the more remarkable since the concept of routine has received much more attention in economics than that of habit. Also, evolutionary economics strongly emphasizes the role of history and historical specificity. One would thus have expected a historical perspective on one of the key concepts much earlier.

THE HISTORICAL CANVAS – AN OVERVIEW

The concept of a 'routine' has some close – and older – cousins: the concepts of 'custom' and 'habit'. These are cousins of a family that could be called 'behavioural predispositions'. All the concepts of this family have in common that they influence individuals' behaviour in such a way that they are predisposed to a certain 'tendency' in their actions. Despite such commonality, there are also, however, important differences between the concepts of custom, habit and routine. The most important is the social nature of customs and routines, as opposed to the individual nature of habits. Customs and routines involve shared habits. While routines involve habits shared within an organization (or by organizations across organizational boundaries), customs however can involve shared habits by individuals that do not have to be members of organizations. This point is placed at the beginning of the chapter because of its importance for a clear understanding. An account of how this understanding has come about is developed in what follows.

There are a number of other concepts that have some overlap with the concept of routines and thus are also in some way or other attached to the wider family of concepts mentioned above: for instance, folkways (Sumner, 1906), conventions, rules, procedures, standard operating procedures (Cyert and March, 1963) and spontaneously evolved rules of conduct

(Hayek, 1973). This chapter does not deal with these concepts in depth, as the focus is on tracing the concept of routines through time – an already complex task. Rather, we will deal with these concepts as far as their similarities or differences with the concept of routines matter, but will limit our attention to pointing out the links between routines and other concepts where that is of interest for better understanding what is in the focus here, the concept of routines.

The concept of routines builds mainly on the older concepts of custom and habit. Thus, it is with those that we commence our reconstruction of the history of the concept of routines. We will take up the analysis in the era of the Enlightenment, where the concept of habit received more systematic attention. We will then look at the reaction to the Enlightenment in the early nineteenth century, and the 'high point' of concepts like habit and custom around the end of the that century, before in detail looking at movements of counter-reaction to this that were culminating in the 1920s: positivism, behaviourism and Scientific Management. In the 1940s we will find the ground prepared for the appearance of the concept of routines.

While concepts of behavioural predispositions such as habits and customs were already present in much earlier writings, the concept of habit received more systematic attention during the eighteenth century (see Funke, 1958) from some of the main protagonists of the Enlightenment like Kant, Rousseau and Hume (Camic, 1986), but also during the reaction to the Enlightenment in the early nineteenth century, namely English utilitarianism and German idealism. It was used by James Mill and Georg F.W. Hegel,[3] who postulated that 'habit is indispensable for the existence of all intellectual life' (1830, p. 143; Camic, 1986, p. 1048). Earlier, it had also been employed by some of the 'founders' of classical economics like, for example, Thomas Malthus (Waller, 1988; Commons, 1934).

Towards the end of the nineteenth century a number of prominent theoreticians in different disciplines of the social sciences made the concept of habit a cornerstone of their theories. This took place in the last decade of the nineteenth century and the following two decades. Among those were Émile Durkheim, Max Weber, Charles Sanders Peirce, William James, Thorstein Veblen and John Commons. The fields in which this took place were psychology, philosophy, sociology and economics.

For Durkheim, habits were 'the real forces which govern us' (Durkheim, 1905–06, p. 152; 1898–1900, p. 80; Camic, 1986, p. 1052):

> There are certain ways in which (differentiated functions) react on one another, which, being more in accordance with the nature of things, are repeated more often and become habits; then the habits, as they acquire force, are transformed

into rules of conduct . . . In other words, a certain selection of rights and duties is made by habitual practice and these end up by becoming obligatory. (Durkheim, 1893, p. 366; Camic, 1986, p. 1053)

Weber expressly put habit in relation to economics by declaring the 'far-reaching economic significance' of habit, and that 'the patterns of use and of relationship among (modern) economic units are determined by habit' (Weber, 1922, pp. 67–8, 78, 89, 320, 335; in Camic, 1986, p. 1058). The emphasis he put on the role of habits for work represented an important contribution to the concept of routines, which for him rests on a habitual foundation (Camic, 1986, p. 1058). Having set up a relationship between habits and efficiency, it seems likely that he thus contributed much to setting the conceptual stage for Taylorism.

Much in the same vein, and also around the turn of the century, the American pragmatist school presented another form of counter-reaction to over-rationalistic concepts of human behaviour. Peirce finally and decidedly broke with empiricism and 'actually made Habit and Custom, instead of intellect and sensation, the foundation of all science' (Commons, 1934, p. 150). He made habit a central concept in American pragmatist theory. In doing so, he 'set the direction for (a) new conception of the mind by developing a theory of knowledge which was at radical variance with both the rationalism of Descartes and the simple empiricism of Locke' (Twomey, 1998, p. 437). This direction is opposed to the 'monolithic perspective on the mind, which does not distinguish between different levels of thought and behaviour' (Twomey, 1998, p. 436).

As James in particular has elaborated, instincts, habits and conscious reasoning are different levels that emerge from and interact with each other. Habits are thus put at the very basis of human intelligence and problem-solving by conserving intellectual effort and increasing efficiency by allowing individuals to concentrate their efforts on new or unique circumstances (Waller, 1988). Peirce, however, made further contributions to the notion of habit. First, he used the concept of habit to situate action in time, thus providing the foundation of a dynamic theory of action: 'Time, with Hume is successive mathematical *points* of time, each without duration. Time with Peirce is an *instant* of time containing in itself past, present, and future' (Commons, 1934, p. 150). In this way, customs originate in the past, are changing in the present, and entail the expectation that practices will be repeated in the future (Commons, 1934). As a second major contribution, Peirce drew a connection between the level of action and the cognitive level (Hodgson, 1999a, p. 119): habit does not merely reinforce belief, but the 'essence of belief is the establishment of habit' (Peirce, 1934, pp. 255–6). A third contribution to this line of reasoning, drawing a connection between repetition and the establishment of expectations, is elaborated further below.

James, another eminent pragmatist, differed from Peirce with regard to the role of psychological and biological elements in the definition of habit. While Peirce was of the opinion that physiological explanations were unlikely to generate anything but probabilistic explanations of habitual behaviour, James was one of the strongest proponents of the psychological and biological definition of habit and developed this aspect further (James, 1890 [1950], p. 107; Waller, 1988, p. 540; Twomey, 1998, p. 437).

The pragmatist school in philosophy had an important influence on the American institutionalist school in economics. For Thorstein Veblen, human behaviour was dominated by habits of thought (Hodgson, 1994a), comprised of irreducible instincts and learned habits (Twomey, 1998). The concept of 'habit' was one of the fundamental theoretical concepts and the basis of his economic analysis (Dyer, 1984). The point his work made very strongly is that economists must consider habitual action (Samuels, 1990). For example, all economic change has ultimately to be traced back to a change in habits of thought (Veblen, 1898). Likewise, habit is central for the analysis of institutions. For Veblen, 'institutions involve congealed habits' (Hodgson, 1994b, p. 304): 'institutions are an outgrowth of habit. The growth of culture is a cumulative sequence of habituation, and the ways and means of it are the habitual response of human nature to exigencies' (Veblen, 1919, p. 241). Veblen's stance has to be considered nothing less than an 'intellectual revolution' (Hodgson, 1999b, p. 97).

However, Veblen made further contributions to the concept of habit and that of routine. First, in contrast to Peirce, he focused on the social dimensions of habit (Waller, 1988), as well as on their cognitive dimension (Hodgson, 1993b). Second, he applied a dynamic perspective to habits and thus began building them into a *dynamic* theoretical concept. For example, the crucial argument in *Theory of the Leisure Class* hinges on the idea that habits form only by long-continued use (Veblen, 1899 [1970], p. 49). It was not only duration, but also the strength and stability, or resistance to change, of habits, that were dynamic parameters brought up by Veblen (Waller, 1988). He then developed this dynamic perspective into an evolutionary one: observing that habits and routines have a stable and inert quality and often sustain their important characteristics through time, Veblen proposed to view them as evolutionary adaptations to changing environmental conditions in an explicitly evolutionary perspective (Hodgson, 1993b; 1994a). For Veblen, a dynamic perspective took the form of 'a genetic account of an unfolding process' (Veblen, 1898, p. 388).

In the 1920s the institutional school was the dominant economic school in the USA, and concepts of habitual behavioural dispositions, leading to recurrent action patterns, were among its key concepts. However, the 1920s also saw the rise of developments in the social sciences that ultimately discredited the institutionalist school, and with it the family of concepts mentioned.[4]

Those developments were, first, the counter-reaction against the application of evolutionary theory to economics (initiated by Veblen (1898 and 1899 [1970])). An origin of this was the ideological misuse of evolutionary theory in 'social Darwinism'. It manifested itself for example in anthropology (Franz Boas, Alfred Kroeber, Margaret Mead), where Boas's school – arguing against the relevance of biological influences such as instincts, as opposed to social influences (culture) – had become dominant in the 1920s. The second development was positivism (Auguste Comte), which had caught on widely since the turn of the century and also became dominant in the 1920s (as with the Vienna Circle). The third (related) development was the rise of behaviourism (founded in 1913 by John B. Watson), which denounced instinct, like anything else that could not be measured and tested directly, as unscientific. The publication of *Behaviorism* in 1924 by Watson signifies the end of instinct psychology and thus destroys, together with the other developments described, the foundations of institutionalism. These three developments all also contributed to the discrediting of concepts like habits and customs, as they were often interpreted to be connected in some way to instincts or thought to be intangible, both of which made them 'unscientific' according to these new currents of thinking. Finally, the Great Crash of 1929 and the ensuing depression made the institutionalist school, already bereft of its foundations, look very unattractive, as opposed to the technocratic versions of Keynesianism. This in the 1930s largely sealed the fate of the institutionalist school and thus of the family of concepts mentioned as well.

Parallel to these more general changes, concepts of general behavioural disposition like habit, custom and instinct came under attack more directly as well during that time. The concept of habit, used extensively in American sociology until around 1918, was in the following two decades 'purposefully excised from the conceptual structure of the field' (Camic, 1986, pp. 1039–40).

In conclusion, the situation with regard to the central importance of concepts of general behavioural disposition like habit, custom and instinct had changed completely. The broad developments described above had also led to a massive reorientation in the general philosophy and theory of science: positivism had led to a focus on empirical, tangible matters; the counter-reaction against evolutionary theory led to economics being modelled after the scientific ideal of the natural sciences, the goal being to find ubiquitously valid laws; behaviourism led to the method of measurement.

A good example of this 'new' focus was Scientific Management, which since the publication of Frederick Taylor's main work in 1911[5] – thus more or less parallel to the developments described above – diffused widely and soon had become the dominant management paradigm. In Scientific Management, the goal of eradicating inefficiencies (Taylor, 1911) led to a clear focus on details (Brown, 1932)[6] and on concrete application[7] (Hiscox, 1923); the gathering together, tabulation and reduction to rules, laws and formulae of all knowledge relating to the functioning of the enterprise was central (Nyland, 1996); the replacement of rule of thumb by science was one 'absolutey essential' element of Scientific Management (Nyland, 1996, p. 987); and finally, there was an obsession with measurement (particularly by Frank Gilbreth).

Although Taylorism with its strong emphasis on rational behaviour and fighting 'rules of thumb' (Taylor 1911 [1993], p. 16; Merkle, 1980, p. 288) thus on the one hand presented an antipode to institutionalism,[8] where the precursors of routines originated, on the other hand it made a very interesting contribution to the formation of the concept of routines. 'Habit' was not only an important concept in Taylorism[9] – it had become a central concept, as Taylor made it an objective to train workers into new working habits (Taylor, 1911 [1993]; see also White, 1927).

The most important contribution of Taylorism, however, might lie in the fact that in the pursuit of its goal to find best-practice procedures or 'principles of increasing efficiency by the analysis of routines and procedures' (Urwick and Breck, 1945, p. 141) it introduced precisely those routines, procedures and action patterns as an analytical perspective and unit of analysis. Taylor and the Scientific Management movement he initiated first introduced an analytical perspective on the organization of work that was characterized by being extremely detailed: this has been described as the 'minute subdivision of tasks', 'the microdivision of labor' (Merkle, 1980, p. 288), analyzing tasks in their smallest detail (Warner, 1996). However, it has to be noted that the connection of this analytical perspective of a detailed action pattern with the term 'routine' has taken place only rarely (see for example Hiscox 1924; Hiscox and Stirling 1920 [1959][10]), respectively implicitly.[11] This might be because much attention was focused on the division of activities into the smallest steps and their measurement and 'optimization', and not on more theoretically oriented questions like the unit of analysis.

Second, Taylor stressed routines much more than earlier thinkers because of his drive for the systemization of the flow of production, based on abstract laws and rules (leading to regular and repetitive movements, not movements influenced by personal judgments and rules of thumb). The degree of 'routinization and standardization' came to serve as an indication of Scientific Management (Merkle, 1980). Nonetheless, it seems highly likely that because recurrent patterns of action were the centre focus of a movement that from the 1910s onwards became the dominant management paradigm, an at least implicit connection between the term 'routine' and the notion of a detailed, recurring pattern of action had been widely established.

Summing up the developments in this era, a parallel development had taken place: concepts of habitual behavioural disposition such as habit and custom as well as their theoretical foundations by the end of the 1930s had become completely discredited.[12] However, almost at the same time there developed the first seed of a concept of recurrent action pattern that most likely has not been connected with the earlier ones because the analytical perspective had shifted to detailed and precisely specified action patterns[13] (as opposed to more general and potential behavioural predispositions), as became clear in the relatively large 'how-to' literature of the 1920s and 1930s, which covers 'standing instructions' (Hiscox, 1923) for areas such as, for example, production planning (Hiscox, 1924), business correspondence (Osborne, 1930), administration (Hiscox and Stirling, 1920) and public issues (Brown, 1932).

Contrary to the analytical perspective of Scientific Management – focused on workflow and on formal aspects of organization – Chester Barnard (1938) developed an alternative view which also made use of the concept of habit and can be interpreted as another stepping stone for the concept of routines because of two contributions.

One of Barnard's contributions was to advocate a *dynamic* analysis in understanding 'organization . . . [as] always an impersonal system of coordinated human efforts' (Barnard, 1938 [1968], p. 94). In doing so, he gave the counter-reaction against the rationalist approach to organization a precise direction: understanding a formal organization as a concrete social process by which social action is accomplished (Rothwell, 1996). He thus shifted the analytical perspective to dynamics. A second contribution of Barnard's consisted of pointing out a weakness in Taylor's system: the neglect of tacit knowledge and informal aspects. He not only filled this gap but in doing so brought habits back onto centre stage. At the beginning of the 1940s, that is, after the impact of Taylorism and the publication of Barnard's book, the ground for the emergence of the *concept* of routines seemed to have been prepared.

The *term* 'routines' did emerge earlier, however. Maybe the earliest appearance in the economic literature was in 1926. In this year, the second edition of Schumpeter's *Theorie der wirtschaftlichen Entwicklung* (translated in 1934 as *The Theory of Economic Development*) was published. As developed elsewhere (Becker and Knudsen, 2002), Schumpeter substantially and systematically changed the content of this book both between the first and the second German editions, as well as between the second German edition (from which the English translation was made with his active participation) and the English translation. One of the changes that can be traced throughout these three editions of *Theorie* is the emergence of the term 'Routine' in the second edition – in passages that are inserted in the new edition – and the translation of a number of different German terms as 'routine' in the English edition. In both instances, this leads to a consistent rise of the term 'routine' within the same book: while in 1911 (the first German edition) there were very few instances in which it was used, in 1934 (the English edition) the term 'routine' (as well as ideas that are connected with it today) were much more prominent.

Maybe the most famous of the passages added in 1926 (the second edition of *Theorie*) is the following:

> Where the boundaries of routine stop, many people can go no further, and the rest can only do so in a highly variable manner. The assumption that conduct is prompt and rational is in all cases a fiction. But it proves to be sufficiently near to reality, if things have time to hammer logic into men. (Schumpeter, 1934, p. 80; cf. Schumpeter, 1926, p. 118; for other passages on routines see Schumpeter, 1926, p. 122, 123, 124, 351).

Some of the terms that were translated as 'routine' in the English edition of 1934 were 'in reality' ('in der Wirklichkeit') (1926, p. 150; 1934, p. 104); 'automatism' ('Automatismus') (1926, p. 112; 1934, p. 75); 'channel' ('Bahn') (1926, p. 112; 1934, p. 98); 'administrative work' ('Verwaltungsarbeit') (1926, p. 113; 1934, p. 76); 'running down of checklists' ('das Erledigen von Qualifikationslisten') (1926, p. 115; 1934, p. 77); 'habitual' ('Gewohntes') (1926, p. 119 n.; 1934, p. 81 n.); and 'commonalities' ('Alltäglichkeiten') (1926, p. 123; 1934, p. 84). It is obvious that Schumpeter did not yet have a clear *concept* of routines in mind, albeit he decided to use the term, which seemed to take on some significance in the economic literature in the mid-1930s. In a letter of 1934 – the same year that many different German terms were translated as 'routine' in the translation of *Theorie* – Schumpeter gives us a hint as to what kind of significance the term 'routine' was taking on at that time. There, he emphasized the 'technique of production and the methods and ways of commerce' and 'the emergence in the practice of economic life of new ways of doing things' (letter to S. Colum Gilfillan of 18 May 1934, reproduced in Hedtke and Swedberg, 2000, p. 265). This indicates that Schumpeter had focused on methods, ways and techniques in economic life.

This was in 1934. By 1940 Stene wrote: 'Organization routine is that part of any organization's activities which has become habitual because of repetition and which is followed regularly without specific directions or detailed supervision by any member of the organization' (Stene, 1940, p. 1129; cited in Simon, 1947 [1997], p. 100). Note how the concept is connected to the behavioural level, that is, routine consists of activities. Also, note that while in 1934 Schumpeter had used the term 'routine' rather loosely and his interest was focused on 'ways of doing things in the practice of *economic life*', in 1940 we see the use of the term 'organization routine', that is, an application to organizations. It is not by chance, it seems, that Stene's contribution had the title 'Public administration – an approach to a science of administration' and appeared in the *American Political Science Review*. Notably, Simon referred to Stene (1940) in his 1947 book *Administrative Behavior* (Simon 1947 [1997], p. 100). In the economic literature (broadly speaking), the term 'routine', therefore, emerged in the second half of the 1920s. In the mid-1930s, an increasing focus on the 'way of doing things' and economic practices can be noted, combined with an increase in the use of the term 'routine'. However, it is in 1940 that Stene applies the term 'routine' to the study of (adminstrative) organization and puts it in a distinctively organizational context. Herbert Simon then picked it up in his 1947 book, from where it diffused into organization theory. The 'birth' of the concept of routines is thus closely linked to the 'birth' of the study of economic organization.

From the mid-1940s onwards a growing number of authors were using the concept as well:[14] Ludwik Fleck (1946, p. 120);[15] Fritz Machlup (1946, p. 521, 524–5); Edith Penrose (1952, p. 817);[16] Michael Polanyi (1958, p. 76); James March and Herbert Simon (1958, p. 45); George Richardson (1960, p. 52); Richard Cyert and James March (1963);[17] Arthur Koestler (1967). Finally[18] Sidney Winter (1964), 'return(ing) to the ideas of Veblen (1919) and the "old" institutionalists concerning the centrality of habit and routine in economic life',[19] introduced the concept against a Simonian backdrop of satisficing behaviour and search: 'When the firm is doing well, it will not expend time and money on "search activity"'. Thus if a firm is behaving according to a routine that is actually viable, given the existing competition of other organization forms and the character of the environment, it will not be inclined to depart from the routine' (Winter, 1964, p. 264). The accompanying footnote presents his definition of routines: 'I use the word "routine" here to mean a pattern of behavior that is followed repeatedly, but is subject to change if conditions change. If the patterns of behaviour were *not* subject change, then description of it would be a characterization of the firm's organizational form' (Winter, 1964, p. 264 n.). Thus, for Winter the concept of routines presented a qualification of 'patterns of behavior' in general. They matter because of their strong link to satisficing behaviour and search activity. Together with Richard Nelson, he developed the concept of routines through the 1970s (Winter, 1975; Nelson and Winter, 1973, 1980), culminating in their 1982 *An Evolutionary Theory of Economic Change* (Nelson and Winter, 1982) in which routines occupy a central role as units of inheritance: 'Our general term for all regular and predictable behavioral patterns of firms is "routine". . . . In our evolutionary theory, these routines play the role that genes play in biological evolutionary theory' (Nelson and Winter, 1982, p. 14). It is this book that presents the first extensive treatment of routines at the organizational level of analysis (Raub, 1998) and drew large-scale attention to it.

Since the reception of Nelson and Winter (1982) there has been a rapid increase in the literature on routines and in the use of the concept of routines. For some authors the concept takes a central position in their work (for example Michael D. Cohen, Giovanni Dosi, Massimo Egidi, Geoffrey M. Hodgson, Franco Malerba, Luigi Marengo, J.S. Metcalfe, Richard Nelson, Massimo Warglien and Sidney Winter).

KEY ELEMENTS OF THE CONCEPT OF 'ROUTINES'

The objective of this article is to contribute to our understanding of the concept of routine through illuminating its historical origin. One reason this can contribute to understanding is that underlying ideas can be made clearer by reference to their origins. Also, originally important ideas and aspects that have been 'lost' and forgotten over time can be brought to light again. In order to achieve this objective, it is necessary but not sufficient to just paint a broad canvas. It will be necessary to carve out of history the basic underlying structures – if not every detail, then much more importantly some very clear contours and shapes. In particular, we will attempt to assemble and trace the ideas that have been underlying the notion of a 'routine' when it was formed. Because they have preceded the concept of 'routines', have paved the way for its development, played a role in its formation and have been 'absorbed' and shaped the concept, they are key elements of the concept of 'routines'. The ideas that can be most clearly traced through time and that have become 'building blocks' of the concept of 'routines' are the collective (social) nature of routines, the repetitiveness of routines, and the non-rational and self-actuating nature of routines. These three characteristics can not only be shown to have had a major influence on the development of the concept of routines; they also still bear a mark on it today.

Before we start to trace each of these three characteristics of routines through history, a word on the role of the cognitive dimension is necessary. As shown in Becker (2001; 2004), routines are seen as implying the cognitive as well as the behavioural level. Still today there is ambiguity on the question of which of the two levels the concept of routines refers to – or whether it refers to both. Because of this lack of consensus, therefore, it is *not* a key characteristic of the concept of routines to be a cognitive-level or a behavioural-level concept. However, for the further discussion it will be helpful to keep in mind that a number of related concepts quite clearly refer to the cognitive level, which helps to distinguish them from the concept of routines. Probably the most important of those is the concept of rules. Rules are cognitive in the sense that they stand for something that influences behaviour, but are not themselves just behaviour. There are explicit and non-explicit (because they are not articulable or out of the reach of consciousness) rules.

Now, without further distinguishing these concepts amongst themselves, the concepts of conventions, norms, procedures and standard operating procedures seem – generally – to be in the cognitive realm: they inform and constrain expressed behaviour. The concept closest to routines is that of 'standard procedure' (March and Simon, 1958) or 'standard operating procedure' (Cyert and March, 1963 [1992]). Standard operating procedures are explicit, change slowly and thereby give stability to the organization. Due to this characteristic, they give direction to activities that are constantly recurring. They influence (and in many cases dictate) the decisions made in the organization (Cyert and March, 1963 [1992], p. 122). Note how standard operating procedures are situated on the cognitive level, which distinguishes them from routines. Let us now turn to tracing the three key characteristics of routines over time.

The Repetitiveness of Routines

Writing in the age of Enlightenment, Edmund Burke was one of the earliest authors who emphasized the aspect of repetition. Burke made 'repetition', 'the principle of rhythm', and 'imitation' important topics in thinking about habits and customs (Kramnick, 1977). The contribution of this move cannot be underestimated, as it provided the very first steps towards a framework for analysing concepts of behavioural predisposition, which later would also come to include routines. Further, he also provided a link to creativity, pointing out that 'if everyone imitated previous patterns there would be no change' (Kramnick, 1977, p. 95–6). Burke was thus one of the first to direct attention to the processes of imitation and repetition, suggesting some analytical inroads to them as well. For example, he pointed out that 'repetition causes an expectation of another (incident)' (Burke, 1757 [1958], p. 140), that 'variation itself must be continually varied' (Burke, 1757 [1958], p. 156), and that the degree of variation is important: 'Nothing long continued in the same manner, nothing very suddenly varied can be beautiful (Burke, 1757 [1958], p. 156). This was a substantial contribution indeed and as such might be regarded an appropriate historical starting point for a reconstruction of this aspect of the concept of routine.

The aspect of repetition was also emphasized where the concept of habit featured in Enlightenment thought. Hume for example made the point strongly: '. . . we call every thing custom, which proceeds from a past repetition, without any new reasoning or conclusion' (quoted in Commons, 1934, p. 146). Immanuel Kant argued in the same vein as Hume in this regard. In making the claim that 'all of our knowledge begins with experience . . . but the basic categories of our experience are not learned from experience but instead are brought to experience as *a priori* organizing principles' (Solomon and Higgins, 1996, p. 208), he emphasized the importance of precedence and repetition.

In the second half of the nineteenth century, the aspect of repetition was given a narrower meaning. Although the image of habits as a fixed, mechanical reaction to stimuli had already been existent in the 1780s (Camic, 1986), it was in the course of the nineteenth century that the concept of habit became to be equated more exclusively with activities of a relatively elementary type (Camic, 1986). This change was due to two developments: first, it was due to the influence of evolutionary biology, where the term 'habit' was used for describing the elementary behaviours of lower species. Both Jean-Baptiste Lamarck and Charles Darwin used the term in this sense, talking for example about the 'habits of British insects' (Darwin, 1859, p. 11). Second, the science of psychology – newly emerging in the nineteenth century – was fascinated with the study of 'reflex action' and physiological experimentalism and conceptualized habit accordingly; that is, it equated habit with reflex action and even went so far as to suggest that habits were certain neural pathways (Camic, 1986).

Those two developments led to an equation between habit and elementary behaviour, which was dovetailing with the fascination physiologists had for the experimental study of 'reflex action'. What took place was thus a physiologization of the concept of habit because the physiological literature had long since adopted habit as the standard synonym for acquired reflexes (Camic, 1986). The concept of habit was in this way being 'appropriated' by the biophysical sciences (Camic, 1986). Later, Taylor built on this narrow understanding of habits. In his endeavour to systematize the flow of production, based on abstract laws and rules, he contrasted regular and repetitive movements with movements influenced by personal judgments and rules of thumb. Routinization and standardization thereby became indicators of Scientific Management (Merkle, 1980). Thus, Taylor had introduced another important relationship of repetition: that between repetition and *personal judgment*.

Not all authors, however, used the concept in this very narrow sense. Peirce, for example, also emphasized repetition but pointed out another important aspect of it: customs originate in the past, are changing in the present, and entail the *expectation* that practices will be repeated in the future (Commons, 1934). Peirce established the link between repetition and the establishment of expectations as a crucial and important aspect of habits. For him, 'the essence of belief is the establishment of habit' (Peirce, 1934, pp. 255–6). The aspect of repetition has featured in the work of Commons as well: 'Custom is the mere repetition, duplication, and variability of practices and transactions' (Commons, 1934, p. 44).

In the 1940s, when the concept of 'routine' started to appear, the aspect of repetition was central: 'Organization routine is that part of any organization's activities which has become habitual because of repetition and which is followed regularly without specific directions or detailed supervision by any member of the organization' (Stene, 1940, p. 1129).

In the same year as Edwin Stene's paper was published (1940), George Katona published a paper mentioning routines (Katona, 1940). In it, he made an interesting distinction, which he developed further six years later (Katona, 1946). On the one side of the distinction is 'a routine response which in some cases we cannot distinguish from the results obtained by drill' (Katona, 1940, p. 252). (Drill means the repetition of something.) He contrasted this with 'real understanding' as the origin of a routine response (Katona, 1940, p. 252). Thus, not only did he make the *origin* of routines an issue, he also proposed two alternative origins: by mere repetition ('drill'), and by understanding. His (very early) contributions to the concept are not exhausted with this, though. Having identified two potential origins of routines, he also had a hypothesis about the *process* of routinization. In the first case, it obviously consists of repetition of an activity. In the second case, a routine develops when

> principles, well understood in their original context, tend to be carried over from one situation to another. This is the most important explanation of routine or conventional action, in contrast to purely repetitive action, never fully understood or understandable, such as tapping the typewriter here for 's' and there for 't'. (Katona, 1946, p. 49)

Thus, Katona has further specified the definition of routines: routines are not activity patterns which develop through mere repetition ('purely repetitive action'). They are activity patterns that had once been understood in their original context and then have been carried over to other (temporal) contexts.[20] In the 1946 article he set routines in yet another contrast and thus introduced another distinction: he set 'genuine business decisions in contradistinction to inflexible routine actions' (Katona, 1946,

p. 46). Genuine decisions, however, require judgment. Thus, his distinction is reminiscent of Taylor's contrasting regular and repetitive movements with movements influenced by personal judgments and rules of thumb. Katona – in 1940 Taylor should still have been fresh on his mind – thus galvanized this opposition and at the same time made the following a characteristic of routines: they do not require judgment.

But there was a second implication following on from this dichotomy between 'genuine decisions and inflexible routine actions': whereas decisions have to be 'guided by definite expectations' (Katona, 1946, p. 55), routines are characterized by not requiring an underlying expectation: 'Business actions are frequently routine in the sense that expectations or changes in expectations play hardly any role in determining them' (Katona, 1946, p. 53).The expectations in turn 'may also be routine, consisting of carrying over principles that were understood to be appropriate under previous different circumstances' (Katona, 1946, p. 57).

Over a series of publications (1940, 1946, 1951) Katona developed a three-level hierarchy of business activity. On the first level, there are mechanistic, repetitive actions. They are the result of drill. On the second level, there is routine behaviour or routine procedure. It is characterized by the idea that something that has been understood once in the original situation is being carried over to other situations (see particularly Katona, 1940). On the third level, there are 'genuine decisions'. These are guided by expectations (see particularly Katona, 1946).

The Non-Rational and Self-Actuating Nature of Routines

Amongst many other things, Hume has also pointed out that there are limits to reason. For instance, there are some things that reason can *not* provide, such as delivering assurances (Solomon and Higgins, 1996). In arguing that there are limits to reason, Hume breached the assumption that *all* behaviour is governed by ratio and established the possibility of non-rational behaviour.[21] Hume himself made a proposal for how to fill the gap he breached: he proposed that what reason cannot do, nature would do for us anyway. If reason cannot guarantee us knowledge, nature nevertheless provides us with the good sense to make our way in the world (cf. Solomon and Higgins, 1996). In doing so, he pointed in the direction of instincts. But he was also more specific: '. . . we call every thing custom, which proceeds from a past repetition, without any new reasoning or conclusion' (quoted in Commons, 1934, p. 146). Custom is a form of non-rational behaviour.

Custom (Burke, 1757 [1958], p. 101, 103, 148) and habit (Burke, 1757 [1958], p. 103, 104) were also playing an important role in the works of Edmund Burke (Kramnick, 1977). He characterized them as forms of behaviour brought about 'without any intervention of the reasoning faculty, but solely from our natural constitution' (Burke, 1757 [1958], p. 49; cf. also Kramnick, 1977, p. 25, 32). In doing so, he as well characterized them as non-rational concepts.

Finally, Kant – a contemporary of Hume and Burke – opened the same gap and filled it with something pointing towards a member of the family of behavioural predispositions: 'inclinations' which 'naturally' lead to actions (Solomon and Higgins, 1996, p. 211). But Kant also provided something else that is very important in our context: arguments for establishing the possibility of the coexistence of *both* forms of predisposed behaviour and forms of behaviour not limited by such predispositions at the same time. As Solomon and Higgins have put it: 'Not all actions are motivated by the inclinations, however. People have the capacity to *will*' (Solomon and Higgins, 1996, p. 211).

This was the situation at the end of the eighteenth century. The possibility of non-rational behaviour, as also coexisting with rational behaviour, had been floated. 'Inclinations' (Kant) and other types of 'natural behaviour' (Hume) had been given as examples of such non-rational behaviour. Burke and Hume had concretized these 'natural' behaviours: They are habits and customs.

In the mid-nineteenth century, Henry Sumner Maine extended this characteristic of the non-rationality of habit (Maine, 1871, p. 66) and custom (Maine, 1861, pp. 5, 8; 1871, pp. 54, 66). For Maine, custom denoted something characterized by self-enforcement (Maine, 1871, pp. 67, 68), and by unintentional changes (Maine, 1871, pp. 70–71). This is an important extension of the idea of non-rationality: it has the implication that habitual behaviour, although human behaviour, might not be completely accessible to (conscious) control.[22] Instead, it has a self-actuating quality and is only loosely coupled with intention (if at all).[23]

At the end of the nineteenth century, one author took a decisive step and reversed perspectives on the rationality of behaviour: Charles Sanders Peirce 'actually made Habit and Custom, instead of intellect and sensation, the foundation of all science' (Commons, 1934, p. 150). In doing so, he not only broke with empiricism, but also drove home the point that not only are there rational *and* non-rational forms of behaviour – but that the non-rational forms might actually be the more important, more fundamental ones. Veblen, amongst others, had followed this 'habitual turn'. He saw human nature as comprised of irreducible instincts and learned habits (Twomey, 1998), and made habit a fundamental theoretical concept and put it at the basis of his economic analysis (Dyer, 1984). For instance, in his work he attempted to trace back all economic change to changes in habits of thought (Veblen, 1898).

Just a little after the time when Peirce was writing, Vilfredo Pareto drew a distinction between 'logical' and 'non-logical' behaviour[24] which he developed in 1897 (Finer, 1966) and systematized in his *Manuel d'Economie Politique* (1909) and *Trattato di Sociologia Generale* (1916). He made two important contributions: first, he acknowledged that 'in actual behaviour the different categories are nearly always mixed, and a given action may to a large extent be non-logical while yet being to a smaller extent logical; or vice versa' (Pareto, 1909, § 3). Second, however, he proceeded to excise the analysis of non-logical behaviour from the nascent field of economics, to whose development he contributed much at a critical time: habits and other 'non-logical' concepts (that is, concepts not applying rationality) were excluded from economic analysis and relegated to sociology or psychology. Thus, although the idea began to take form, it was excised from economics.

There were remnants at least in the field of management, however. Barnard, for example, writing in 1938, emphasized *informal*, not just formal aspects of organizations (Barnard, 1938 [1968]; Rothwell, 1996). It is informal mechanisms that deal with know-how and behavioural (we would now call it 'tacit') knowledge (Barnard, 1938 [1968]). These informal mechanisms consist of 'habitual experience' and 'habits' (Barnard, 1938 [1968], p. 307). Not only did he (still) speak of intuitional (as opposed to logical) processes. Also, these were 'indispensable' (Barnard, 1938 [1968], p. 313). In this way, routines seemed to have countered the Tayloristic drive for closely directed and supervized action. Thus, another contribution of Taylorism could have been to have drawn some attention to its opposite aspects by 'overemphasizing' the explicit, tangible, measurable, supervized and directed aspects of action.

This was the situation at the beginning of the 1940s when the notion of 'routine' appeared. One of the characteristics routines had when they were 'introduced' was that they are self-actuating: 'Organization routine is that part of any organization's activities which has become habitual because of repetition and which is followed regularly *without specific directions or detailed supervision* by any member of the organization' (Stene, 1940, p. 1129; cited in Simon 1947 [1997], p. 100; emphasis added).

The non-rational characteristic is also clearly present in a concept related to that of routines, also arising around the 1940s: Hayek's 'spontaneously evolved rules of conduct'. Hayek (1973) sees rules as spontaneously evolved from social interactions over time. These rules then guide behaviour, thereby leading to a social order that is not designed. The social order, therefore, is not a deliberate construction of human reason. It is non-rational. Because Hayek suggests that there is some mechanism of cultural evolution that can be expected to systematically select for appropriate rules (Vanberg, 1994), the social order is not the product of a rational process, but of an unconscious evolutionary process (cf. Ioannides, 2000). Not only the social order – the 'product' of the spontaneously evolved rules of conduct – is non-rational; also the rules themselves. The reason is that they are not fully articulable. As Hayek says, they are 'supra-conscious', inarticulable, tacit. Thus, they are not fully accessible to conscious deliberation, and therefore not fully available for rational calculation.

Despite this similarity between the concepts of routines and spontaneously evolved rules of conduct, however, there are important differences between the concepts. The most important difference seems to be that for Hayek, rules are clearly distinguished from action. Much of his theory is concerned with the interplay between the order of rules and the order of actions (Vanberg, 1994). While routines also involve rules (at least to the extent that the recurrent activity might be induced by rule-following), the concept of routines appears to primarily refer to the level of action. See for example Stene's definition in the previous paragraph. Although 'spontaneously evolved rules' differ from routines in being on the cognitive, not the behavioural level, the similarities between the two concepts indicate how the notion of non-rationality was a core characteristic of concepts belonging to the family of concepts considered here.

One more aspect of the rational/non-rational behaviour dichotomy is worth noting here: there have consistently been hints that the two types of behaviour might form a continuum, each presenting one end of the spectrum. Pareto for instance, although introducing the distinction between logical and non-logical behaviour (Pareto, 1909; 1916), acknowledged that 'in actual behaviour the different categories are nearly always mixed, and a given action may to a large extent be non-logical while yet being to a smaller extent logical; or vice versa' (Pareto, 1909, § 3). This idea was not a one-off. Barnard has developed it as well. He proposed a continuum of mental processes and argued that:

> a great variety of mental processes is required, ranging from the very rapid intuitional . . . to the formal logical processes of scientific reasoning. All these processes appear to be required in any kind of work; the differences are in the relative emphasis upon the various parts of the scale of processes. (Barnard, 1938 [1968], p. 312)

With the formal, logical end of the continuum already having received plenty of attention, he then called for an analysis of the other extreme of the continuum, for a 'habitual analysis' (Barnard, 1938 [1968], p. 313).

The Collective (Social) Nature of Routines

The third core characteristic of routines started to crystallize in the first decades of the twentieth century: the collective (social) nature of routines.[25] Already the concept of habit had a social dimension for some authors. Veblen, for example, focused on the social dimensions of habit (Waller, 1988), as well as on their cognitive dimension (Hodgson, 1993b). John Commons later introduced a distinction along social/individual lines, making clear that 'habit' is at the individual and 'custom' at the collective level: 'Habit is repetition by one person. Custom is repetition by the continuing group of changing persons. It has a coercive effect on individuals' (Commons, 1934, p. 155; also Commons, 1924 [1974], p. 300). This distinction also manifested itself when he shifted the 'ultimate unit of economic investigation from commodities and individuals to transactions between individuals' (Commons, 1934, p. 73) – that is, from commodities to processes and more precisely, to *inter*action. *Trans*actions are *inter*actions. Interactions involve at least two parties. This emphasis on the collectiveness of customs and the distinction between collective customs and individual habits was a contribution that had not been made that clearly before (cf. Lorenz, 2000). Thus, by the 1930s – when we can note an increase in the use of the term 'routine' and shortly before the appearance of the concept of a 'routine' and the emergence of a science of economic organization – the ground seems to have been well prepared for a collective concept.

It is significant for tracing the collective, social character of the concept of a 'routine' that when it emerged it emerged in the context of the study of economic organization. The fact that it was seen in connection with economic organization and organizations clearly infuses it with a collective, social character. It is important to keep this origin of the concept in mind.

Stene (1940) is very clear on the point that routines refer to organizational activities. In his study of organizational decision-making, Gordon (1945) found that many of the decisions with which economic theory is concerned are made by routinized procedures, while corporate executives actually spend their time on matters of greater importance (see Nelson and Winter, 1982, p. 16 n.). Thus, Gordon also situates routines in an organizational context. More than that, for Gordon, routines clearly are collective processes. Simon (1947 [1997], p. 100), too, when he mentioned routines (quoting Stene, 1940), introduced them as 'artificial organization counterpart' of habits. This was a clear message that routines are collective, social, phenomena. However, just a little further on in the text he says: 'If a formal criterion were needed, it might be said that a matter has become part of the organization routine when it is settled by reference to accepted or approved practices rather than by consideration of the alternatives or their merits' (Simon, 1947 [1997], p. 100).

Although Simon introduced routines precisely with the distinguishing criterion (from habits) of collectivity, he presented this in a way that could easily be misinterpreted. Instead of emphasizing the collective aspect more, he picked up the question of rationality of behaviour: 'consideration of the alternatives of their merits'. Thus, the point about the collectivity of routines – although clearly made by Simon – easily got lost because it was presented in a way that could easily be misinterpreted.[26] Instead – although not diminishing the argument about routines as collective phenomena – Simon has been emphasizing the non-rational aspects more, as he explains in his comment in the 1997 edition. In one sentence, the thesis of chapters IV and V is this: 'The central concern of administrative theory is with the boundary between the rational and the nonrational aspects of human social behaviour' (Simon, 1947 [1997], p. 118). This illustrates the point well: he takes the social nature of the behaviour studied (and also of routines) for granted, and instead (or because of that) emphasized the rational aspects.[27]

This has led to an unfortunate and unintended effect: Simon, one crucial early contributor introducing the concept of routines in management and economics, made use of such an emphasis that it made it easy for the collective nature of routines to escape attention.[28] This emphasis turned out to be written in a book which came to be one of the most influential and most widely read books in management. It was thus greatly influencing perception of the young concept of routines. Furthermore, because this statement was Simon's and he subsequently developed a *cognitive* theory, it was even easier to lose sight of the collective dimension of routines – although clearly stated by Simon. Indeed, this is what has happened: although in principle clearly stated, the collective nature of routines has sometimes been neglected (cf. Lorenz, 2000). So much so, in fact, that some authors seem to have forgotten about it and confusion on this point has resulted, to the extent that a very recent conceptual work on routines complained about the 'complete absence of an institutional dimension in the [Nelson and Winter] theory of 1982' (Mangolte, 1997, p. 8) and had the research objective of 'establishing the necessity of a redefinition of the concept of routines in a more institutionalist perspective and to formulate, in the most rigorous complete way possible, this redefinition' (Mangolte, 1997, p. 11). A further reason for this confusion might have been that – as we have seen – the concept of 'routine' builds on both that of 'custom' and that of 'habit'. However, habit is individual while custom is collective. Because the individual/collective aspect has simply slipped attention, this tension has never been discussed and is still today a source of ambiguity.

CONCLUSION

The concept of 'routines' has built on the older concepts of 'habits' and 'customs'. At the beginning of the twentieth century, both these concepts were well established in American pragmatism and American institutionalism, respectively. Subsequently, the Taylorist movement represented an important impulse for reassessing these concepts and their legacy. In the first place, Taylorism emphasized rational management and thus led to a suppression of ideas of behavioural predispositions such as habits and customs. Its focus on analyzing and rationalizing work processes, however, opened another inroad for ideas associated with these concepts. In the economic literature, the term 'routine' started to crop up in the late 1920s, indicating that these ideas took the shape of the concept of 'routines'. In the 1940s, the term 'routine', which for a long time already had been used in a number of commonsensical meanings, then crystallized into a theoretical concept put to use in the social sciences. This crystallization took place in the nascent field of 'administrative behaviour' (see the important contributions of Stene (1940) and Simon (1947 [1997])).

In this process, the concept of routine assumed some of its defining characteristics: its repetitive, non-rational and self-actuating nature. However, it also acquired a characteristic that set it in distinction from particularly the concept of 'habit': its collective nature. Unfortunately, this last characteristic has sometimes not received much attention, resulting in ambiguity. Historically, the three characteristics 'repetitiveness', 'collectiveness', and 'non-rationality and self-actuatedness' form the core of the concept of 'routines'. It is important to be clear about the relevance of each of those characteristics and to take care to not lose sight of any one of them. As for the collective character of routines, there consistently has been some confusion in the literature. The historical analysis shows that we are justified in setting the record straight and to point out that the concept of organizational routines has an important collective dimension. This has been the criterion that was the crucial one for distinguishing it from the already existing concept of habit when it was formed in the 1940s. As this chapter has attempted to show, some of the ambiguity surrounding the concept today can be dissolved quite easily by firmly grounding our understanding of the concept in history. The concept of routines has a long legacy and well-established fundaments in the social sciences, and to take this into account helps to distinguish more clearly which are the important characteristics of the concept.

Probably the most important result of the historical reconstruction is that a concept with the three characteristics of repetitiveness, collectiveness and non-rationality and self-actuatedness has long played a role in the social sciences. While one can use various terms to denote this concept, one

254 *Flexibility, routines and production in economics and social sciences*

should take care not to mix and water down the 'substance' of the concept – repetitiveness, collectiveness and self-actuatedness and non-rationality. If we depart from these characteristics, we should do it in a discussion that documents why we do so and that allows for linking this modern discussion to the historical one.

While this chapter has helped to make clearer the ideas that historically have underlied the concept, what is needed now is a terminological convention of the use of the term 'routine'. The Santa Fe meeting (Cohen et al., 1996) was a first attempt to bring together key participants of the debate to work on precisely that, and others have ensued over the last years (see Becker et al. (2005), and the Industrial and Corporate Change Special Section on Organizational Routines in the same issue). More such efforts are needed. The chapter also points to questions on the research agenda on routines. Having carved out historical key characteristics of the concept, we should now establish the limits of these criteria. For instance, with regard to repetitiveness: how 'similar' do repetitions have to be to be counted as the 'same' routine? With regard to self-actuatedness: what degree of deliberation is 'acceptable' in a routine to still qualify as a routine? By working along such questions, the historical characteristics could be linked to the modern discussion. Also, the questions present one way to work on operationalizing the concept of routines.

When the concept of routines was made popular by Nelson and Winter (1982), it was introduced as the equivalent of the gene in the social realm. Against the history of the concept it becomes clear that this idea was 'put on top' of already rich – if sometimes implicit – historical baggage. Articulating this baggage shows that the idea of routines as genes sits somewhat uneasily. While the idea itself is important, the historical reconstruction raises the question of whether it is a good move to call the equivalent of the gene a 'routine' (in this context note Winter's use of the term 'quasi-genetic traits' (Cohen et al., 1996)).

NOTES

1. University of Southern Denmark, Department of Management and Marketing, Campusvej 55, DK-5230 Odense M, Denmark. email m.becker.97@cantab.net. I am grateful to Geoff Hodgson, Stavros Ioannides, Thorbjørn Knudsen, Klaus Nielsen, Dylan Sutherland and participants of the 2000 EAEPE meetings for discussion and helpful comments. However, any ommissions and errors are my own. Support for this research by the British Economic and Social Research Council (ESRC) and the Cambridge Political Economy Society Trust is gratefully acknowledged.
2. The other two, of course, being selection and variation.
3. There are some links of influence from Hegel to Ralph Waldo Emerson, who in turn had a profound influence on the American pragmatists (Solomon and Higgins, 1996).

4. In its general part, this section draws heavily on Hodgson (1999b).
5. More precisely since Louis Brandeis, a famous lawyer at that time, had claimed in 1910 that the railroads could save one million dollars a day by applying Taylor's methods.
6. O.M. Brown, R.S. Osborne and W.J. Hiscox are British authors. The later date of their publications is explained by the fact that 'the historical heyday of Taylorism in Britain was not 1911 or 1915, but in the interwar years' (Littler, 1978, p. 187).
7. 'System is an embodiment of principles, and principles must necessarily be broad. Routine is the application of system to everyday affairs, and the application must of necessity cover detail. System implies, but routine must transform the implication into something tangible and understandable to all' (Hiscox, 1923, p. vii).
8. As a theoretical movement in general, however, it was not completely opposed to institutionalism. Although Commons held Taylorism as too radical, Veblen was in favour of Taylorism. I am indebted to Geoff Hodgson for pointing this out to me.
9. Note that a possible reason for the attention to the concept of habit could have been that Gantt, for example, who was one of the only four 'original' Taylorites recognized by Taylor himself, was influenced by the works of Veblen, which he read in 1916 (Merkle, 1980, p. 70). The same is true for other members of the inner circle of 'Taylorites' (Nyland, 1996, p. 990).
10. This publication has seen at least five editions and seems to have been very popular and in use for at least four decades. Maybe this can serve as an indication for how the concept 'survived' over this period.
11. The term 'routine' seems to have been around for some time, mostly with the meaning or connotation of being opposed to creative acts (see for example Hobson, 1914, p. 304, 305).
12. It should be noted, however, that this thread had not been severed completely, and that it – albeit very thinly – passed through time, from William James (1890) to John Dewey (1930) and to Simon (1947 [1997]). Also, contributions of Keynes (1936), and Hall and Hitch (1939) mention habitual behaviour. In 1928, Young recognized that 'at any given time routine and inertia play a very large part in the organisation and conduct of industrial operations' (Young, 1928, p. 531).
13. This shift might well have been supported by the developments in pragmatist philosophy at that time, whereby in the meantime Dewey had developed pragmatism into a more instrumentalist direction, putting more emphasis on practice and on the actual ways in which we learn things by *doing* them (Solomon and Higgins, 1996). While still being in the pragmatist tradition of recognizing habit as a central category, this more instrumental orientation seems to fit well to the development of a more 'micro'-perspective in Taylorism.
14. At about the same time as routines became an object of published research, the concept of 'folkways' (Sumner, 1906) was also findings its way into a business context with the publication of *Factory Folkways* (Ellsworth, 1952). Folkways were seen as 'customary patterns of behavior' that are characteristic elements of an institution (Ellsworth, 1952, p. 93, 98). They themselves are characterized by being an integrated practice, not a bundle of isolated activities (Ellsworth, 1952).
15. 'The epoch of "discoveries" was followed by the epoch of "routine", with established methods, with a specific acquired fund of experience and skill' (Fleck, 1946, p. 120).
16. 'The importance of routine as a means of taking care of some aspects of life in order that others maybe given more attention has frequently been stressed' (Penrose, 1952, p. 817).
17. Although Cyert and March do not use the term 'routine' in this piece, their 'standard operating procedure' is very close to what has been described so far.
18. In the 1940s there was a relevant development in biology as well: the Neo-Darwinian synthesis was becoming dominant. This led to the publication of a small number of papers discussing evolutionary ideas in the context of economics in the 1950s (Alchian, Enke, Friedman, Boulding, Penrose). In parallel, the rehabilitation of the concept of instinct was slowly beginning with the works of Nikolaus Tinbergen in the 1950s and Konrad Lorenz in the 1960s.
19. Hodgson 1998b, p. 43.
20. This criterion also featured in the 1940 article (Katona, 1940).

21. Note that I use the term 'non-rational' to refer to behavior not driven by ratio, but rather by other motives such as precedent, emotion, etc. In this sense, non-rational does not equal 'irrational'. Behavior that was motivated by motives other than rational calculation can well turn out to be rational (in the sense of a choice that 'makes sense' from a rational point of view). In other words, I use the term to refer to the process, not the outcome.

22. Maine made this point in relation to law, emphasizing the extent to which law (consisting in large part in customs) could *not* be used for the purpose of social engineering (Maine, 1871, pp. 70–71).

23. Maine's second contribution to the concept was to take a dynamic perspective on the origin of customs and habits. He saw a development from the specific to the general (Maine, 1861, p. 9), and an evolution from habit to custom to law (Maine, 1861, pp. 5, 8). The last step takes place at the moment of codification: 'The customs at once altered their character. . . . Usage, once recorded upon evidence given, immediately becomes written and fixed law. Nor is it any longer obeyed as usage. It is henceforth obeyed as the law administered by a British Court, and has thus really become a command of the sovereign' (Maine, 1871, p. 72). One implication identified by him is the different speed of adaptation of customs and laws. In this evolutionary perspective, he also makes a distinction between 'customs which do and customs which do not correspond to practices' (Maine, 1871, p. 59). The evolutionary contribution of Maine's, however, has not really been taken up. For example, W.G. Sumner, writing on *Folkways* in 1906 (Sumner, 1906), did barely refer to Maine in his work, although one could have suspected this to be the case with a work so closely related in the subject matter. Also, after the First World War in different disciplines the evolutionary approach was more or less eclipsed completely (see Cocks (1988) for sociology, Hodgson (1999b) for economics), which did not help to revive interest in Maine and his ideas.

24. Pareto's criterion as to what is logical and what is non-logical is a comparison: a comparison between the ends–means relationship as seen by the performer and as seen by the observer. Where the two correspond, the action was considered to be logical (Finer, 1966).

25. Note that 'collective nature' refers to a distinctly collective dimension that organizational routines have. For instance, how smoothly individuals participating in a planning routine cooperate is a quality of the planning routine (referring to the interaction between the participants), not of any of the individual participants themselves. Saying that organizational routines have such a distinctly collective dimension does not mean to say they do not have micro-foundations. Rather, the idea is that such a collective dimension is an emergent property that emerges from the interaction of individuals.

26. This is also supported by the fact that in the following section Simon takes up the issues of triggers, that is, he does not come back to the 'collective' point.

27. There is a reference to Pareto (1935; the English translation of Pareto 1916, in which he introduces the logical/non-logical behaviour distinction) in the same book (Simon 1947 [1997], p. 72 n.).

28. In his 1997 comments Simon supports this interpretation: 'Because I used logic . . . as a central metaphor to describe the decision-making process, many readers of *Administrative Behavior* have concluded that the theory advanced here applies only to "logical" decision-making, and not to decisions that involve intuition and judgment. That was certainly not my intent' (Simon 1947 [1997], p. 131).

REFERENCES

Barnard, Chester I. (1938), *The Functions of the Executive* [1968], Cambridge, MA: Harvard University Press.

Becker, Markus C. (2001), *The Roles of Routines in Organizations – An Empirical and Taxonomic Investigation*, PhD Thesis, Cambridge University.

Becker, Markus C. (2004), 'Organizational routines: a review of the literature', *Industrial and Corporate Change*, **13** (4), 643–77.

Becker, Markus C. and Thorbjørn Knudsen (2002), 'Schumpeter 1911: farsighted visions of economic development', *American Journal of Economics and Sociology*, **61** (2), 387–403.

Becker, Markus C., Nathalie Lazaric, Richard R. Nelson and Sidney G. Winter (2005), 'Applying organizational routines in analyzing organizations', *Industrial and Corporate Change*, **14** (5), 775–91.

Brown, Oswald M. (1932), *The Routine of a Public Issue*, Cambridge: Heffer & Sons.

Burke, Edmund (1757), *A Philosophical Enquiry into the Origin of our Ideas of the Sublime and Beautiful* [1958], London: Routledge and Kegan Paul.

Camic, Charles (1986), 'The matter of habit', *American Journal of Sociology*, **91** (54), 1039–87.

Cocks, R.C.J. (1988), *Sir Henry Maine – A Study in Victorian Jurisprudence*, Cambridge: Cambridge University Press.

Cohen, Michael and Paul Bacdayan (1994), 'Organizational routines are stored as procedural memory: evidence from a laboratory study', *Organization Science*, **5** (4), 554–68.

Cohen, Michael D., Roger Burkhart, Giovanni Dosi, Massimo Egidi, Luigi Marengo, Massimo Warglien and Sidney Winter (1996), 'Routines and other recurring action patterns of organizations: contemporary research issues', *Industrial and Corporate Change*, **5** (3), 653–98.

Commons, John R. (1924), *Legal Foundations of Capitalism* [1974], Clifton: Augustus Kelly.

Commons, John R. (1934), *Institutional Economics*, New York: Macmillan.

Cyert, Richard M. and James G. March (1963), *A Behavioral Theory of the Firm* [1992], 2nd edn, Oxford: Blackwell.

Darwin, Charles R. (1859), *On the Origin of Species by Means of Natural Selection, or the Preservation of Favoured Races in the Struggle for Life*, 1st edn. London: Murray.

Dewey, John (1930), *Human Nature and Conduct*, New York: Modern Library.

Dosi, Giovanni (1988), 'Sources, procedures, and microeconomic effects of innovation', *Journal of Economic Literature*, **26**, 1120–71.

Durkheim, Émile (1893), *The Division of Labour in Society* [1933/1964], Ann Arbor, MI: University of Michigan Press.

Durkheim, Émile (1898–1900), *Professional Ethics and Civic Morals* [1958], Glencoe, IL: Free Press.

Durkheim, Émile (1905–06), 'The evolution and the role of secondary education in France', in Émile Durkheim (ed.), *Education and Society* [1956], Glencoe, IL: Free Press.

Dyer, A.W. (1984), 'The habit of work – a theoretical exploration', *Journal of Economic Issues*, **18** (2), 557–64, reprinted in John C. Wood (ed.) (1993), *Thorstein Veblen – Critical Assessments*, London: Routledge, pp. 495–501.

Egidi, Massimo (1992), 'Organizational learning, problem solving and the division of labour', in Herbert A. Simon, Massimo Egidi, Robin Marris and Ricardo Viale (eds), *Economics, Bounded Rationality and the Cognitive Revolution*, Aldershot, UK and Brookfield, US: Edward Elgar, pp. 148–73.

Egidi, Massimo (1993), 'Routines, hierarchies of problems, procedural behaviour some evidence from experiments', unpublished paper, University of Trento.

Ellsworth, John S. (1952), *Factory Folkways – A Study of Institutional Structure and Change*, New Haven, CT: Yale Unversity Press.

Finer, S.E. (1966), 'Introduction', in S.E. Finer (ed.), *Vilfredo Pareto – Sociological Writings*, London: Pall Mall Press, pp. 3–95.

Fleck, Ludwik (1946), 'Problems of the science of science', *Zycie Nauki 1*, Warsaw, reprinted in Robert S. Cohen and Thomas Schnelle (eds), *Cognition and Fact – Materials on Ludwik Fleck*, Dordrecht: D. Reidel Publishing Co.

Funke, Gerhard (1958), 'Gewohnheit', *Archiv für Begriffsgeschichte* [1961], 3, Bonn: Bouvier.

Gordon, R.A. (1945), *Business Leadership in the Large Corporation* [1961], Berkeley and Los Angeles: University of California Press.

Hall, R.L. and C.J. Hitch (1939), 'Price Theory and Business Behavior', *Oxford Economic Papers*, **2**, 12–45.

Hayek, Friedrich A. (1973), 'Law, legislation and liberty', *Rules and Order*, Vol. I, London: Routledge & Kegan Paul.

Hedtke, Ulrich and Richard Swedberg (eds) (2000), *Joseph A. Schumpeter – Briefe/Letters*, Tübingen: Mohr Siebeck.

Hegel, Georg F.W. (1830), *Philosophy of Mind* [1971], Oxford: Clarendon.

Hiscox, W.J. (1923), *Workshop Routine – Its Principles and Application with Special Reference to 'Standing Instructions'*, London: Chapman & Hall.

Hiscox, W.J. (1923), *Factory Lay-Out, Planning and Progress*, London: Pitman & Sons.

Hiscox, W.J. and James Stirling (1920), 'Factory', *Administration in Practice* [1959], London: Pitman & Sons.

Hobson, J.A. (1914), 'The creative factor in production', Ch. IV, pp. 44–59 and 'The social will as an economic force', Ch. XX, pp. 301–9, in J.A. Hobson, *Work and Wealth: A Human Valuation*, London: Macmillan, reprinted in Geoffrey M. Hodgson (ed.) (1999), *The Foundation of Evolutionary Economics: 1890–1973*, Vol. 2. Cheltenham, UK and Northampton, MA, USA: Edward Elgar, pp. 5–29.

Hodgson, Geoffrey (1993a), *Economics and Evolution*, Cambridge: Polity Press.

Hodgson, Geoffrey (1993b), 'Institutional economics: surveying the "old" and the "new"', *Metroeconomica*, **44** (1), 1–28, reprinted in Geoffrey M. Hodgson (ed.), *The Economics of Institutions*, Aldershot, UK and Brookfield, US: Edward Elgar, pp. 50–77.

Hodgson, Geoffrey M. (1994a), 'Precursors of modern evolutionary economics: Marx, Marshall, Veblen, and Schumpeter', in Richard England (ed.), *Evolutionary Concepts in Contemporary Economics*, Ann Arbor: University of Michigan Press, pp. 9–35.

Hodgson, Geoffrey M. (1994b), 'Habits', in Geoffrey Hodgson, Warren Samuels and Marc Tool (eds), *The Elgar Companion to Institutional and Evolutionary Economics*, Vol. 1, Aldershot, UK and Brookfield, US: Edward Elgar; pp. 302–5.

Hodgson, Geoffrey M. (1988a), 'The approach of institutional economics', *Journal of Economic Literature*, **36** (March), 166–192.

Hodgson, Geoffrey M. (1998), 'Evolutionary and competence-based theories of the firm', *Journal of Economic Studies*, **25** (1), 25–56.

Hodgson, Geoffrey M. (1999a), *Economics and Utopia – Why the Learning Economy is Not the End of History*, London: Routledge.

Hodgson, Geoffrey M. (1999b), *Evolution and Institutions – On Evolutionary Economics and the Evolution of Economics*, Cheltenham, UK and Northampton, MA, USA: Edward Elgar.

Hume, David (1739–40/2003), *A Treatise on Human Nature*, Mineola, NY: Dover Publications.

Ioannides, Stavros (2000), 'Austrian economics, socialism and impure forms of economic organisation', *Review of Political Economy*, **12** (1), 45–71.

James, William (1890), *The Principles of Psychology* [1950], New York: Dover Publications.

Kant, Immanuel (1909/2004), *Critique of Practical Reason*, Mineola, NY: Dover Publications.

Katona, George (1940), *Organizing and Memorizing – Studies in the Psychology of Learning and Teaching*, New York: Columbia University Press.

Katona, George (1946), 'Psychological analysis of business decisions and expectations', *American Economic Review*, **36** (1), 44–62.

Katona, George (1951), *Psychological Analysis of Economic Behavior*, New York: McGraw-Hill.

Keynes, John Maynard (1936), *The General Theory of Employment, Interest and Money*, London: Macmillan.

Koestler, Arthur (1967), *The Ghost in the Machine*, London: Hutchinson.

Kramnick, Issac (1977), *The Rage of Edmund Burke – Portrait of An Ambivalent Conservative*, New York: Basic Books.

Littler, Craig R. (1978), 'Understanding Taylorism', *British Journal of Sociology*, **29** (2), 186–207.

Lorenz, Edward (2000), 'Organisational routines in the light of 'old' evolutionary economics: bringing politics back into the study of organisational learning', *European Journal of Economic and Social Systems*, **14** (2), 191–207.

Machlup, Fritz (1946), 'Marginal analysis and empirical research', *American Economic Review*, **36** (4), 519–54.

Maine, Henry Sumner (1861), *Ancient Law – Its Connection with the Early History of Society, and its Relation to Modern Ideas*, London: John Murry.

Maine, Henry Sumner (1871), *Village-Communities in the East and West*, London: John Murray.

Malerba, Franco and Luigi Orsenigo (1996), 'Technological regimes and firm behavior', in Giovanni Dosi and Franco Malerba (eds), *Organization and Strategy in the Evolution of the Enterprise*, Houndmills: Macmillan, pp. 42–71.

Mangolte, Pierre-André (1997), 'Le Concept de "Routine Organisationelle" entre Cognition et Institution', these pour le doctorat en science economiques, Université Paris-Nord, U.F.R. de Sciences Economiques et de Gestion, Centre de Recherche en Economie Industrielle.

March, James and Herbert Simon (1958), *Organizations* [1993], Oxford: Blackwell.

Marengo, Luigi (1996), 'Structure, competence and learning in an adaptive model of the firm', in Giovanni Dosi and Franco Malerba (eds.), *Organization and Strategy in the Evolution of the Enterprise*, Houndmills: Macmillan, pp. 124–54.

Merkle, Judith A. (1980), *Management and Ideology – The Legacy of the International Scientific Management Movement*, Berkeley and Los Angeles: University of California Press.

Nelson, Richard R. (1995), 'Recent evolutionary theorizing about economic change', *Journal of Economic Literature*, **33** (March), 48–90.

Nelson, Richard and Sidney Winter (1973), 'Toward an evolutionary theory of economic capabilities', *American Economic Review (Papers and Proceedings)*, **68** (2), 440–49, reprinted in Geoffrey M. Hodgson (ed.) (1999), *The Foundation* *of Evolutionary Economics: 1890–1973*, Vol. 2, Cheltenham, UK and Northampton, MA, USA: Edward Elgar, pp. 408–19.

Nelson, Richard and Sidney Winter (1982), *An Evolutionary Theory of Economic Change*, Cambridge, MA: Belknap Press of Harvard University Press.

Nyland, Christopher (1996), 'Taylorism, John R. Commons, and the Hoxie Report', *Journal of Economic Issues*, **30** (4), 985–1016.

Osborne, R.S. (1930), *Modern Business Routine Explained and Illustrated*, 2 Vols, London: Effingham Wilson.

Pareto, Vilfredo (1909), *Manuel d'Economie Politique*, English trans. by Derrick Mirfin, in S.E. Finer (1966), *Vilfredo Pareto – Sociological Writings*, London: Pall Mall Press, pp. 143–64.

Pareto, Vilfredo (1916), *Trattato di Sociologia Generale*, English trans. by Derrick Mirfin, in S.E. Finer (1966), *Vilfredo Pareto – Sociological Writings*, London: Pall Mall Press, pp. 167–283.

Peirce, Charles Sanders (1934), *Collected Papers of Charles Sanders Peirce*, in C. Hartshorne and P. Weiss (ed.), *Pramatism and Pragmaticism*, Vol. 5, Cambridge, MA: Harvard University Press.

Penrose, Edith T. (1952), 'Biological analogies in the theory of the firm', *American Economic Review*, **42** (5), 804–19, reprinted in Geoffrey M. Hodgson (ed.) (1999), *The Foundation of Evolutionary Economics: 1890–1973*, Vol. 2, Cheltenham, UK and Northampton, MA, USA: Edward Elgar, pp. 264–79.

Polanyi, Michael (1958), *Personal Knowledge*, London: Routledge & Kegan Paul.

Raub, Steffen (1998), 'Towards a knowledge-based model of organizational competences', PhD Thesis, Université de Geneve.

Reynaud, Bénédicte (1998), 'Les propriétés des routines: outils pragmatiques de décision et modes de coordination collective', *Sociologie du travail*, **4**, 465–77.

Richardson, George B. (1960), *Information and Investment – A Study in the Working of the Competitive Economy*, Oxford: Oxford University Press.

Rothwell, Sheila G. (1996), 'Barnard, Chester I', in Malcolm Warner (ed.), *International Encyclopedia of Business and Management*, Vol. 1, London: Routledge, pp. 345–50.

Rutherford, Malcom (1994), *Institutions in Economics – The Old and the New Institutionalism*, Cambridge: Cambridge University Press.

Samuels, W.J. (ed.) (1990), *Economics as Discourse: An Analysis of the Language of Economists*, Boston: Kluwer.

Schumpeter, Joseph A. (1911), *Theorie der wirtschaftlichen Entwicklung*, Leipzig: Duncker & Humbolt.

Schumpeter, Joseph A. (1926), *Theorie der wirtschaftlichen Entwicklung*, 2nd edn, München: Duncker & Humblot.

Schumpeter, Joseph A. (1934), *The Theory of Economic Development*, Cambridge, MA: Harvard University Press.

Simon, Herbert A. (1947), *Administrative Behavior* [1997], 4th edn., New York: The Free Press.

Solomon, Robert C. and Kathleen M. Higgins (1996), *A Short History of Philosophy*, Oxford: Oxford University Press.

Stene, Edwin O. (1940), 'Public administration – an approach to a science of Administration', *American Political Science Review*, **34** (6), 1124–37.

Sumner, William Graham (1906), *Folkways – A Study on the Sociological Importance of Usages, Manners, Customes, Mores, and Manners*, Boston: Ginn.

Taylor, Frederick Winslow (1911), *The Principles of Scientific Management* [1993], London: Routledge/Thoemmes Press.

Twomey, Paul (1998), 'Reviving Veblenian economic psychology', *Cambridge Journal of Economics*, **22**, 433–48.

Urwick, L. and E.F.L. Breck (1945), *The Making of Scientific Management*, London: Management Publications Trust.

Vanberg, Viktor (1994), *Rules and Choice in Economics*, Routledge, London.

Veblen, Thorstein (1898), 'Why is economics not an evolutionary science?', *Quarterly Journal of Economics*, **XII** (July), 373–97, reprinted in Geoffrey M. Hodgson (ed.) (1999), *The Foundation of Evolutionary Economics: 1890–1973*, Vol. 1, Cheltenham, UK and Northampton, MA, USA, pp. 163–87.

Veblen, Thorstein (1899), *The Theory of the Leisure Class – An Economic Study of Institutions* [1970], London: Unwin.

Veblen, Thorstein (1919), *The Place of Science in Modern Civilization* [1990], Brunswick, NJ: Transaction Publishers.

Waller, W.T. Jr. (1988), 'The concept of habit in economic analysis', *Journal of Economic Issues*, **22** (1), 1113–26, reprinted in John C. Wood (ed.) (1993), *Thorstein Veblen – Critical Assessments*, Vol. 2, London: Routledge, pp. 539–51.

Warner, Malcolm (1996), 'Taylor, Frederick Winslow', in Malcolm Warner (ed.), *International Encyclopedia of Business and Management*, Vol. 5, London: Routledge, pp. 4782–6.

Watson, John B. (1924/1998), *Behaviorism*, New Brunswick, NJ: Transaction Publishers.

Weber, Max (1922), *Economy and Society* [1978], Berkeley, CA: University of California Press.

White, Percival (1927), *Scientific Marketing Management – Its Principles and Methods*, London: Harper & Brothers.

Winter, Sidney G. (1964), 'Economic "Natural Selection" and the Theory of the Firm', *Yale Economic Esssays*, **4** (1), 225–72.

Winter, Sidney G. (1975), 'Optimization and evolution in the theory of the firm', in Richard H. Day and Theodore Groves (eds), *Adaptive Economic Models*, New York: Academic Press, pp. 73–118.

Winter, Sidney (1986), 'The research program of the behavioral theory of the firm: orthodox critique and evolutionary perspective', in B. Gilad and S. Kaish (eds), *Handbook of Behavioral Economics, Vol. A: Behavioral Microeconomics*, Greenwich, CT: JAI Press, pp. 151–88.

Winter, Sidney (1987), 'Knowledge and competence as strategic assets', in David Teece (ed.), *The Competitive Challenge – Strategies for Industrial Innovation and Renewal*, Cambridge, MA: Ballinger, pp. 159–84.

Winter, Sidney, G. (1990), 'Survival, selection, and inheritance in evolutionary theories of organization', in Jitendra V. Singh (ed.), *Organizational Evolution – New Directions*, Newbury Park, CA: Sage, pp. 269–97.

Winter, Sidney G. (1995), 'Four Rs of profitability: rents, resources, routines, and replication', in Cynthia Montgomery (ed.), *Resource-Based and Evolutionary Theories of the Firm – Towards a Synthesis*, Dordrecht: Kluwer, pp. 147–78.

Young, Allyn (1928), 'Increasing returns and economic progress', *Economic Journal*, **38** (152), 527–42.

11. Complementarity, cognition and capabilities: towards an evolutionary theory of production

Guido Buenstorf

INTRODUCTION

Production is one of the core activities in any economy. Economists, however, show little interest in a realistic representation of the production process. The production functions of standard models do not seriously attempt to capture details of actual production processes. Also, in recent evolutionary approaches to economics the production process is rarely studied in its own right. Evolutionary economics tends to deal with production only inasmuch as is necessary for the study of related issues such as growth, innovation and economic organization. Take for example the seminal contribution made by Nelson and Winter (1982). Their representation of the firm is meant to capture behavioural aspects identified in organization theory, and to allow for an evolutionary concept of competition as a selection process. Production is modelled by a set of input coefficients that are subject to stochastic changes caused by innovation. The representation of the production process thus remains at a similarly stylized level as in standard models. Similarly, in the tradition of evolutionary growth models originating from Nelson and Winter (1982), the modelling of the firm's actual production activities is not at centre stage (cf. the discussion in Silverberg and Verspagen, 1995).

An analogous argument moreover holds for the knowledge- or capability-based approach in the theory of the firm. This strand of literature has been characterized as the 'rebirth of production in the theory of economic organization' (Langlois and Foss, 1999) because it recognizes that the firm's production-relevant knowledge (its 'capabilities'), and the way it is organized, are crucial determinants of both the boundaries and the performance of the firm. This is a significant departure from earlier approaches to economic organization that had almost exclusively focused on governance problems. Nonetheless, the details of production processes that give rise to issues such as the tacitness of knowledge and the reliance on routines in problem solving are not systematically explored within the capabilities approach.

This chapter is a contribution to an evolutionary theory of production. It is based on a disaggregated representation of the production process. Although it does not present a unified theory, it does suggest several building blocks of such a theory. In doing so, the analysis uses concepts from economics, engineering, and psychology. The structure of the argument is as follows. The second section deals with technological interdependence between various elements and stages of the production process. Technological interdependence complicates changes to production technologies because it causes compatibility problems. The chapter then turns to behavioural aspects that underlie the productive activities of firms. I argue that inertial tendencies may be caused by the properties of cognitive and communicative processes. Findings on cognition and communication are reviewed in the third and fourth sections, respectively. Their implications for production theory are then discussed in the fifth section. Based on this line of reasoning, I suggest in the following section that if one approaches production from a dynamic perspective, there are significant parallels to the problem of technological competition under increasing returns to adoption. Subsequently, some relevant approaches to formal modelling are discussed. The final section presents concluding remarks.

This chapter focuses on the dynamics of production processes based on learning and technological change. It should be briefly noted that, although the emphasis on technological change is shared by the majority of approaches to evolutionary economics, this emphasis does not exhaust the range of issues relevant to an evolutionary theory of production. There are good reasons to question not only the high degree of aggregation in standard production models, but also the validity of the kinds of aggregates considered. This would lead to an inquiry into the nature of outputs and inputs of production, and would suggest, for example, a reconsideration of the notion of factors of production (Weissmahr, 1992; Witt, 1997a). These issues are not covered in this chapter. They are dealt with in detail elsewhere (Buenstorf, 2004). The present discussion of behavioural aspects is moreover limited to the processes relevant to the acquisition, communication and use of knowledge. It cannot do justice to the richness of individual and organizational determinants of production performance. Other relevant factors that are neglected here include issues of individual motivation as well as the effects of labour relations within the firm.

TECHNOLOGICAL INTERDEPENDENCE AND COMPLEMENTARY INPUTS TO PRODUCTION

Technology has network characteristics (Rosenberg, 1969, 1979). Most products are made from multiple components, and production processes typically consist of several stages ('operations'), in which various inputs are used. Individual product components are interdependent, and so are operations. These elements of the production process have to be coordinated into a coherent whole to obtain a useful product. And even if the static problem of coordinating components and operations has been solved, there remains a dynamic problem of how technological changes can be introduced to the process, as changes made to one element frequently affect the performance of related elements.

The multi-dimensionality of production processes is recognized by several fields and disciplines. To deal with multi-component products, the concept of product 'architecture' has been developed by management scholars. A product's architecture is defined by the arrangement of its functional elements, the way in which the various functions relate to the physical components of the product, and the nature of the interfaces that connect individual physical components (Ulrich, 1995). It has been studied how different kinds of architectures affect the feasibility of innovations (ibid.). Management theorists have, moreover, suggested that the ability of firms to cope with an innovation depends on how the innovation affects the components and/or the architecture of the product (Henderson and Clark, 1990).

The sequential character of production processes is taken into consideration by authors from quite different backgrounds. Georgescu-Roegen (1971, Ch. 9) adopts a sequential perspective to analyze how different temporal setups of production activities affect the utilization of 'fund factors' (that is, inputs that do not enter the product but provide services in production, for example machines and workers). Scazzieri (1993) uses this kind of approach to study interdependences between the scale and organization of production. Landesmann and Scazzieri (1996) take this as their point of departure for developing a general framework of production in terms of tasks, factors and material flows.

A sequential perspective also underlies the way in which production is characterized in engineering. Engineers analytically subdivide production processes into sequences of separable operations that are then analyzed in detail (cf. Todd, Allen and Alting, 1994). At the level of engineering, there is frequently an inherent logic in the sequence of operations needed to produce a particular kind of good. Most changes in the material properties of products-in-process must be made before the product's geometry is modified. In turn, changes to the geometry may cause a need for further manipulation of material properties and of surfaces. For example, heat treatment of metals is required to deal with internal stresses caused by previous machining operations.

This example indicates how individual stages of a production process may be interdependent. From a dynamic perspective, interdependence matters because it implies that process innovations introduced at any stage of a sequential production process have to be compatible with all other stages. The most basic requirement is that the modification of one operation must not change the output of this operation beyond the range of variations that the subsequent operation can be adapted to. Buenstorf (2004) has suggested a stylized sequential framework to represent the relationship between changes at the various stages. It distinguishes different kinds of process innovations according to their repercussions on other operations.

If a production process is characterized by substantial interdependence among its elements (product components and/or operations), changes made to one element will affect other elements as soon as they go beyond mere increases in productivity (such as those caused by workers' learning by doing, in performing operations). The interdependence effects of technological changes can be classified into three broad categories. First, the new element A may make it more expensive, or even impossible, to apply element B in the same way as before. This kind of effect may be called an incompatibility between elements A and B. Incompatibilities with other elements of a production process often delay the introduction of new components, operations, or inputs. For example, the introduction of automated workpiece handling in the later stages of a manufacturing process may be prevented by the lack of dimensional precision achieved in earlier stages (cf. Buenstorf, 2005). Similarly, using a stronger engine in an existing car model typically requires adaptations to the vehicle's brakes and the transmission. Or it may be frustrated simply because the engine is too large to fit into the existing engine compartment.

The second, opposite, possibility is that the new element A decreases the cost of element B. As illustrations of this kind of interdependence effect, consider a new, lighter component lowering the requirements for the structural stability of the product's overall design, or the introduction of a precision-machining operation reducing the need for subsequent finishing operations. In these cases, interdependence gives rise to a complementarity between A and B. More precisely, the complementarity can be characterized as 'direct' or 'static', in order to distinguish it from the third form of interdependence, which is accordingly called an 'indirect' or 'dynamic' complementarity. The latter is present if the introduction of A does not decrease the cost of B, but facilitates future cost-reducing changes to be made to *B*. In the literature on general purpose technologies this kind of interdependence is referred to as 'innovational complementarity' (Bresnahan and Trajtenberg, 1995).

The above considerations suggest that in multi-element production processes, changes made to an individual element cannot be analyzed in isolation, but their effects on other elements have to be taken into consideration. In an evolutionary perspective, another issue is relevant: the question of how learning can be expected to alter the degree of interdependence over the life cycle of products and technologies. Two counteracting effects of learning on interdependence can be distinguished: the mutual adaptation of elements and the broadening of the knowledge base that underlies the process.

With increasing experience, the coordination among the individual elements of a production process tends to be enhanced by learning by doing and deliberate incremental innovations. Mutual adaptation of elements is a straightforward strategy for increasing the productivity of the overall process. If it is followed, the elements will over time become increasingly interdependent. Development activities will focus on features that improve the coordination, whereas those dimensions of the elements that are not needed in the particular context are minimized. Fine-tuning elements to the specific requirements posed by other elements tends to reduce the generality of their application, however. Miniaturized laptop computers, for example, contain custom-made components that frequently exhibit compatibility problems with standardized external components. These considerations suggest that technological change based on learning by doing and using (Rosenberg, 1982) and on incremental innovation tends to be localized, that is, restricted to the specific combinations of elements in use. At the same time, mutual adaptation of elements reduces the feasibility of modifying or replacing individual components or operations. Innovations in elements that are not adapted to the other ones, for example because they derive from innovations made in another industry, will require modifications of other elements before they can be adopted. In the limit, only the entire process can be replaced by another process but not single elements.

This tendency of learning and incremental innovations to increase the degree of interdependence among elements is counteracted by the effect that learning has on the underlying knowledge base. Learning may not only allow for the fine-tuning of a production process, but it may also enhance the understanding of the principles and regularities underlying the technology in use. In other words, the knowledge base of the production process is broadened. One consequence of the broadened knowledge base is to allow for a wider range of applications for the respective production process. It is a pervasive feature of real-world technologies that their range of application has increased over their life cycle. Insofar as learning by doing does result in such a broadened knowledge base, then, it will reduce the degree of technological interdependence, as broader knowledge about the process opens new opportunities for adapting the overall process to changes made in individual elements.

There is a prima facie tension between the present emphasis on technological interdependence on the one hand and recent discussions of modularity concepts in management and economics, which seem to imply a diminishing significance of interdependence, on the other. Several authors have suggested the use of modular design principles as a generally advantageous strategy in diverse contexts ranging from product design to organizational setups (Langlois and Robertson, 1992; Baldwin and Clark, 1997; Langlois, 2002, 2003). Modularity can roughly be characterized as the absence of interdependencies between the individual elements of a multi-element system, such that changes in individual elements have no repercussions on other elements. Modularity can be achieved by deliberate design through the *ex ante* specification of interfaces connecting the elements. Changes in the degree of modularity can, moreover, be the consequences of technological change. For example, according to Langlois's (2003) 'vanishing hand' hypothesis, present advances in information and communication technologies increase the degree of organizational modularity of firms (for a less enthusiastic position cf. Robertson and Arunthari, 2002).

Several points have to be considered to appreciate the relationship between the modularity concept and the position taken here (cf. Buenstorf, 2005, for a more elaborate discussion). First, economists often discuss modularity at the organizational level rather than the level of technology. The conditions and effects of interdependence may be quite different at these levels. The trend toward increasing organizational modularity suggested by Langlois (2003) does not necessarily imply reduced interdependence at the technological level. Second, much of the discussion on technological modularity has focused on the product architecture and innovations in product components. By contrast, the relationship among operations within a sequential production process has not captured much attention. Third, and perhaps most importantly, the suggestion that modularity is generally advantageous has not gone unchallenged.

There is substantial evidence suggesting that, while the characteristics of modular designs are very useful in some situations, modularity also has a cost. Modular product designs, for instance, facilitate changes of individual components, but they compromise global performance criteria such as low overall weight and compactness, which require the coordination of the various components (Ulrich, 1995). Changes in the architecture of the product are by definition excluded in a modular design. Moreover, the independence of elements is limited to specific component levels and ranges of variation (Brusoni and Prencipe, 2001). Similar arguments hold for the process dimension of production. In a modular production process, individual operations can be modified independently. Accordingly, changes to the individual operations are facilitated. On the other hand, more drastic changes of the process, which would modify the interfaces between operations or even their entire sequence, are excluded.

These limitations of modularity imply that technological interdependence problems cannot be resolved simply by designing perfectly modular products and processes. Nor is interdependence likely to be eliminated by a global trend toward universal modularity. However, the above discussion has indicated that the degree of interdependence between the various elements of a production process is an important determinant of its technological dynamics. It is itself subject to change over time.

More generally, the arguments of this section reinforce scepticism about highly aggregated models of production. Production processes are complex, interdependent systems, and their elements are not easily reducible to two- or three-factor aggregates. Even more problematic is the assumption of smooth substitutability between aggregate input categories. In real-world production processes, using a little more of x and a little less of y simply does not suffice as a reaction to input price changes. It is more appropriate to assign to input prices an indirect role as focusing devices that affect the direction of search (as in Cimoli and Dosi, 1995). The consideration of interdependencies between the various elements of the production process implies, however, that alternatives to the presently used technology are often difficult to find. Technological interdependence may thus create an inertial tendency in production processes and prevent the perfect adaptation to changing opportunities or constraints.[1]

INERTIAL TENDENCIES IN INDIVIDUAL COGNITION

The previous section has argued that technological interdependence among the elements of a production process gives rise to inertial tendencies in technological change and, moreover, that it causes technological change to be localized in technology space. Technological factors are not the only causes of inertia and localization, however. Inertial tendencies may be further reinforced by individual cognitive processes, by communication between agents, and by organizational characteristics of the firm (which is, after all, the locus of production activities in the economy). In the present section, some evidence from cognitive psychology is reviewed to evaluate how inertia and localization may arise from individual cognitive processes. The argument is based on overviews of cognitive psychology given in Eysenck and Keane (1995), Kellogg (1995) and Anderson (2000). A more detailed review can be found in Buenstorf (2003). The following section will then add findings from social psychology and organization theory on the effects of communication in groups and organizations.

Selectivity of perception and attention is a major determinant of information processing in the human mind (Simon, 1986; Kellogg, 1995, Ch. 2). The senses provide the mind with a large amount of environmental information. The perception of environmental stimuli is biased initially by existing knowledge and expectations. Moreover, because of limited attentional capacities, only a fraction of the perceived stimuli can be attended to and consciously processed. Selection of attended stimuli is guided both by the agent's prior knowledge and by his or her momentary intentions. Selective attention allows humans to focus their cognitive capacities on those stimuli that seem most important at the moment. It thus helps to prevent information overload and enables meaningful behaviour in complex environments. However, since selection is based on prior experience, it may fail to account for changes in environmental conditions.

Perceived stimuli are briefly retained in sensory stores of various kinds (of which auditory and visual ones are most important). Their transfer into permanent memory is facilitated by the existence of auxiliary short-term storage capacities known as rehearsal systems (Anderson, 2000, Ch. 5). These are part of the working memory and have limited capacity, so that only some of the attended stimuli can be rehearsed at a time. The capacity restriction of the rehearsal systems is not perfectly rigid, however. Based on experience with specific kinds of stimuli, the working memory develops the capacity to 'chunk' several related stimuli and to process them as one. The capacity for chunking has been found to be highly domain-specific. Enhanced memory of a particular kind of stimuli based on chunking requires familiarity with this specific kind of stimuli.

The long-term memories of stimuli, and the ability to retrieve them, is subject to a number of factors. First, different forms of processing a stimulus exist, which result in differentially reliable memories (Anderson, 2000, Chs 6–8). Memory is enhanced by semantic processing based on understanding the meaning of a stimulus. By contrast, stimuli are harder to remember if they are processed on the basis of more superficial characteristics. Second, a feedback exists between present goals and deliberate activities on the one hand, and the memory of stimuli on the other. Stimuli that are related to present goals and activities are more likely to gain attention and to be semantically processed than others. This increases their chances of being retained in the memory. In turn, memory affects goals and attention. Third, retrieval of memories is enhanced by elaboration, that is, by redundant associations between specific pieces of information. Finally, cognitive psychologists have shown that the retrieval of memories is a constructive process. Humans can reconstruct memories from their memories of related stimuli even if they cannot access the target memory directly. Based on the use of related memories, they may even infer 'memories' of stimuli that they have not in fact experienced.

To explain these findings on memory and recall, it is helpful to consider how the human mind organizes memories into categories. Apparently, the mind is able to categorize related memories in different ways (Anderson, 2000, Ch. 10). Some categories (known as schemata) form on the basis of associations between the common features of stimuli. The strength of these associations varies gradually, so that they may persist in spite of some contradictory experience. Other categories are learned on the basis of a deliberate hypothesis-testing behaviour, and are more easily overturned if inconsistent with present experience.

The important implication of these findings is that human memory of stimuli is in several ways affected by prior knowledge. Stimuli that are related to earlier experience are easier to understand and to process semantically. Memories may even be distorted by the influence of earlier experience. In addition, prior knowledge has an indirect effect on memory, which operates through the allocation of attention. Because attention is guided by prior knowledge, existing memories influence the selection of stimuli to be attended to. Attention, in turn, facilitates the memory of these new stimuli.

In this context, the distinction between codified and tacit knowledge is relevant. It has a counterpart in cognitive psychology in the distinction made between explicit and implicit memory. Explicit memory stores declarative knowledge of facts and events that can be recalled and verbalized by the agent. By contrast, the content of implicit memory is not recalled consciously. It cannot be expressed in words but is revealed by the agent's behaviour. An important part of implicit memory consists in procedural knowledge of how to perform particular tasks. Various kinds of procedural knowledge exist, including motor skills, perceptual skills and cognitive skills. Implicit memory influences activities and also cognitive processes. The effect of implicit memory on cognition shows, for example, when agents feel familiar with some kind of material without being able to account for that feeling. This feeling of familiarity increases agents' confidence in the accurateness of assertions. Explicit and implicit memories are based on different forms of learning (Reber, 1993; Liebermann, 2000). The acquisition of expertise will be discussed later in this section, which is one particular way of learning implicit knowledge.

Why are the above reflections on human cognition relevant for the analysis of production? The answer is that cognitive processes underlie human problem solving, reasoning and decision-making. These activities play important roles in the professional tasks of engineers and managers involved in designing and supervising production. Accordingly, they warrant some further discussion.

Empirical evidence on problem solving indicates that it is partially reproductive. Prior knowledge influences both the representation of the problem and the way of solving it. The initial state from which problem solving starts is not objectively given but depends on how the problem is conceived of or 'framed'[2] by the agent. The definition and classification of problems proceeds on the basis of prior knowledge. Similarly, there are often several possible ways to tackle a problem. Which one is actually taken depends on the problem-solving strategies (heuristics) available to the agent. The reproductive component of problem solving includes the recall of solutions to earlier problems. Previously acquired knowledge about particular kinds of situations thus affects one's way of solving these kinds of problems. However, the influence of prior knowledge may be relaxed if it frustrates problem solving. In this case, the mind is capable of re-representing the problem and applying different solution methods.

Memory is an important ingredient of expert problem solving. For example, expert chess players use extensive memories of board positions, and of suitable moves to make from these positions. A learned capacity for chunking board positions enables them to process this kind of information more effectively than novices. Another component of expertise consists in the repertoire of domain-specific knowledge that helps experts to classify problems in meaningful ways, and to link different classes of problems to appropriate solution principles. Experts, moreover, possess heuristic knowledge for evaluating new problems within their field of expertise. This ability of experts to cope with non-standard problems, and to develop ad hoc strategies to solve them, is referred to as adaptive expertise (cf. Eysenck and Keane, 1995, Ch. 15). The limits of adaptive expertise tend to be rather narrow, that is, it is restricted to situations that are closely related to the experiences accumulated before. A further empirical feature of expertise is known as metacognition, that is, the capacity for monitoring and evaluating one's own performance. For example, experts are better than novices in evaluating their comprehension of problem-related information. Chunking, classificatory knowledge, adaptive expertise and metacognition all improve problem-solving performance. Experience and prior knowledge may also have detrimental effects on problem solving, however, particularly in variable environments. For example, the repeated use of a tool may give rise to a subjective inability to use it in ways other than its typical use (so-called functional fixedness).

The development of expertise follows a regular pattern (Anderson, 2000, Ch. 9). Initially, agents use general, domain-independent heuristics. By contrast, experienced problem solvers have acquired more efficient (but less universal) domain-specific heuristics. The acquisition of domain-specific heuristics comes with a change in the nature of the underlying knowledge. Explicit factual knowledge is increasingly replaced by implicit procedural knowledge. Problem solving by novices requires active deliberation based on the use of general heuristics in combination with declarative knowledge. In repeated problem solving, particular combinations of declarative knowledge and activities are learned as new heuristics. They are represented as implicit memories and can be activated in later solutions of similar problems. With increasing expertise, problem solving thus changes its character; deliberation is increasingly replaced by retrieval of earlier solutions. The individual steps needed to solve a problem moreover tend to be fused into unitary heuristics.

Finally, problem solving based on expertise becomes increasingly automated. Speed and accuracy of problem solving increase, and less cognitive involvement on the part of the agent is needed. The attentional capacities thus liberated can be employed for other cognitive activities. At the same time, problem solving becomes more susceptible for interruptions, and the capacity of verbally expressing the solution process is reduced or even lost entirely. The domain-specific character of the acquired heuristics limits the range and adaptability of expertise.

In cognitive psychology, the research on problem solving is distinct from that on logical reasoning and decision-making. As regards decision-making, empirical findings of deviations from the predictions of rational choice have found much attention in economics (cf. for example Devetag, 1999). Similarly, experimental evidence on deductive reasoning (the derivation of necessary logical conclusions from a set of premises) shows that agents' abilities for deduction are limited. Valid inferences are frequently not identified, whereas invalid inferences are accepted. Mental models theory (Johnson-Laird, 1985; Legrenzi, Girotto and Johnson-Laird, 1993) provides a possible explanation for these findings (although contesting theories exist, cf. Eysenck and Keane, 1995, Ch. 17). It argues that human reasoning is based on mental models that derive their coherence from the content of the specific situation, not from the underlying logical structure. Mental models are constructed in the working memory. They tend to be based on as little information as possible. Erroneous conclusions may emerge if an agent's mental model neglects crucial information. Such errors are caused by focusing effects, that is, the human tendency to restrict one's thinking to what is explicitly represented in the model.

Mental models theory is able to account for a number of empirical findings. For example, agents perform better in reasoning tasks if realistic contexts are used. According to mental model theory, this is because context information is used to 'flesh out' the mental model with more explicit information, so that focusing effects are counteracted. Similarly, framing effects in decision-making are explained by differences in mental models and consequently in the extent of focusing. In this context, further findings of systematic biases in human use of information for reasoning and decision-making can be noted. Evidence shows that agents overrate the importance of negative versus positive information, and that they rely on case history information more than on statistical evidence (Taylor, Peplau and Sears, 2000, Ch. 2).

By deductive reasoning, no knowledge can be gained in addition to that included in the premises. Inductive reasoning is required to arrive at new hypotheses. According to Holland et al. (1986), induction, too, proceeds on the basis of mental models. These authors stress the impact that prior knowledge, motivation and the specific context have on induction. Based on their concept, Arthur (1994, p. 407) argues for a 'built-in hysteresis' of the process, as agents stick to previously successful models even when they no longer work satisfactorily. The notion of 'hysteresis' runs the risk, however, of overemphasizing the impact of prior knowledge. To appreciate the degree of contingency in inductive reasoning, consider the human capacity for forming analogies, which has been demonstrated as a powerful method of generating innovative solutions to problems. Analogical thinking involves a mapping of the conceptual structure of one set of ideas into another set of ideas. In this way, integrated rather than fragmentary knowledge is transferred so that aspects that were not originally present in the target domain are transferred into it. What particular analogies an individual forms depends on highly idiosyncratic factors.

If one tries to derive a general conclusion from these findings on individual cognition, it is important to note the mixed evidence on inertial tendencies. On the one hand, there are various channels for prior knowledge to affect individual memory and individual cognitive processes. The findings on expert problem solving, moreover, suggest that biases stemming from previous experience are also present in the kind of professional activities that matter for production processes. Some cognitive inertia can therefore be expected in these activities. On the other hand, the human mind is capable of restricting the impact of the past on the present, in particular if 'traditional' approaches to problems are found to be no longer appropriate. This issue will be taken up later in this chapter. Meanwhile, the communication of knowledge among agents will be dealt with in the next section.

COMMUNICATION PROCESSES AND THE TRANSFER OF KNOWLEDGE IN GROUPS AND ORGANIZATIONS

Individual cognitive processes matter for the present discussion because ultimately all problem solutions and innovations are devised and enacted by individual minds. However, solutions to production-related problems and decisions on business practices are not normally made by isolated individuals, but rather within groups of experts. This implies that individuals have to communicate their knowledge to others.

Knowledge transfer can be based on verbal and on non-verbal communication. Verbal communication cannot transmit tacit knowledge but is restricted to declarative knowledge which can be encoded verbally. For verbal communication knowledge has to be encoded by the agent who wants to communicate it, and it has to be decoded by the recipient of the message. Both encoding and decoding are based on the contextual knowledge held by the respective agent. The various biases of individual cognitive representations that were sketched in the previous section also affect the process of communication. When communicating complex problems agents may not be able to encode all relevant knowledge because some of it may be tacit. Even if they do their best to share their knowledge (which of course cannot be taken for granted), encoding, and in consequence communication, is likely to be biased and incomplete (Denzau and North, 1994). Similarly, how well the recipient of the message is able to decode it depends on how well it matches relevant cognitive representations in his or her mind. Decoding of the communicated message is affected by prior knowledge.

The role of prior knowledge in the encoding and decoding of messages implies that communication depends on some shared knowledge of the communicating agents. Knowledge transfer through communication will work better the more similar the backgrounds of the communicating agents are. If their prior knowledge bases differ drastically, communication may fail. At the same time, successful communication increases the similarity of the representations held by the communicating agents. Communication therefore has a self-reinforcing effect on the cognitive representations of agents. Similar knowledge makes effective communication possible and thus favours further convergence of the individual knowledge bases. By contrast, differences in knowledge inhibit communication so that cognitive commonalities are unlikely to develop.

Agents, moreover, also communicate in non-verbal form, and most real-world communication has both verbal and non-verbal components. In contrast to verbal communication, non-verbal communication can also be used to transfer implicit knowledge. The effects of learning based on non-verbal communication are captured by social cognitive learning theory (Bandura, 1986; see also Harris, 1999; Stahl-Rolf, 2000). Social cognitive learning (also known as observational or model learning) is based on observing the behaviour of other agents ('models') as well as its consequences. Social learning requires that attention is paid to the model. Individuals are more likely to gain attention and become models if they are very visible for the observer, and if they have power and status. Social learning, moreover, depends on the observer's ability and willingness to imitate the model. The motivation for imitation may come from the observer's own rewarding experience in imitating the model's behaviour, but also from the 'vicarious reinforcement' (Harris, 1999, p. 197) effected by the rewards that the model gains with the observed behaviour. Social cognitive learning favours the convergence of cognitive representations within groups, including implicit ones such as attitudes, norms and the selection of problem-solving methods, possibly without the group members being aware of the ongoing homogenization.

To communicate their knowledge, humans need not engage in direct, face-to-face interaction. Transfer of knowledge can also take indirect forms. The extreme case of indirect communication is the dissemination of information by print and audio-visual media. Indirect communication via printed media such as books, journals and manuals is mostly in verbal form. It plays an important role in the communication of knowledge within professional communities. In addition, indirect transfer of non-verbal knowledge is feasible with audio-visual media. The basic conditions and cognitive mechanisms of indirect transfer are essentially the same as those for direct transfer. In particular, the problems of faithful encoding and decoding of knowledge and the impact of prior knowledge on interpretation are also present in the indirect transfer of verbally encoded knowledge.

The discussion of communication in groups is not yet specific enough to account for the dynamics of production-relevant knowledge. Most production decisions tend to be made by groups of individuals who are members of the same firm. Firms are loci of divided labour and divided knowledge. As was argued above, lack of communication between agents may make it increasingly difficult for them to understand each other. This also holds within firms. Therefore, communication among firm members is necessary to coordinate their activities and to maintain the coherence of the firm. However, because of the importance of internal communication to the firm's performance, the development of communication channels and flows is not left to the spontaneous processes described above. The firm will rather try to prevent communication breakdown between agents whose activities need to be coordinated, and to channel knowledge flows within the firm according to the requirements of coordination. The structuring effect on knowledge flows is one function of the firm's hierarchical organization. In addition, explicit regulations of communication channels and contents are employed to make sure that particular people get particular information at particular times. This provides a rationale for management instruments such as mandatory reporting schemes.

There is more to communication processes within firms than is shown in such formal prescriptions. Authors from quite different backgrounds have argued that much of the production-relevant knowledge of the firm is tacit and distributed among firm members. This characterization of firm knowledge is the basic premise of the knowledge- (or resource-) based perspective in the theory of the firm.[3] It is, moreover, consistent with the findings of historians of science. For example, Vincenti (1990) concludes from case studies of the aircraft industry that much of engineering knowledge is tacit. Some design problems are tackled on the basis of entirely phenomenological knowledge, without the underlying physical principles being known to the engineers who develop the design. In addition, judgment skills, decision heuristics and knowledge on how to use specific machinery may be tacit and learned on the job only. The communication of such knowledge affects the performance of the firm, and represents a non-trivial management task.

According to Nelson and Winter's (1982, Ch. 5) account of firm behaviour, much of the firm's knowledge is embodied in the regular patterns of behaviour within it, that is, in its 'routines'.[4] They argue (ibid., p. 99) that routines are the locus of the firm's 'memory' and that firms 'remember by doing'. Much like the implicit memory of individuals, the knowledge contained in the firm's routines is not explicitly known to its members but is expressed in their activities. It cannot be reduced to the knowledge of individual employees. Routines allow for effective and coordinated activities of the firm members. By following routines, individual activities are predictable for others who can adapt their own behaviour accordingly. As predictability presupposes regularity, the emphasis on routines highlights the inertial tendencies in firm activities. And even in the change of the firm's activities, routines have an important role to play. In direct analogy to the individual problem-solving heuristics discussed in the third section of this chapter, Nelson and Winter suggest that the firm employs well-defined and persistent routines for its innovation activities. Accordingly, both the present activities of the firm and the ways of changing them depend on the firm's earlier activities.

Back in the 1950s, Edith Penrose emphasized the importance of communicating tacit knowledge for the firm's performance and its capacity to grow (Penrose, 1995). Penrose characterizes the firm as a set of resources. The base of managerial knowledge available to a firm determines in what ways and how effectively it can make use of its resources. However, since managerial knowledge stems from specific experiences made within the firm, it cannot be bought in markets. To the contrary: if new managers are hired from outside, existing management capacities are initially required for their absorbtion into the firm. Managerial knowledge plays a double role in the growth of the firm. On the one hand, its non-tradability restricts the feasible rate of growth. Efficient growth is possible only to the extent that managers learn from their experience and become capable of fulfilling their duties in less time than before. (This implies that although the growth rate of the firm is limited, a tendency for growth is inherent to the firm.) On the other hand, because of learning, a 'pool of unused productive services, resources, and special knowledge' (Penrose, 1995, p. 66) develops in the firm. The nature of this pool affects the direction of firm growth. Each firm focuses its attention on the part of the spectrum of goods that is related to its present knowledge and activities. Its present position provides a 'frame of reference' (ibid., p. 86) for the interpretation of growth opportunities. Its growth is therefore likely to stay close to its present activities. Again, the firm's future is strongly dependent on its past.

In addition to routines and managerial expertise, a third dimension in which the development of firms is affected by the communication of tacit knowledge has been stressed by Witt (1998) in his theory of cognitive leadership. Witt suggests that part of the entrepreneur's role is to provide an interpretative framework (dubbed the 'business conception') for the activities of the firm members. By communicating his or her business conception to the firm members (in social cognitive learning processes, as discussed above), the entrepreneur influences their understanding of the goals of the firm, and also their interpretation of incoming information. Tacit cognitive commonalities among firm members develop on the basis of the shared interpretative framework. In this way, cognitive leadership helps to achieve coordination within the firm and to keep opportunism in check. The sharing of interpretations within the firm comes at a cost, however. As is acknowledged by Witt, cognitive commonalities may compromise the innovative capacity of the firm. The coordination of firm members' cognitive representations 'from above' reduces the variety of individual knowledge bases even beyond the homogenizing effect of group communication. Existing tendencies for inertia and incremental rather than drastic change are further reinforced. If and to what extent these tendencies actually become a problem depends both on the specific organizational structure of the firm and on its attitude toward innovation from within.

So far the argument has focused on the communication of knowledge within the firm. In addition to this 'internal' dimension of firm knowledge, further 'external' difficulties arise in the integration of new knowledge that originated outside its boundaries. This integration is needed if the firm is to learn from its environment. However, because of the partially tacit and therefore 'sticky' character of production knowledge, a firm's capacity to learn from its environment is restricted to specific kinds of knowledge. The notion of 'absorptive capacities' (Cohen and Levinthal, 1990) has been introduced as the aggregate of capabilities that enable a firm to recognize the value of external knowledge, to assimilate it and to apply it to commercial ends. Absorptive capacities are seen as a function of the firm's existing knowledge base. They are generated as a by-product of R&D (research and development) efforts and production activities. According to this view, firms can absorb external knowledge only if it is related to their own prior knowledge. This implies that drastic change based on external knowledge is difficult for the firm to achieve.

Moreover, learning from sources outside the firm, inasmuch as it is possible, is often not automatic and costless but requires deliberate activities on the part of the firm (Malerba, 1992). In a complementary approach, it has been argued that if innovation requires coordination between numerous specialized firms, it may be frustrated by dynamic transaction costs, that is, the costs of acquiring production knowledge from other firms (Langlois, 1992). Arguably, radical innovations are more likely to have such systemic properties than incremental changes in firm practices. Dynamic transaction costs may therefore be an additional cause of a tendency toward local learning and incremental rather than drastic change in firm activities.

COGNITION, COMMUNICATION AND THE DYNAMICS OF PRODUCTION

The above discussion of individual cognition and of communication in groups and organizations suggests that, in addition to the 'objective' inertia of technological systems caused by technological interdependencies, changes in production methods may be further hindered by 'subjective' factors stemming from the behaviour of engineers and managers who develop, produce and market commodities.

A first potential source of behavioural inertia lies in the impact of prior knowledge on individual cognition. Prior knowledge affects problem representation in various, mutually reinforcing, ways. It biases attention as well as memory, and since attention and memory are interdependent (memory affects attention, and attention enhances learning and thus the establishing of memories), there is a tendency for individual knowledge to become increasingly idiosyncratic and inflexible. It may lead to inappropriate problem representations if not all relevant information is attended to or if crucial differences to earlier, seemingly equivalent problems are over-looked. Implicit memory further limits the flexibility of individual cognition. It affects an agent's thinking without the agent being aware of its impact and being able to counteract it.

Prior knowledge also modifies the way in which a problem (in its idiosyncratic representation) is solved. As professional experts, engineers and managers have acquired domain-specific heuristics to handle their tasks. These heuristics are the foundation of their expertise; they enhance the speed and accuracy of problem solving. Acquired expertise may become counterproductive, though, if it does not adapt when problems change or better solutions become available. The capability of adapting problem solving to changing circumstances is restricted by the partially automatic character of heuristics due to proceduralization. Improved problem-solving performance comes with reduced cognitive control of the problem-solving activity, and with a tendency to rely on memory and intuition rather than on deliberation. A loss in the capacity to express one's problem-solving approaches verbally is a natural concomitant of developing expertise. It introduces an element of tacit knowledge into experts' professional activities, and tends to limit their ability to change these activities.

There are limits to the effects of prior knowledge on problem solving and reasoning, however. Sometimes a range of problems that is not too different from previous ones can be covered by adaptive expertise. Metacognition increases the capability of experts to recognize the limitations of their own performance and to seek improvements. Moreover, the human capacity of analogical thinking brings a degree of contingency to problem solving. In making analogies, a random element enters cognition through the idiosyncratic perceptions and experiences of the particular problem solver that often have no systematic relation to his or her professional tasks but nonetheless affect the nature of the analogies actually formed. Finally, of course, feedback from the environment serves as a disciplining factor. Persistent failure of their problem solving methods will motivate agents to change their behaviour (even though there is no guarantee that the agent identifies the correct causes of the failure). If failure is realized, the current representation of the problem may be given up, and the problem solver may return to explicit (but more cumbersome) solution methods. These factors indicate that the wholesale characterization of individual cognition as being path-dependent that is sometimes found in the relevant research literature does not do justice to the capacities of the human mind.

Communication in groups is a second potential cause of 'subjective' inertia in technologies. Engineers and managers are severely limited in what they can achieve individually. They are part of a network of relations to other members of the department or the research lab, other departments of the firm, and to other members of their professional community. For ideas to become relevant they must be communicated to other individuals and gain their support. Historical evidence indicates that an important part of the communication of new technological knowledge takes place within the professional communities of engineers (Vincenti, 1990). Communities play an important role in defining design requirements and performance criteria as well as in selecting which kinds of newly developed solutions to techno-logical problems are actually used by practitioners.

The communication of new technological knowledge is complicated by the limitations discussed above. Individuals selectively attend to stimuli. Both in the communication of verbally encoded information and in model learning, they are more likely to attend to sources of information with high reputation. Since reputation is granted by the community, this implies that persons who are regarded as experts will be attended to more willingly than outsiders. Similarly, engineers would rather rely on information published in respected professional journals and handbooks than on information coming from outside their community. In addition to selective attention, not all attended information will be understood equally well. Misunder-standings will be less frequent for material that is compatible with an agent's pre-existing knowledge than for material which is not.

The characteristics of communication contribute to the homogenization of the communicating agents' cognitive representations. Biases in the com-munication of technological knowledge imply that new knowledge diffuses more easily within the group if it does not fundamentally depart from established traditions but builds on ongoing practices. By contrast, rad-ically new ideas and solutions are harder to communicate. They may not be found acceptable for use in actual production processes, particularly in light of the potential risks involved in investments in new technologies.

Finally, the firm is a third source of subjective inertia. Not only are com-munication processes within the firm subject to the same homogenizing effects as those in groups, as is indicated by the internal and external knowl-edge problems of the firm identified above; these effects are moreover re-inforced by the role of routines within firms, by the tacit character of managerial knowledge and by shared cognitive representations stemming from cognitive leadership. As a consequence, what the firm can do, and what it actually does, is influenced by its prior knowledge. The theoretical arguments for the impact of prior managerial and entrepreneurial knowl-edge on firm growth and innovation are supported by recent empirical work. Several studies of new industries have found that firms with experi-ence in related industries were among the most successful entrants (cf. Klepper and Simons, 2000; Thompson, 2005). At the same time, incumbent firms often have difficulties in coping with radical and architectural innovations. In these kinds of innovations, prior knowledge appears to have a restrictive more than an enabling effect (Henderson and Clark, 1990). Shane (2000) shows that prior experience enables the recognition of entrepreneurial activities, and that the nature of the prior knowledge also affects *which* opportunities a particular agent discovers.

LOCALIZED LEARNING, KNOWLEDGE SPILLOVERS AND MODELS OF TECHNOLOGICAL COMPETITION

What do the above considerations imply for the dynamic representation of production processes? Technological interdependence suggests that radical changes in production methods will often result in incompatibility problems, and also that cognitive and communicative processes appear to favour incremental over radical change. A tendency for 'localized' technological change (Atkinson and Stiglitz, 1969) can thus be deduced from the above discussion; that is, for technological change limited to production processes that are closely related to the one presently in use.

Because of its implications for knowledge spillovers between firms, the firm's 'external' knowledge problem is, moreover, relevant for the dynamic representation of production processes. Beginning with Arrow (1962), learning by doing is often found in macroeconomic models. This modelling approach implicitly combines two assumptions: first, that knowledge 'flows' between points in time, as learning is based on experience, and second, that knowledge 'flows' between separate firms and industries. However, the notion of absorptive capacities (Cohen and Levinthal, 1990; see above) suggests that knowledge spillovers are more circumscribed than is assumed in these kinds of models. The firm can absorb external knowledge only if it already possesses some related prior knowledge. This implies that not only the innovation activities of the individual firm are localized, but also the knowledge spillovers between firms.[5]

If both the firm's own innovations and its capacity for integrating external knowledge are localized, then the changes in productivity of a technology are a function of its installed base. The more widespread the use of a technology, the more dynamic it will tend to be. If, furthermore, only a small number of alternative technologies exist for a particular production process (which is a plausible assumption in light of the interdependence problems discussed previously), then the dynamics of technological change will give rise to network effects even for technologies that have no network characteristics otherwise. The adoption of a technological alternative by one producer then causes a positive externality for other producers working with the same technological alternative. Technologies with the above characteristics fulfill the conditions for network technologies as identified by David (1987, 1992): technical interrelatedness between components of the system that give rise to compatibility problems and increasing returns at the system level. Consequently, their dynamics may be represented by models of technological competition under increasing returns to adoption. These considerations suggest that stochastic models of technological competition with network externalities are more generally applicable than often assumed.[6] Technologies with localized learning do differ from 'ordinary' network technologies however, in that learning requires time (that is, network externalities always have a temporal structure).

Models of technological competition under increasing returns to adoption can, moreover, be classified along (at least) two dimensions. First, they assume either synchronous or asynchronous entry of the competing technologies. And second, they model network externalities either as global for the respective technological alternatives (that is, all users of a technology benefit from the learning of all other users of the same technology), or as localized even within the range of uses of the individual technologies. In the latter case, not all users of a technology benefit from the improvements introduced by another user of the same technology, but only a subset of them does. In other words, heterogeneity exists also within the respective technological alternatives. (Of course, based on the above assumption that knowledge can at best spill over within each technological alternative, the users of the other alternative will in no case benefit from the improvements.)

Brian Arthur's (1989) well-known model is an example of technological competition with synchronous entry and global network externalities (within the alternatives). It does not model a production problem, but more generally an adoption decision made according to a criterion of superiority. The model can be applied to a production context if the superiority criterion is interpreted as a measure of the relative productivity of alternative production technologies. In Arthur's model, two kinds of agents and two alternative technologies are present. Each kind of agent inherently prefers a different one of the two competing technologies. Because of increasing returns to adoption, however, benefits from widespread use of a technology may overcompensate the inherent preference that one group originally had for the competing alternative. The more widespread technology then becomes the superior alternative for both groups of agents. Under specific modelling assumptions (of an infinite number of agents chooses between the technologies once and for all, with the probability of choosing each alternative being equal to its market share), the technology that happens to be adopted more widely in the early phase of the industry will dominate the industry forever, even if it is technologically inferior to the alternative. Put more technically, the dynamic system exhibits non-ergodicity, that is, there exists a region of the phase space that cannot be left by the system once it is entered.

Whereas Arthur's model considers the case of two alternatives competing for a 'virgin' market, Witt (1997b) notes that real-world competition between technological alternatives often involves a struggle between an incumbent technology and a newly entering one, that is, a situation of asynchronous entry. Although the entrant technology may be technologically superior, it is disadvantaged by the increasing returns to adoption that the incumbent technology has already generated. To account for this kind of situation, Witt proposes a model in which a finite number of agents choose between two alternative technologies and where agents can reconsider their choice and switch their technology. In this model, no lock-in to one of the technologies occurs. The new technology can spread and capture the entire market if it is able to overcome a critical threshold of market share, which is a function of its relative inherent productivity. Although Witt interprets the problem of network externalities narrowly and does not consider localized learning as a potential source of increasing returns to adoption, the model seems suitable for doing so.

Both Arthur's and Witt's models consider global network externalities (that is, each user of a technological alternative benefits from each additional user of the same alternative). There is no heterogeneity within the respective technological alternatives. Heterogeneity within the alternatives can be represented by modelling local network externalities. As an example, consider David and Foray's (1994) model of the diffusion of a standard. In this model, a set of organizations is connected through a set of transactional lines. Each organization decides whether or not to adopt a standard. Through the set of transactional lines, the structure of relations between the organizations is specified. Each organization reacts with a specific probability (so-called receptivity) to the adoption decisions of its direct neighbours. Moreover, whether a line is able to transmit influences from one organization to another depends on a threshold value (called connectivity), which is also a stochastic variable. Below some critical values of both receptivity and connectivity, isolated adoption decisions cannot spread in the system. By contrast, lock-in to complete spread of the standard is realized only in the limiting case of both probabilities equalling one.

Similar models can be devised to represent the localization of technological change within the alternative technologies. Durlauf (1993) uses a related methodology in a growth model in which a number of industries choose between two alternative technologies that are characterized by low and high production volumes respectively. Starting from an all low-volume situation, the decision to adopt the high-volume technology follows a transition probability that is a function of the adoption decisions previously made within a specific range of neighbouring industries. One result of the model is that high-volume regimes are less likely to emerge for larger ranges of interdependence; that is, if a large number of earlier switches by neighbouring industries is required in order to induce the deciding industry also to switch.

The above examples indicate ways of modelling the dynamics of production technologies that correspond to different entry and spillover conditions. At the same time, all these models using stochastic dynamic processes share a common shortcoming. They are highly stylized and capture only some particular elements of production decisions. Accordingly, although the underlying assumptions about the dynamics of the process are congenial to modelling the considerations of this chapter, there is a long way to go to turn them into more realistic models of production.

CONCLUSIONS: FROM CHOICE OF TECHNIQUE TO ENDOGENOUS PRODUCTIVITY

It was the aim of this chapter to discuss the building blocks of a dynamic theory of production. To this purpose, the chapter started from two characteristics of production technologies that give rise to a tendency toward incremental rather than more radical change. First, technological interdependence between elements of the technology that prevent the modification of individual elements unless other elements are also modified, and second, a tendency toward localized learning based on properties of individual cognition, communication processes and effects of organizational structure. It has been argued that technology-specific incremental change, in combination with inter-firm learning, gives rise to technological dynamics analogous to those familiar from models of network industries. Various approaches to model these dynamics from a production perspective have been discussed.

If one adopts the dynamic perspective of this chapter, the short-run choice-of-technique problem that figures so prominently in the economics of production is essentially turned on its head. The relative superiority of technologies is no longer taken as exogenously given but is the endogenous result of earlier learning. The more learning has focused on a specific technology in the past, the more likely that specific technology is superior to alternative technologies. In an evolutionary view, technologies are not chosen because they are superior to the available alternatives, but they are superior to the alternatives because they have been chosen before. Learning and incremental innovation may thus result in technological path dependence even if network externalities proper are absent.

NOTES

1. The thrust of the present argument is perfectly compatible with Potts's (2000) insistence on the non-integral character of abstract economic space.
2. The notion of 'framing' originally stems from research on decision-making under uncertainty. It has been shown that decisions in logically equivalent situations may differ because agents interpret the situations in different ways (for example, as potential gains versus potential losses; cf. Tversky and Kahneman, 1981).
3. For surveys of this literature see Langlois and Foss (1999) and Rathe and Witt (2001).
4. Nelson and Winter's argument is similar to the present one in that the discussion of routines also starts from individual skills (1982, Ch. 4). In their concept, however, individual cognitive processes have a metaphorical role more than an explanatory one (cf. also Foss, 2001).
5. In addition to spillovers based on the absorption of external knowledge by the firm, other routes of potential spillovers exist; for example, the inter-firm mobility of employees and the knowledge-diffusing role of the professional communities of which employees are members. As with direct knowledge spillovers between firms, knowledge flowing through these channels is likely to result in localized technological change.
6. Network technologies and the problem of potential 'lock-in' to an inferior technology have received much attention in the context of direct compatibility problems or network externalities as sources of increasing returns to adoption (such as in the well-known examples of typewriter keyboards and VCR systems). It has to be noted, however, that already Arthur's (1984, 1989) original argument for increasing returns to adoption was based on the assumption that learning by doing causes the productivity of the alternative technologies to increase with more widespread use.

REFERENCES

Anderson, J.R. (2000), *Learning and Memory*, 2nd edn, New York: John Wiley and Sons.
Arrow, K.J. (1962), 'The economic implications of learning by doing', *Review of Economic Studies*, **29**, 155–73.
Arthur, W.B. (1984), 'Competing technologies and economic prediction', *Options*, **2**, 10–13.
Arthur, W.B. (1989), 'Competing technologies, increasing returns, and lock-in by historical events', *Economic Journal*, **99**, 116–31.
Arthur, W.B. (1994), 'Inductive reasoning and bounded rationality', *American Economic Association Papers and Proceedings*, **84**, 406–11.
Atkinson, A.B and J.E. Stiglitz (1969), 'A new view of technological change', *Economic Journal*, **79**, 573–78.
Baldwin, C.Y. and K.B. Clark (1997), 'Managing in an age of modularity', *Harvard Business Review*, September–October, 84–93.
Bandura, A. (1986), *Social Foundations of Thought and Action*, Englewood Cliffs, NJ: Prentice-Hall.

Bresnahan, T. and M. Trajtenberg (1995), 'General purpose technologies "Engines of growth"?', *Journal of Econometrics*, **65**, 83–108.

Brusoni, S. and A. Prencipe (2001), 'Unpacking the black box of modularity: technologies, products and organizations', *Industrial and Corporate Change*, **10**, 179–205.

Buenstorf, G. (2003), 'Processes of knowledge sharing: from cognitive psychology to economics', in E. Helmstädter (ed.), *The Economics of Knowledge Sharing. A New Institutional Approach*, Cheltenham, UK and Northampton, MA, USA: Edward Elgar, pp. 74–99.

Buenstorf, G. (2004), *Energy Use in Production: A Long-Term Analysis*, Cheltenham, UK and Northampton, MA, USA: Edward Elgar.

Buenstorf, G. (2005), 'Sequential production, modular and technological change', *Structural Change and Economic Dynamics*, **16**, 221–41.

Cimoli, M. and G. Dosi (1995), 'Technological paradigms, patterns of learning and development: an introductory roadmap', *Journal of Evolutionary Economics*, **5**, 243–68.

Cohen, W.M. and D.A. Levinthal (1990), 'Absorptive capacity: a new perspective on learning and innovation', *Administrative Science Quarterly*, **35**, 128–52.

David, P.A. (1987), 'Some new standards for the economics of standardization in the information age', in P. Dasgupta and P. Stoneman (eds), *Economic Policy and Technological Performance*, Cambridge: Cambridge University Press, pp. 206–39.

David, P.A. (1992), 'Heroes, herds and hysteresis in technological history: Thomas Edison and "The battle of the systems" reconsidered', *Industrial and Corporate Change*, **1**, 129–80.

David, P.A. and D. Foray (1994), 'Percolation structures, Markov random fields and the economics of EDI standards diffusion', in G. Pogorel (ed.), *Global Telecommunications Strategies and Technological Changes*, Amsterdam: New-Holland, pp. 135–70.

Denzau, A.T. and D.C. North (1994), 'Shared mental models: ideologies and institutions', *Kyklos*, **47**, 3–31.

Devetag, M.G. (1999), 'From utilities to mental models: a critical survey on decision rules and cognition in consumer choice', *Industrial and Corporate Change*, **8**, 289–351.

Durlauf, S.N. (1993), 'Nonergodic economic growth', *Review of Economic Studies*, **60**, 349–66.

Eysenck, M.W. and M.T. Keane (1995), *Cognitive Psychology: A Student's Handbook*, 3rd edn., Hove: Psychology Press.

Foss, N.J. (2001), 'Simon's grand theme and the economics of organization', *Journal of Management and Governance*, **5**, 216–23.

Georgescu-Roegen, N. (1971), *The Entropy Law and the Economic Process*, Cambridge, MA and London: Harvard University Press.

Harris, R.J. (1999), *A Cognitive Psychology of Mass Communication*, 3rd edn., Mahwah, NJ and London: Lawrence Erlbaum Associates.

Henderson, R.M. and K.B. Clark (1990), 'Architectural innovation: the reconfiguration of existing product technologies and the failure of established firms', *Administrative Science Quarterly*, **35**, 9–30.

Holland, J.H., K.J. Holyak, R.E. Nisbett and P.R. Thagard (1986), *Induction: Processes of Inference, Learning, and Discovery*, Cambridge, MA and London: MIT Press.

Johnson-Laird, P.N. (1985), 'Mental models', in A.M. Aitkenhead and J.M. Slack (eds), *Issues in Cognitive Modeling*, Hillsdale, NJ: Lawrence Erlbaum, pp. 81–99.

Kellogg, R.T. (1995), *Cognitive Psychology*, Thousand Oaks, CA: Sage.

Klepper, S. and K.L. Simons (2000), 'Dominance by birthright: entry of prior radio producers and competitive ramifications in the US television receiver industry', *Strategic Management Journal*, **21**, 997–1016.

Landesmann, M. and R. Scazzieri (1996), 'The production process: description and analysis', in M. Landesmann and R. Scazzieri (eds), *Production and Economic Dynamics*, Cambridge, UK and New York: Cambridge University Press, pp. 191–228.

Langlois, R.N. (1992), 'Transaction-cost economics in real time', *Industrial and Corporate Change*, **1**, 99–127.

Langlois, R.N. (2002), 'Modularity in technology and organization', *Journal of Economic Behavior and Organization*, **49**, 19–38.

Langlois, R.N. (2003), 'The vanishing hand: the changing dynamics of industrial capitalism', *Industrial and Corporate Change*, **12**, 351–85.

Langlois, R.N. and N.J. Foss (1999), 'Capabilities and governance: the rebirth of production in the theory of economic organization', *Kyklos*, **52**, 201–18.

Langlois, R.N. and P.L. Robertson (1992), 'Networks and innovation in a modular system: lessons from the microcomputer and stereo component industries', *Research Policy*, **21**, 297–313.

Legrenzi, P., V. Girotto and P.N. Jonson-Laird (1993), 'Focussing in reasoning and decision making', *Cognition*, **49**, 37–66.

Lieberman, M.D. (2000), 'Intuition: a social cognitive neuroscience approach', *Psychological Bulletin*, **126**, 109–37.

Malerba, F. (1992), 'Learning by firms and incremental technical change', *Economic Journal*, **102**, 845–59.

Nelson, R.R. and S.G. Winter (1982), *An Evolutionary Theory of Economic Change*, Cambridge, MA and London: Belknap Press of Harvard University Press.

Penrose, E.T. (1995), *The Theory of the Growth of the Firm*, 2nd edn., Oxford: Oxford University Press.

Potts, J. (2000), *The New Evolutionary Microeconomics. Complexity, Competence and Adaptive Behaviour*, Cheltenham, UK and Northampton, MA, USA: Edward Elgar.

Rathe, K. and U. Witt (2001), 'The nature of the firm – static versus developmental interpretations', *Journal of Management and Governance*, **5**, 331–51.

Reber, A.S. (1993), *Implicit Learning and Tacit Knowledge*, New York and Oxford: Oxford University Press and Clarendon Press.

Robertson, P.L. and S. Arunthari (2002), 'The steady hand: what do managers really do?', University of Wollongong, mimeo.

Rosenberg, N. (1969), 'The direction of technological change: inducement mechanisms and focusing devices', *Economic Development and Cultural Change*, **18**, 1–24.

Rosenberg, N. (1979), 'Technological interdependence in the American economy', *Technology and Culture*, **20**, 25–50.

Rosenberg, N. (1982), 'Learning by using', in N. Rosenberg (ed.), *Inside the Black Box: Technology and Economics*, Cambridge, UK and New York: Cambridge University Press, pp. 120–40.

Scazzieri, R. (1993), *A Theory of Production. Tasks, Processes, and Technical Practices*, Oxford: Clarendon Press.

Shane, S. (2000), 'Prior knowledge and the discovery of entrepreneurial opportunities', *Organization Science*, **11**, 448–60.

Silverberg, G. and B. Verspagen (1995), 'Evolutionary theorizing on economic growth', *Laxenburg: International Institute for Applied Systems Analysis (IIASA)*, Working Paper no. 95–78.

Simon, H.A. (1986), 'Rationality in psychology and economics', *Journal of Business*, **59**, S209–24.

Stahl-Rolf, S.R. (2000), 'Persistence and change of economic institutions. A social-cognitive approach', in B. Nooteboom and P.P. Saviotti (eds), *Technology and Knowledge: From the Firm to Innovation Systems*, Cheltenham, UK and Northampton, MA, USA: Edward Elgar, pp. 263–84.

Taylor, S.E., L.A. Peplau and D.O. Sears (2000), *Social Psychology*, 10th edn., Upper Saddle River, NJ: Prentice Hall.

Thompson, P. (2005), 'Selection and firm survival: evidence from the shipbuilding industry, 1825–1914', *Review of Economics and Statistics*, **87**, 26–36.

Todd, R.H., D.K. Allen and L. Alting (1994), *Fundamental Principles of Manufacturing Processes*, New York: Industrial Press.

Tversky, A. and D. Kahneman (1981), 'The framing of decisions and the psychology of choice', *Science*, **211** (January), 453–8.

Ulrich, K. (1995), 'The role of product architecture in the manufacturing firm', *Research Policy*, **24**, 419–40.

Vincenti, W.G. (1990), *What Engineers Know and How They Know It. Analytical Studies from Aeronautical History*, Baltimore, MD and London: Johns Hopkins University Press.

Weissmahr, J.A. (1992), 'The factors of production of evolutionary economics', in U. Witt (ed.), *Explaining Process and Change*, Ann Arbor, MI: University of Michigan Press, pp. 67–79.

Witt, U. (1997a), 'Self-organization in economics – what is new?', *Structural Change and Economic Dynamics*, **8**, 489–507.

Witt, U. (1997b), ' "Lock-in" vs. "critical masses" – industrial change under network externalities', *International Journal of Industrial Organization*, **15**, 753–74.

Witt, U. (1998), 'Imagination and leadership – the neglected dimension of an evolutionary theory of the firm', *Journal of Economic Behavior and Organization*, **35**, 161–77.

Index

altruism 150–51, 166, 220
American
   institutionalism 97, 98, 100, 101–2,
     107, 125, 126, 130–31, 197,
     237–8
   pragmatist theory 236, 237
   sociology 238
Anderson, J. 269, 270, 272
anthropology
   cross-disciplinary learning 32, 206
   and evolutionary theory 238
   general theory 113
   methodology 175, 176, 177
   nomothetical discipline 5, 6
   and social capital 169, 171
   sociality in 173–6, 177
appropriateness 19, 20, 99, 105, 106
Aristotle 146, 152–8, 177
   mean as balancing commitments
     157–8
   virtue ethics 152–3
Arrow, K. 113, 117–18, 121, 169, 170,
   171, 281
Arthur, Brian 273, 282–3
atomism 166, 167, 175
Ayres, C. 98

Backhouse, R. 47
Balibar, E. 69
Bandura, A. 275
Barnard, C. 240, 249, 250–51
Baron, J. and M. Hannan 11, 16
barter economy 119–20, 124, 128, 196
Bauman, Z. 80
Becker, Gary 6, 8–9, 16, 19, 33, 56, 73,
   145–6, 147, 187
Becker, Markus C. 25, 233–61
Beckert, J. 17, 99, 105
behavioural predispositions 83, 234,
   235, 238, 241–3, 244, 272–3
   inclinations 248
   logical and non-logical 249

non-rational 247–50
   see also individualism; routines
Ben-Ner, A. and L. Putterman 53
Binmore, K. 34
biochemistry 37
biology 115, 117
   cellular 37, 48
   cross-disciplinary learning 32–5, 37,
     38, 41, 46, 48–51, 206
   epigenetic rules 43–7, 48, 51–2, 53
   evolutionary *see* evolutionary
     biology
   habitual behaviour 237, 238, 245
   historical specificity 124
   molecular 37
   ontological aspect 33, 34
   and preference patterns 33
   serious 40, 42–6, 48, 49, 50, 53
   subdisciplines 37
Bogason, P. 92
bottom-up synthesis 49–50
Boulding, K. 153
bounded rationality 18, 19
Bourdieu, P. 5, 17, 73, 221
Boyer, R. 229
Brinton, M. and V. Nee 91
Buchanan, J. 149
Buenstorf, Guido 25, 262–88
Burke, E. 244–5, 247–8
Burke, K. 141
business economics 7, 16, 77, 77–8,
   79–80
   business enterprise 77, 188, 198–205
   routines in 233, 247
   see also organization theory

Camic, C. 71, 235–6, 238, 245
Campbell, J. 19, 91, 92, 100, 106
capitalism 224
   American 130
   and feudalism 122, 123
   general equilibrium theory 114, 196

realism 101, 103, 131–2
reason 247
reductionism 47, 48–51, 83, 98, 166,
    169, 171, 175–8, 221
reflex action study 245
Regulation School 229
revealed preference theory 42
'rhetoric' movement 35, 113
Ricardo, D. 65, 113
Robbins, Lionel 8, 42, 64, 71, 72, 126,
    127, 131
Robinson Crusoe 141
Rosenbaum, C. 221
routines
    cognitive dimension 243–4
    collective social nature of 251–2
    and decision-making 251
    in firms 233, 242, 276
    history of concept 233–61
    and individualism 234
    and institutionalism 252
    and judgement 246–7
    key elements 243–52
    non-rational and self-actuating
        nature of 247–50, 252
    in psychology 235, 249
    repetitiveness of 237, 242, 244–7
    in social sciences 235
    time element 236
    understanding of 246–7
    see also custom and habit
rules of conduct 234–5, 239, 244, 245,
    249–50
Rutherford, M. 91, 233

Sagoff, M. 189
Samuelson, P. 42, 72
satisficing 18, 19–20, 242
    see also decision-making; rational
        choice theory; problem-solving
Savage, L. 42
scarcity 114, 127, 148, 153, 179,
    196–7
Schmoller, G. 125
Schumpeter, Joseph A. 75, 98, 99, 103,
    114, 194, 206–7, 229, 233, 240–41,
    242
science
    explanatory unification 112–13,
        115–16, 117

general theory 113
    realism in 132
Scientific Management 235, 239–40,
    245
Scott, W. 92, 106
self-regulating market system 65, 67,
    68, 129–31, 192–3, 196, 198, 219,
    225
Sen, A. 146, 149, 150–51, 152
Simon, Herbert 17, 19, 43, 77, 81, 149,
    242, 244, 249, 251–2, 253, 269
Skocpol, T. 95
Smith, Adam 64, 65–6, 67, 69, 75, 113,
    128, 129, 153, 154, 156
social capital theory 17, 19, 74, 79–82
    and anthropology 169, 171
    and community 168, 170, 171
    and individualism 168–71
    meaning of 168–70
    or sociality 163–84
social choice theory 6, 19
social class 67, 68
social cognitive learning theory 275
social-constructivist institutionalism
    93, 94, 95, 97, 99, 100, 103
social contract 64
social conventions 16, 96, 107, 234, 244
Social Costs of Business Enterprise
    (Kapp) 188, 198–205
social justice 72
social norms 17, 20, 164–5, 167, 168,
    169, 170, 171, 176
social ontology, Durkheim and Weber
    68–71
social order 64, 65, 66, 68, 78, 250
social psychology 34–5, 37
social reforms 5, 69, 70
social relations, economic role of 17,
    99, 176
Social Science Information 12
social sciences
    Anglo-American 186
    and causality 177–8
    cognitive turn in 91
    cultural turn in 91
    disciplinary boundaries 186–9
    and economics, boundaries between
        11, 15, 16–20, 81
    and economics, methodological
        contrasts 163–84